ACCA

PAPER F4

CORPORATE AND BUSINESS LAW (ENGLISH)

PRACTICE & REVISION KIT

BPP Learning Media is the **sole ACCA Platinum Approved Learning Partner – content** for the ACCA qualification. In this, **the only Paper F4 Practice and Revision Kit to be reviewed by the examiner**:

- We discuss the **best strategies** for revising and taking your ACCA exams
- We show you how to be **well prepared** for your exam
- We give you **lots of great guidance** on tackling questions
- We show you how you can **build your own exams**
- We provide you with **three** mock exams including the **December 2010 exam**
- We provide the **ACCA examiner's answers** as well as our own to the June and December 2010 exams as an additional revision aid

Our **i-Pass** product also supports this paper.

FOR EXAMS IN 2011

BPP LEARNING MEDIA

First edition 2007
Fifth edition January 2011

ISBN 9780 7517 9399 4
(previous ISBN 9780 7517 8050 5)

e-ISBN 9780 7517 8721 4

British Library Cataloguing-in-Publication Data
A catalogue record for this book
is available from the British Library

Published by

BPP Learning Media Ltd
BPP House, Aldine Place
London W12 8AA

www.bpp.com/learningmedia

Printed in the United Kingdom

We are grateful to the Association of Chartered Certified Accountants for permission to reproduce past examination questions. The suggested solutions in the exam answer bank have been prepared by BPP Learning Media Ltd, except where otherwise stated.

Contents

Page

Finding questions

Helping you with your revision – the ONLY F4 Practice and Revision Kit to be reviewed by the examiner!

Revising F4

Planning your question practice

Questions and answers

Exam practice

Review Form

Question index

The headings in this checklist/index indicate the main topics of questions, but questions may cover several different topics.

Questions set under the old syllabus 2.2 paper are included because their style and content reflect the F4 exam. Some questions have been amended to reflect the current exam format.

Planning your question practice

Our guidance from page xxi shows you how to organise your question practice, either by attempting questions from each syllabus area or **by building your own exams** – tackling questions as a series of practice exams.

Using your BPP Learning Media products

This Kit gives you the question practice and guidance you need in the exam. Our other products can also help you pass:

- **Learning to Learn Accountancy** gives further valuable advice on revision
- **Passcards** provide you with clear topic summaries and exam tips
- **Success CDs** help you revise on the move
- **i-Pass CDs** offer tests of knowledge against the clock

You can purchase these products by visiting www.bpp.com/mybpp.

Topic index

Listed below are the key Paper F4 syllabus topics and the numbers of the questions in this Kit covering those topics.

If you need to concentrate your practice and revision on certain topics or if you want to attempt all available questions that refer to a particular subject, you will find this index useful.

Helping you with your revision – the ONLY F4 Practice and Revision Kit to be reviewed by the examiner!

BPP Learning Media – the sole Platinum Approved Learning Partner - content

As ACCA's **sole Platinum Approved Learning Partner – content**, BPP Learning Media gives you the **unique opportunity** to use **examiner-reviewed** revision materials for the 2011 exams. By incorporating the examiner's comments and suggestions regarding syllabus coverage, the BPP Learning Media Practice and Revision Kit provides excellent, **ACCA-approved** support for your revision.

Tackling revision and the exam

Using feedback obtained from ACCA examiners as part of their review:

- We look at the dos and don'ts of revising for, and taking, ACCA exams
- We focus on Paper F4; we discuss revising the syllabus, what to do (and what not to do) in the exam, how to approach different types of question and ways of obtaining easy marks

Selecting questions

We provide signposts to help you plan your revision.

- A full **question index**
- A **topic index** listing all the questions that cover key topics, so that you can locate the questions that provide practice on these topics, and see the different ways in which they might be examined
- **BPP's question plan** highlighting the most important questions and explaining why you should attempt them
- **Build your own exams**, showing how you can practise questions in a series of exams

Making the most of question practice

At BPP Learning Media we realise that you need more than just questions and model answers to get the most from your question practice.

- Our **Top tips** included for certain questions provide essential advice on tackling questions, presenting answers and the key points that answers need to include
- We show you how you can pick up **Easy marks** on some questions, as we know that picking up all readily available marks often can make the difference between passing and failing
- We include **marking guides** to show you what the examiner rewards
- We include **examiners' comments** to show you where students struggled or performed well in the actual exam
- We refer to the **2010 BPP Study Text** (for exams in 2011) for detailed coverage of the topics covered in questions
- In a bank at the end of this Kit we include the **examiner's answers** to the June and December 2010 papers. Used in conjunction with our answers they provide an indication of all possible points that could be made, issues that could be covered and approaches to adopt.

Attempting mock exams

There are three mock exams that provide practice at coping with the pressures of the exam day. We strongly recommend that you attempt them under exam conditions. **Mock exams 1 and 2** reflect the question styles and syllabus coverage of the exam; **Mock exam 3** is the December 2010 paper.

Revising F4

Topics to revise

Although the examiner, David Kelly, sets challenging questions, the styles of question he uses are now familiar because he has been the law examiner for many years. He has also provided very detailed suggested answers, which show all the detail required to score very highly indeed.

As with most examiners, David Kelly has warned against question-spotting and trying to predict the topics that will be included in the exam. He has on occasions examined the same topic in two successive sittings. He regards few areas as off-limits, and all of the major areas of the syllabus can and have been tested.

The exam consists of ten compulsory questions. You must therefore revise the syllabus fully, even omitting one topic area could potentially cause you to fail the exam.

The examiner expects you to show your basic knowledge in the seven knowledge-based questions he will set in each exam, but you will be rewarded for showing that you have thought about the way the law operates. Marks can be given for critical insights into the way the law works in practice as opposed to regurgitating standard chunks of text. The three scenario-based questions will require you to **identify** the legal issues, **state** the law, **apply** and **conclude**. You should practise this ISAC approach when attempting such questions as it will give your answer balance and demonstrates logical thought and application.

There are certain topics that were examined particularly frequently and thoroughly under the old syllabus and we have seen this continue under the new syllabus:

- Operation of the English legal system (courts, precedent, sources of law)
- Contract formation, contents, breach and remedies
- Employment law (duties and dismissal)
- Company formation and constitution
- The duties, powers and role of directors
- Share capital
- Company administration and liquidation
- Insider dealing and money laundering

Negligence and corporate governance are relatively new syllabus areas which you should consider highly examinable.

Question practice

You should use the Passcards and any brief notes you have to revise the syllabus, but you mustn't spend all your revision time passively reading. **Question practice is vital**; doing as many questions as you can in full will help develop your ability to analyse scenarios and produce relevant discussion and recommendations. The question plan on page xxi tells you what questions to cover so that you can choose questions covering a variety of syllabus areas.

Passing the F4 exam

Displaying the right qualities

The examiner will expect you to display the following qualities.

Qualities required	
Read and answer the question set	If, for instance, the question asks you to set out the ways in which agency can be formed, do not waste time describing the different types of authority that an agent has, or the rights of the agent. You'll score nothing. In fact, as time goes on, ACCA law questions are becoming more and more focused – so watch out!
Knowledge of the law	70% of the marks available in this paper are for showing that you have knowledge of the relevant law. All knowledge-based questions ask for basic knowledge of very specific topics.
Application of the law	30% of the marks are available for the scenario questions. These require application of law to the analysis of scenarios. This sounds more complicated than it is. Usually the scenario relates directly to the law and is generally quite easy to answer. Sketching the relationship between parties in the scenario will help you understand it.
Communication	There are few if any numbers in law exams, and this is a problem for some students. It shouldn't be. Being an accountant is as much about knowledge and the communication of knowledge as it is about numbers and what they represent. If you're nervous about not having the comfort blanket of numbers in the exam, it's particularly important that you practise: • Reading law questions so that you identify exactly what it is the examiner is seeking • Planning law answers so that you get all your points into them, in a logical order (this helps you to be accurate and comprehensive) • Writing law answers so that you feel confident in your ability to get your knowledge across effectively. Get someone else to read your answers and then give you feedback on whether the answers are communicating clearly.

Avoiding weaknesses

David Kelly has emphasised the importance of good exam technique and setting out answers clearly. He has mentioned that the following shortcomings should be avoided:

- Unclear question labelling, it is sometimes difficult for the marker to actually recognise which question is being answered
- Not starting each question on a new page
- Not using both sides of the paper, thus leading to bulkier scripts
- Using additional booklets to no great effect, by simply repeating information
- Producing long general essay answers to problem questions which contain little information relating to the specific issues raised in the question

Using the reading time

The ACCA allows you 15 minutes reading time for Fundamentals papers F4-F9 and all Professional level papers. How you use this time is up to you, but here are some possible options:

- Speed read through the question paper, jotting down any ideas that come to you about any of the questions
- Decide the order which you're likely to tackle questions (see below)
- Spend the remainder of reading time reading the question(s) you'll do first in detail, analysing scenarios, jotting down plans (any plans written on the question paper should be reproduced in the answer booklet)
- When you start writing, get straight on with the questions you've planned in detail

Choosing the order to tackle the questions

As all ten questions are compulsory, it is important for you to decide which order to attempt them. Since each question carries equal marks you may prefer to attempt the questions that you are more confident about first. This means you will build up marks early on giving you a solid base to tackle the harder questions later. However do not spend too long on the questions you are confident about as you need to spend an equal amount of time on them all. You cannot pass the exam answering three or four questions well and the rest poorly.

An alternative strategy is to answer all questions in strict order. You could use the time saved choosing the order by starting to plan your answers. You may prefer to use this method if you find yourself spending too long on your favourite questions as it forces you to spend an equal time on each before moving on.

Tackling questions

You'll improve your chances by following a step-by-step approach to answering questions such as the following.

Step 1 **Read the requirement**

Identify the knowledge areas being tested and see precisely what the examiner wants you to do. This will help you focus on what's important, especially if there is a scenario. Identify and make sure you understand the action verbs in the requirement. These are mostly 'explain', (which means: make clear and intelligible or state the meaning of). In scenario questions you may be asked to 'analyse' (which means examine in detail the structure of) or 'advise' (which means: to 'inform' or 'notify').

Step 2 **Check the mark allocation**

This shows the depth of answer anticipated and you should use it to allocate time across parts of the question and decide where to slot in knowledge to avoid repeating yourself.

Step 3 **Read scenarios carefully**

Identify which information is relevant to each part. Read the scenario and jot down key points on the page: who's who, the key issues at stake, the alternatives open to the parties for resolving any dispute (eg damages, rectification etc), and conclusion.

Step 4 **Plan your answer**

Consider the number and priority of points you will make. Use the ISAC approach when answering scenario questions.

- **Identify** the legal issues
- **State** the relevant law
- **Apply** the law
- **Conclude** with justification

Step 5 **Write your answer**

Stick carefully to the time allocation for each question, and for each part of each question.

Gaining the easy marks

Most marks in this paper are available for setting out the legal rules that apply to each topic. These are 'easy marks' – if you know the rules! In the scenario questions, there are often easy marks available for identifying who is who, stating the key issues and reaching a reasoned conclusion.

To get these 'easy' marks:

- Make sure that you plan gaining these marks as a priority. Try to identify them as you read the questions and write them down
- State the law clearly, in as simple language as you can (you're not a lawyer standing up in a courtroom: you need to impress the examiner with your knowledge of the law, not with fancy 'legalese'). Learn as many basic definitions as you can.

Exam information

The exam paper

Format of the exam

	Number of marks
10 compulsory questions of 10 marks each	100
Three questions will involve a short scenario	
	100

Time allowed: 3 hours

The examination will comprise of questions drawn across all syllabus areas. The scenario questions will normally require you to analyse a situation from a legal point of view and give advice.

December 2010

1 Legislation
2 Remedies for breach of contract
3 Negligence – terms
4 Issuing shares
5 Company registers and accounting records
6 Directors' duties
7 Unfair dismissal
8 Intention
9 Dividend payments
10 Partnership dissolution

This exam is included in this kit as Mock Exam 3.

June 2010

		Question in this kit
1	Civil court system	3
2	Offer – terms	15
3	Duty of care	40
4	Registering a plc	65
5	Debentures and charges	83
6	Company secretary	86
7	Employee or self-employed	46
8	Consideration	26
9	Partnership	58
10	Share allotment and directors' duties	81

Examiner's comments

The structure of the examination paper, as usual, consisted of ten compulsory questions, each carrying 10 marks, although some were subdivided into smaller subsections. The first seven questions were essentially knowledge based, while the latter three were problem-based scenarios requiring both legal analysis and application of the appropriate law. The firsts point to make about the general structure of answers is that it is pleasing to note that the number of candidates who failed to do all or even the majority of questions was considerably down on previous sessions. Although there were a sizeable proportion of candidates who did not do the entire question, the vast majority managed to make an attempt at answering all of the questions. Even where they got the answer wrong they at least recognised what the questions were about, which is itself an improvement on past performance. Where candidates failed to attempt all of the questions this appeared to be as a result of a general lack of knowledge in relation to particular questions, rather than based on any time pressure or structural difficulties in the questions (the issue of time pressure will be considered in relation to question ten below). That being said it is still a fact that the last three problem scenario based questions provide the greatest ground for concern. Too many candidates were let down by their performance in those questions, which continues to suggest a general lack of analysis and application skills if not general knowledge.

However it would appear that some candidates still engaged in question spotting and as a result supplied prepared, but inappropriate, answers to some questions. This was particularly the case in response to questions one and ten, as will be considered further below in the detailed question analysis. However the way question ten was dealt with did give rise to particular concern. Candidates clearly are aware of the syllabus content and the structure of the paper, which has been maintained over a number of years. However the fact that question ten has on a number of occasions been the slot for questions relating to criminal aspects of company regulation meant that a significant number of produced answers relating to various aspects of the criminal law, rather than on directors' duties, which was the actual subject of the question.

Many candidates still fail to read the question asked and provide general prepared answers on a topic area encapsulating the specific question topic. As a result they still spend time providing unnecessary material or even worse, completely irrelevant material.

Question in this kit

December 2009

1	Interpreting statutes	9
2	Postal rule and privity of contract	22
3	Damages	37
4	Auditors' duty of care	41
5	Companies and limited liability	62
6	Winding up and administration	101
7	Duties of employers and employees	47
8	Exclusion clauses	31
9	Directors' liability	92
10	Fraudulent and wrongful trading	108

Examiner's comments

The structure, as usual, consisted of ten compulsory questions. The first seven questions were essentially knowledge based, while the latter three were problem-based scenarios requiring both legal analysis and application of the appropriate law. The firsts point to make about the general structure of answers is that far too many candidates did not complete all ten questions, the result of which was to make it increasingly difficult, depending on the number of questions not attempted, for the candidates in question to gain sufficient marks to pass overall. However, it would seem from an analysis of the papers that this particular problem was the result of a lack of knowledge in relation to particular questions, rather than based on any time pressure, a point emphasised by a number of markers. A second related point to mention is that the questions that tended to be missed out were the last three problem scenario based questions, which would suggest a lack of analysis and application skills if not general knowledge.

It would appear that some candidates engaged in question spotting and as a result supplied prepared but inappropriate answers to some questions. As will be mentioned further in relation particularly to questions 4, 5 and 8 many candidates did not read the question sufficiently closely and as a result either spent time providing unnecessary material or even worse, completely irrelevant material.

June 2009

		Question in this kit
1	Judicial precedent – terms	6
2	Consideration	24
3	Representations, express and implied terms	28
4	Company names and 'passing off'	71
5	Capital maintenance and reducing capital	77
6	Director disqualification under CDDA 1986	89
7	Redundancy	48
8	Anticipatory breach of contract	33
9	Directors' duties	97
10	Insider dealing and money laundering	110

Examiner's comments

As usual, this paper was made up of ten compulsory questions, each of ten marks, although many of them were subdivided into distinct parts. This format seems to have settled down and to meet with candidates' approval from the way they tackle it. However, it is a matter of some concern that a significant number of candidates are not completing, or even attempting, all ten questions. This does not appear to be an issue of time-management but lack of knowledge, which might reflect a failed effort of candidates to question spot. This point has been made in the past, but it clearly has to be repeated for every session: if you do not do all the questions you greatly reduce your chances of passing the exam. The syllabus is wide, but you have to cover it all; question/area spotting is a dangerous game to play. All questions were done very well by a number of candidates across the board; although the reverse of that is equally true in that all questions were done inadequately by a number of candidates across the board.

Question in this kit

December 2008

1	Sources of law	4
2	Anticipatory breach of contract	32
3	Contributory negligence and *volenti non fit injuria*	43
4	Share capital	76
5	Ordinary, special and written resolutions	84
6	Duty to promote the success of the company	91
7	Fair and constructive dismissal	50
8	Contract formation	12
9	Amending articles of association	70
10	Partnership liability	56

Examiner's comments

This paper gave rise to the worst level of performance from candidates for a number of years. A couple of the questions required a subtlety of approach that was beyond the ability of students at this level (question 9 being the cited example), however there were many marks available for basic knowledge and indeed question 9 could have been passed well, without the need for the subtly provided in the model answer. This was due to the lack of legal knowledge exhibited by candidates. Even in question such as number eight, in which most candidates achieved a reasonable mark, it was noticeable the extent to which candidates simply did not support their analysis with the legal authority of, in this instance, cases. However markers commented that this lack of legal authority was a shortcoming throughout the paper.

Question in this kit

June 2008

1	Common law and legislation	8
2	Offer and invitation to treat	16
3	Standard of care	42
4	Separate legal personality	63
5	Ordinary and preferences shares, debentures	75
6	Types of director	93
7	Employment and self-employment	45
8	Contract law remedies for breach	34
9	Partnership liability	57
10	Insider dealing	106

Examiner's comments

The main reason for any inadequate performance in the paper was a complete lack of knowledge on the part of the candidates. The questions provided ample opportunity for candidates to demonstrate both knowledge and understanding. Some candidates clearly find 10 compulsory questions challenging and try to question spot, which, as a general rule, has disastrous consequences. However, the format of the paper suits the stronger candidate.

Question in this kit

December 2007

Please note that question 4 is not included in this kit because the subject matter is now out of date.

Examiner's comments

This is the first report on an examination conducted under the new syllabus and format. The change in format seems to have been less problematic than the change in syllabus with most candidates answering all of the questions, although it has to be said with various degrees of success. Some candidates are treating the three problem/application questions at the end of the paper in the same way as they dealt with the previous 20 mark problem questions, with the effect that the candidates are spending too much time dealing with these questions to the detriment of their general performance. This appears to be a particular concern with candidates who start their papers with the problem questions. Candidates should be made aware that these questions are worth no more than the other questions and they should be encouraged to manage their time better in making sure they have sufficient time to deal with all the questions equally well. It is always surprising the extent to which students will pursue marginal marks at the end of an answer rather than turn their attention to the easier marks to be had be answering a new question.

As for the syllabus change, the introduction of tort law appears to have completely passed by the majority of candidates, who insisted in answering the tort question as if it were a contract question.

Question in this kit

Pilot paper

Analysis of past papers

The table below provides details of when each element of the syllabus has been examined and the question number and section in which each element appeared.

Covered in Text chapter		Dec 2010	Jun 2010	Dec 2009	June 2009	Dec 2008	June 2008	Dec 2007	Pilot Paper
	ESSENTIAL ELEMENTS OF THE LEGAL SYSTEM								
1	The English legal system		1					1	
2	Sources of English law	1		1	1	1	1		1
3	Human rights								
	THE LAW OF OBLIGATIONS								
4, 5	Formation of contracts	8	2, 8	2	2	8	2	2, 8	8
6	Terms of contract			8	3				2
7	Breach of contract	2		3	8	2	8		
8	Torts	3	3			3	3	3	3
9	Professional negligence			4					
	EMPLOYMENT LAW								
10	Employment contract		7	7			7		
11	Dismissal and redundancy	7			7	7		6	7
	THE FORMATION AND CONSTITUTION OF BUSINESS ORGANISATIONS								
12	Agency law								
13	Organisations and legal personality	10	9	5		10	4,9		
14	Company formation	5	4						4
15	Constitution of a company				4	9		4	
	CAPITAL AND THE FINANCING OF COMPANIES								
16	Share capital	4	10			4	5		9
17	Borrowing and loan capital		5				5		
18	Capital maintenance and dividend law	9			5			5	
	MANAGEMENT, ADMINISTRATION AND REGULATION OF COMPANIES								
19	Company directors and other company officers	6	6, 10	9	6,9	6	6	7, 10	
20	Company meetings and resolutions					5			5
	LEGAL IMPLICATIONS OF COMPANIES IN DIFFICULTY OR IN CRISIS								
21	Insolvency and administration			6				9	
	GOVERNANCE AND ETHICAL ISSUES RELATING TO BUSINESS								
22	Corporate governance								6
23	Fraudulent behaviour			10	10		10		10

Useful websites

The websites below provide additional sources of information of relevance to your studies of *Corporate and Business Law.*

- www.accaglobal.com

  ACCA's website. The students' section of the website is invaluable for detailed information about the qualification, past issues of Student Accountant (including technical articles) and even interviews with the examiners.

- www.bpp.com

  Our website provides information about BPP products and services, with a link to the ACCA website.

- www.ft.com

  This website provides information about current international business. You can search for information and articles on specific industry groups as well as individual companies.

- www.lawreports.co.uk

  The Incorporated Council of Law Reporting

- www.lawrights.co.uk

  Source of free legal information

- www.lawsociety.org.uk

  Law Society

- www.bbc.co.uk

  The website of the BBC carries general business information as well as programme-related content.

The Supreme Court for the United Kingdom

The **Constitutional Reform Act 2005** has severed the link between the **legislative** and **judicial** functions of the House of Lords. A **Supreme Court** for the United Kingdom has been established and it opened for business at the start of the legal year in October 2009. It consists of **12 judges** known as *'Justices of the Supreme Court'* and its members include a **President** and a **Deputy President**.

Its **role** is to take over the House of Lords' appellate function – in other words to hear civil and criminal case appeals. However, the House of Lords continues with its existing **legislative role**.

To avoid confusion in answers to questions in this kit, the House of Lords is referred to where that institution decided a particular case. Future decisions made by the Supreme Court will be noted as such.

Planning your question practice

We have already stressed that question practice should be right at the centre of your revision. Whilst you will spend some time looking at your notes and Paper F4 Passcards, you should spend the majority of your revision time practising questions.

We recommend two ways in which you can practise questions.

- Use **BPP Learning Media's question plan** to work systematically through the syllabus and attempt key and other questions on a section-by-section basis
- **Build your own exams** – attempt questions as a series of practice exams

These ways are suggestions and simply following them is no guarantee of success. You or your college may prefer an alternative but equally valid approach.

BPP Learning Media's question plan

The BPP Learning Media plan below requires you to devote a **minimum of 25 hours** to revision of Paper F4. Any time you can spend over and above this should only increase your chances of success.

Step 1 **Review your notes** and the chapter summaries in the Paper F4 **Passcards** for each section of the syllabus.

Step 2 **Answer the key questions** for that section. These questions have boxes round the question number in the table below and you should answer them in full. Even if you are short of time you must attempt these questions if you want to pass the exam. You should complete your answers without referring to our solutions.

Step 3 **Attempt the other questions** in that section. For some questions we have suggested that you prepare **answer plans or do the calculations** rather than full solutions. Planning an answer means that you should spend about 40% of the time allowance for the questions brainstorming the question and drawing up a list of points to be included in the answer.

Step 4 Attempt **Mock exams 1, 2 and 3** under strict exam conditions.

Syllabus section	2010 Passcards chapters	Questions in this Kit	Comments	Done ☑
Revision period 1				
English legal system				
Types of law and the court system	1	1	These concepts could easily be examined, spend some time planning out an answer to them.	☐
		2	A good question, thoroughly testing knowledge of the English courts.	☐
Sources of law	2	4, 5, 6, 8	These questions cover the key areas of sources of law and precedent. Questions could easily be set requiring their explanation and their advantages and disadvantages.	☐
Delegated legislation	2	10	Students often find this topic difficult. Make a good attempt at this Pilot Paper question.	☐
Human Rights Act	3	11	Questions on the Human Rights Act may not come up often, but when they do they could be similar to this.	☐
Revision period 2				
Formation of contract				
Contract formation	4, 5	12, 14, 15, 16, 17, 20, 22	These questions comprehensively cover the issue of contract formation. Try at least five of them in full and plan two others.	☐
Consideration	5	24, 26	Consideration is likely to feature quite frequently in the exam as it is central to contract law. Attempt these questions as they are good practice for this tricky area.	☐
Revision period 3				
Terms of contract and breach				
Terms of a contract	6	27	This Pilot Paper question covers the key issues in relation to the content of contracts. A similar question could easily come up and the examiner would expect you to earn high marks on it.	☐
Exclusion clauses	6	29, 30	Question 29 is a useful example of a question on exclusion clauses as it covers most of the main areas. Question 30 illustrates the type of scenario question that could be set on this area of law.	☐
Breach	7	32	This question makes you think about breach, which is likely to be examined quite frequently. Do this question in full.	☐
Damages	7	33, 34, 36, 37	Exams may include questions on damages alone and remedies generally. Remoteness of damage and the measure of damages are other popular areas. Practising these questions will prepare you well.	☐

Syllabus section	2010 Passcards chapters	Questions in this Kit	Comments	Done ☑
Revision period 4				
Tort and negligence				
Negligence	8	39, 40, 42, 43	These questions are a good test of remoteness of damage, duty of care and defences which are key areas of negligence.	☐
Professional negligence	8,9	41	Professional negligence is not examined frequently, but you need to be aware of the main issues.	☐
Revision period 5				
Employment law				
Employees or independent contractors	10	45	This June 2008 question covers this important practical issue and explores the importance of the distinction.	☐
Employment contracts	10	46, 47	These questions quickly deal with employment contracts and duties of employers.	
Redundancy	11	48	The examiner included a specific question on redundancy in the Pilot Paper and examined it again in June 2009, so it is clearly important. It could appear as either a scenario or knowledge-based question.	☐
Dismissal	11	49, 50 51	Unfair and constructive dismissal are key terms so make sure that you know the difference between them. Try these questions in full.	☐
Revision period 6				
Agency and business associations				
Agents	12	54	Questions on agency are likely to cover authority as this is the main area where disputes occur. This question covers all types of authority.	☐
Partnership	13	55, 56, 57, 61 59	Questions on partnership can take various forms. They may test your understanding of authority and liability of partners or how they may be terminated. These questions cover them all.	☐
Incorporation	13	60, 63	The advantages and disadvantages of incorporation are also very popular with the examiner. The veil of incorporation is also important and is covered in Question 63 from June 2008.	☐

Syllabus section	2010 Passcards chapters	Questions in this Kit	Comments	Done ☑
Revision period 7				
Company formation				
Company formation	14	65	This question focuses particularly on plcs, but as you know, ltd companies are very similar except for the trading certificate requirement. This subject matter is very popular with the examiner, and was examined a number of times under the old syllabus.	☐
Types of company	13,14	72	The examiner may set questions that test your knowledge of quite basic terms, such as this one on types of company. Plan an answer by jotting down the key points that you would make	
Company constitution	15	68, 69, 70	These questions are typical of the questions the examiner has set before and are therefore good practice. They require you to have a good knowledge of the documents of a company's constitution. You might find scenario questions in company law draw on knowledge of what is contained in an objects clause and the articles in general, so it is important to work on your knowledge of them.	☐
Company names	15	71	This is a good question and it requires a quite detailed knowledge of the law. If this is an area you struggle with, work through this question in full.	☐
Company registers and records	14	66	You may be set a similar question on this syllabus area as there are not many ways the examiner could test it. Have a good attempt at it and revisit any registers or records you omit.	☐
Revision period 8				
Company finance				
Shares and capital maintenance	16	75, 76, 77, 78	Make sure that you get the basics right in these questions as if they come up in the exam you should expect to score highly. Question 78 covers all you need to know about class rights and will prepare you well for a topic students always struggle with.	
Dividends	18	82	Dividends can be examined in isolation or as part of a larger question. They are important, but can be complex, so have a good attempt at this question.	☐
Debentures and charges	17	83	You should be able to answer a knowledge-based question on loan capital well. You may find an exam question asking you to compare and contrast shares and debentures as sources of capital.	☐

Syllabus section	2010 Passcards chapters	Questions in this Kit	Comments	Done ☑
Revision period 9				
Company administration				
Resolutions	20	84	It is vital to know all about resolutions. They may be relevant in a scenario question where shareholders are taking various actions or in an explain question such as this. You should aim to get full marks as you just need to repeat text book knowledge.	
Meetings	20	85	This is a good example of the type of knowledge-based question you may see on meetings.	☐
Revision period 10				
Company management				
Company secretary	19	86	You must be prepared to answer questions like this comprehensively.	☐
Auditors	19	95 94	The rules on auditors are quite straightforward. Put your knowledge to the test by producing answering this.	
Directors	19	88, 89, 90, 92, 93	These questions comprehensively cover all aspects of directors and are extremely good practice for the type of company law question you should expect in the exam.	☐
Revision period 11				
Winding up				
Compulsory winding up	21	99	Winding up is an area which might seem daunting, but easy marks can be gained. Work through this in full.	☐
Voluntary winding up	21	98	Question 98 gives good practice of the skills needed to answer questions in this area. It is quite a difficult question, so take your time.	☐
Administration	21	100	Administration may seem like a strange concept, but just remember that it is an attempt to save the company – not another form of liquidation. This section is probably about as hard as questions will get in this area so it is good preparation for the exam.	☐
Revision period 12				
Governance and ethical issues				
Corporate governance	22	103 104	Governance can be examined in many ways. This question focuses on the basics and links into the duties of directors.	☐
Criminal offences	23	106, 107, 108, 109 110	These questions cover the key criminal offences that you must understand. Produce quality answers for them all.	☐

Build your own exams

Having revised your notes and the BPP Passcards, you can attempt the questions in the Kit as a series of practice exams. You can organise the questions in the following ways.

- Either you can attempt complete past exam papers; recent papers are listed below:

	Pilot paper Q in kit	*Dec 07 Q in Kit*	*June 08 Q in kit*	*Dec 08 Q in kit*	*June 09 Q in kit*	*Dec 09 Q in kit*	*June 10 Q in kit*
1	10	2	8	4	6	9	3
2	27	23	16	32	24	22	15
3	40	39	42	43	28	37	40
4	65	68*	63	76	71	41	65
5	85	82	75	84	77	62	83
6	103	49	93	91	89	101	86
7	48	95	45	50	48	47	46
8	19	14	34	12	33	31	26
9	79	102	57	70	97	92	58
10	105	96	106	56	110	108	81

* Note. Question 4 from the December 2007 exam is not included in this kit as it is out of date under the Companies Act 2006. Question 63 should be attempted instead as a suitable replacement.

- Or you can make up practice exams, either yourself or using the suggestions we have listed below.

	Practice Exam				
	1	*2*	*3*	*4*	*5*
1	2	3	4	6	8
2	15	16	22	27	28
3	39	40	41	42	43
4	54	55	62	63	45
5	94	95	73	74	75
6	84	85	86	88	90
7	45	46	47	48	49
8	34	33	30	26	21
9	79	80	58	57	56
10	105	106	108	110	102

Questions

ESSENTIAL ELEMENTS OF THE LEGAL SYSTEM

Questions 1 to 11 cover the essential elements of the legal system, the subject of Part A of the BPP Study Text for Paper F4.

1 Types of law — 18 mins

Briefly explain the following types of law.

(a) Common law and equity **(4 marks)**
(b) Civil law **(3 marks)**
(c) Criminal law **(3 marks)**

(Total = 10 marks)

---

2 Legal system and courts (12/07) — 18 mins

(a) In relation to the English legal system distinguish between the following:
   (i) criminal law
   (ii) civil law **(5 marks)**
(b) Explain the jurisdiction of the courts dealing with criminal and civil law. **(5 marks)**

(Total = 10 marks)

---

3 Civil courts (6/10) — 18 mins

Describe the structure and functions of the main civil courts in the English legal system, including the Supreme Court. **(10 marks)**

---

4 Contemporary sources of law (12/08) — 18 mins

In relation to the English legal system, explain the main sources of contemporary law. **(10 marks)**

---

5 Precedent — 18 mins

(a) Explain the doctrine of precedent within the English legal system. **(2 marks)**
(b) Explain the hierarchy of the courts within the English legal system in relation to the operation of precedent. **(3 marks)**
(c) Discuss the relative advantages and disadvantages of the doctrine of precedent. **(5 marks)**

(Total = 10 marks)

---

6 Precedent; terms (6/09) — 18 mins

Explain and distinguish between the following terms in relation to the doctrine of precedent in the English legal system:

(a) *Ratio decidendi* and *obiter dictum* **(4 marks)**
(b) Binding precedent and persuasive precedent **(6 marks)**

(Total = 10 marks)

---

7 Legal terms (2.2 6/05) **18 mins**

Explain the distinction between the following terms in relation to the doctrine of precedent in the English legal system:

(a) *Ratio decendi* and *obiter dictum* **(5 marks)**
(b) Reversing, overruling and distinguishing **(5 marks)**

(Total = 10 marks)

---

8 Common law and legislation (6/08) **18 mins**

In relation to the English legal system explain the following sources of law:

(a) Common law **(6 marks)**
(b) Legislation **(4 marks)**

(Total = 10 marks)

---

9 Statutory interpretation (12/09) **18 mins**

In relation to the courts' powers to interpret legislation, explain and differentiate between:

(a) The literal approach, including the golden rule; and **(5 marks)**
(b) The purposive approach, including the mischief rule **(5 marks)**

(Total = 10 marks)

---

10 Delegated legislation (Pilot Paper) **18 mins**

Explain the meaning and effect of delegated legislation, and evaluate its advantages and disadvantages, and how it is controlled by both Parliament and the courts. **(10 marks)**

---

11 Sources of law and the Human Rights Act 1998 **18 mins**

In relation to sources of English law, explain:

(a) Case law (common law) **(4 marks)**
(b) Statute (legislation) **(3 marks)**
(c) In what ways has the Human Rights Act 1998 had an impact on case law and statute? **(3 marks)**

(Total = 10 marks)

THE LAW OF OBLIGATIONS

Questions 12 to 44 cover the law of obligations, the subject of Part B of the BPP Study Text for Paper F4.

12 Alvin (12/08) — 18 mins

Alvin runs a business selling expensive cars. Last Monday he mistakenly placed a notice on one car indicating that it was for sale for £5,000 when in fact its real price was £25,000. Bert later noticed the sign and, recognising what a bargain it was, immediately indicated to Alvin that he accepted the offer and would take the car for the indicated amount. Alvin, however, told Bert that there had been a mistake and that the true price of the car was £25,000. Bert insisted that he was entitled to get the car at the lower price, and when Alvin would not give it to him at that price Bert said that he would sue Alvin.

After Bert had left, Alvin changed the price on the car to £25,000 and subsequently Cat came in and said she would like to buy the car, but that she would have to arrange finance.

On Tuesday Del came by and offered Alvin the full £25,000 cash there and then and Alvin sold it to him.

Required

Advise Alvin, Bert, Cat and Del as to their rights and liabilities in the law of contract. **(10 marks)**

13 Ann's art (2.2 12/01 amended) — 18 mins

On Friday 10 December the following notice is placed in the window of Ann's art gallery: '2 copies of a very rare Blake print – £15,000 each'. Chas and Dave are very keen to acquire the prints but think that the price is too high. They each offer Ann £12,000 for a copy but she refuses to sell the prints at that price, although she says she will accept £13,500. She also says she will keep her offer to them open until 12 o'clock on the following Monday, 13 December, if they each pay her £100. Chas and Dave agree and each hands over £100. On the Saturday before the deadline Chas and Dave have to leave the country on business but before they do so each posts a letter stating that he agrees to buy one of the prints at the agreed price of £13,500. Chas's letter arrives at 9.30 on the Monday morning but Dave's letter is delayed and arrives on the morning of Tuesday 14 December. In any event Ann had already sold both prints to Eve on Saturday 11 December for a total price of £30,000.

Required

Advise Ann on whether or not she has an enforceable contract with Chas and Dave. **(10 marks)**

14 Ali (12/07) — 18 mins

Ali is an antiques dealer and one Saturday in November 20X7 he put a vase in the window of his shop with a sign which stated 'exceptional piece of 19th century pottery – on offer for £500'.

Ben happened to notice the vase as he walked past the shop and thought he would like to have it. Unfortunately, as he was late for an important meeting, he could not go into the shop to buy it, but as soon as his meeting was finished he wrote to Ali agreeing to buy the vase for the stated price of £500. The letter was posted at 11:30 am.

Later on the same day, Chet visited Ali's shop and said he would like the vase but was only willing to pay £400 for it. Ali replied that he would accept £450 for the vase, but Chet insisted that he was only willing to pay £400 and left the shop. However, on his journey home Chet realised that £450 was actually a very good price for the vase and he immediately wrote to Ali agreeing to buy it for that price. His letter was posted at 12:30 pm.

Just before closing time at 5 pm. Di came into Ali's shop and she also offered £400 for the vase. This time Ali agreed to sell the vase at that price and Di promised to return the following Monday with the money. On Monday morning Ali received both of the letters from Ben and Chet before Di could arrive to pay and collect the vase.

Required

From the point of view of the law of contract advise Ali as to his legal relations with Ben, Chet and Di. **(10 marks)**

15 Offers, counter-offers and unilateral offers (6/10) 18 mins

In relation to the law of contract:

(a) Define an offer **(5 marks)**

(b) Explain the specific meaning and effect of:

(i) a counter-offer **(3 marks)**

(ii) a unilateral offer **(2 marks)**

(Total = 10 marks)

16 Offers and invitations to treat (6/08) 18 mins

In relation to contract law explain the meaning and effect of:

(a) An offer **(4 marks)**

(b) An invitation to treat **(6 marks)**

(Total = 10 marks)

17 Acceptance and revocation of offer (2.2 6/03) 18 mins

Explain in relation to the law of contract:

(a) The rules relating to acceptance of an offer **(5 marks)**

(b) The rules relating to revocation of an offer **(5 marks)**

(Total = 10 marks)

18 Ace Ltd (2.2 6/07 amended) 18 mins

Ace Ltd had been having difficulties in developing software for its new internet service Brag.com. As the time for delivering the service, 1 May 20X7, approached, Ace Ltd placed the following notice in the January edition of its company journal:

'£10,000 reward to any employee who can design a solution to the Brag problem before 1 April.'

The journal was distributed to all employees of Ace Ltd.

Cid, a self employed computer expert, who was married to an employee of Ace Ltd, read the journal and thought that he could solve the problem so started work on it.

Ed, a computer software expert employed by Ace Ltd, but not involved with the Brag.com project, saw the advert and decided to work on it in his own time after reading the journal.

However, before anyone could solve the problem, Ace Ltd decided to cancel the Brag.com project and placed a note in the March edition of its journal cancelling the reward for overcoming the Brag.com problems.

Required

Analyse the scenario from the perspective of contract law and advise Cid and Ed, each of whom managed to solve the Brag.com problem after the cancellation of the reward but before the original deadline. **(10 marks)**

19 Al (Pilot Paper) **18 mins**

Al operates a small business manufacturing specialist engine filters. In January he placed an advertisement in a car trade magazine stating that he would supply filters at £60 per filter, but would consider a reduction in the price for substantial orders. He received a letter from Bash Cars plc requesting his terms of supply for 1,000 filters. Al replied, offering to supply the filters at a cost of £50 each. Bash Cars plc responded to Al's letter stating that they accepted his offer but that they would only pay £45 per filter. Al wrote back to Bash Cars plc stating that he would supply the filters but only at the original price of £50. When Al's letter arrived, the purchasing director of Bash Cars plc did not notice the alteration of the price and ordered the 1,000 filters from Al, which he supplied.

Required

Analyse the situation from the perspective of contract law and in particular advise Al what price he is entitled to claim from Bash Cars plc. **(10 marks)**

---

20 Presumption and rebuttal (2.2 12/05) **18 mins**

In relation to the intention to create contractual relations explain:

(a) The meaning of the terms 'presumption' and 'rebuttal' **(2 marks)**

(b) How presumption and rebuttal operate in the context of:

(i) domestic and social agreements **(4 marks)**

(ii) business agreements **(4 marks)**

(Total = 10 marks)

---

21 Alan (2.2 12/04 amended) **18 mins**

Alan is a qualified accountant. Last year he agreed with his father Ben, who owns a small manufacturing business, that he would prepare his tax return for him for a fee of £500. Alan did the accountancy work and Ben submitted the accounts to the tax authorities. Ben now refuses to pay Alan, saying that it is not right for a son to charge his father for doing him a favour.

Two years ago Alan separated from his wife Cath. As part of the written agreement between them, Alan agreed to pay Cath £1,000 per month in order to maintain her and their daughter Dawn. The money also had to be used to pay off the mortgage on the house that Alan and Cath jointly owned. Alan promised that when the mortgage was paid off he would transfer his share of the property to Cath. Now, however, although the mortgage has been paid off, Alan refuses to transfer his title in the house to Cath.

Required

Briefly analyse the above situation from the point of view of contract law and advise Alan whether:

(a) Alan can require Ben to pay him for his accountancy work

(b) Cath can require Alan to transfer his part of the house to her **(10 marks)**

---

22 Privity and the postal rule (12/09) **18 mins**

In relation to the law of contract, explain:

(a) The postal rule **(5 marks)**

(b) The doctrine of privity **(5 marks)**

(Total = 10 marks)

---

23 Privity and intention (12/07) — 18 mins

In relation to the law of contract explain the meaning and effect of:

(a) The doctrine of privity (6 marks)

(b) The intention to create legal relations (4 marks)

(Total = 10 marks)

24 Consideration (6/09) — 18 mins

In relation to the law of contract:

(a) Define and explain consideration (3 marks)

(b) Explain the following statements regarding consideration:

(i) consideration must be sufficient but does not have to be adequate (3 marks)

(ii) past consideration is not good consideration (4 marks)

(Total = 10 marks)

25 Forms of consideration (2.2 12/02) — 18 mins

(a) Define consideration as it is understood in English contract law. (3 marks)

(b) Explain and distinguish between the following terms:

(i) executory consideration (2 marks)

(ii) executed consideration (2 marks)

(iii) past consideration (3 marks)

(Total = 10 marks)

26 Ami, Bry and Cis (6/10) — 18 mins

In January 20X0 Ami took over an old warehouse with the intention of opening an art gallery. As the warehouse had to be converted, Ami entered into two contracts, one with Bry to do all the necessary plastering and one with Cis, who was to do all the necessary painting. Both Bry and Cis were to be paid £5,000. Both received initial payments of £1,000 and agreed to have the work completed on 31 March, as the art gallery had to be ready for its first exhibition on 1 May.

At the end of February, Bry told Ami that he would not complete the plastering in time unless she agreed to increase his payment by a further £1,000. Ami agreed to pay the increased sum in order to ensure that the job was done on time. She then thought it was only fair that she should increase the amount of money promised to Cis by the same amount.

However, on completion of the work on time Ami refused to make either of the additional payments to Bry or Cis, beyond the original contractual price.

Required

Advise Bry and Cis whether they have any rights in law to enforce Ami's promise to pay them an extra £1,000.

(10 marks)

27 Types of term I (Pilot Paper) **18 mins**

In relation to the contents of a contract explain the following:

(a) Terms **(2 marks)**
(b) Conditions **(3 marks)**
(c) Warranties **(3 marks)**
(d) Innominate terms **(2 marks)**

(Total = 10 marks)

---

28 Types of term II (6/09) **18 mins**

In relation to the law of contract, distinguish between and explain the effect of:

(a) A term and a mere representation **(3 marks)**

(b) Express and implied terms, paying particular regard to the circumstances under which terms may be implied in contracts **(7 marks)**

(Total = 10 marks)

---

29 Exclusion clauses (2.2 6/02) **18 mins**

(a) Explain the meaning of exclusion clauses, also known as exemption clauses, in contract law. **(2 marks)**

(b) How are such clauses controlled:

(i) at common law **(4 marks)**
(ii) by statute? **(4 marks)**

(Total = 10 marks)

---

30 Seller Ltd and Transport Ltd **18 mins**

Seller Ltd had used the services of Transport Ltd ten times in the past year. On this occasion, the managing director of Seller Ltd telephoned the offices of Transport Ltd and arranged for the transportation of some expensive machinery to a customer. Transport Ltd confirmed the order by sending a notice to this effect. Unfortunately, due to driver error, the vehicle carrying Seller Ltd's equipment crashed and the equipment was badly damaged. Transport Ltd has advised Seller Ltd that it intends to rely on the following clause:

'Transport Ltd will not accept any liability for loss or damage caused to customers' property during transportation, no matter how the loss or damage was caused. Customers are advised to take out their own insurance.'

Transport Ltd has pointed out that the clause appears in a notice prominently displayed outside the entrance to the company's offices, and is reproduced on the back of all invoices, receipts and confirmation of order notices issued by the company.

Required

In the context of the law of contract, advise Seller Ltd whether Transport Ltd will be able to rely on the clause to avoid liability for the damaged goods. **(10 marks)**

---

31 Bash Ltd (12/09) **18 mins**

Whilst at work Andy always parked his car in a car park operated by Bash Ltd. On the entry to the car park just in front of the payment machine there is a large sign in fluorescent red paint which states:

'These premises are not staffed by our employees and may be dangerous. Clients use these facilities strictly at their own risk and Bash Ltd accept no liability whatsoever for any damage or injury sustained by either those using this facility or their vehicles or property, no matter how caused.'

Andy was aware of the sign, but had never paid much attention to it. However, one day he returned to his car to find that it had been badly damaged by a towing vehicle driven by an employee of Bash Ltd. Whilst on his way to the car park office to complain he was hit by the same towing vehicle, which was clearly being driven dangerously by one of Bash Ltd's employees. As a result, not only was his car severely damaged, but he suffered a broken leg and was off work for eight weeks.

Bash Ltd has accepted that its employee was negligent on both counts but denies any liability, relying on the exclusion clause.

Required

On the understanding that the clause excluding Bash Ltd's liability was incorporated into its contract with Andy, advise Andy whether there is any action he can take against Bash Ltd. **(10 marks)**

---

32 Breach of contact (12/08) **18 mins**

In relation to the law of contract, explain what is meant by breach of contract, paying attention to anticipatory breach. **(10 marks)**

---

33 Arti (6/09) **18 mins**

In January 20X8 Arti entered in a contractual agreement with Bee Ltd to write a study manual for an international accountancy body's award. The manual was to cover the period from September 20X8 till June 20X9, and it was a term of the contract that the text be supplied by 31 June 20X8 so that it could be printed in time for September. By 30 May, Arti had not yet started on the text and indeed he had written to Bee Ltd stating that he was too busy to write the text.

Bee Ltd was extremely perturbed by the news, especially as it had acquired the contract to supply all of the accountancy body's study manuals and had already incurred extensive preliminary expenses in relation to the publication of the new manual.

Required

In the context of the law of contract, advise Bee Ltd whether they can take any action against Arti. **(10 marks)**

---

34 Astride (6/08) **18 mins**

Astride entered into a contract with Bild Ltd to construct a wall around the garden of a house she had just purchased. The wall was to be three metres high to block out a view of a rubbish tip. The wall was due to be finished in May and Astride entered into another contract with Chris to landscape the garden starting on 1 June.

Bild Ltd finished the wall on 25 May. However when Astride came to examine it for the first time she found that it was only 2.5 metres high and that the rubbish tip was still visible from the top of her garden.

On 1 June, Chris informed Astride that he was too busy to landscape her garden and that she would have to get someone else to do it. The only person available, however, will charge Astride £500 more than Chris had agreed for doing the work.

Required

Analyse the scenario from the perspective of the law of contract, advising Astride:

(a) Whether she can require Bild Ltd to reconstruct the garden wall in order to make it the agreed height, and if not, what alternative action is available to her. **(5 marks)**

(b) Whether she can require Chris to undertake the work on the garden, and if not, what alternative action is available to her. **(5 marks)**

(Total = 10 marks)

---

35 Remedies for breach (2.2 12/02 and 12/04) — 18 mins

State and explain the remedies available for breach of contract. **(10 marks)**

---

36 Remoteness and measure of damages (2.2 6/04) — 18 mins

In the law of contract describe the rules relating to:

(a) Remoteness of damage **(5 marks)**

(b) The measure of damages **(5 marks)**

(Total = 10 marks)

---

37 Liquidated damages, penalty clauses and mitigation (12/09) — 18 mins

In relation to remedies for breach of contract, explain:

(a) The difference between liquidated damages and penalty clauses **(7 marks)**

(b) The duty to mitigate losses **(3 marks)**

(Total = 10 marks)

---

38 Roger and Lulu — 18 mins

Roger regularly takes part in a sport which involves fighting with wooden sticks. He has been successful in many fights but recently took part in one in which he lost to Jack. The fight took place under the necessary safety regulations and was stopped before Roger was hurt too badly. However, soon after the fight it was clear that he had received severe brain damage and he now has difficulty talking.

Lulu used a public toilet at her local train station. Unfortunately the lock was defective and she was stuck inside. In a hurry to escape she attempted to climb out of the window (despite a warning notice not to do so) and fell to the ground outside, injuring her head.

Required

Assuming the fight organisers and the train station have breached their duty of care, do they have any defences that will limit or eliminate their liability for the injuries caused to Roger and Lulu? **(10 marks)**

---

39 Remoteness of damage (12/07) — 18 mins

In relation to the law of tort explain the concept of 'remoteness of damage'. **(10 marks)**

---

40 Duty of care (Pilot Paper, 6/10) — 18 mins

In relation to the tort of negligence explain the meaning of 'duty of care'. **(10 marks)**

41 An auditor's duty of care (12/09) — 18 mins

In relation to the law of negligence, explain the extent of a company auditor's duty of care and to whom any such duty is owed. **(10 marks)**

42 Standard of care (6/08) — 18 mins

In relation to the tort of negligence explain the standard of care owed by one person to another. **(10 marks)**

43 Defences (12/08) — 18 mins

In relation to defences in the tort of negligence, explain the meaning of:

(a) Contributory negligence **(5 marks)**
(b) *Volenti non fit injuria* (consent) **(5 marks)**

(Total = 10 marks)

44 Accountants4U — 18 mins

Sally is the audit partner of Accountants4U and regularly advises on takeovers. She was asked to speak at a board meeting of GWZ Ltd which was planning a takeover of THT Ltd (a client of Sally's) as the latest audited accounts showed very good profits. During the meeting she said that she 'absolutely stood by the results of THT Ltd' which she had signed off.

The takeover went ahead, but soon after GWZ Ltd found that THT Ltd was in fact close to insolvency rather than being profitable. It is now looking to sue Accountants4U for negligence.

Advise Sally as to whether or not her firm would be liable for a claim of negligence brought by GWZ Ltd.

(10 marks)

EMPLOYMENT LAW

Questions 45 to 53 cover employment law, the subject of Part C of the BPP Study Text for Paper F4.

45 Employed v self-employed (6/08) — 18 mins

In relation to employment law:

(a) Explain why it is important to distinguish between contracts of service and contracts for services **(4 marks)**

(b) State how the courts decide whether someone is an employee or is self-employed **(6 marks)**

(Total = 10 marks)

---

46 Employment contracts (6/10) — 18 mins

In the context of employment law, state how the courts decide whether someone is self-employed or is an employee. **(10 marks)**

---

47 Employer and employee duties (12/09) — 18 mins

In the context of contracts of employment, explain the common law duties imposed on:

(a) Employers **(6 marks)**

(b) Employees **(4 marks)**

(Total = 10 marks)

---

48 Redundancy (Pilot Paper, 6/09) — 18 mins

In relation to employment law, explain the meaning of redundancy and the rules that govern it. **(10 marks)**

---

49 Constructive and unfair dismissal (12/07) — 18 mins

In relation to employment law explain:

(a) The meaning of 'constructive dismissal' **(5 marks)**

(b) The remedies available in relation to a successful claim for unfair dismissal **(5 marks)**

(Total = 10 marks)

---

50 Fair and constructive dismissal (12/08) — 18 mins

In relation to employment law, explain:

(a) The grounds upon which dismissal may be fair **(5 marks)**

(b) The meaning and effect of constructive dismissal **(5 marks)**

(Total = 10 marks)

---

51 Fine Ltd **18 mins**

Fine Ltd specialises in providing software to the financial services industry. It has two offices, one in Edinburgh and the other, its main office, in London. In January 20X3, Gus was employed as a software designer attached to the Edinburgh office. However, in May 20X4, Gus was informed that he was to be transferred to the head office in London, which is more than 350 miles from his usual workplace.

Gus refused to accept the transfer on the basis that he had been employed to work in Edinburgh not London. Consequently, on 1 June 20X4 he wrote to Fine Ltd terminating his contract with them.

Required

Analyse the scenario from the point of view of employment law and in particular advise Gus as to:

(a) His rights on the termination of his contract of employment with Fine Ltd **(6 marks)**

(b) Any remedies which might be available to him **(4 marks)**

(Total = 10 marks)

52 Grace and Fawn Ltd (2.2 12/02 amended) **18 mins**

Fawn Ltd manufactures clothes and sells them through its own retail shop. Grace, who is 33 years old, has been employed by Fawn Ltd for three years as manager of the shop. Grace has just been told that her services are no longer required as Fawn Ltd has decided to close its store and concentrate solely on manufacturing. Grace has also been told that she will not receive any recompense for her job loss.

Required

Advise Grace as to the likelihood of her successfully claiming for redundancy. **(10 marks)**

53 Impact College (2.2 12/05 amended) **18 mins**

Impact College Ltd provides private tuition. The college is managed by Jack, who also has responsibility for personnel matters. The College has lost a considerable number of its clients in recent years and the decision has been taken to reduce the staff numbers by ten. Fred, Gale and Hilda are amongst the 60 lecturers currently employed by Impact College Ltd. They have all worked for Impact College for the past six years. Fred has been the staff trade union representative for the past three years and has had several confrontations with Jack as to the working conditions of the college's employees. Gale has been off work twice in the past four years on maternity leave, to Jack's stated annoyance, and is pregnant once again. Last year Hilda reported the college for breaching health and safety requirements and the college was fined a substantial amount of money. It has transpired that Fred, Gale and Hilda are amongst the ten members of staff to be selected for dismissal by the college and they all suspect that Jack has pursued a personal vendetta against them.

Required

Advise Fred, Gale and Hilda as to whether they have been dismissed for an automatically unfair reason. **(10 marks)**

THE FORMATION AND CONSTITUTION OF BUSINESS ORGANISATIONS

Questions 54 to 72 cover the formation and constitution of business organisations, the subject of Part D of the BPP Study Text for Paper F4.

54 Types of authority (2.2 12/01) 18 mins

Explain the meaning of the following terms with regard to the law of agency:

(a) Express authority **(3 marks)**

(b) Implied authority **(3 marks)**

(c) Ostensible/apparent authority **(4 marks)**

(Total = 10 marks)

55 Unlimited and limited partnerships 18 mins

(a) Briefly discuss what an unlimited partnership is. **(4 marks)**

(b) What is meant by 'apparent authority' in the context of partnership law? **(3 marks)**

(c) What are the main requirements of a limited liability partnership with regard to formation and publicity of information? **(3 marks)**

(Total = 10 marks)

56 Ham, Sam and Tam (12/08) 18 mins

Ham, Sam and Tam formed a partnership to run a petrol station. The partnership agreement expressly stated that the partnership business was to be limited exclusively to the sale of petrol.

In January 20X8 Sam received £10,000 from the partnership's bank drawn on its overdraft facility. He told the bank that the money was to finance a short-term partnership debt but in fact he used the money to pay for a round the world cruise. In February Tam entered into a £15,000 contract on behalf of the partnership to buy some used cars, which he hoped to sell from the garage forecourt. In March the partnership's bank refused to honour its cheque for the payment of its monthly petrol account, on the basis that there were no funds in its account and it had reached its overdraft facility.

Required

Advise Ham, Sam and Tam as to their various rights and liabilities in relation to partnership law. **(10 marks)**

57 Clare, Dan and Eve (6/08) 18 mins

Clare, Dan and Eve formed a partnership 10 years ago, although Clare was a sleeping partner and never had anything to do with running the business. Last year Dan retired from the partnership. Eve has subsequently entered into two large contracts. The first one was with a longstanding customer Greg, who had dealt with the partnership for some five years. The second contract was with a new customer Hugh. Both believed that Dan was still a partner in the business. Both contracts have gone badly wrong leaving the partnership owing £50,000 to both Greg and Hugh. Unfortunately the business assets will only cover the first £50,000 of the debt.

Required

Explain the potential liabilities of Clare, Dan, and Eve for the partnership debts. **(10 marks)**

58 Chi, Di and Fi (6/10) **18 mins**

Chi, Di and Fi formed an ordinary partnership to run an art gallery. Each of them paid £100,000 into the business. As Fi had no prospect of raising any more money it was agreed between them that her maximum liability for any partnership debts would be fixed at her original contribution of £100,000. The partnership agreement specifically restricted the scope of the partnership business to the sale of 'paintings, sculptures and other works of art.' In January 20X0 Chi took £10,000 from the partnership's bank drawn on its overdraft facility. She had told the bank that the money was to finance a short-term partnership debt but in fact she used the money to pay for a holiday. In February Di entered into a £25,000 contract on behalf of the partnership to buy some books, which she hoped to sell in the gallery.

Required

Advise Chi, Di and Fi as to their various rights and liabilities in relation to the operation of the business under partnership law. **(10 marks)**

---

59 Partnership liability **18 mins**

Describe the liability of partners for partnership debts in a:

(a) Traditional partnership **(2 marks)**
(b) Limited partnership **(4 marks)**
(c) Limited liability partnership **(4 marks)**

(Total = 10 marks)

---

60 Partnership v company (2.2 12/01 amended) **18 mins**

Consider the advantages of the registered company as against the partnership as a form of business organisation. **(10 marks)**

---

61 Termination of partnerships (2.2 12/02) **18 mins**

Detail the grounds upon which a partnership can be terminated. **(10 marks)**

---

62 Limited liability and types of company (12/09) **18 mins**

In relation to company law:

(a) Explain the meaning of limited liability **(3 marks)**
(b) Explain and distinguish between:
  (i) unlimited companies **(2 marks)**
  (ii) companies limited by guarantee **(2 marks)**
  (iii) companies limited by shares **(3 marks)**

(Total = 10 marks)

---

63 Separate personality (6/08) **18 mins**

In the context of company law explain:

(a) The doctrine of separate personality and its consequences **(6 marks)**
(b) The circumstances under which separate personality will be ignored **(4 marks)**

(Total = 10 marks)

---

64 Mick (2.2 12/05 amended) **18 mins**

Mick has operated a house building business as a sole trader for a number of years. Now his accountant has recommended that he should consider registering as a company in order to gain the benefits of separate personality. He is unclear as to what is meant by this and seeks advice on how he would go about registering.

Required

(a) Explain the concept of corporate personality **(5 marks)**

(b) Detail the procedures and the documentation required to register a private limited company **(5 marks)**

(Total = 10 marks)

---

65 Public companies (Pilot Paper, 6/10) **18 mins**

Explain the documents necessary, and the procedure to be followed, in registering a public limited company under the provisions of the Companies Act 2006. **(10 marks)**

---

66 Company registers and accounting records (2.2 6/02 amended) **18 mins**

(a) List and explain the purpose of the various registers that have to be kept by a company. **(5 marks)**

(b) Describe the accounting records that have to be maintained by a company. **(5 marks)**

(Total = 10 marks)

---

67 Eden plc (2.2 6/05 amended) **18 mins**

Don was instrumental in forming Eden plc, which was registered and received its trading certificate in December 20X4. It has subsequently come to the attention of the board of directors that the following events had taken place prior to the incorporation of the company:

(a) Don entered into a contract in the company's name to buy computer equipment, which the board of directors do not wish to honour.

(b) Don entered into a contract in the company's name to develop a particular patent, which the board of directors of Eden wish to pursue but in relation to which the other party does not wish to proceed.

(c) Don entered into an agreement with Fad Ltd for business equipment. The agreement was made 'subject to adoption by Eden plc' but now Eden plc does not wish to pursue the agreement.

Required

Analyse the situation from the perspective of the law relating to company promoters and in particular advise the parties involved in the transactions detailed. **(10 marks)**

---

68 Objects clause (2.2 6/05 amended) **18 mins**

In relation to the company's constitution explain:

(a) The extent of a company's objects **(3 marks)**

(b) The meaning and effect of the doctrine of *ultra vires* **(7 marks)**

(Total = 10 marks)

---

69 Articles (2.2 6/04 amended) 18 mins

Explain the meaning and effect of a company's articles of association, paying particular attention to the following issues.

(a) The nature of model articles of association (2 marks)
(b) The effect of the articles on both members and non-members (4 marks)
(c) The procedure for altering the articles of association (4 marks)

(Total = 10 marks)

---

70 Fred (12/08) 18 mins

Fred is a member of Glad Ltd, a small publishing company, holding 100 of its 500 shares; the other 400 shares are held by four other members.

It has recently become apparent that Fred has set up a rival business to Glad Ltd and the other members have decided that he should be expelled from the company.

To that end they propose to alter the articles of association to include a new power to 'require any member to transfer their shares for fair value to the other members upon the passing of a resolution so to do'.

Required

Advise the parties concerned whether or not the proposed change to the articles is legally enforceable and whether or not it can be used to force Fred to sell his shares. (10 marks)

---

71 Company names (6/09) 18 mins

In relation to company law, explain:

(a) The limitations on the use of company names (4 marks)
(b) The tort of 'passing off' (4 marks)
(c) The role of the company names adjudicators under the Companies Act 2006 (2 marks)

(Total = 10 marks)

---

72 Various terms (2.2 6/06) 18 mins

Explain the meaning and consequence of the following terms when found at the end of the names of business organisations:

(a) LLP (3 marks)
(b) Ltd (3 marks)
(c) plc (4 marks)

(Total = 10 marks)

CAPITAL AND THE FINANCING OF COMPANIES

Questions 73 to 83 cover capital and the financing of companies, the subject of Part E of the BPP Study Text for Paper F4.

73 Discount and premium (2.2 12/01) — 18 mins

With regard to payment for shares explain the meaning and effect of the following:

(a) Issuing shares at a discount **(6 marks)**
(b) The share premium account **(4 marks)**

(Total = 10 marks)

---

74 Capital terms I (2.2 12/03 amended) — 18 mins

In relation to a company's shares explain the following:

(a) Nominal value **(2 marks)**
(b) Market value **(2 marks)**
(c) Issued capital **(3 marks)**
(d) Paid up capital **(3 marks)**

(Total = 10 marks)

---

75 Shares and debentures (6/08) — 18 mins

In relation to company law explain the meaning of the following:

(a) Ordinary shares **(3 marks)**
(b) Preference shares **(3 marks)**
(c) Debentures **(4 marks)**

(Total = 10 marks)

---

76 Capital terms II (12/08) — 18 mins

In relation to a company's shares, explain the following:

(a) The statement of capital and initial shareholdings **(4 marks)**
(b) Authorised minimum issued capital in a public company **(2 marks)**
(c) Paid-up capital **(2 marks)**
(d) The difference between nominal value and market value **(2 marks)**

(Total = 10 marks)

---

77 Capital maintenance and reducing share capital (6/09) — 18 mins

In relation to company law, explain:

(a) The doctrine of capital maintenance **(4 marks)**

(b) The circumstances under which both a private and a public company can reduce its capital and the procedure to be followed **(6 marks)**

(Total = 10 marks)

---

78 Class rights (2.2 12/02) **18 mins**

In company law:

(a) Explain the meaning of class rights in relation to company shares providing examples of such rights **(6 marks)**

(b) State how such rights can be altered **(4 marks)**

(Total = 10 marks)

---

79 Flop Ltd (Pilot Paper) **18 mins**

Flop Ltd was in financial difficulties. In January, in order to raise capital, it issued 10,000 £1 shares to Gus, but only asked him to pay 75 pence per share at the time of issue. The directors of Flop Ltd intended asking Gus for the other 25 pence per share at a later date. However, in June it realised that it needed even more than the £2,500 it could raise from Gus's existing shareholding. So in order to persuade Gus to provide the needed money Flop Ltd told him that if he bought a further 10,000 shares he would only have to pay a total of 50 pence for each £1 share, and it would write off the money owed on the original share purchase.

Gus agreed to this, but the injection of cash did not save Flop Ltd and in December it went into insolvent liquidation, owing a considerable amount of money.

Required

Explain any potential liability that Gus might have on the shares he holds in Flop Ltd. **(10 marks)**

---

80 Lux Ltd (2.2 6/07 amended) **18 mins**

In 20X5 two newspaper companies, Kudos Ltd and Lux Ltd, entered into negotiations in an attempt to safeguard their independent positions. As a result, an agreement was reached and a contractual document drawn up to the effect that:

(i) Kudos Ltd was to purchase 15% of Lux Ltd's ordinary share capital and 20% of its preference shares, which carry a preferred dividend of 10%

(ii) Mat, the current deputy editor of Kudos Ltd's paper, was to be appointed as the editor of Lux Ltd's paper, with a contract of employment for five years at a salary of £50,000 per year

Following the agreement the articles of Lux Ltd were altered so as to accommodate all of the above terms.

The majority of the board of directors of Lux Ltd have become disenchanted with their link with Kudos Ltd and want to agree terms for a link with another paper, News Ltd. In order to facilitate this new allegiance they propose:

(a) To remove Mat from his position as editor of the Lux paper
(b) To reduce the dividend on all preference shares to 5%

Required

Advise the directors of Lux Ltd generally as to the nature of class rights and in particular as to the legality of, and procedure for, pursuing their proposals. **(10 marks)**

---

81 Gilt Ltd (6/10) **18 mins**

Gilt Ltd is a small company with an issued share capital of 100,000 £1 shares held by 100 members.

Harry, the managing director of Gilt Ltd, has been approached by Itt plc in respect of its making a takeover bid for Gilt Ltd. Itt plc has given Harry what is described as a facility fee of £50,000 for ensuring that the takeover is successful.

At the next board meeting Harry convinces the other directors that the takeover bid is in the long-term interest of Gilt Ltd, but they are concerned that the holders of the majority of the issued share capital will not approve of the takeover.

In order to ensure the success of the takeover, the directors of Gilt Ltd agree that they should allot sufficient new shares to Itt plc to ensure that a new majority of members will support the takeover.

After the allocation of the shares to Itt plc a general meeting is called to consider the takeover and it is approved, with Itt plc voting in favour.

May, a substantial shareholder in Gilt Ltd, has subsequently found out about the actions of Itt plc, Harry and the other directors.

Required

Advise May as to the legality of the share allotment and as to what action can be taken against Harry. **(10 marks)**

---

82 Dividends (12/07) **18 mins**

In relation to the rules governing the payment of company dividends explain:

(a) How dividends may be properly funded **(4 marks)**
(b) The rules which apply to public limited companies **(3 marks)**
(c) The consequences of any dividend being paid in breach of those rules **(3 marks)**

(Total = 10 marks)

---

83 Debentures and charges (6/10) **18 mins**

Explain the meaning of the following terms in company law:

(a) A debenture **(3 marks)**
(b) A fixed charge **(3 marks)**
(c) A floating charge **(4 marks)**

(Total = 10 marks)

MANAGEMENT, ADMINISTRATION AND REGULATION OF COMPANIES

Questions 84 to 97 cover management, administration and regulation of companies, the subject of Part F of the BPP Study Text for Paper F4.

84 Resolutions (12/08) 18 mins

In relation to private companies, explain the meaning of, and the procedure for passing, the following:

(a) An ordinary and a special resolution **(5 marks)**
(b) A written resolution **(5 marks)**

(Total = 10 marks)

85 Meetings (Pilot Paper) 18 mins

In relation to company law explain and distinguish between the following:

(a) Annual general meeting **(5 marks)**
(b) Other general meetings **(2 marks)**
(c) Class meeting **(3 marks)**

(Total = 10 marks)

86 Company secretary (6/10) 18 mins

In the context of corporate governance, explain the rules relating to the appointment, duties and powers of a company secretary in a public limited company. **(10 marks)**

87 Implied authority and company secretary (2.2 6/07) 18 mins

In relation to the law of agency:

(a) Explain the meaning of implied authority **(6 marks)**
(b) Explain the extent of the implied authority of a company secretary **(4 marks)**

(Total = 10 marks)

88 Appointment and removal (2.2 12/03) 18 mins

In company law explain:

(a) How a director of a company may be appointed **(3 marks)**
(b) How a director may be removed from his position **(7 marks)**

(Total = 10 marks)

89 Statutory grounds for disqualifying directors (6/09) 18 mins

Explain the grounds upon which a person may be disqualified under the Company Directors Disqualification Act 1986. **(10 marks)**

90 Statutory duties — 18 mins

Briefly explain any five of the statutory duties owed by directors to their companies. **(10 marks)**

91 Promoting success (12/08) — 18 mins

In relation to the Companies Act 2006, explain the duty of directors to promote the success of the company, and to whom such a duty is owed. **(10 marks)**

92 Caz (12/09) — 18 mins

Caz is a director of Dull plc, but she also carries out her own business as a wholesale supplier of specialist metals under the name of Era Ltd.

Last year Dull plc entered into a contract to buy a large consignment of metal from Era Ltd. Caz attended the board meeting that approved the contract and voted in favour of it, without revealing any link with Era Ltd.

Required

Analyse the situation explaining any potential liability that Caz may have in relation to the sale of the metal to Dull plc by Era Ltd. **(10 marks)**

93 Directors (6/08) — 18 mins

In relation to company law distinguish between:

(a) Executive directors **(4 marks)**
(b) Non-executive directors **(3 marks)**
(c) Shadow directors **(3 marks)**

(Total = 10 marks)

94 Auditors I (2.2 6/03) — 18 mins

Explain the role of public company auditors paying particular regard to their appointment, removal, rights and duties. **(10 marks)**

95 Auditors II (12/07) — 18 mins

In the context of corporate governance explain the role of the external company auditors, paying particular regard to the following issues:

(a) Their qualifications
(b) Their powers
(c) Their duties **(10 marks)**

96 Katch Ltd (12/07) **18 mins**

Katch Ltd is a small private company. Although there are three members of its board of directors, the actual day-to-day running of the business is left to one of them, Len, who simply reports back to the board on the business he has transacted. Len refers to himself as the managing director of Katch Ltd, although he has never been officially appointed as such.

Six months ago Len entered into a contract on Katch Ltd's behalf with Mo to produce some advertising material for the company. However Katch Ltd did not wish to proceed with the advertising campaign and the board of directors have refused to pay Mo, claiming that Len did not have the necessary authority to enter into the contract with him.

Required

Analyse the situation with regard to the authority of Len to make contracts on behalf of Katch Ltd, and in particular advise whether or not Katch Ltd is liable to Mo. **(10 marks)**

---

97 Clean Ltd (6/09) **18 mins**

Clean Ltd was established some five years ago to manufacture industrial solvents and cleaning solutions, and Des was appointed managing director.

The company's main contract was with Dank plc a large industrial conglomerate.

In the course of its research activity, Clean Ltd's scientists developed a new super glue. Des was very keen to pursue the manufacture of the glue but the board of directors overruled him and decided that the company should stick to its core business.

The managing director of Dank plc is a friend of Des's and has told him that Dank plc will not be renewing its contract with Clean Ltd as he is not happy with its performance. He also told Des that he would be happy to continue to deal with him, if only he was not linked to Clean Ltd.

Following that discussion Des resigned from his position as managing director of Clean Ltd and set up his own company, Flush Ltd which later entered into a contract with Dank plc to replace Clean Ltd. Flush Ltd also manufactures the new glue discovered by Clean Ltd's scientists, which has proved to be very profitable.

Required

In the context of company law, advise the board of Clean Ltd as to whether they can take any action against Des or Flush Ltd. **(10 marks)**

LEGAL IMPLICATIONS OF COMPANIES IN DIFFICULTY OR IN CRISIS

Questions 98 to 102 cover the legal implications of companies in difficulty or in crisis, the subject of Part G of the BPP Study Text for Paper F4.

98 Liquidation (2.2 12/04 amended) — 18 mins

In the context of company liquidation:

(a) State and explain the two main grounds under which a company may be wound up under Section 122 of the Insolvency Act 1986. **(5 marks)**

(b) What are the distinguishing characteristics of a creditors' voluntary winding up? **(5 marks)**

(Total = 10 marks)

99 Compulsory winding up — 18 mins

What is the immediate legal effect of an order of the court for the compulsory winding up of a company? **(10 marks)**

100 Lazy Days — 18 mins

Lazy Days Ltd is a coach tour company. It recently leased a fleet of five brand new 'Executive style' coaches ahead of an anticipated increase in business. The coaches cost a total of £20,000 a month to lease, and on top of this, the business also has to pay its overheads including staff costs – a total of £15,000 per month. The increase in business did not materialise and Lazy Days is only generating £28,000 of revenue per month. The coach trips are going out on average 50% full of passengers.

Noelle, the Finance director is increasingly concerned about the situation and has called a meeting of the board of directors to discuss the situation and the possibility of putting the business into administration.

Advise Noelle of:

(a) The purpose and effect of an administration order **(3 marks)**

(b) The procedure to be followed when applying for administration **(5 marks)**

(c) Whether or not it is likely that an administration order would be granted for Lazy Days Ltd **(2 marks)**

(Total = 10 marks)

101 Compulsory winding up and administration (12/09) — 18 mins

In the context of companies in financial difficulty, distinguish between and explain the operation of:

(a) Compulsory winding up **(4 marks)**

(b) Administration **(6 marks)**

(Total = 10 marks)

102 Earl (12/07) 18 mins

Earl has been employed by Flash Ltd for the past 20 years. During that time he has also invested in the company in the form of shares and debentures. Earl owns 5,000 ordinary shares in Flash Ltd. The shares are of £1 nominal value and are paid up to the extent of 75%. The debentures, to the value of £5,000, are secured by a fixed charge against the land on which Flash Ltd's factory is built.

In April it was announced that Flash Ltd was going into immediate insolvent liquidation, owing considerable amounts of money to trade creditors. As a result of the suddenness of the decision to liquidate the company, none of the employees received their last month's wages. In Earl's case this amounted to £2,000.

Required

Advise Earl as to his rights and liabilities in relation to Flash Ltd in regard to:

(a) His unpaid wages **(3 marks)**

(b) His shareholding **(3 marks)**

(c) His debentures **(4 marks)**

(Total = 10 marks)

GOVERNANCE AND ETHICAL ISSUES RELATING TO BUSINESS

Questions 103 to 110 cover governance and ethical issues relating to business, the subject of Part H of the BPP Study Text for Paper F4.

103 Directors and corporate governance (Pilot Paper) 18 mins

(a) Explain briefly what is meant by 'corporate governance'. **(4 marks)**

(b) Within the context of corporate governance examine the role of, and relationship between, executive directors and non-executive directors. **(6 marks)**

(Total = 10 marks)

---

104 UK Corporate Governance Code 18 mins

Explain how the UK Corporate Governance Code attempts to regulate a board of directors. **(10 marks)**

---

105 Huge plc (Pilot Paper) 18 mins

In January the board of directors of Huge plc decided to make a takeover bid for Large plc. After the decision was taken, but before it is announced, the following chain of events occurs:

(i) Slye, a director of Huge plc, buys shares in Large plc

(ii) Slye tells his friend Mate about the likelihood of the takeover and Mate buys shares in Large plc

(iii) at a dinner party Slye, without actually telling him about the takeover proposal, advises his brother Tim to buy shares in Large plc and Tim does so

Required

Consider the legal position of Slye, Mate and Tim under the law relating to insider dealing. **(10 marks)**

---

106 Sid and Vic (6/08) 18 mins

Sid is a director of two listed public companies in which he has substantial shareholdings: Trend plc and Umber plc.

The annual reports of both Trend plc and Umber plc have just been drawn up although not yet disclosed. They show that Trend plc has made a surprisingly big loss and that Umber plc has made an equally surprising big profit. On the basis of this information Sid sold his shares in Trend plc and bought shares in Umber plc. He also advised his brother to buy shares in Umber plc.

Vic who is also a shareholder in both companies sold a significant number of shares in Umber plc only the day before its annual report was published.

Required

(a) Analyse the above scenario from the perspective of the law relating to insider dealing **(8 marks)**

(b) In particular advise Vic as to his position **(2 marks)**

(Total = 10 marks)

---

107 Wrongful trading (2.2 12/05) 18 mins

Explain the meaning and effect of 'wrongful trading' under s.214 of the Insolvency Act 1986. **(10 marks)**

---

108 Fran, Gram and Hen (12/09) — 18 mins

Fran, Gram and Hen registered a private limited company Ire Ltd in January 20X5 with a share capital of £300, which was equally divided between them, with each of them becoming a director of the company.

Although the company did manage to make a small profit in its first year of trading, it was never a great success and in its second year of trading it made a loss of £10,000.

At that time Fran said he thought the company should cease trading and be wound up. Gram and Hen, however, were insistent that the company would be profitable in the long-term so they agreed to carry on the business, with Fran taking less of a part in the day-to-day management of the business, although retaining his position as a company director.

In the course of the next three years Gram and Hen falsified Ire Ltd's accounts to disguise the fact that the company had continued to suffer losses, until it became obvious that they could no longer hide the company's debts and that it would have to go into insolvent liquidation, with debts of £100,000.

Required

Advise Fran, Gram and Hen as to any potential liability they might face as regards:

(a) Fraudulent trading, under both criminal and civil law **(5 marks)**
(b) Wrongful trading under s.214 of the Insolvency Act 1986 **(5 marks)**

(Total = 10 marks)

---

109 Money laundering (2.2 12/05) — 18 mins

(a) Explain the term 'money laundering' and how such activity is conducted. **(5 marks)**
(b) Explain how the Proceeds of Crime Act 2002 seeks to control money laundering. **(5 marks)**

(Total = 10 marks)

---

110 Greg (6/09) — 18 mins

Greg is a member of the board of directors of Huge plc. He also controls a private limited company Imp Ltd through which he operates a management consultancy business. He also owns all the shares in Jet Ltd through which he conducts an investment business.

When Greg learns that Huge plc is going to make a take-over bid for Kop plc he arranges for Jet Ltd to buy a large number of shares in Kop plc on the London Stock Exchange on which it makes a large profit when it sells them after the takeover bid is announced. He then arranges for Jet Ltd to transfer the profit to Imp Ltd as the charge for supposed consultancy work. The money is then transferred to Greg through the declaration of dividends by Imp Ltd.

Required

Analyse the above conduct from the perspective of criminal law paying particular attention to the issues of:

(a) Insider dealing; and **(5 marks)**
(b) Money laundering **(5 marks)**

(Total = 10 marks)

Answers

1 Types of law

Text Reference. Chapter 1

Top tips. Even though you are not asked for it, defining law at the start of your answer will show the marker that you have thought about the question and provides a good base to build the rest of your answer on. Do not go into too much detail about each type of law – remember there are limited marks available for each, though part (a) is worth slightly more as both common law and equity are needed in the answer. Writing too much will not earn you extra marks and will cost you valuable time.

Easy marks. A brief definition and explanation of each type of law will earn you enough marks to pass.

Law is a **formal control mechanism**. It provides a structure for dealing with and resolving disputes that may arise, as well as providing some deterrent to those wishing to disrupt social order.

(a) **Common law**

Common law developed in England during the period following the Norman Conquest. It was made by judges who travelled around the country to keep the King's peace and made law by **amalgamating local customary laws** into one 'law of the land'. Today, the concept of **precedent** continues as this key feature of common law is what distinguishes it from other legal systems.

Remedies under common law are monetary, and are known as **damages**.

Equity

Common law does not provide justice to the wronged person if monetary compensation is **not a suitable remedy**. For example, where a person needs to **stop** another person's behaviour or to force them to **act** as they agreed to, **equity** provides remedies to achieve this and other non-monetary resolutions.

Equity developed two or three hundred years after common law as a system to resolve such disputes and to therefore introduce **fairness** into the legal system.

(b) **Civil law**

Civil law exists to regulate disputes over the rights and obligations of persons dealing with each other and seeks to compensate injured parties.

It is therefore a form of **private law** (between individuals) and there is no concept of punishment. The object is to **compensate** the wronged person for the damage they suffered. Where civil cases go to court, the case must be proved on the balance of probability. The object is to convince the court that it is more probable than not that the assertions of the wronged person are true. However, both parties may choose to settle the dispute out of court should they wish.

(c) **Criminal law**

In **criminal cases**, the state prosecutes the wrongdoer for a crime that they have committed. A crime is conduct that is prohibited by the law.

It is therefore a form of **public law** (between the State and individuals). The State is the prosecutor because it is the community as a whole which suffers as a result of the law being broken. Persons guilty of crime may be **punished** by fines payable to the State, imprisonment, or a community-based punishment. In a criminal trial, the burden of proof to convict the accused rests with the prosecution, which must prove its case beyond reasonable doubt.

In the UK, the police take the initial decision to **prosecute**, but this is then reviewed by the Crown Prosecution Service. However, some prosecutions are started by the Director of Public Prosecutions, who is the head of the Crown Prosecution Service.

2 Legal system and courts

Text reference. Chapter 1

Top tips. It is very easy to write too much when answering this question. You will only have about 9 minutes to answer Part (a) and the same period of time for Part (b) so ensure your answer sticks strictly to the facts. It may help you to quickly list a selection of facts for each part before writing your answer so you do not become distracted and begin to waffle.

Easy marks. Stating the nature of criminal and civil law in Part (a) and remembering the appeals procedure for each court system in Part (b).

Examiner's comments. There was often an attempt to consider certain relevant factors such as criminal proceedings are brought by the state and civil proceedings by the individual and the aim of criminal proceedings is to punish by fines or imprisonment while civil proceedings aim to compensate by way of damages. Also there was some mention of the different standards of proof. A small number noted the different methods of citation and the fact that different courts are involved. The outcome was that many candidates produced a reasonable response. Some candidates thought that the death penalty was still carried out in England.

Marking scheme

		Marks
(a)	A thorough to comprehensive explanation of the difference between the two types of law.	3–5
	Ranging from some but little knowledge down to no understanding at all of the differences.	0–2
(b)	Full explanation of both court systems.	4–5
	Some explanation of the courts in both systems.	2–3
	Little or no knowledge of either court system or, at the higher end of this grade, some knowledge of one of the systems.	0–1

(a) (i) **Criminal law**

A **crime** is conduct prohibited by the law. In a **criminal case** the State is the prosecutor because it is the community as a whole which suffers as a result of the law being broken. Persons guilty of crime may be punished by **fines** payable to the State, **imprisonment**, or a **community-based** punishment. Criminal cases are usually referred to as *R v Jones*. The prosecution is brought in the name of the Crown against the alleged wrongdoer, the **accused**. In a criminal trial, the **burden of proof** to convict the accused rests with the **prosecution**, which must prove its case **beyond reasonable doubt**.

(ii) **Civil law**

Civil law exists to **regulate disputes** over the **rights** and **obligations** of persons dealing with each other, and seeks to compensate injured parties. It is a form of **private law** and covers areas such as tort, contract and employment law. In civil proceedings, the case must be proved on the **balance of probability,** the object is to convince the court that it is more probable than not that a person's assertions are true. There is no concept of **punishment**, and **compensation** is paid to the wronged person. Both parties may choose to **settle** the dispute **out of court** should they wish.

Terminology in civil cases is different from that in criminal cases. The **claimant** sues the **defendant**. A civil case would therefore be referred to as, for example, *Smith v Megacorp plc.*

It is not an act or event which creates the distinction between criminal and civil law, but the **legal consequences**. A single event might give rise to both criminal and civil proceedings.

(b) **Jurisdiction of criminal courts**

All criminal cases begin in **Magistrates' Courts** where the case is introduced into the system. Certain types of offence are known as **indictable offences**; these are serious offences and can only be heard in a Crown Court. Other, less serious **summary offences** are heard summarily in the Magistrates' Court. Where an offence falls in between the two it can be **'triable either way':** this means the defendant will have the choice to be tried by the Magistrate or at the Crown Court in front of a **jury**.

Where the decision in a **criminal case** is appealed against, a court further up the hierarchy will hear it. **Appeals** from Magistrates' Courts are either to the **Crown Court** or the **Queen's Bench Division** (QBD) of the **High Court**. Appeals can be by way of **'case stated'**, on the basis that the law was misinterpreted by the Magistrate.

Appeals against **conviction** or **sentence** from the **Crown Court** are heard at the **Court of Appeal** and this may in turn be appealed to the **Supreme Court**. Case stated appeals from the Crown Court are made to QBD.

Jurisdiction of civil courts

The nature of the case and the size of the claim will determine which court hears a civil case. **County Courts** deal with almost every kind of civil case that is **small** or which are deemed to be **'Fast Track'** cases. The case is heard by a Circuit Judge assisted by District Judges.

Complicated cases or those which are deemed to be **'Multi Track'** cases are heard at the **High Court**. The **Queen's Bench Division** hears cases of **contract** and **tort**. The **Family Division** hears cases involving **children** and **matrimonial** issues such as divorce. The **Chancery Division** hears cases concerning **trusts**, **bankruptcy** and **corporate** matters.

Appeals are to the **Civil Division** of the **Court of Appeal** and are heard by three judges who will decide the outcome by a majority. As with criminal cases, a further appeal to the **Supreme Court** may be permitted.

3 Civil courts

Text reference. Chapter 1.

Top tips. Before you start a question like this it is worth drawing a rough diagram of the civil court system to use as a plan. This will help to ensure that you don't forget any of the courts involved. Keep your answer strictly to the civil courts - you will gain no marks for discussing the criminal courts.

Easy marks. Stating and describing each court.

ACCA examiner's answers. The ACCA examiner's answer to this question can be found at the back of this kit.

Examiners' comments. A number of candidates produced answers about the doctrine of precedent and although their answers did refer to the hierarchical structure of the courts, there was much that was not necessary in their answers.

Other common errors were that candidates sometimes got mixed up with the hierarchical structure and thought that the divisions of the High Court were actually parts of the Magistrates' Court. There was also frequent reference to the House of Lords, which demonstrated a lack of knowledge on the reform of the UK judicial system. In some instances candidates completely misinterpreted the question and wrote all they knew on Acts of Parliament and what stages a bill had to be passed through before becoming an Act, or they described at great length the literal rule and golden rule.

Marking scheme

This question requires candidates to describe the structure and functions of the main civil courts in the English legal system.

8–10 marks:	A thorough to complete description of the various civil courts with an explanation of their relationships and function. At this level it is required that answers make reference to the Supreme Court.
5–7 marks:	A less detailed treatment of the court structure but still covering the main courts. This represents the maximum mark that can be achieved without reference to the Supreme Court.
3–4 marks:	Weak answer, perhaps just providing a sketch of the court structure with no explanation of that structure.
0–2 marks:	Little or no understanding of the topic.

The courts in the English legal system which have a **civil jurisdiction** are as follows.

Magistrates' Court

The **Magistrates' Court** is mainly a criminal court, but it also has original jurisdiction in a number of civil cases, particularly family proceedings. It hears many domestic issues such as proceedings for the financial provision for parties to a marriage and children, the custody or supervision of children and guardianship, and adoption orders. It will also hear claims for recovery of unpaid local authority charges and council tax.

County Court

The **County Court** only hears civil cases, but deals with virtually every type of civil matter arising within the geographical area which it serves. In some types of case, its jurisdiction is concurrent with that of the High Court. The main limits to its jurisdiction are financial. It is involved in hearing the following:

- Actions in **contract** and **tort**
- **Equitable matters** concerning trusts, mortgages and partnership dissolution
- Disputes concerning **land**
- Undefended **matrimonial** cases
- **Probate** matters
- **Miscellaneous** matters conferred by various statutes, for example, the Consumer Credit Act 1974
- Some **bankruptcy**, company **winding-up** and **admiralty** cases.

High Court

The **High Court** also deals with civil cases at first instance. It is divided into three sections.

The **Queen's Bench Division** deals with common law matters, such as contract and tort. It also includes a Commercial Court and an Admiralty Court (to deal with shipping cases). A Divisional Court of the QBD has an appellate jurisdiction on cases from Magistrates' Courts.

The **Chancery Division** of the High Court deals with equity matters such as trusts, mortgages, bankruptcy, taxation, probate and partnerships. It also has a special Companies Court which deals with liquidations and other company proceedings, and a Patents Court.

The **Family Division** of the High Court deals with matrimonial cases, family property and proceedings relating to children. The Family Division also has a limited appellate function in that it hears some appeals on domestic matters from the Magistrates' Courts.

Appeal courts

The civil courts which have an exclusively **appellate jurisdiction** are the **Civil Division of the Court of Appeal** and the **Supreme Court**.

Court of Appeal

The **Court of Appeal** hears appeals from the High Court, County Courts and several special tribunals. It reviews the evidence and the legal opinions and makes its decisions based on them. Cases are usually heard by three judges sitting together (known as Lord Justices of Appeal).

Supreme Court

The **Supreme Court** is the highest court of appeal in the English legal system. Cases are heard by Justices of the Supreme Court. The court hears appeals from the Court of Appeal, and also appeals from the High Court under the 'leapfrog procedure' where leave to appeal is granted.

4 Contemporary sources of law

Text reference. Chapter 2.

Top tips. Take a minute or two at the start of the question to clarify in your own mind what points you need to include. Ensure your answer refers to the 'contemporary' sources of law rather than historical ones.

Easy marks. Make sure that you include and explain each source in your answer. Don't just state what they are.

Examiner's comments. This question required the candidates to consider the various sources of contemporary UK law. The better answers displayed a competent understanding of what was required. There was firstly, a reference to legislation being formulated by Parliament, along with the process involved. Many answers continued with a rather detailed coverage of delegated legislation- examples, advantages and disadvantages. On precedent the good answers explained the nature of judicial precedent including the legal rule on which a judicial decision is based – ratio decidendi comparing that with other statements of law which do not form the basis of the decision - obiter dicta. However most coverage concerned the hierarchy of authority as a factor in determining the importance of a precedent.

Marking scheme

In order to get full marks candidates must deal well with each of the three areas and not confine themselves to an extended treatment of only one, or two of them. Also the question asks for a consideration of the main sources of contemporary law. It would be inappropriate, therefore, to present an extended treatment of the role of custom as a source of law, to the exclusion of a more detailed treatment of the other sources. The following marking scheme details the way in which marks would be allocated in relation to this question.

Each major part would be notionally allocated 3 marks, with the additional mark for a particularly good treatment of one of the sources or reference to some other source.

8–10 marks:	Thorough treatment of the three major sources with perhaps reference to other sources such as custom or perhaps the role of the Law Commission, although the latter is certainly not necessary.
5–7 marks:	Thorough treatment of two of the sources, or a less complete treatment of the three.
2–4 marks:	Some understanding but lacking in detail. Perhaps unbalanced answer, focusing on only one aspect of the question and ignoring the others.
0–1 mark:	Shows little understanding of the subject matter of the question.

Sources of English law

There are **three main sources of English law**, namely **legislation** (statute), **case law** and **custom**. Broadly speaking, legislation is made by the legislature in Parliament and case law is 'made' and developed in the courts. Therefore, as both of these sources create law today, they can be considered contemporary. However, local customs, which developed historically and have generally existed for a very long time, are not considered to be contemporary.

Legislation

Statute law is made by **Parliament**. Parliament may make law as it sees fit – it may repeal earlier statutes, overrule case law developed in the courts or make law in new areas previously unregulated. The validity of an Act of Parliament cannot be questioned *(Cheney v Conn 1968)*. This principle of Parliamentary sovereignty has been reduced somewhat by the UK's membership of the European Union which requires its laws to be brought into line with the EU's treaties and directives. Additionally, the Human Rights Act 1998 requires new laws to be compatible with the European Convention on Human Rights.

Additional material

The paragraph below is not vital for your answer. We have included it for the sake of completeness. It would probably only be worth 1 mark if included in your answer.

A proposal for legislation is first aired in a **Green Paper**. After comments are received, a **White Paper** is issued. This is then put into draft form as a **Bill** and introduced into the House of Commons or the House of Lords. Once a Bill has passed through the necessary stages in one House, it is introduced into the other House. In each, the successive stages are the **first reading** (publication only), **second reading** (debate), **Committee stage** (examination by a Standing Committee), **report stage** (approval by the full House) and **third reading** (final approval). Finally, a Bill receives the **Royal Assent** prior to becoming an Act of Parliament.

Statute law may be **'fresh' legislation** or it may be a **consolidation of existing statutes** and their amendments, for example the Companies Act 2006. It may also be a codification of existing statutory and case law, for example the Sale of Goods Act 1979.

The courts are **bound to apply** relevant statute law and cannot choose to disregard or rewrite it. Whatever the nature of the legislation, the role of judges to **interpret and apply it** is the same. Judicial interpretation might be needed because of ambiguity in drafting or uncertainty as to whether a particular set of facts are within the scope of a statute, or where unforeseeable developments have occurred since the statute was passed.

The **complexity** of much modern legislation means that, in many instances, there is a **great deal of detail** which cannot conveniently be included in an Act. Therefore, legislation often gives power to a minister or public body, such as a local authority, to make laws for specified purposes in the form of statutory instruments, bye-laws and Rules of Court. Such **delegated legislation** has the same legal force and effect as the empowering Act itself.

Case law

Case law is law which is made in the **courts** according to the rules of **common law and equity**. Both common law and equity are the product of decisions in the courts made by judges who interpret and apply previous cases based on a principle of consistency, the doctrine of *stare decisis* or **binding precedent**.

This doctrine provides that once a principle of law has been decided in court, it becomes a precedent which, generally speaking, **binds the lower courts in cases with materially the same facts**. If the facts of the case are not materially the same as those of the relevant precedent, the precedent may be 'distinguished' and not followed.

In order to be a binding precedent, a decision must be based on a **proposition of law** and not a question of fact. It must **form part of the ratio decidendi** of the case; this is 'any rule of law expressly or impliedly treated by the judge as a necessary step in reaching his conclusion, having regard to the line of reasoning adopted by him, or a necessary part of his direction to the jury' (Cross).

Statements which announce **legal principle** but **do not form part of the ratio decidendi** and statements which are based on **hypothetical facts** are not precedents but are *obiter dicta* and of persuasive authority only.

Whether the doctrine of binding precedent applies depends on the **status of the court** dealing with the case and that of the court which delivered the 'precedent' judgment. There is a **hierarchy of courts** with the lower courts being bound to follow the decisions of the higher courts. Therefore, for example, Magistrates' Courts and County Courts are bound by decisions of the High Court, the Court of Appeal and the Supreme Court.

5 Precedent

Text reference. Chapter 2.

Top tips. Allocate your time to all parts of the question carefully. Notice that part (c) asks you about the advantages and disadvantages of binding precedent, so you do not need to include those in part (a).

Easy marks. Include a mention of all of the courts in the structure to maximise the breadth of your answer. In part (c) be sure to discuss both the advantages and disadvantages, as there will be marks for both. You can't earn marks if you don't address the specific issues asked for.

Marking scheme

This question requires candidates to explain the doctrine of precedent, the hierarchical structure of the English court system and the operation of the doctrine of precedent. It is essential that all aspects of the question be dealt with.

6-10 marks	A good to full explanation of the doctrine of precedent together with a description of the position and relationship of the various courts within the hierarchy will result in full marks. The more full the explanation and the more detailed the description, the higher will be the marks awarded.
0-5 marks	Unbalanced answer, perhaps lacking in detail in relation to the court structure or the operation of precedent. A mere diagram of the court structure will gain no more than 2 marks at most.

(a) **Binding precedent**

The doctrine of **binding precedent**, or *stare decisis*, is essential to the English legal system. It provides that in determining any case, where the facts of the case are materially the same as in a previous case heard by a superior (or sometimes equal) court, then the court will be bound by any proposition of law which formed part of the *ratio decidendi* of that previous case. The purpose of the doctrine is to provide **coherency**, **consistency** and, therefore, **predictability** and **fairness** in the development of case law.

Ratio decidendi* and *obiter dicta

Only a **proposition of law**, as opposed to a statement of fact, will be binding. The *ratio decidendi* of a case has been defined as 'any rule of law, express or implied, treated by a judge as a necessary step in reaching his conclusion, having regard to the line of reasoning adopted by him, or a necessary part of his direction to the jury' (Cross). The *ratio decidendi* is often difficult to identify and should be contrasted with *obiter dicta;* these might be propositions of law which do not form part of the basis for the decision, or statements based on hypothetical facts rather than the actual facts before the court. *Obiter dicta* are of persuasive authority only and do not bind later courts.

(b) The **hierarchy of the courts** is as follows.

Magistrates', County and Crown Courts

Decisions of the **Magistrates' Courts** and **County Courts** do not constitute precedent and are therefore not binding on any court, but each of these courts is bound by decisions of the High Court, Court of Appeal and the Supreme Court. The **Crown Court** is also bound by the superior courts and its decisions are of persuasive authority only.

High Court

A decision of the **High Court** (an individual judge) binds all lower courts, but does not bind another High Court judge. However, it is of persuasive authority and tends to be followed in practice. A decision of a **Divisional Court of the High Court** binds any other divisional court as well as a judge sitting alone. A Divisional Court decision usually binds another Divisional Court, although in rare circumstances it may have regard to the exceptions available to the Court of Appeal arising from the *Bristol Aeroplane* case.

Court of Appeal

The **Court of Appeal's** decisions are binding on all English courts (except the Supreme Court). The Court is normally bound by its own previous majority and unanimous decisions, by those of its predecessors and by those of the Supreme Court.

Supreme Court

The **Supreme Court** stands at the apex of the English judicial system. Its decisions are binding on all other English courts. It generally regards itself as bound by its own earlier decisions but it reserves the right to depart from its own precedents in exceptional cases, although this discretion is rarely exercised.

(c) There are a number of widely accepted **advantages** to the doctrine of binding precedent.

Certainty

The doctrine helps to ensure certainty, fairness and predictability of decisions. The need for costly and time-consuming litigation can be avoided where the facts of a case are so materially similar to those of a previous case that the outcome can be foretold. The doctrine also gives guidance to judges and leads to consistency in decisions from different judges in different courts and in different parts of the country.

Clarity

Since only propositions of law forming part of the ratio decidendi of a case constitute binding precedent, it should be the case that the doctrine gives rise to a healthy source of statements of legal principle that can helpfully and clearly be applied to new cases generally. This leads to a saving of time for all concerned, in that cases do not need to be put before the courts and argued again.

Flexibility

The doctrine allows the law to grow and be developed in accordance with changing needs and circumstances of society and allows a much more flexible judge-made law than Parliament-enacted legislation.

Practicality

Another advantage of the doctrine of judicial precedent sometimes put forward is that it has its roots in tried and tested cases and not in theory, as is often the case with new legislation. As a result, there should perhaps be less uncertainty and misunderstanding in its application.

A number of **disadvantages** can also be identified.

Inflexibility

It can be argued that with certainty comes rigidity, inflexibility and undesirable decisions being reached because judges are obliged to apply earlier decisions. This makes the law more complicated especially where judges are clearly at pains to avoid being bound by a precedent which would cause such a result.

Lack of clarity

There may also be a lack of clarity. Although possibly not strictly a 'disadvantage' of the doctrine, the criticism is sometimes made that these propositions of law are often not clear enough and there may appear to be conflicting propositions in the same judgment or discrepancies between propositions reached in more than one case.

Uncertainty

There can also be uncertainty, because there are only a finite number of precedents available and so it is often not possible to predict exactly how a court may decide a particular case.

Unconstitutional

It may also be argued that the doctrine is unconstitutional. It is sometimes said that the flexibility given to unelected judges is too great as it effectively allows them to make law not just to apply law.

Complexity

The disadvantage of the level of detail often contained in judgments is that the bulk of material makes subsequent reading, digesting and application of judges' decisions unnecessarily difficult and complicated. The distinguishing of cases can also become more tenuous the more detail is included.

6 Precedent; terms

Text reference. Chapters 1 and 2.

Top tips. Make it easy for the marker to award you marks by using a separate paragraph to explain each type of precedent – give each paragraph a header too.

Easy marks. Defining each type of precedent.

Examiner's comments. This question required candidates to consider the doctrine of precedent and in particular to explain particular terms operative within that doctrine. On the whole it was done fairly well. However the greatest shortcoming was in relation to the lack of information about the hierarchy of the courts within the English legal system and the implications this has for the doctrine of precedent.

Marking scheme

This question requires candidates to consider the doctrine of precedent and in particular to explain particular terms operative within that doctrine.

(a)	3–4 marks	A thorough, to complete answer, explaining the meaning of the two terms.
	0–2 marks	A less than complete answer, probably unbalanced, focusing only on one of the terms, or lacking in detail.
(b)	4–6 marks	Thorough treatment of the topic. Clearly explaining the meaning of the two types of precedent.
	2–3 marks	Less thorough answer, but showing a reasonable understanding of the topic of precedent.
	0–1 mark	Weak answer, perhaps showing some knowledge but little understanding of the topic generally.

(a) **Judgements**

A judgement in a case will start with a description of the facts and probably a review of earlier precedents. The judge will then make **statements of law applicable to the legal problems** raised by the material facts. Statements are classed as either **ratio decidendi** or **obiter dicta**.

Ratio decidendi

Statements, which if used as the **basis for the decision**, are known as the **ratio decidendi** of the case. This is the vital element that **binds future judges**.

Obiter dicta

Statements made by a judge which are said 'by the way' are known as **obiter dicta**. They **do not form part of the ratio decidendi** and are not binding in future cases as they are merely persuasive.

There are **two types** of obiter dicta:

- A judge's statements of **legal principle** that do not form the basis of the decision.
- A judge's statements that are not based on the material facts, but on **hypothetical facts**.

It is not always easy to distinguish the **ratio decidendi and obiter dicta**. In decisions of appeal courts, where there are several separate judgements, the members of the court may reach the same conclusion but give different reasons. Many judges indicate in their speeches which comments are 'ratio' and which are 'obiter'.

(b) **Judicial precedent**

Case law in England is based on the system of judicial precedent which states that **principles of English law do not become inoperative through the lapse of time**. Precedent, or the principle of consistency, is expressed in the maxim **stare decisis**, which means 'to stand by a decision'. In any later case to which a legal principle is relevant, the same principle should (subject to certain exceptions) be applied.

Court hierarchy

The **court system** in the UK is split into those courts which deal with **civil law** cases and those which deal with **criminal law cases**. Cases begin in Courts of First instance, which in civil cases is usually the **County Court** and in the criminal system is the **Magistrates' Court**. Decisions of these courts can be appealed to courts higher up in the hierarchy which include the relevant Division of the **High Court** and **Court of Appeal**. The final appeal court in the UK is the **Supreme Court**. Decisions of the courts in the hierarchy create two types of judicial precedent, **binding** and **persuasive**.

Binding precedent

Binding precedent means that a judge is bound to apply a decision from an earlier case to the facts of the case before them, provided, among other conditions, there is no material difference between the current case and the previous case which created the 'binding' precedent.

Persuasive precedent

Apart from binding precedents, reported conclusions of any court may be treated as **persuasive precedents** in future cases. Persuasive precedents may be, but need not be, followed in a later case. This is because a court of higher status is free to disregard the verdict of a court of lower status.

Where an earlier decision was made by a lower court, a judge can **overrule** the earlier ratio decidendi if they disagree with the lower court's statement of the law. **The outcome of the earlier judgement remains the same, but will not be followed in future**.

If the decision of a lower court is appealed to a higher one, the higher court may **reverse** the decision if they feel the lower court has wrongly interpreted the law. **When a decision is reversed through appeal, the higher court is usually also overruling the lower court's statement of the law**.

7 Legal terms

Text reference. Chapter 2.

Top tips. Don't forget that you are required to highlight the *differences* between the terms.

Easy marks. There are five easy marks available just for addressing each of the terms.

Examiner's comments. Many answers in part (a) only provided a translation of the two Latin terms and did not expand upon them and explain their different effects. Answers to part (b) tended to be unsatisfactory, as few candidates could explain that reversing relates to decisions and over-ruling relates to *ratios*.

Marking scheme

This question requires candidates to consider the doctrine of precedent and in particular to explain particular terms operative within that doctrine.

(a)	3–5 marks	A thorough, to complete answer, explaining the meaning of the two terms.
	0–2 marks	A less than complete answer, probably unbalanced, focusing only on one of the terms, or lacking in detail.
(b)	3–5 marks	A thorough answer demonstrating a clear understanding of the three terms.
	0–2 marks	A less than complete answer, probably unbalanced, focusing only on one or two of the terms, or lacking in detail.

(a) **Binding precedent**

The doctrine of **binding precedent**, or *stare decisis*, provides that in determining any case, where the facts of the case are materially the same as in a previous case heard by a superior (or sometimes equal) court, then the court will be bound by any proposition of law which formed part of the *ratio decidendi* of that previous case.

In practice, the doctrine means that decisions of the Magistrates' and County Courts are not binding on anyone but they are bound by decisions of the High Court, Court of Appeal and the Supreme Court.

The purpose of the doctrine is to provide coherency, consistency and, therefore, predictability and fairness in the development of case law. A comprehensive, consistent and objective system of reporting of cases is necessary for the doctrine to operate, as this enables lawyers to have access to previous relevant cases.

Ratio decidendi

Only a **proposition of law**, as opposed to a statement of fact, will be binding. The *ratio decidendi* of a case has been defined as 'any rule of law, express or implied, treated by a judge as a necessary step in reaching his conclusion, having regard to the line of reasoning adopted by him, or a necessary part of his direction to the jury' (Cross).

Obiter dictum

The *ratio decidendi* is often difficult to identify and should be contrasted with *obiter dicta* which might be propositions of law which do not form part of the basis for the decision or statements based on hypothetical facts rather than the actual facts before the court. *Obiter dicta* are of **persuasive authority** only and do not bind later courts. This means that they may be taken into account, but need not necessarily be followed.

Differences

It is not always easy to **distinguish** between the *ratio decidendi* and the *obiter dicta*. Judges do not always make clear in their comments whether a particular statement or conclusion is 'ratio' or 'obiter'. Indeed, in a case heard by more than one judge, each judge may provide a different ratio decidendi in support of a common decision.

(b) **Precedent**

When a case is decided, the **principle underlying that decision becomes a precedent**. In later cases, judges will look to that precedent and may be bound to make their decisions in accordance with the doctrine of judicial precedent. In certain circumstances, however, a judge may not wish to follow an earlier decision and it may be open to them to reverse, overrule or distinguish the precedent.

Reversing

Once a decision has been reached in a case by the court of first instance (the court where the case was originally heard), the party against whom the court's finding is reached may decide, or be given leave, to appeal against the decision. If the appellate court decides that the original decision was incorrect, it is said to '**reverse**' the original decision. The original decision cannot subsequently form a precedent. For example, where the Court of Appeal reverses a decision of the High Court, the first decision cannot be a precedent but the reversed decision becomes one instead.

Overruling

Following the example given above; if the first decision (by the High Court) had been reached by following precedent, then in reversing that decision, the Court of Appeal also '**overrules**' that earlier precedent which formed the *ratio decidendi.* It can be seen that overruling involves an earlier case, rather than a case which is the subject of an appeal. Higher courts may overrule the decisions of lower courts, depriving those earlier decisions of their precedent status.

When a decision is overruled, the **law is changed with retrospective effect**. Judges are usually cautious before overruling a long-standing precedent, but this is sometimes necessary, for example where what is acceptable within a particular society changes.

Distinguishing

For a precedent to be followed, the facts of the previous case and the case under consideration must be materially the same. To the extent that there are significant differences in the material facts between the two cases, the previous case may be '**distinguished**' and therefore not followed.

8 Common law and legislation

Text reference. Chapters 1 and 2.

Top tips. This is a very straightforward question that requires you to explain two sources of English law. The answer below provides far more detail than you would be expected to produce in the exam, and is designed to cover a wide range of possible answers.

Before writing your answer to each part, quickly list all of the points that you need to make. Aim for one point per mark. This will enable you to write your answer quickly and keep it focused on the question in hand.

According to the examiner's model answer for part (a), you would also gain marks if you explained some advantages and disadvantages of common law - although this was not specifically asked for in the question.

In part (b), you would also gain marks if you explained the rules of statutory interpretation – again not specifically required by the question.

Easy marks. Basic marks are available for defining the sources of law.

Examiner's comments. This question dealt with a central aspect of the English legal system. It was divided into two parts with part (a) referring to the common law and part (b) referring to legislation. As has been the case for a number of years candidates did not do particularly well in this question which is surprising given that the first question is always on aspects of the legal system. Of concern was the fact that a number of candidates simply did not do this question.

Marking scheme

(a)	4–6 marks	Good explanation of the common law. Examples used to highlight answers.
	2–3 marks	Sound understanding but perhaps no examples.
	0–1 marks	Little knowledge only about the topic.
(b)	3–4 marks	Good awareness of the meaning and effect of legislation.
	0–2 marks	Limited knowledge only about the topic.

(a) **Common law**

Common law is the earliest element of the English legal system. It is a system of rigid rules laid down by the **Royal Courts** following the Norman Conquest. The 'law of the land' was created by **judges** who travelled around the country keeping the King's peace. By applying and amalgamating **local customary laws**, a body of legal rules common to the whole country was created.

The doctrine of **judicial precedent** underpins the common law and English law generally. A key principle is that **legal principles do not become inoperative through the lapse of time**. This doctrine means that a judge is bound to apply a decision from an earlier case to the facts of the case before him. This is provided that there is no material difference between the cases and that the previous case created a '**binding' precedent**.

When making a judgement, a judge will make various statements. These statements are either classed as **ratio decidendi** or **obiter dicta**. Judgements start with a description of the facts of the case and probably a review of earlier precedents.

The judge will then make **statements of law applicable to the legal problems** raised by the material facts. The facts which are used **as the basis for the decision are known as the ratio decidendi**. This is the **vital element that binds future judges**.

However, if there are significant differences between the earlier and current cases, the court may **distinguish the earlier case on the facts** and thereby **avoid following it as a precedent**.

Obiter dicta means something said 'by the way' and does not bind future judges, but it may have persuasive authority. There are two types of obiter; firstly, statements of **legal principle** that do not form the basis of the decision and secondly, statements that are not based on the material facts, but on **hypothetical facts**.

Remedies under common law are **monetary**, and are known as **damages**.

(b) **Legislation**

Whilst the judiciary is responsible for the creation of common law, **Parliament** is responsible for **statute law** and therefore it is the supreme source of law in the UK. Statute law is usually made in areas so **complicated** or **unique** that suitable common law alternatives are unlikely, or would take an unacceptable length of time to develop. Company law is one example of an area of law created by statute.

In addition to making new law, Parliament may make the law clearer by passing **codifying** statutes. These put case law on a statutory basis (such as the Sale of Goods Act 1979). It may also pass **consolidating** statutes that incorporate an original statute and its successive amendments into a single piece of legislation (such as the Employment Rights Act 1996 or the Companies Act 2006).

A proposal for legislation can be brought by the Government, a backbench MP, or a peer. A Government bill may be aired in public in a **Government Green** or **White Paper** and may be introduced into either the House of Commons or the House of Lords. When it has passed through various stages in one House it must then go through the same stages in the other House.

Delegated legislation

Powers may be given to a minister, or public body such as a local authority, to make **subordinate or delegated legislation**. Delegated legislation has the same force of law as statute but it is often used where the law is highly technical (requiring expert input) or where it is too time-consuming for Parliament to go into enough detail.

As delegated legislation is often created by unelected individuals or bodies there are controls over it. It may have to be approved by an **affirmative resolution** of Parliament and/or be **laid** before Parliament for 40 days before it takes effect.

There are standing **Scrutiny Committees** of both Houses whose duty it is to examine delegated legislation from a technical point of view and they may raise objections if necessary. However they have no authority to object to its nature or content.

Delegated legislation may be **challenged** in the courts. Firstly, on the grounds that Parliament exceeded its authority to delegate and has acted *ultra vires*, or secondly, that the legislation has been made without due compliance with the correct procedure.

The **Human Rights Act 1998 (HRA)** gives courts power to **strike out** any delegated legislation that runs contrary to the HRA.

9 Statutory interpretation

Text reference. Chapter 2.

Top tips. You should have been able to gain good marks in both parts of this question if you revised this area properly. To pass this exam, you are required to demonstrate an understanding of the law and legal process, not just list the facts or rules you have read in your Study Text. To do this, it is often worth including a general introductory paragraph or two to explain the background of your answer, before going into the detail later on.

Easy marks. This question tests specific rules of statutory interpretation, so make sure that you are certain in your understanding of them, then be clear and concise in your explanation of them and their differences.

Examiner's comments. Although the question requires answers to focus on the two main general approaches, it also requires an explanation of the various traditional rules of statutory interpretation employed by the courts. The format of the question was new but the vast majority of candidates were able to deal with it with little difficulty, indeed many candidates provided considerations of the general approaches as well as the specific rules and were able to explain their relationship and history. Even those who were not totally aware of the general division between literal and purposive approaches were able to give an explanation of the standard rules and usually to provide case authorities in support/as examples.

Where candidates performed unsatisfactorily in this question they tended to treat it as a general question about the English Legal System and to describe court structures and/or operation of the doctrine of precedent.

Marking scheme

This question requires candidates to consider the powers of judges to interpret legislation and the rules they apply in exercising such interpretative powers. Although the question requires answers to focus on the two main general approaches, it also requires an explanation of the various traditional rules of statutory interpretation employed by the courts.

(a) Requires a consideration of the literal approach, including the golden rule.

3–5 marks	Full detailed explanation with supporting cases or examples.
1–2 marks	Limited knowledge of the topic; perhaps lacking detail or cases/examples.
0 mark	No knowledge on the topic under consideration.

(b) Requires a consideration of the purposive approach, including the mischief rule.

3–5 marks	Full detailed explanation with supporting cases or examples.
1–2 marks	Limited knowledge of the topic; perhaps lacking detail or cases/examples.
0 mark	No knowledge on the topic under consideration.

Candidates may simply produce a global answer considering the traditional rules and will be marked according to the content provided.

Statutory interpretation

Although the working of a **piece of legislation is carefully scrutinised** at all stages of its development, from its initial drafting through to the various stages of its passage through the two Houses of Parliament, **difficulties may nonetheless be encountered in its application**.

When the statue comes to be applied in the courts, there may be uncertainty over the **precise meaning** of a word or whether a particular term applied to the circumstances of the case. The applicability of legislative provisions may be uncertain when **unforeseeable or unforeseen developments** have occurred since the legislation was enacted.

It is the **role of the judiciary to apply the law made by Parliament as legislation**. The courts are therefore required to determine the meaning of such legislation. In doing so, they will apply a number of well-established rules and principles to interpret the statute.

Rules of statutory interpretation

The following approaches to and rules of statutory interpretation have been developed by the courts:

(a) **The literal approach, including the golden rule**

The most important guide to the application of the statute is the wording of that statute. Under the **literal approach**, words are to be given their literal, or plain and ordinary meaning. This means that if the words used are clear, the courts must apply them even if they find the consequences distasteful. Therefore in *Whitely v Chapell 1868*, a statute made it an offence to impersonate any person entitled to vote at an election. The accused was acquitted because they impersonated a dead person (who clearly was not entitled to vote).

Part of the literal approach is the **golden rule,** which states that words should be given their literal meaning unless this would lead to manifest absurdity or inconsistency with the rest of the statute. Therefore the golden rule can be distinguished from the general literal approach as it adds a degree of 'common sense' to interpretation of the statute.

(b) **The purposive approach, including the mischief rule**

Under the **purposive approach**, the words of a statute are interpreted not only in their ordinary, literal and grammatical sense, but also bearing in mind the purpose of the legislation, ie what is it trying to achieve? An example is seen in *Gardiner v Sevenoaks RDC 1950* when it was held that the term 'premises' should include a cave where film was stored, as the purpose of the Act concerned was the safety of people in premises.

The **mischief rule** takes a similar approach to interpretation. By applying this rule, a judge will consider what mischief the Act was trying to prevent and in that regard it is designed to remedy a weakness in the legislation by ensuring the correct interpretation is the one which achieves its aims.

10 Delegated legislation

Text reference. Chapter 2.

Top tips. Notice that this question effectively asks you four separate things: (i) the meaning of delegated legislation, (ii) its effect, (iii) its advantages and disadvantages and (iv) how it is controlled by Parliament and the courts. It is important that you acknowledge all four of these requirements and make sure that you attempt them.

Easy marks. The easy marks for this question spring from the point made above, ie that you must attempt all the requirements that the question specifically asks for.

Marking scheme

6–10 marks	A thorough answer which explains the meaning of delegated legislation and how it is introduced. The perceived advantages and disadvantages should be considered and all aspects of control should be mentioned. For full marks reference should be made to the Human Rights Act 1998.
0–5 marks	A less complete answer, perhaps lacking in detail or unbalanced in that it does not deal with some aspects of the question.

Meaning of delegated legislation

In the UK, it is **Parliament** which has sole power to create new legislation. However, the complexity of much modern legislation means that, in many instances, there is a great deal of detail which cannot conveniently be included in an Act of Parliament. The time available to Parliament is limited and the volume of legislation that is required to regulate a complex modern society is extremely high.

Therefore, much modern legislation contains sections allowing for the full scope of legal rules to be completed by Parliament's delegates who are normally ministers, government commissions or local authorities. The legislation is often enabling in nature, which means that it sets out the broad objectives and purpose of the Act, leaving the detail to be delegated to individuals or bodies outside Parliament. Therefore, **delegated legislation is law made by some subordinate person, body or authority to whom Parliament has delegated its legislative powers.**

Effect of delegated legislation

The effect of delegated legislation can be as wide as Parliament sees fit. Delegated legislation is usually encountered in one of a number of specific forms.

- **Statutory instruments**: Most often, these laws take the form of statutory instruments, made by government ministers to whom enabling legislation has delegated the relevant powers.
- **Bye-laws**: These are made by local authorities and apply within a specific locality.
- **Rules of Court**: these may be made by the judiciary to control court procedure.
- **Professional rules**: Parliament also gives powers to various professional bodies, such as the ACCA, in connection with the regulation by the professional body of the conduct of its members.
- **Orders in Council**: these contain rules which are often laid down by the Privy Council.

Advantages of delegated legislation

Delegated legislation can be extremely effective, but it also has drawbacks. The principal advantages, which make it an effective form of legislation, are as follows:

Volume of work

Without delegated legislation, Parliament would be overwhelmed by the **volume of work**. Delegated legislation therefore enables Parliament to concentrate on the broader principles of the legislative framework, rather than getting bogged down in details.

Speed

The use of delegated legislation enables new laws to be passed much more **quickly**, especially advantageous in times of **emergency**.

Expertise

The subject of new legislation is often highly detailed, **technical and complex**. It therefore makes sense for the exact content and wording to be arrived at by consultation with professional, commercial or industrial groups outside parliament who have the relevant **expertise**.

Tidier primary legislation

It also means that the **primary legislation is more concise** because the details are left to other delegated legislation documentation.

Flexibility

Delegation leads to **greater flexibility**, because regulations can be altered later without the need to revert to Parliament.

Disadvantages of delegated legislation

There is also some disadvantage inherent in passing legislative powers into the hands of persons outside Parliament itself.

Volume

The **volume of delegated legislation** means that it can become difficult for Parliament (and others) to keep track of the effect of the legislation that it has enabled.

Unconstitutional

Although Parliament is ultimately responsible for the legislation that is in force, it is likely that much of the detail has actually been drafted and finalised by individual ministers or by civil servants. Since civil servants are **unelected**, the degree to which law-making powers should be delegated to them is a matter for some debate.

It is therefore important that delegated legislation is **properly controlled** and that control is exercised by the courts and by Parliament.

Control over delegated legislation

Ultra vires

The power to make delegated legislation is conferred by the enabling Act of Parliament and this also defines the extent of that power. A statutory instrument may be **challenged** in the courts on the grounds that it is ***ultra vires*** – in other words that it exceeds the prescribed limits or that it has been made without due compliance with the correct procedure. In this way they may be said to exercise some degree of control over it.

Human Rights Act 1998

The **Human Rights Act 1998**, implementing the European Convention on Human Rights, introduced an additional check on delegated legislation. In any proceedings in which a court determines whether a provision of primary legislation is compatible with a Convention right, **the court may declare the provision incompatible with the Convention right** but cannot declare it invalid. However, in any proceedings in which a court determines whether a provision of delegated legislation is compatible with a Convention right, it may declare the delegated legislation itself to be invalid and therefore of no effect.

Parliament

Parliament can also exercise some control over delegated legislation. This is achieved by means of providing for statutory instruments to be **laid before Parliament for 40 days** before they take effect and for members to propose (within forty days) a resolution of veto if there are objections. Alternatively, some regulations must be affirmatively approved by Parliament before they take effect. In addition, there are standing committees ('Scrutiny Committees') of both Houses of Parliament whose duty it is to examine statutory instruments with a view to raising objections if necessary (usually on the grounds that the instrument is obscure, expensive or retrospective).

11 Sources of law and the Human Rights Act 1998

Text reference. Chapters 1, 2 and 3.

Top tips. Don't fall into the trap of trying to write everything you know about the two types of law and how the Act has had an impact on them. Instead make sure you cover the basics only as that's all you have time for.

Easy marks. Stating the main impact of the Human Rights Act 1998 on each type of law.

(a) **Case law (common law)**

Common law is the earliest element of the English legal system. It is a system of rigid rules laid down by the **Royal Courts** following the Norman Conquest. The 'law of the land' was created by **judges** who travelled around the country keeping the King's peace. By applying and amalgamating **local customary laws**, a body of legal rules common to the whole country was created.

The doctrine of **judicial precedent** underpins the common law and English law generally. A key principle is that **legal principles do not become inoperative through the lapse of time**. This doctrine means that a judge is bound to apply a decision from an earlier case to the facts of the case before him. This is provided that there is no material difference between the cases and that the previous case created a '**binding**' **precedent**.

When making a judgement, a judge will make various statements. These statements are either classed as **ratio decidendi** or **obiter dicta**. Judgements start with a description of the facts of the case and probably a review of earlier precedents. The judge will then make **statements of law applicable to the legal problems** raised by the material facts. The facts which are used **as the basis for the decision are known as the ratio decidendi**. This is the **vital element that binds future judges**.

However, if there are significant differences between the earlier and current cases, the court may **distinguish the earlier case on the facts** and thereby **avoid following it as a precedent**.

Obiter dicta means something said 'by the way' and does not bind future judges, but it may have persuasive authority. There are two types of obiter; firstly, statements of **legal principle** that do not form the basis of the decision and secondly, statements that are not based on the material facts, but on **hypothetical facts**.

Remedies under common law are **monetary**, and are known as **damages**.

(b) **Statute (legislation)**

Whilst the judiciary is responsible for the creation of common law, **Parliament** is responsible for **statute law** and therefore it is the supreme source of law in the UK. Statute law is usually made in areas so **complicated** or **unique** that suitable common law alternatives are unlikely, or would take an unacceptable length of time to develop. Company law is one example of an area of law created by statute.

In addition to making new law, Parliament may make the law clearer by passing **codifying** statutes. These put case law on a statutory basis (such as the Sale of Goods Act 1979). It may also pass **consolidating** statutes that incorporate an original statute and its successive amendments into a single piece of legislation (such as the Employment Rights Act 1996 or the Companies Act 2006).

A proposal for legislation can be brought by the Government, a backbench MP, or a peer. A Government bill may be aired in public in a **Government Green** or **White Paper** and may be introduced into either the House of Commons or the House of Lords. When it has passed through various stages in one House it must then go through the same stages in the other House.

(c) **Impact of the Human Rights Act 1998 on case law and statute**

The main impact of the Human Rights Act on case law and statute is that UK courts are now required to **interpret** UK law in a way that is **compatible** with the European Convention on Human Rights.

This means that the courts must take into account the previous decisions of the **European Court of Human Rights** when interpreting any UK law. If a court feels that a provision of primary legislation (ie an Act of Parliament) is incompatible with the Convention it can make a declaration of incompatibility but it is then up to the Government to take action to remedy the incompatibility. Courts also have the power to **strike out** any incompatible **secondary (delegated) legislation**.

12 Alvin

Text reference. Chapter 4.

Top tips. The answer to this question looks straightforward, and indeed it is. However, you cannot earn enough marks to pass by rushing straight into a conclusion – make sure you follow the correct approach. **Identify** the legal issues, **state** the law, **apply** the law and then **conclude**.

Easy marks. This is a very simple question and you should have no trouble passing it by stating and applying the basic principles of contract formation.

Examiner's comments. Answers broke the question down into a statement of relevant law and then applying that law to the three customers – Bert, Cat and Del. Credit was given for a brief statement of the key essentials for a valid contract, and then the distinction between an offer and an invitation to treat. The vast majority of students rightly identified that Alvin's notice was in fact an invitation to treat, correctly citing or describing the case of *Fisher v Bell*. However, in applying the law to the scenario, many candidates jumped straight into dealing with each customer as though Alvin's notice was an offer and therefore Alvin was the offeror. Some of these students then went on to reach the correct conclusions – that Bert and Cat had no right to sue Alvin as no contract had been made.

Generally speaking, marks were gained by dealing with Bert since that is when candidates went into detail about Alvin's offer being an invitation to treat, to which Bert responded by making an offer, which Alvin was at liberty to accept or reject. Some students became confused at this stage by saying that Alvin could revoke his offer of £5,000 as long as it was before Bert's acceptance; whereas some candidates kept on track by treating the notice as an invitation to treat which was not capable of acceptance. Therefore Alvin was free to change the price on the notice.

Cat's scenario was more problematic for candidates. Many candidates did not specifically identify the issue concerning the option contract, which would have obliged Alvin to honour any promise he makes to keep the offer open if Cat had paid some consideration for him to do so. The reason for this is that a promise to keep an offer open is only binding where there is a separate contract to this effect. However many candidates did cover the issue of Cat's failure to give consideration so credit was given accordingly. Most students also correctly identified that Alvin did not, in any case, expressly accept Cat's offer. Some candidates raised the issue of counter-offer, but the question was not inviting a discussion of counter-offer.

Del's scenario was a simple case of legally enforceable contract being entered into, with Del being the offeror and Alvin being the offeree. For some reason, many candidates just simply restated the facts given in the question rather than actually concluding that a contract had been reached because the essentials for a contract were all present.

Marking scheme

This question asks candidates to analyse the scenario provided in the light of the rules relating to the formation of a contract. In particular it requires an examination of the distinction between offer and invitation to treat, and the operation of option contracts.

8–10 marks: A thorough treatment of all of the rules relating to the formation of contracts together with a clear and correct application of those rules to the problem scenario. Cases will be expected to be provided at this level.

5–7 marks: Good analysis and case support, although perhaps limited in appreciation.

3–4 marks: Recognition of the areas covered by the question, but lacking in detail.

0–2 marks: Very weak answers which might recognise what the question is about but show no ability to analyse or answer the problem as set out.

Alvin and Bert

Issue

Alvin has been threatened with legal action by Bert for not selling him the car when Bert apparently accepted Alvin's offer. The issue appears to be whether or not a valid offer was made by Alvin in the first place.

Relevant law

For a contract to be valid there must be an **offer** made by the offeror and **acceptance** from the offeree. An offer is a definite promise to be bound on specific terms. It does not have to be made to a particular person and may be made to a class of persons or to the world at large.

Statements that initiate negotiations are not offers but are known as **invitations to treat**. They are not capable of being accepted and therefore cannot form a legally binding agreement.

According to Bert, a contract was formed when he accepted Alvin's **offer,** which he believes was made by the **price notice** that Alvin attached to the car. It must therefore be considered whether or not the price notice is a **valid offer** or an **invitation to treat**.

In *Fisher v Bell 1961* it was held that an article for sale with a **price attached** to it is not a valid offer but an invitation to treat.

Application of law and conclusion

Alvin's price notice cannot be considered a valid offer. Legally, Bert made an offer when he 'accepted' to purchase the car for £5,000. As Alvin did not accept this offer, there is no contract between Alvin and Bert and Alvin **cannot be sued** for not selling Bert the car.

Alvin and Cat

Issue

Cat said she wanted to purchase the car at full price but required Alvin to wait until she could arrange finance. Alvin subsequently sold the car for cash to Del. The issues here are whether or not Alvin made an offer to Cat which he would need to revoke in order to sell the car to Del, whether or not Alvin accepted Cat's offer to buy the car, and whether or not there was an option contract.

Relevant law

If an offer exists, an offeror may **revoke** their offer at any time before acceptance, *Payne v Cave 1789.* Even if they undertake to keep their offer open for a specified time, they may nonetheless revoke it within that time. This is unless a **separate contract** exists under which the offeror has agreed to keep it open. However, in this case, Alvin is not the offeror because the price notice is just an invitation to treat. Therefore he has no offer to revoke and the rules on revocation do not apply. If Cat's expression of interest in buying the car could be treated as an offer in response to the invitation to treat, Alvin has not accepted her offer so again there is no contract.

Application of law and conclusion

The question becomes whether or not Alvin and Cat formed a separate contract by which Alvin agreed to wait for Cat to arrange finance to purchase the car. Such contracts are known as **option contracts** and are formed in the same way as any other contract. From the facts of the case, it does not appear that such a contract was formed as **Cat did not provide any consideration** in return for Alvin keeping the invitation to treat open. Therefore Alvin was free to sell the car to Del, as no contract of any form existed between Alvin and Cat.

Alvin and Del

A valid contract was formed between Alvin and Del. Del **offered the full price** to Alvin who accepted it. Del provided **cash payment** as **consideration**, in return for the car provided by Del.

13 Ann's art

Text reference. Chapter 4.

Top tips. This scenario question is typical of the type of question you must expect in the exam. It requires you to analyse the scenario and apply principles of contract law to it. You must not expect there to be one simple and obvious answer to a question like this. Comparing this situation to case law you are aware of will help you identify what is most likely to be the case here.

Imagine the process (say) Dave's solicitor will go through – analysing case law, trying to build up his own case. He would compare the facts to *Carlill v Carbolic Smokeball Co*, etc ... so must you. In this instance you must consider the scenario from each person's point of view (Ann, Chas, Dave, Eve). What case would each try to build? Each point raised would be relevant in this answer.

You will probably find it useful, as we have in our answer, to consider the various elements of contract separately: agreement (offer and acceptance), consideration, intention (if relevant ... in this commercial situation it is a fair assumption that the parties intended legal relations and it does not merit being mentioned).

Easy marks. The only easy marks are for stating the basic rules and definitions – learn them!

Marking scheme

	Marks
Agreement	1
Offer	2
Invitations to treat	2
Acceptance	2
Postal rule	2
Conclusion	1
	10

Agreement

For an agreement to constitute a valid and binding contract, it must comprise a valid **acceptance** of a valid **offer** made with the **intention of creating legal relations** and being supported by valid **consideration**.

Offer

An offer is a definite promise to be bound on specific terms. It must be certain in its terms (*Gunthing v Lynn 1831*) and can be made to a particular person or to a class of persons, in which case it is only open for those persons to whom the offer is made to accept it.

However, an offer can be made to the **world at large** (*Carlill v Carbolic Smoke Ball Co 1893*) in which case anyone can accept it. It must be more than a mere supply of information (*Harvey v Facey 1893*) or statement of intention (*Harris v Nickerson 1873*).

Invitation to treat

An invitation to treat, on the other hand, is an indication that a person is prepared to receive offers with a view to entering into a binding contract. It is generally accepted that goods displayed in a shop window give rise to an invitation to treat rather than an offer (*Fisher v Bell 1961*).

Ann

The notice in Ann's window is therefore almost certainly an invitation to treat and an offer was made in response to this invitation to treat when Chas and Dave offer £12,000 for the prints.

Acceptance

Acceptance must be an **unqualified agreement** to the terms of the offer and must not introduce new terms (in which case it is a counter-offer). Similarly, a purported acceptance which is actually a request for further information or one which is made 'subject to contract' will not constitute valid acceptance.

Acceptance of an offer may be by express words or be inferred from conduct (*Brogden v Metropolitan Railway Co 1877*). It may only be made by a person authorised to do so, usually the offeree or their authorised agent.

Ann

Ann is entitled to accept or reject Chas's and Dave's offers and she rejects them, but at the same time makes a **counter-offer** that she will sell the prints for £13,500 each. Likewise, Chas and Dave are free to accept or reject this counter-offer which destroys the original offer of £12,000 (*Hyde v Wrench 1840*).

The arrangements whereby Ann agrees to keep the offers open until noon on Monday amount to separate option agreements supported by consideration in Chas and Dave each paying £100. These collateral contracts are binding on both parties. The offer to sell at £13,500 has still to be accepted in order to make the main contract of sale binding also.

Communication of acceptance

Generally speaking, **acceptance must be communicated to the offeror** before it can be effective, unless the offeror expressly waives the need for communication (as in *Carlill's* case). The offeror may stipulate the sole means of communication in which case only compliance with their terms will suffice.

If the offeror specifies a means of communication but does not make it absolutely compulsory, then acceptance by another means which is equally expeditious and does not disadvantage the offeror in any way will be sufficient (*Yates Building Co v R J Pulleyn and Sons (York) 1975*).

The postal rule

Communication of acceptance by post is subject to the **postal rule** established in *Adams v Lindsell 1818*. This provides that where the use of the post is in the contemplation of both parties and the acceptance is correctly addressed and stamped and is actually put in the post, then **acceptance will be valid and effective once posted** and it is irrelevant whether the offeror actually receives the letter.

There is no need for the offer to specifically state that acceptance must be communicated by post – whether this was in the **contemplation of the parties** may be deduced from the circumstances. Clearly if it is evident that the parties did not intend the postal rule to apply then the rule will be excluded.

Ann

In this case, **Ann does not stipulate the means by which acceptance of her offer is to be communicated**. It can be argued, however, that since the parties so far have communicated face to face, it was to be expected that Chas and Dave would again visit the shop by Monday if they wished to purchase the prints at £13,500 a piece.

In the case of Chas, his acceptance arrives within the stipulated time in any event and an enforceable contract for sale exists from this point. It is probable that Dave, however, has not entered into an enforceable contract for sale with Ann because his acceptance has not been communicated by noon on Monday and the postal rule was not in the reasonable contemplation of the parties.

14 Ali

Text reference. Chapters 4 and 5

Top tips. Answering this question is very simple if you read it carefully. Questions such as this typically include three issues for you to spot and advise on. When you **identify** an issue you need to **state** the relevant law in your answer, **apply** it to the scenario and **conclude**. Answers to scenario questions may therefore be shorter than other questions since marks are awarded for application.

Easy marks. Identifying and stating the law on window displays, counter-offers and executory consideration.

Examiner's comments. The question tended to be done reasonably well with most candidates achieving a pass mark on the basis of their recognition of the law involved in the scenario and their application of that law.

Marking scheme

	Marks
A thorough analysis of the scenario focusing on the appropriate rules of law and applying them accurately. It is extremely likely that cases will be cited in support of the analysis and/or application.	8–10
A clear understanding of the general law but perhaps lacking in detail or unbalanced in only dealing with some issues.	5–7
Some, but limited, understanding of the law or completely lacking in application.	2–4
Little or no knowledge of the relevant law.	0–1

Issues

The **issues in the scenario** concerning Ali, Ben, Chet and Di are in regard to **contractual offer** and **acceptance**, the elements that forms a **valid agreement**, and **consideration**.

Advertisements

An **advertisement** in a shop window is considered in law to be an **invitation to treat**, so the seller is under no obligation to sell the product. An offer is legally a definite promise to be bound on specific terms; it was held in *Fisher v Bell 1961* that having goods in a window did not amount to offering them for sale.

Acceptance

Acceptance must be an **unqualified agreement to the terms of the offer**. A purported acceptance which introduces any new terms is a counter-offer, which has the effect of terminating the original offer: *Hyde v Wrench 1840.*

Consideration

Executory consideration is a promise given for a promise. It can be defined as 'that which is to take place at some future time'. For instance, consideration for the delivery of goods is executory if it is a promise to pay at a future date. The consideration in support of each promise is the other promise, not a performed act, but it is valid consideration nonetheless.

Applying the law to the scenario we can determine the following:

Ben

Ali's advertisement is an invitation to treat, not an offer, therefore Ben cannot accept it as such. Ben's letter however is legally an offer to Ali to buy the vase. Therefore Ben has no contract to buy the vase.

Chet

Chet made an offer to buy the vase from Ali for £400 which Ali did not accept. By introducing new terms (a price of £450) Ali made a counter-offer to Chet. Chet rejected this offer and therefore made no agreement to buy the vase from Ali. Subsequently he could not then accept a counter-offer that he has already rejected and therefore he has no contract to buy the vase.

Di

Di made a valid offer to Ali to buy the vase for £400 which was accepted. Di's promise to pay Ali and Ali's promise to provide the vase to Di on Monday are both executory consideration, which is valid to support a contract. Therefore Di has a contract to buy the vase from Ali which will be valid unless and until she fails to pay for the vase on Monday. In that event Ali will be free to sell the vase to Ben, Chet or anyone else.

15 Offers, counter-offers and unilateral offers

Text reference. Chapter 4.

Top tips. Where possible you should always refer to case law or statute to back up your answers. The examiner's comments below reinforce the importance of this.

Easy marks. You can almost pass this question by providing good definitions supported with case law.

ACCA examiner's answers. The ACCA examiner's answer to this question can be found at the back of this kit.

Examiner's comments. Part (a) was well done. Most candidates were comfortable describing an offer and drew distinctions between an offer and an invitation to treat, with excellent examples and a good grasp of the statements in *Carlill v Carbollic Smoke Ball*. Candidates were clearly well prepared for this aspect of the question.

In part b (i), again, answers to this question were sound with the majority of candidates being able to describe the characteristics of a counter-offer, its effect, reference to *Hyde v Wrench* and contrast with a request for information. In a high number of instances, candidates were awarded full marks on this section.

Part b (ii) was not well answered and demonstrated that candidates did not really understand the terminology. Answers given ranged from *Dunlop v Selfridge* and privity of contract, to Sale of Goods Act and exclusion clauses. Only a small number of candidates were able to describe the characteristics of a unilateral offer and, where they did, answers were sound and made reference to relevant cases such as *Errington v Errington* and *Carlill*.

Marking scheme

This question is divided into three parts and requires candidate to explain the meaning of three elements in contract law: offer, counter-offer and unilateral offer.

(a) 3–5 marks A good to complete answer explaining the meaning of an offer.

1–2 marks For some indication as to the meaning of offer.

(b) (i) 2–3 marks Awarded for explanation of the meaning and effect of counter-offer depending on clarity of explanation.

1 mark For some knowledge.

(ii) 2 marks For a good to complete explanation of the meaning and effect of a unilateral offer.

1 mark Some idea about unilateral offers but lacking in detail.

(a) **Offers**

In the law of contract, an **offer is a definite promise to another to be bound on specific terms**. It is a promise which is capable of acceptance so as to form a binding contract. It cannot be in vague terms, for example a promise to buy a horse if it is 'lucky' *(Gunthing v Lynn 1831)*.

An offer can be made to an **individual**, a **class of persons** or to the **world at large** and it can be accepted by the conduct of the offeree *(Carlill v Carbolic Smoke Ball Co 1893).*

Once an offer has been accepted, a **binding contract is created**. Either party (the offeror, who made the offer) or the offeree (who accepted the offer) may legally enforce the promise of the other. Not all statements which appear to be offers are capable of acceptance to form a valid contract. Legitimate offers should be distinguished from supplies of information, statements of intention and invitations to treat.

Supply of information

A mere **supply of information** is not an offer, because there is no intention to be bound. For example, stating the minimum price that one would consider if a sale were to be agreed does not constitute an offer *(Harvey v Facey 1893).*

Statement of intention

Similarly a mere **statement of intention**, for example that an event such as an auction is to take place, is not the same as an offer *(Harris v Nickerson 1873).* Only an offer made with the intention that it shall become binding when accepted may be accepted so as to form a binding contract.

Invitation to treat

An **invitation to treat**, on the other hand, is an indication that someone is prepared to receive offers with the view to forming a binding contract. In the usual example, when a person displays goods for sale, they are not making an offer but are inviting other persons to make them an offer to buy the goods which they can then choose whether or not to accept. There is no binding contract until this offer is made and, in turn, accepted.

(b) (i) **Counter-offers**

A **counter-offer** occurs when the person to whom the offer was made proposes new or amended terms. This has the effect of terminating the original offer: *Hyde v Wrench 1840.*

However, it is possible to respond to an offer by making a **request for information**. Such requests can include whether or not other terms would be acceptable. Such requests are not considered a counter-offer and the original offer will stand: *Stevenson v McLean 1880.*

(ii) **Unilateral offers**

A **unilateral offer** is a promise made in return for an act, and if accepted forms a **unilateral contract**. An example of a unilateral offer is in the case of *Carlill v Carbolic Smoke Ball Co 1893* where the act of the claimant in using a smoke ball was enough to be considered valid acceptance of the offer of money made by the defendant.

16 Offers and invitations to treat

Text reference. Chapter 4

Top tips. This question requires the repetition of textbook knowledge on two of the basic principles of contract law. The examiner often sets questions, like this, where parts (a) and (b) are related. Make sure your answer to part (a) does not cover the material required in part (b). Note how the answer makes reference to case law where appropriate.

Easy marks. Defining offer, invitations to treat, and the use of examples and cases.

Examiner's comments. ... the best answers defined offer in positive terms and went on to consider several of the many issues that could have been properly raised in relation to it. They then went on to deal with invitation to treat as a distinct issue in part (b). These best answers invariably provided case authorities or examples in support of their explanations.

Marking scheme

This question in two parts requires candidates to explain the meaning of offer and invitation to treat within the common law.

(a) Carries 4 marks as follows:

3–4 marks	Thorough to complete explanation of the meaning of offer. It is expected that cases will be cited in support, although examples will be acceptable.
1–2 marks	Some but limited knowledge of the topic. Perhaps uncertain as to meaning or lacking in detailed explanation or authority.
0 marks	No understanding whatsoever.

(b) Carries 6 marks.

4–6 marks	Thorough to complete explanation of the meaning of invitation to treat. It is expected that cases will be cited in support, although examples will be acceptable.
2–3 marks	Some but limited knowledge of the topic. Perhaps uncertain as to meaning or lacking in detailed explanation or authority.
0–1 marks	Very little or no understanding whatsoever.

(a) **Offer**

The first **essential element** in the formation of a binding contract is **agreement**. This is usually evidenced by **offer** and **acceptance**. Offers are made by an offeror to an offeree and are **definite promises to be bound on specific terms**.

They may be **express** or **implied statements** of the terms on which the maker is prepared to be **contractually bound** if it is accepted unconditionally. Therefore, if accepted, offers result in legally binding contracts. Statements that are too vague are not offers (*Gunthing v Lynn 1831)*.

Offers may be made to **one person**, to a **class of persons** or to the **world at large** *(Carlill v Carbolic Smoke Ball Co 1893)*, and only the person or one of the persons to whom it is made may accept it.

Not all statements are offers, even if they appear or purport to be. True offers must be **distinguished** from a mere **supply of information** and from **statements of intention**.

An example of a **supply of information** can be found in the case of *Harvey v Facey 1893*. In this case, a telegram stating the minimum price an individual would accept for a property was held not to be an offer.

Statements of intention are also not classed as offers. An example is the advertising of an event such as an auction. Potential buyers may not sue the auctioneer if the auction does not take place: *Harris v Nickerson 1873*.

(b) **Invitations to treat**

An **invitation to treat** can be defined as 'an indication that a person is prepared to receive offers with a view to entering into a binding contract'

Invitations to treat are **not capable of acceptance** and therefore cannot form a valid agreement. Those who make them are not obliged to accept any offers that result from them. In legal terms, the person who receives an invitation treat becomes an offeror if they respond to the invitation. The maker of the invitation to treat becomes an offeree.

Examples of invitations to treat include

Auction sales

Offers are made by bidders stating the price at which they are prepared to buy and acceptance takes place by the fall of the auctioneer's hammer: *Payne v Cave 1789*.

Advertisements (for example, price lists or newspaper advertisements)

An advertisement of goods for sale is usually an attempt to induce offer *(Partridge v Crittenden 1968)*.

Displaying goods for sale

Displaying goods in a shop window *(Fisher v Bell 1961)* or on the open shelves of a self-service shop or advertising goods for sale, is normally an invitation to treat (*Pharmaceutical Society of Great Britain v Boots Cash Chemists (Southern) 1952)*.

An invitation for tenders

A **tender** is an estimate submitted in response to a prior request. When a person tenders for a contract they are making an offer to the person who has advertised a contract as being available. An invitation for tenders does not generally amount to an offer to contract with the person quoting the lowest price, except where the person inviting tenders actually makes it clear that they are making an offer.

17 Acceptance and revocation of offer

Text reference. Chapter 4.

Top tips. Each part of this question is worth five marks, which means that you can only spend nine minutes on them. Don't give in to the temptation to over-run on part (a) and therefore not leaving yourself enough time to do justice to part (b), which is equally straightforward. The examiner will not allow you to score over the mark allocation on one part of a question even if you devote all your time to it and produce a brilliant answer.

Easy marks. Get the easy marks by writing the rules on acceptance and revocation down, and if possible citing a case or quoting an illustration in support.

Examiner's comments. This was the most popular question in the entire exam. The main criticism of candidates was that some produced irrelevant material, for example on invitations to treat, therefore wasting their time.

Marking scheme

This question requires an explanation of the rules relating to the acceptance and revocation of offers in contract law. Marks will not be transferred between parts.

(a)	3-5 marks	A good to complete answer dealing with most if not all of the issues relating to acceptance of offers
	0-2 marks	A less detailed answer, perhaps recognising what the question relates to but lacking in detailed knowledge of the rules.
(b)	3-5 marks	A good to complete answer dealing with most if not all of the issues relating to revocation of offers
	0-2 marks	A less detailed answer, perhaps recognising what the question relates to but lacking in detailed knowledge of the rules

(a) **Acceptance**

Valid acceptance of a valid offer is one of the essentials of a contract.

An acceptance must be an **unqualified agreement** that corresponds to the terms of the offer. If a purported acceptance in fact introduces new terms then it is a 'counter-offer' (which might then be accepted by the original offeror) and not an acceptance. Therefore in *Hyde v Wrench 1840*, where an offer was made to sell land for £1,000 and the claimant made a counter-offer of £950 but later sought to accept the original offer, it was held that the claimant's counter-offer had terminated the original offer.

Method of acceptance

The acceptance may be by express words or be inferred from conduct *(Brogden v Metropolitan Railway Co 1877)*. In a unilateral contract (as in *Carlill v Carbolic Smoke Ball Co 1893*), **performance of the act** required by the offer or advertisement constitutes acceptance. There must be some act on the part of the offeree since **passive inaction or silence is not capable of constituting acceptance** *(Felthouse v Bindley 1862)*.

Request for information

A response to an offer which is actually a **request for further information** will not constitute acceptance. Acceptance made 'subject to contract' will not amount to a valid acceptance until the proposed formal contract has been signed.

Communications

Acceptance of an offer may only be made by a **person authorised to do so**, usually the offeree or their authorised agent. Generally speaking, acceptance must be **communicated** to the offeror before it can be effective, unless the offeror expressly waives the need for communication (as in *Carlill's case*). The offeror may stipulate the sole means of communication in which case only compliance with their terms will suffice. If the offeror specifies a means of communication but does not make it absolutely compulsory, then acceptance by another means which is equally expeditious and does not disadvantage the offeror in any way will be sufficient *(Yates Building Co v R J Pulleyn and Sons (York) 1975)*.

Postal rule

Communication of acceptance by post is subject to the **postal rule** established in *Adams v Lindsell 1818*. This provides that where the use of the post is in the contemplation of both parties and the acceptance is correctly addressed and stamped and is actually put in the post, then acceptance will be valid and effective once posted and it is irrelevant whether the offeror actually receives the letter.

There is no need for the offer to specifically state that acceptance must be communicated by post – whether this was in the contemplation of the parties may be deduced from the circumstances. For example if the offer was itself made by post *(Household Fire and Carriage Accident Insurance Co v Grant 1879)*.

Clearly if it is evident that the parties did not intend the postal rule to apply then the rule will be excluded (*Holwell Securities v Hughes 1974)*.

(b) **Revocation**

The offeror may 'revoke' (or cancel) the offer **at any time prior to acceptance** *(Payne v Cave 1789)* unless by a separate option agreement, they agreed to keep the offer open for a certain period of time *(Routledge v Grant 1828*). Once accepted, an offer cannot be revoked. Equally, once an offer has been revoked, it is no longer available for acceptance.

Method of revocation

Revocation may be made by an express statement to that effect or may be **implied** from an act of the offeror indicating that the offer is no longer in force (for example sale of the goods to a third party).

Communication

Whatever form it takes, it is essential that the revocation is **communicated to the offeree** in order to be effective. Revocation of an offer may be communicated by the offeror or by any third party who is a sufficiently reliable informant *(Dickinson v Dodds 1876)*.

Postal rule

While a **postal acceptance of an offer** is usually effective from the time of posting, a postal revocation of an offer does not take effect until **received by the offeree** (ie communicated to the offeree). Therefore, where a letter of revocation crosses in the post with a letter of acceptance, a legally binding contract will have been formed from the time the letter of acceptance was posted *(Byrne v Van Tienhoven 1880)*.

Where an offer is intended to be accepted by conduct (a unilateral offer), it has been held that the offer cannot be revoked once the offeree has begun to perform the necessary act required to accept the contract *(Errington v Errington 1953)*.

18 Ace Ltd

Text reference. Chapter 4

Top tips. As with all scenario questions, the correct approach is to **Identify** the area of law, **State** the relevant law, **Apply** the law and **Conclude**. Ensure you always follow this method.

Explaining the *Carlill* case is important to demonstrate an understanding of how the law works, but you could have explained the law without reference to this case.

Easy marks. Defining offer and acceptance and stating relevant cases to support your answer present you with an easy source of marks. If you knew the case law well then your application to the facts in this question should have been straightforward.

Issue

Cid and Ed wish to claim the £10,000 reward but Ace Ltd will seek to counter this claim on the grounds that no contract was formed (there was a **lack of offer and acceptance**).

Offer

An offer is a **definite promise** to be bound on **specific terms**. It can be an express or implied statement of the terms on which the maker is prepared to be contractually bound. It does not have to be made to a particular person; it may be made to a class of persons or to the world at large.

Acceptance

Acceptance is a positive act by a person to whom an offer has been made which brings a binding contract into effect. Contracts usually come into **effect** once the offeree has **accepted** the terms presented to them. This is the point of no return; after acceptance, the offeror **cannot revoke** their offer and both parties will be **bound** by the terms that they have agreed.

Case law

Carlill v Carbolic Smoke Ball Co 1893 is considered the **key case** on offer and acceptance and it is relevant to Cid and Ed's situation.

In this case the manufacturers of a medicinal product (a smoke ball) advertised that if the smoke ball was used as directed and the person using it caught influenza, they would pay them £100. To show that they were serious, the manufacturer deposited £1,000 in a bank account to be used for any claims arising. The claimant used the smoke ball as instructed and subsequently caught influenza.

The case is important as it established several points of law. First **offers do not need to be addressed to a particular person** but can be made to the whole world. Secondly mere '**sales puff**', which consumers are not expected to take seriously, can **become an offer** when the offeror makes some indication that it **should be taken seriously** – in this case the deposit of £1,000 into the bank. Thirdly **acceptance does not need to be communicated to the offeror** in cases such as this. Acceptance will result from a person following the terms of the offer (in this case using the smoke ball).

The *Carlill* case is an example of a **unilateral contract**, in other words a contract where the terms of the offer are fulfilled by the acts of the offeree. As acceptance is not necessarily communicated to the offeror as they are subject to slightly different rules than bi-lateral contracts, the most pertinent difference being on revocation of an offer.

Usually an offeror may **revoke** their offer at **any time before acceptance** *(Routledge v Grant 1828)*. However this is not the case in **unilateral contracts** and **revocation is not possible** once the offeree has begun to **perform** the task specified in the offer (*Errington v Errington 1953)*.

Ace Ltd

Ace Ltd will attempt to **deny the existence of a contract** on the following grounds:

- That the offer in the journal **should not be taken seriously**
- That the offer was **not validly accepted** by Cid and Ed
- That the offer was **validly revoked**

Whilst not quite the same as the *Carlill* case as there is no reward, the offer in the journal could quite easily be argued to be serious since it was made in an **employee journal** and employees should **reasonably expect** the journal's contents to be serious. That the offer was not validly accepted would be dismissed on the facts contained in the *Carlill* case. Notification of acceptance is not required; **performance of the task is enough**. Valid revocation would be dismissed as a unilateral contract was made and therefore **revocation is not possible** once performance has commenced, as per *Errington v Errington 1953*.

Cid

Ace Ltd will claim that the offer was not made to Cid. The terms of the offer clearly state that it is open to **employees of Ace Ltd only** and therefore in this respect the facts differ from that of the *Carlill* case. Offers can be made to the world at large but where they are addressed to a specific group of people then only those within that group can accept them. Therefore Cid has no claim on the reward.

Ed

Ed is an employee and therefore **included in the terms of the offer**. As mentioned above, Ace Ltd is **not permitted to revoke** the offer and therefore since he solved the problem before the deadline he is entitled to the reward.

19 Al

Text reference. Chapter 4.

Top tips. Questions such as this can seem complicated as there are many events occurring. Keep a clear head and try to draw a timeline with the types of events and the order in which they occur. This will help you follow the story and decide what events are offers, counter-offers and acceptance.

Easy marks. Stating the law on offer and acceptance.

Marking scheme

8–10 marks	A complete answer, highlighting and dealing with all of the issues presented in the problem scenario. It is most likely that cases will be referred to, and they will be credited.
5–7 marks	An accurate recognition of the problems inherent in the question, together with an attempt to apply the appropriate legal rules to the situation.
2–4 marks	An ability to recognise some, although not all, of the key issues and suggest appropriate legal responses to them. A recognition of the area of law but no attempt to apply that law.
0–1 marks	Very weak answer showing no, or very little, understanding of the question.

Valid acceptance of a valid offer is one of the essentials of a contract.

Offer

An **offer is a definite promise to another to be bound on specific terms**. It is a promise which is capable of acceptance so as to form a binding contract. It cannot be in its vague terms, for example a promise to buy a horse if it is 'lucky' *(Gunthing v Lynn 1831)*. An offer can be made to an individual, a class of persons or to the world at large and it can be accepted by the conduct of the offeree *(Carlill v Carbolic Smoke Ball Co 1893)*.

Once an offer has been accepted, a **binding contract** is created. Either party (the offeror, who made the offer or the offeree, who accepted the offer) may legally enforce the promise of the other.

Supply of information

A mere **supply of information** is not an offer, because there is no intention to be bound. For example, stating the minimum price that one would consider if a sale were to be agreed does not constitute an offer *(Harvey v Facey 1893)*.

Statement of intention

Similarly, a mere **statement of intention**, for example, that an event such as an auction is to take place, is not the same as an offer *(Harris v Nickerson 1873)*. Only an offer made with the intention that it shall become binding when accepted may be accepted so as to form a binding contract.

Invitation to treat

An **invitation to treat**, on the other hand, is an indication that someone is prepared to receive offers with the view to forming a binding contract. In the usual example, when a person displays goods for sale, they are not making an offer but are inviting another person to make them an offer to buy the goods which they can then choose whether or not to accept. There is no binding contract until this offer is made and, in turn, accepted.

Advertisement

Therefore, an **advertisement** for the sale of goods is treated as an attempt to induce offers (*Partridge v Crittenden*, where an advert in a magazine was held to be an invitation to treat and not an offer).

Acceptance

The acceptance of an offer must be an **unqualified agreement** to the terms of the offer. If it in fact introduces new terms then it is a counter-offer (which might then be accepted by the original offeror) and not an acceptance. Therefore, in *Hyde v Wrench 1840* (where an offer was made to sell land for £1,000 and the claimant made a counter-offer of £950 but later sought to accept the original offer) it was held that the claimant's counter-offer had terminated the original offer.

Al

Applying this to Al's situation it is clear that Al's **advertisement** is an invitation to treat and the first letter from Bash Cars plc requesting terms was a **request for information** and therefore neither constituted an offer.

The first offer was the letter by Al stating that he offered to sell the filters at £50. Bash Cars could have accepted this offer, but replied with a **counter-offer** (as it changed the price to £45). This counter-offer destroys Al's offer. Al replied with his own counter-offer when he restated his terms and Bash Cars was free to reject this offer, but instead sent in an order for 1,000 filters which constituted **acceptance** of Al's counter-offer.

Therefore Al and Bash Cars plc have entered into a **binding contract** for Al to supply 1,000 filters at £50.

20 Presumption and rebuttal

Text reference. Chapter 5.

Top tips. At first glance, this looks quite a difficult question. However if you take just a minute to think about it, you will see that it is not so intimidating and covers quite an easy area of law.

Easy marks. This question looks quite intimidating and daunting because it contains some real legal jargon: 'presumption' and 'rebuttal'. However, all it is asking you is when it is presumed that there is intention to create legal relations, and when it is not, and what can cause those presumptions to be rebutted, or overridden. There will be easy marks available for quoting the relevant cases (which should be familiar).

Examiner's comments. Many candidates could not specifically explain the terms, as required by part (a) of the question, but almost explained them by default in part (b), where they were able to set out what they knew of these situations. This indicates that candidates memorise answers to questions but cannot then cope with the questions if they are set in a different order from that expected.

Marking scheme

8-10 marks	Thorough treatment of the two contexts with appropriate use of cases.
5-7 marks	Good treatment of one of the contexts but less complete treatment of the other.
0-4 marks	Very unbalanced answer, focusing on only one aspect of the question and ignoring the other, or one which shows little understanding of the subject matter of the question and simply cites a number of cases in an unstructured way.

(a) **Presumption**

In a legal context, a **presumption** is an assumption of fact accepted by the courts until disproved. The court is entitled to assume a fact to be true until such time as there is a greater weight of evidence which disproves the presumption.

Rebuttal

If the presumption is disproved or outweighed, it is said to be rebutted. A witness can present facts to persuade the judge that the presumption is not true. For example, an accused person is presumed innocent until proven guilty. The presumption of innocence is rebuttable.

(b) **Intention**

No agreement can constitute a contract unless there is evidence, express or implied, of the **intention** of the parties that their agreement should give rise to legally binding obligations. The parties may make an **express statement** in making an agreement, that it is or it is not intended to create legal relations (*Rose & Frank v Crompton 1923*) but this is unusual. Usually courts must interpret the agreement which the parties have made by objective criteria and legally rebuttable presumptions, depending on the relationship of the parties.

Presumption

There are **two basic presumptions**, the first relating to **family and social arrangements** and the second relating to **commercial agreements**. Both presumptions may be **rebutted** by evidence to the contrary.

(i) **Family and social arrangements**

Domestic agreements are generally regarded as **informal** rather than contractual, unless the facts indicate otherwise. At one time, it was firmly considered that in an agreement made in a domestic context there was no implied intention to create legal relations if none had been expressed. Therefore an agreement by a husband to pay an allowance to his wife during his absence abroad was not legally binding *(Balfour v Balfour 1919)*. Similarly, in *Jones v Padavatton 1969*, a mother promised her daughter a monthly allowance if the daughter would return to England to study law. The daughter did so and the mother refused to pay the allowance. It was held that there was no intention to create legal relations and that the agreement was not therefore legally binding.

The presumption is, however, **rebuttable** and the courts may decide that there is an intention to create legal relations in an agreement between husband and wife, especially if they are no longer **living together** or if there is **other evidence** that legal relations were intended. For example, the agreement being formally drawn up and signed *(Merritt v Merritt 1970)*. Also, where the agreement relates to **property matters**, it is perhaps more likely that the courts will infer an intention to create legal relations.

In other relationships, such as those involving **relatives** or **friends**, the presumption is more likely to be rebutted where there is a '**mutuality in the arrangements**' amounting to a joint enterprise. For example where persons jointly enter a competition (*Simpkins v Pays 1955*). In this case, a woman, her granddaughter and a paying lodger took part in a weekly competition in a newspaper, which they entered in the grandmother's name. One week they won £750 and the lodger was denied a third share. It was held that there was a mutuality of agreement and that this was not a 'friendly adventure' but a contract and enforceable.

(ii) **Commercial arrangements**

In **commercial agreements**, the courts will normally infer that there is **an intention to create legal relations** unless there is evidence to the contrary.

In *Edwards v Skyways 1964* an agreement entered into to make an **'ex-gratia' payment** as part of a larger negotiation was held to be legally binding. In *Carlill v Carbolic Smoke Ball Co 1893*, the manufacturer argued – unsuccessfully – that their offer to pay a sum of money to any user of their medicine (who was not protected by it) was a mere **'puff'** not intended to create a legally binding agreement. The court held that their assurance that they had deposited money in a bank account to meet claims was evidence of an intention to create legal relations.

Some commercial agreements may be described by the parties as **'binding in honour only'**. This amounts to an express denial of intention to create legal relations and is effective to rebut the presumption *(Jones v Vernon Pools 1938)*.

As mentioned above, in *Rose and Frank v Crompton 1923*, a statement that the arrangement was not subject to legal jurisdiction was held to be effective. **'Letters of comfort'** given to creditors of subsidiary companies are presumed to be statements of present intentions only and are not legally binding *(Kleinwort Benson Ltd v Malaysia Mining Corpn Bhd 1989)*.

21 Alan

Text reference. Chapter 5.

Top tips. Read the question carefully at least twice. It contains two mini scenarios and you must address each of them. The question tries to help you to appreciate this, by asking you two specific questions, but it does not give you a mark allocation for the separate parts. In each of the scenarios, make sure that you:

- **Identify** the issue
- **State** the law
- **Apply** the law
- **Conclude** and advise the parties concerned

Easy marks. You can gain easy marks in this question by identifying the legal issues for each of the problems. That demonstrates to the examiner that you can recognise the law. Then try to illustrate your answer by reference to similar cases. Don't forget to advise the parties concerned on the basis of the points that you have made.

Marking scheme

This question requires candidates to analyse a situation from the perspective of contract law. In particular it requires an understanding, explanation and application of the law relating to the need for an intention to create legal relations in the creation of contractual relations. Marks will be allocated as follows.

9-10 marks	Thorough explanation of the law relating to intention to create legal relations relevant to the scenario, with case authorities or examples. Good and accurate application of the law to the particular issues raised in the problem.
7-8 marks	Good treatment of the topic but perhaps not dealing with all the issues raised or lacking in some knowledge or application. Perhaps lacking balance.
5-6 marks	Lacking in detail in some or all aspects or lacking in application
0-4 marks	Some but little knowledge of the topic with little appropriate action

Contracts

A **contract** is a **legally binding agreement** resulting from the **valid acceptance** of a **valid offer** supported by **consideration**. In addition, no agreement can constitute a contract unless there is evidence, express or implied, of the intention of the parties that their agreement should give rise to legally binding obligations.

The parties may make an **express statement** in making an agreement, that it is or it is not intended to create legal relations. In one leading case, a written agreement stated that the agreement itself was 'not subject to legal jurisdiction' *(Rose & Frank v Crompton 1923)* and that statement was legally effective.

However, in many cases, the parties do not express any intention and in those circumstances the **courts** must **interpret the agreement** which the parties have made by objective criteria and legal rebuttable presumptions, depending on the relationship of the parties.

There are **two basic presumptions**, the first relating to **family** and **social arrangements** and the second relating to **commercial agreements**. Both presumptions may be rebutted by evidence to the contrary.

Domestic and social agreements

Domestic agreements are generally regarded as **informal** rather than contractual, unless the facts indicate otherwise. Therefore an agreement by a husband to pay an allowance to his wife during his absence abroad was not legally binding *(Balfour v Balfour 1919).*

The **presumption** is, however, **rebuttable** and the courts may decide that there is an intention to create legal relations in an agreement between husband and wife, especially if they are no longer living together and/or if there is other evidence that legal relations were intended. For example, where the agreement is formally drawn up and signed *(Merritt v Merritt 1970).* Also, where the agreement relates to property matters, it is perhaps more likely that the courts will infer an intention to create legal relations.

Business agreements

In **commercial agreements**, the **courts** will normally infer that there **is an intention to create legal relations** unless there is evidence to the contrary. In *Edwards v Skyways 1964* an agreement entered into to make an 'ex-gratia' payment as part of a larger negotiation was held to be legally binding. In *Carlill v Carbolic Smoke Ball Co 1893*, the manufacturer argued, unsuccessfully, that their offer to pay a sum of money to any user of their medicine (who was not protected by it) was a mere 'puff' not intended to create a legally binding agreement. The court held that their assurance that they had deposited money in a bank account to meet claims was evidence of an intention to create legal relations.

Some commercial agreements may be described by the parties as '**binding in honour only**'. This amounts to an express denial of intention to create legal relations and is effective to rebut the presumption *(Jones v Vernon Pools 1938).* As mentioned above, in *Rose and Frank v Crompton 1923*, a statement that the arrangement was not subject to legal jurisdiction was held to be effective.

Applying the above principles to the facts of the scenario, the following may be observed.

(a) **Alan and Ben**

Alan and Ben are son and father and so it may be thought that the presumption that this is a '**domestic and social**' **arrangement**, involving family relations, should apply. However, it is clear from the facts of the case that there is an intention to enter into a business relationship with an expectation of consideration on both sides. It is likely that a court would find that Ben should pay for the work.

(b) **Cath**

The presumption in arrangements between **husband and wife**, as evidenced by the *Balfour* case, is that there is no intention to enter into legal relations. However, the case in the scenario involves a situation which resembles the *Merritt case*, in that the husband and wife are separating and the agreement is contained in a signed document. It is likely that a court would find that Cath could enforce the agreement against Alan.

22 Privity and the postal rule

Text reference. Chapters 4 and 5.

Top tips. Each part of this question is worth five marks, which means that you can only spend nine minutes on them. Don't give in to the temptation to over-run on part (a) and therefore not leave yourself enough time to do justice to part (b), which is equally straightforward. The examiner will not allow you to score over the mark allocation on one part of a question even if you devote all your time to it and produce a brilliant answer.

Your answer to part (b) could have also validly mentioned trustees, statutory exceptions, agency and covenants as exceptions to privity rules.

Easy marks. Get the easy marks by stating what the postal rule and privity of contract are, and if possible citing a case and the 1999 Act, or quoting an illustration in support.

Examiner's comments. Although it has to be admitted that the postal rule is probably of reduced relevance in modern time of electronic communication, it is still in the syllabus and in textbooks and still appears to be popular with students if the answers in this examination are a guide. Candidates, and there were many good answers to this question, were able to locate the postal rule as an exception to the general rule of acceptance of offers and had little difficulty in gaining 5 marks by explaining its operation and, importantly, when it cannot be used.

Although not done quite as well as part (a), this part on the doctrine of privity was still done fairly well nonetheless. The majority of candidates were able to explain the effect of the doctrine for, both parties to contracts and outsiders and had little difficulty in providing at least some examples of the circumstances under which the doctrine could be avoided. As might be expected reference to Beswick v Beswick was common, but it was particularly pleasing to see candidates making reference to collateral contracts and Shanklin Pier v Detel Products Ltd.

Marking scheme

This question is divided into two parts relating to distinct aspects of the law of contract.

(a)	4–5 marks	A good to excellent understanding of the postal rule demonstrated by references to cases or examples.
	2–3 marks	Some, but limited, understanding of the topic, or clear understanding of only one aspect.
	0–1 mark	Little or no knowledge of the topic.
(b)	4–5 marks	A good to excellent understanding of privity demonstrated by references to cases or examples.
	2–3 marks	Some, but limited, understanding of the topic, or clear understanding of only one aspect.
	0–1 mark	Little or no knowledge of the topic.

(a) **The postal rule**

The postal rule in contract law covers situations when the use of the post was in the contemplation of both parties and one or either of the parties uses the post to communicate with the other. It is necessary because it covers problems caused by delays in the postal system or if mail is lost altogether.

It applies where one party accepts an offer, or where the offeror decides to revoke their offer.

Acceptance

Communication of acceptance by post is subject to the rule established in *Adams v Lindsell 1818*. This provides that where the use of the post is in the contemplation of both parties and the acceptance is correctly addressed and stamped and is actually put in the post, then acceptance will be valid and effective once posted and it is irrelevant whether the offeror actually receives the letter.

There is no need for the offer to specifically state that acceptance must be communicated by post – whether this was in the contemplation of the parties may be deduced from the circumstances. For example if the offer was itself made by post (*Household Fire and Carriage Accident Insurance Co v Grant 1879*).

Clearly if it was evident that the parties did not intend the postal rule to apply then the rule will be excluded (*Holwell Securities v Hughes 1974*).

Revocation

While a postal acceptance of an offer is usually effective from the time of posting, a postal revocation of an offer does not take effect until received by the offeree (ie communicated to the offeree). Therefore, where a letter of revocation crosses in the post with a letter of acceptance, a legally binding contract will have been formed from the time the letter of acceptance was posted (*Bryne v Van Tienhoven 1880*).

(b) **Privity of contract**

The term '**privity of contract**' is a general rule which means that only a person who is a party to a contract has enforceable rights or obligations under it. **Third parties** generally have no right to sue on a contract (*Dunlop v Selfridge 1915)*. If a party to a contract imposes a condition for the benefit of a third party or obtains a promise of a benefit for a third party, then that party (not the third party) can usually enforce it. However damages cannot be recovered on the third party's behalf, since a claimant can only recover damages for a loss they have suffered.

Exceptions

There are some **exceptions** to the rule that third parties cannot enforce a contract.

Where the contract has been validly assigned to the third party

Benefit from a contract can be re-assigned from the original beneficiary to a third party if the assignment is in writing, if it transfers the same to the new beneficiary and if it has the consent of the other party.

Where they sue in another capacity

In *Beswick v Beswick 1968* a widow was able to sue in her capacity as administrator of her late husband's estate rather then purely as his wife.

Where the contract is a collateral contract

In *Shanklin Pier v Detel Products Ltd 1951* the owners of a pier were able to sue the suppliers of paint used by contactors to paint the pier. The paint supplier confirmed to the contractor that the paint was suitable for the job but this did not turn out to be true. The pier owners were able to sue the paint suppliers, even though they were not party to the contract for the sale of the pant, as they were party to the collateral contract between them and the contractors responsible for painting the pier.

Where there is foreseeable loss to a third party

In *Linden Gardens Trust Ltd v Lenesta Sludge Disposals Ltd 1994* a third party was in the contemplation of both parties at the time the contract was made. As it was reasonably foreseeable that the third party may suffer a loss as a result of breach of contract the claimants successfully sued contractors for poor workmanship on behalf of the third party.

Where the Contracts (Rights of Third Parties) Act 1999 applies

Under this Act, a third party may enforce a contract's terms either if the contract expressly provides for this, or if a benefit is conferred on the third party under the contract, unless it appears that the contracting parties did not intend for the beneficiary to have the right to enforce the contract.

23 Privity and intention

Text reference. Chapter 5

Top tips. Privity of contract and intention to create legal relations are two areas of law which may seem complicated when really they are not. When thinking of privity think private - third parties have few rights to sue on contracts they are not party to. When explaining intention remember that social agreements are not usually legally binding, and that commercial contracts are binding unless the contrary is proved.

Easy marks. Stating the nature of privity in Part (a) and the two rebuttable presumptions in Part (b).

Examiner's comments. On the whole the question was reasonably well answered. Part (b) was answered better than part (a). In respect of the former, many candidates were able to give a full account of the relevant principles and provide case authorities in support of their explanations. In contrast, whilst many candidates could state the basic principle of privity and some could cite the case of Dunlop v Selfridge to explain it, their knowledge of the exceptions to the rule left much to be desired. A surprising number knew very little and indeed many confused privity with the unrelated concept of privacy.

Marking scheme

	Marks
A thorough understanding of both topics demonstrated by references to cases or examples.	8–10
A clear understanding of both topics but perhaps lacking in detail.	5–7
Alternatively, an unbalanced answer showing good understanding of one part but less in the other.	
Some, but limited, understanding of both topics, or clear understanding of only one of the topics.	2–4
Little or no knowledge of either of the topics	0–1

(a) **Privity of contract**

The term '**privity of contract**' is a general rule which means that only a person who is a party to a contract has enforceable rights or obligations under it. **Third parties** generally have no right to sue on a contract (*Dunlop v Selfridge 1915*). If a party to a contract imposes a condition for the benefit of a third party or obtains a promise of a benefit for a third party, then that party (not the third party) can usually enforce it. However damages cannot be recovered on the third party's behalf, since a claimant can only recover damages for a loss they have suffered.

Exceptions

There are some **exceptions** to the rule that third parties cannot enforce a contract.

Where the contract has been validly assigned to the third party

Benefit from a contract can be re-assigned from the original beneficiary to a third party if the assignment is in writing, if it transfers the same or no more benefits to the new beneficiary and if it has the consent of the other party.

Where they act in another capacity

In *Beswick v Beswick 1968* a widow was able to sue in her capacity as administrator of her late husband's estate rather than purely as his wife.

Where the contract is a collateral contract

In *Shanklin Pier v Detel Products Ltd 1951* the owners of a pier were able to sue the suppliers of paint used by contractors to paint the pier. The paint supplier confirmed to the contractors that the paint was suitable for the job but this did not turn out to be true. The pier owners were able to sue the paint suppliers, even though they were not party to the contract for the sale of the paint, as they were party to the collateral contract between them and the contractors responsible for painting the pier.

Where there is foreseeable loss to a third party

In *Linden Gardens Trust Ltd v Lenesta Sludge Disposals Ltd 1994* a third party was in the contemplation of both parties at the time the contract was made. As it was reasonably foreseeable that the third party may suffer a loss as a result of breach of contract the claimants successfully sued contractors for poor workmanship on behalf of the third party.

Where the Contracts (Rights of Third Parties) Act 1999 applies

Under this Act, a third party may enforce a contract's terms where the contract expressly provides for this, or where a benefit is conferred on them by the contract (unless it appears that the contracting parties did not intend for the beneficiary to have the right to enforce the contract).

(b) **Intention to create legal relations**

The law recognises that only certain contracts are intended to have **legal effect**. If every agreement made was legally binding then the courts would be overrun by litigation.

Where there is no express statement as to whether or not legal relations are intended, the courts apply one of two **rebuttable presumptions** to a case.

- **Social, domestic and family arrangements** are not usually intended to be *binding: Balfour v Balfour 1919*
- **Commercial agreements** are usually intended by the parties involved to be legally binding: *Edwards v Skyways Ltd 1964*

The word **'presumption**' means it is assumed that something is the case, for example it is presumed that social arrangements are not deemed to be legally binding. **'Rebuttable'** means that the presumption can in some cases be refuted.

For example in *Merritt v Merritt 1970* a **domestic case** between husband and wife was deemed to involve a legally binding agreement because that is what the facts and circumstances suggested. In *Rose and Frank v Crompton 1923* a **commercial agreement** was found not to be legally binding since the contract explicitly stated this was so.

24 Consideration

Text reference. Chapter 5.

Top tips. It is important to allocate your time correctly to the different parts of the question. The last part is worth 40% of the whole, so devote enough time to it.

Easy marks. This is a very straightforward question, and the easy marks lie in the cases that you can cite in support of the definitions and explanations that you provide.

Examiner's comments. Part (a) required an explanation of consideration and on the whole it was done very well, with the majority of candidates either giving quotations from appropriate cases or providing examples of consideration.

Part (b) was divided into two separate elements. Part (i) focused on the meaning of and difference between sufficiency and adequacy. By and large candidates were much clearer as regards the issue of adequacy and only a relative few were able to give a clear or detailed explanation of the requirement relating to sufficiency. Part (ii) on past consideration was done fairly well and most candidates were able to cite *McArdle*. However, only a few went further to consider the exceptions to the general rule as set out in such cases as *Lampleigh*.

(a) **Consideration**

Consideration is an **essential element of all binding contracts**, except those made by deed. This is based on the idea that the contractual promise should not be gratuitous but should have an element of bargain about it, even though the courts will not weigh up the relative values of each party's promise or act. Broadly speaking, the doctrine of consideration provides that one party must know that they have bought **the other party's promise**, either by performing some act of their own or by offering a promise of their own.

Consideration has been defined as follows: 'an **act** or **forbearance** of one party, or the promise thereof, is the price for which the promise of the other is bought, and the promise thus given for value is enforceable' *(Dunlop v Selfridge 1915)*. An alternative definition was given in *Currie v Misa 1875:* 'A valuable consideration in the sense of the law may consist either in some **right, interest, profit** or **benefit** accruing to one party, or some **forbearance**, **detriment, loss** or **responsibility** given, suffered or undertaken by the other.'

Types of consideration

Consideration may validly be **executed** or **executory** but cannot be past. **Executed consideration** is a performed, or executed, act in return for a promise. **Executory consideration** is a promise given for a promise (and will be valid before either party performs their promise). Both executed and executory consideration are provided at the time when the promise is given.

Consideration must '**move from the promisee**' which means that the price of a promise **must be paid by the person who seeks to enforce the promise**, ie the promisee *(Tweddle v Atkinson 1861)*. The promisor need not receive any benefit from the promisee.

(b) (i) **Adequacy**

The fact that consideration need not be **adequate** means that it does not have to be of a value appropriate to the promise. The courts will not seek to weigh up the comparative values of the promises, nor will they provide a remedy for someone who simply makes a poor bargain.

In *Chappell & Co v Nestle Co 1960*, chocolate wrappers were held to be good consideration because they were identifiable even though they had no economic value. A nominal rent is sufficient consideration even if it is inadequate as rent in the open market *(Thomas v Thomas 1842)*.

Sufficiency

If consideration is to be **sufficient**, it must be more than the contracting parties were legally obliged to do in any event.

For example in *Glasbrook Bros. v Glamorgan CC 1925*, the policing of a football match was considered to be sufficient consideration to expect payment as more police were supplied than would normally be the case.

Other considerations

Additional incentives from the promisee to encourage performance of existing contractual or statutory obligations are not sufficient consideration *(Stilk v Myrick 1809)*. However, in *Williams v Roffey Bros & Nicholls (Contractors) Ltd 1990*, where the promise to pay extra was given to avoid liability under a penalty clause, the courts held that the mutual benefit derived was sufficient to constitute valid consideration.

(ii) **Past consideration**

Subject to some exceptions, anything which has already been done when the promise is made is '**past consideration**' and is not sufficient *(Re McArdle 1951)*. Where one party to an existing contract makes a further promise, even if it is directly related to the previous bargain, it will be held to have been made on past consideration *(Roscorla v Thomas 1842)*.

There are some exceptions where **past consideration will suffice** to make the promise enforceable:

- Under s27 **Bills of Exchange Act 1882**, past consideration is sufficient to create liability on a bill of exchange;
- Where a request for services is made, it may be **implied** that the person requesting them was also promising to pay for them. Where that person promises a specific reward after the services have been performed, that promise will be treated as fixing the amount promised rather than as a new promise *(Lampleigh v Braithwaite 1615)*. The court will need to be satisfied, however, that both parties have assumed, during their negotiations, that the services being requested would have to paid for *(Re Casey's Patents 1892)*.

25 Forms of consideration

Text reference. Chapter 5.

Top tips. It is important to notice the mark allocation in this type of question, as there are four separate parts and it is all too easy to overrun on one of them, limiting the time available on the others.

Easy marks. Defining consideration in part (a), and explaining the three types of consideration in part (b).

Examiner's comments. This was the most popular question on the paper. Candidates tended to score higher marks where they gave definitions, cases or examples. Some candidates were confused between executory and executed consideration, and in part (b)(ii) some just cited *Re McArdle* without explaining the legal principle.

Marking scheme

			Marks
(a)	Price of the other person's promise (or similar explanation)	1	
	Cases or examples	2	
			3
(b)	*Executory consideration*		
	A promise for a promise	1	
	Example	1	
			2
	Executed consideration		
	Definition and example		2
	Past consideration		
	Explanation	1	
	Cases or example	1	
	Exceptions to the rule	1	
			3
			10

(a) **Consideration**

Consideration, like a valid offer and acceptance and an intention to create legal relations, is an essential element of all binding contracts, except those made by deed. This is based on the idea that the contractual promise should not be gratuitous but should have an element of bargain about it, even though the court will not concern itself with the fairness of the bargain made. Broadly speaking, the doctrine of consideration provides that one party must know that they have bought **the other party's promise**, either by performing some act of their own or by offering a promise of their own.

In *Dunlop v Selfridge 1915*, consideration was defined as follows: 'an act or forbearance of one party, or the promise thereof, is the price for which the promise of the other is bought, and the promise thus given for value is enforceable'. An alternative definition was given in *Currie v Misa 1875*. 'A valuable consideration in the sense of the law may consist either in some **right, interest, profit or benefit** accruing to one party, or some **forbearance, detriment, loss or responsibility** given, suffered or undertaken by the other.'

Adequacy and sufficiency

Consideration must be **sufficient but it need not be adequate**. That is to say that it does not have to be of a value appropriate to the promise. The courts will not seek to weigh up the comparative values of the promises, nor will they provide a remedy for someone who simply makes a poor bargain. In *Chappell & Co v Nestle Co 1960*, chocolate wrappers were held to be good consideration because they were identifiable even though they had no economic value to Nestle.

(b) It is often said that consideration may validly be **executed or executory but cannot be past**. Both executed and executory consideration are provided at the time when the promise is given.

(i) **Executory consideration** is a promise given for a promise (and will be valid before either party performs their promise). Therefore, the consideration in support of each promise is the other party's promise rather than a performed act. If one party agrees to pay for goods which the other party agrees to deliver, that constitutes sufficient consideration so that if either party withdraws without the other's consent, that is breach of contract.

(ii) **Executed consideration** is a performed, or executed, act in return for a promise. Therefore, in reward cases, for example, a promise to pay a reward when an act is done becomes enforceable only when that act is performed.

(iii) Subject to some exceptions, anything which has already been done when the promise is made is '**past consideration**' and is not enforceable (*Re McArdle 1951*). Where one party to an existing contract makes a further promise, even if it is directly related to the previous bargain, it will be held to have been made on past consideration (*Roscorla v Thomas 1842*).

There are, however, some **exceptions** where past consideration will suffice to make the promise enforceable, including:

Bills of Exchange Act 1882

Under s 27 bills of Exchange Act 1882, past consideration is sufficient to create liability on a bill of exchange; and

Request for Services

Where a request for services is made, it may be implied that the person requesting them was also promising to pay for them. In which case, where that person promises a specific reward after the services have been performed, that promise will be treated as fixing the amount promised rather than as a new promise *(Lampleigh v Braithwaite 1615)*. The courts will need to be satisfied, however, that both parties must have assumed, during their negotiations, that the services requested would be paid for (*Re Casey's Patents 1892*).

26 Ami, Bry and Cis

Text reference. Chapter 5.

Top tips. Following the ISAC approach will gain you the majority of the marks in this question as it enables you to address the main issues raised by it. See the examiner's comments below.

Easy marks. Identifying consideration and breach of contract as the main points at hand will gain you some basic marks.

ACCA examiner's answers. The ACCA examiner's answer to this question can be found at the back of this kit.

Examiner's comments. It was refreshing to see that candidates had adopted a sensible approach in stating the relevant law, applying it to the scenario and then drawing reasonable conclusions, linked to their interpretation and analysis.

Marking scheme

Marks for this question will be awarded on the basis of a general knowledge of the law together with an ability to analyse the problem scenario and apply the general legal principles to the particular situation of the problem. In particular marks will be given for explanations of consideration, the law relating to existing duties and how those rules may be avoided. Knowledge of specific cases is not a requirement.

8–10 marks:	Accurate analysis of the situation together with a detailed knowledge of the general legal principles involved linked to a sound application of those principles.
5–7 marks:	Sound knowledge of the law but perhaps lacking in application or alternatively not showing a sufficiently clear understanding of the legal principles involved.
3–4 marks:	Weak or unbalanced answer. Perhaps aware of the nature of the problem but lacking in clear knowledge of the principles or deficient in relation to how those principles should be applied.
0–2 marks:	Very weak answer. Perhaps mentioning some of the issues involved in the question but failing to consider them in any detail or merely recounting the facts of some of the cases with no attempt to derive principles or apply them.

Issue

Ami agreed to pay Bry and Cis an extra £1,000 each on top of their contracted fee of £5,000 each in order for their work to be completed on time. The work was completed on time but Ami is refusing to pay Bry and Cis their extra £1,000 and it therefore appears that Ami is in **breach of contract**. However, for agreements to be legally binding, both parties must provide **sufficient consideration**.

The law

Consideration does not have to be adequate (of fair value) but it must be **sufficient**. Ami's offer of £1,000 is clearly sufficient for a promise by Bry and Cis to complete their work on time, so attention must turn to whether Bry's and Cis's agreement to fulfil their **existing contractual obligations** (of completing their work by 31 March) is sufficient as well.

It is established law that the **performance of an existing obligation is no consideration** for a promise of reward (*Stilk v Myrick 1809)*. However, where a party does more than merely performing an existing obligation, this is sufficient consideration (*Hartley v Ponsonby 1857)*.

Where a party receives some **practical benefit** from the other's performance then this is acceptable as consideration providing there was no duress or fraud involved (*Williams v Roffey Bros & Nicholls (Contractors) Ltd 1990)*.

Application

Bry would argue that Ami received some **practical benefit** from her agreement to pay him an additional £1,000 as the work was completed on time. However it seems that Ami was **under duress** from Bry as he stated that he would not complete the work on time unless she paid him the extra money. This left Ami with no choice but to agree to the extra payment.

As far as Cis is concerned, Ami merely offered him an extra £1,000 **without him having to provide any consideration** in return. She received no practical benefit from Cis's performance of his existing obligation.

Conclusion

Neither Bry nor Cis provided **valid consideration** for the extra £1,000 Ami promised to pay them, therefore Ami is not in breach of contract by refusing to pay it.

27 Types of term I

Text reference. Chapter 6.

Top tips. Notice the mark allocation to the four parts of the question and make sure that you give them each the appropriate amount of time. At 1.8 minutes a mark, you should spend about 5½ minutes on a 3 mark section and about 3½ minutes on a 2 mark section. Do not be tempted to over-run as you will then lose the chance to do well on the other parts of the question.

Our answer to part (d) is far longer than you would be expected to produce in the exam but covers the subject comprehensively for revision purposes.

Easy marks. Make sure that you attempt each of the parts of the question in order to get the easy marks available for the definitions and the illustrative cases. Don't forget the easy marks for explaining the effects of breach of the different types of terms.

Marking scheme

8–10 marks	Thorough explanation of the meaning of terms generally together with an explanation of the three categories of terms with reference to appropriate cases or examples.
5–7 marks	Reasonable treatment of terms generally and one or even two of the types of terms, or a less complete treatment of all the elements.
0–4 marks	Very unbalanced answer, focusing on only one aspect of the question and ignoring the others, or one which shows little understanding of the subject matter of the question.

(a) **Terms**

Contractual terms are statements or promises which are incorporated into a contract. The contracting parties are contractually bound to observe and perform contractual terms and in the event of breach, the injured party's remedies will depend on whether the term is classified as a **condition** or a **warranty**.

(b) **Conditions**

A **condition** is a vital term of the contract which goes right to the heart of the contract, breach of which allows the innocent party to treat the agreement as **terminated and sue for damages**. Alternatively, they may elect to affirm the contract, in which case they can still sue for damages for any loss but must continue with their own obligations.

In the leading case of *Poussard v Spiers 1876* it was held that failure by an opera singer to appear on the opening night of a series of performances amounted to breach of a condition and the producer had been entitled to treat the contract for the remaining performances as discharged.

(c) **Warranties**

A **warranty** is a subsidiary contractual term which is less fundamental and breach of it gives only a **right to damages**, not to treat the contract as discharged. If a party to the contract attempts to repudiate the contract following a breach of warranty, this will amount to a wrongful repudiation. This would therefore make the party initially in breach open to a claim for breach of contract.

In contrast to the *Poussard* case, above, the case of *Bettini v Gye 1876* involved an opera singer who was booked to arrive six days before the first performance in order to attend rehearsals. He arrived three days before the first performance and it was held that this was a breach of a warranty. The defendants were not entitled to treat the contract as discharged and were ordered to compensate the claimant, whose services they had refused to accept.

(d) **Innominate terms**

In the absence of any express provision describing the contractual term as a condition or warranty (or any statutory provision which implies certain conditions and warranties), the court will seek to construe what was the **intention of the parties at the time of the contract**.

Where the intention is not clear, then the term is described as an **innominate term** and must be interpreted in the light of the actual effect of the breach. If the effect of the breach is to deprive the injured party of 'substantially the whole benefit of the contract' then the term will be treated as a condition giving rise to a right to treat the contract as repudiated and sue for damages. If the effect of the breach is not so severe, the injured party's rights will be the same as for breach of an express warranty.

In the case of *Hong Kong Fir Shipping Co Ltd v Kawasaki Kisa Kaisha Ltd 1962*, a term that provided for the claimants to supply a ship which was 'in every way fitted for ordinary cargo service' was held to be innominate as it could not automatically be construed as either a condition or a warranty. The court held that the effect of the breach of this innominate term (the ship was not available for 7 out of 24 months) was insufficient to be regarded as breach of condition and did not justify terminating the contract.

28 Types of term II

Text reference. Chapter 6.

Top tips. It is important that you clearly distinguish between the two legal terms in each part – make sure the marker knows you are aware of the differences!

Easy marks. Defining each of the four terms.

Examiner's comments. This question required candidates to consider the law relating to terms in contracts. Part (a) specifically required the candidate to distinguish between terms and mere representations while part (b) required them to explain the difference between express and implied terms in contracts.

Part (a) tended to be answered fairly well and most candidates were able to distinguish between terms and representations, although some candidates spent too much time in developing extended answers on the various types of terms.

Part (b) was also fairly well answered and most candidates were aware of the various sources of implied terms and their effects. Perhaps not surprisingly less detail was provided about express terms.

Marking scheme

(a)	2–3 marks	A good explanation of the distinction between terms and representations. No reference to misrepresentation is needed.
	0–1 mark	Very little knowledge of the meaning of the concepts.
(b)	5–7 marks	Thorough treatment of the topic. Clearly distinguishing between the two types of terms and explaining most, if not all of the ways in which terms may be implied into contracts.
	2–4 marks	Less thorough answer, but showing a reasonable understanding of the topic.
	0–1 mark	Weak answer, perhaps showing some knowledge but little understanding of the topic generally.

(a) **Terms and representations**

Contractual terms are statements or promises which are incorporated into a contract. The contracting parties are contractually bound to observe and perform contractual terms and in the event of breach, the injured party's remedies will depend on whether the term is classified as a **condition** (vital to the contract) or a **warranty** (subsidiary to the main purpose of the contract) .

A **representation** is something which induces the formation of a contract but which does not become a **term** of the contract. The importance of the distinction is that different remedies are available depending on whether a term is broken or a representation turns out to be untrue. If the statement is made by a person with **special knowledge** it is more likely to be treated as a contract term (*Dick Bentley Productions v Arnold Smith Motors 1965*).

(b) **Express and implied terms**

An **express term** may be defined as any term which has been included by the parties. It may be written or oral. The court will ascertain as a question of fact whether any oral statement constitutes a term of the contract or simply a representation. An apparently binding legal agreement must be **complete and certain in its terms** to be a valid contract (*Scammell v Ouston 1941*).

Implied terms

An **implied term** is one which is deemed to form part of a contract even though not expressly stated by the parties, whether orally or in writing. Terms may be implied by the courts, (as necessary to give effect to the parties' presumed intentions), by statute, or in accordance with relevant trade practices. Implied terms can normally be excluded or varied by the parties save where this is prevented by relevant statutory provisions.

Court

The usual reason for a **court** to imply a term in a contract is in order to **give business efficacy** to that contract. In such cases the term which is implied will be one which, it appears to the court, the parties inadvertently omitted or which is so obvious that it goes without saying and it can be assumed that the parties simply took it for granted that such a term would apply. The courts will be keen to prevent the failure of an otherwise sound contract and to implement the manifest intention of the parties *(The Moorcock 1889).* The courts have also established a number of implied terms into employment contracts concerning employers' and employees' duties.

Statute

Terms will be **implied by statute** where that is the expressed intention of the legislation, for example under the **Sale of Goods Act 1979**, terms are implied as to the vendor's title and the description and quality of the goods in a contract for the sale of goods.

Custom and practice

The parties may be considered to have entered into a contract **subject to a custom or practice of their trade**. In *Hutton v Warren 1836*, the defendant landlord gave the claimant, a tenant farmer, notice to quit the farm but insisted that the tenant should continue to farm the land during the period of notice. The tenant asked for 'a fair allowance' for seeds and labour from which they received no benefit (as they left before harvest time). It was held that by custom they were bound to farm the land until the end of the tenancy, but they were also entitled to a fair allowance for seeds and labour. However, any express term overrides a term which might be implied by custom *(Les Affreteurs v Walford 1919).*

29 Exclusion clauses

Text reference. Chapter 6.

Top tips. It is important to spend a little time planning before embarking on this question, especially for part (b). You need to clarify in your own mind the differences between statutory and common law control of exclusion clauses, so that you can produce a logical and well-structured answer.

Easy marks. There are few easy marks unless you know all the rules on exclusion clauses. The easiest marks are to define exclusion clauses and state their aim.

Examiner's comments. Candidates did not pay heed to the mark allocations for the different parts of this question, and did not equate their efforts in relation to the marks indicated for each part of the question. Candidates tended to score better marks on parts (a) and (b)(i) and seemed happier dealing with the common law rather than the statutory points. The Unfair Contract Terms Act and the Unfair Terms in Consumer Contracts Regulations were essential for a full discussion of this area of the law.

Marking scheme

				Marks
(a)	Definition		1	
	Aim of law is to protect the weaker party		1	
				2
(b)	(i)	Proper incorporation into contract	1	
		If document signed	1/2	
		Effect of misrepresentation	1/2	
		Cases (½ each)	1	
		Contra proferentem rule	1	
				4
	(ii)	Unfair Contract Terms Act	1	
		No exclusion for death or injury	1	
		Other examples of terms	1	
		Unfair Terms in Consumer Contracts Regulations	1	
				4
				10

(a) **Exclusion clauses**

An exclusion clause, or exemption clause, can be defined as '**a clause in a contract which purports to exclude liability altogether or to restrict it by limiting damages or by imposing other onerous conditions**'. As a general principle of contract law, the courts will not usually interfere where two parties negotiate a contract from positions of comparable bargaining strength. However, the law will seek to **protect a weaker party**, for example in the case of standard term contracts put forward by the party in the stronger bargaining position. The validity of exclusion clauses is governed by the common law, the Unfair Contract Terms Act 1977 and a number of other statutory regulations.

(b) (i) **Control by common law**

The **common law** provides that an exclusion clause must be properly incorporated into a contract, or in a document which is an integral part of the contract, before it can be effective (*Chapelton v Barry UDC 1940*). Provided this is the case, a term cannot usually be disputed if the **document has been signed**, even if the signatory could not read the terms (*L'Estrange v Graucob 1934*), unless the party putting forward the document gives a misleading explanation of the term's effects (*Curtis v Chemical Cleaning Co 1951*).

Unsigned contracts

In the case of an **unsigned contract**, then it must be shown either that the party affected actually **knew of the clause** or that the person seeking to rely on the exemption clause has taken reasonable steps to bring the existence of the clause to the attention of the other party at the time of or before the contract was made. Therefore, sign on a hotel room wall was not incorporated into the contract between hotel and client since it was not seen until after the contract was made (*Olley v Marlborough Court 1949*).

Nature of the liability

The court will have regard to the **nature of the liability** which is being excluded when deciding whether a clause has been effectively incorporated. If the terms are particularly unusual or wide, a more prominent notice may be necessary (*Thornton v Shoe Lane Parking Ltd 1971*).

Prior notice

Prior notice of the terms is not necessary, however, where the parties have had previous consistent dealings and the documents used previously contained similar terms (even if the claimant has never read them (J *Spurling Ltd v Bradshaw 1956*)).

Previous dealings

Where there have been **previous dealings**, but not on a consistent basis, then the party to be bound by the term must be sufficiently aware of it at the time of making the latest contract (*Hollier v Rambler Motors 1972*). A particularly unusual or onerous term must be highlighted if it is to be incorporated into the contract (*Interfoto Picture Library Ltd v Stiletto Visual Programmes Ltd 1988*).

Interpretation

At common law, under the *contra proferentem* rule, the courts **interpret exclusion clauses strictly** and in favour of the weaker party. They presume that the clause is not intended to defeat the main purpose of the contract. A general exemption will not be interpreted so as to cover negligence (*Hollier v Rambler Motors 1972*) unless to do so is the only means by which the clause is given meaning (*Alderslade v Hendon Laundry 1945*).

(ii) **Control by statute**

The scope of the common law in governing exclusion clauses has been significantly curtailed by extensive **statutory provisions**. The main statutory limitations on exclusion clauses are contained in the **Unfair Contract Terms Act 1977**. The Act applies to clauses inserted into most agreements by commercial concerns or businesses and provides that some clauses shall be void and some valid only as far as they are reasonable.

Personal injury and death

Liability for **personal injury** or **death** due to negligence may never be excluded (s 2(1)). An exemption for loss due to negligence in other circumstances will be valid only insofar as it is reasonable (s 2). 'Negligence' covers breach of contractual obligations of skill and care and the common law duty of skill and care.

Reasonableness

Reasonableness is to be considered with reference to the factors in s 11 and s 2. The court will consider the relative strength of the parties' bargaining power, whether an inducement was offered to the customer, whether the customer knew or ought to have known of the exemption clause and whether compliance with the contract's terms was practicable.

Burden of proof

The **burden of proof** lies with the person relying on the clause and the court will consider the factors outlined above in reaching a decision. This will be a matter of fact.

Sale of goods

A term in a **guarantee of goods** which excludes or limits liability for loss or damage caused by a defect of the goods in consumer use (s 5) will be void, as will a clause in any contract for the sale of goods which excludes the condition that the seller has a right to sell the goods (s 6). Likewise a clause which purports to exclude or limit liability for breach of the conditions relating to **description**, **quality, fitness** or **sample** (ss 6 and 7) will be **void** in a consumer contract and subject to the reasonableness test in a non-consumer contract.

Unfair terms in consumer contracts

In addition to UCTA, the **Unfair Terms in Consumer Contracts Regulations 1999** apply to consumer contracts for the supply of goods and services and to terms which have not been individually negotiated. An **unfair term** is any term which causes a **significant imbalance** in the parties' rights and obligations under the contract to the detriment of the consumer. The courts will have regard to similar factors as those under UCTA and whether the supplier dealt fairly and equitably with the consumer.

30 Seller Ltd and Transport Ltd

Text reference. Chapter 6.

Top tips. This is quite a straightforward problem if you have revised this area thoroughly. A lack of technical knowledge will cost you marks. There is plenty of case law on the topic and you should refer to it.

Easy marks. Remembering and stating relevant cases to support your answer.

Marking scheme

	Marks
Incorporation of the clause	
– By signature	1
– Notice/nature	2
– Course of dealings	3
Statute law restrictions	2
Conclusion	2
	10

Issue

To **enforce the exclusion clause**, Transport Ltd will need to prove that it is validly incorporated into the contract with Seller Ltd and that its use is not restricted.

Incorporation of exclusion clauses

There are three ways in which exclusion clauses can be incorporated into contracts: by **signature**, by **notice** and by a **course of dealing**.

Signature

The terms may be incorporated into the contract by the **signature** of the other party on a document bearing the terms. The signatory is taken to know of the terms, even if they could not read them (*L'Estrange v Graucob 1934*).

Notice

With regard to incorporation by **notice**, it must be shown that the person seeking to rely on the exclusion clause has taken reasonable steps to bring the existence of the clause to the attention of the other party **at the time the contract was made**. Only in limited circumstances will the courts allow the incorporation of a term after the contract has been made. Therefore a sign on a hotel room wall was not incorporated into the contract between hotel and client since it was not seen until after the contract was made (*Olley v Marlborough Court 1949*).

Nature of the liability

The court will have regard to the **nature of the liability** which is being excluded when deciding whether a clause has been effectively incorporated. If the terms are particularly unusual or wide, a more prominent notice may be necessary. For example, in *Thornton v Shoe Lane Parking Ltd 1971* a notice excluding liability for injury in an automatic car park was not sufficiently displayed or referred to at the time the contract was made.

Course of dealing

Where the parties deal frequently in **transactions of a similar nature** and on the **same terms**, the courts are ready to hold that the exclusion clause has been incorporated into the latest agreement by virtue of its being present in the previous dealings, even if the claimant had never read it. The position is not as straightforward where the previous dealings have not been on a consistent basis (eg *Hollier v Rambler Motors 1972* which concerned a consumer contract).

Seller Ltd

In the case of Seller Ltd and Transport Ltd, the court will consider each of these tests. There is no evidence that Transport Ltd's exclusion clause has been incorporated by **signature**.

With regard to incorporation by **notice**, it seems that visitors to Transport Ltd's premises will be made aware of the clause by virtue of the 'notice prominently displayed'.

However as the order was placed by telephone, it is unlikely that Transport Ltd can use this in its defence. Equally, the notice provided with the confirmation of order is provided **too late** to be incorporated into the contract, as the contract has already been concluded by this stage. Following *Olley v Marlborough Court 1949*, this precludes incorporation of the clause by notice to the other party.

The court will also consider the fact that there have been **previous dealings** between the parties and will need to determine whether ten dealings are enough to constitute a regular and consistent course of dealing. In *Hollier v Rambler Motors 1972* a course of dealing which amounted to three or four transactions over five years was held not to be sufficient, but ten dealings in the past year are probably enough to establish previous dealing and to validly incorporate the clause.

Statutory restrictions

Statute law imposes some very important restrictions on the use of validly incorporated exclusion clauses. The **Unfair Contract Terms Act 1977**, which applies to clauses covering business liability, divides these clauses into two types; those which are **void** and those which are valid only as far as they are **reasonable**.

In deciding **reasonableness**, the court will consider the relative strength of the parties' **bargaining power**, whether an **inducement** was offered to the customer, whether the customer **knew** or ought to have **known** of the **exclusion clause** and whether **compliance** with the contract's terms was **practicable** (Sch 2 of the 1977 Act).

An exclusion for loss due to negligence in a **business contract** will be valid only insofar as it is **reasonable** (s 2 of the 1977 Act).

Seller Ltd

In Seller Ltd's case, both parties appear to have **equal bargaining power**, **no inducement** was offered to Seller Ltd and **compliance with the term is practical** (in business, insurance is commonly taken out against such risks). Therefore it appears likely that Transport Ltd will be able to rely on the exclusion clause.

31 Bash Ltd

Text reference. Chapter 6.

Top tips. Read the question carefully at least twice. Highlight the question paper for key points or annotate the margin. Make sure that you identify the issues involved and are fully familiar with the scenario before you start your answer.

Easy marks. Try to have some breadth in your thought processes here. Most candidates will think quite easily of the common law rules here with regard to exclusion clauses, but don't forget the statutory rules as well. There are easy marks available for referring, for example, to the Unfair Contract Terms Act.

Examiner's comments. To quote one marker; '[T]he rubric clearly asks candidates to assume that the exclusion clause was properly incorporated into the contract. The facts of the scenario were drawn up so as to achieve that. Despite this, many candidates devoted most of their effort to a regurgitation of the common law rules of incorporation…given that this was strictly irrelevant it was not possible to give more than minimal marks in respect of this part of the answer…many students seemed to know little about the statutory rules, in particular the Unfair Contract Terms Act 1977. So there existed a paradox. Candidates seemed to know a lot about what was irrelevant, but not enough about what was relevant.'

Marking scheme

This question requires candidates to apply the law relating to exclusion clauses to a specific problem scenario. Marks will be awarded for both knowledge and application, but application is essential.

8–10 marks	The best candidates should provide a clear understanding of the legal control of exclusion clauses and be able to apply the law. Some detailed reference should be made to the provisions of the Unfair Contract Terms Act (UCTA) 1997 and the very best answers will at least mention the Unfair Terms in Consumer Contracts Regulations 1999. Cases or examples should be used to demonstrate points made.
5–7 marks	Weaker candidates may show little detailed knowledge of the legislation but be able to consider the UCTA generally.
3–4 marks	Some but limited knowledge of the appropriate law or lacking in application.
0–2 marks	The poorest candidates will provide nothing but the briefest reference to the legislation.

Exclusion clauses

An **exclusion** or **exemption clause**, can be defined as 'a clause in a contract which purports to exclude liability altogether or to restrict it by limiting damages or by imposing other onerous conditions.

As a general principle of contract law, the **courts will not usually interfere** where two parties negotiate a contract from positions of **comparable bargaining strength**. However, the law will seek to protect a weaker party, for example in the case of **standard term contracts** put forward by the party in the stronger bargaining position. The validity of exclusion clauses is governed by the common law, the **Unfair Contract Terms Act 1977** and a number of other statutory regulations.

Usually it is necessary to determine whether the exclusion clause that Bash Ltd is seeking to rely on has been **properly incorporated** into the contract with Andy. However, as we are told that the term has been properly incorporated we shall move on to consider whether or not the term is successful in protecting Bash Ltd from liability.

Liability

The **Unfair Contract Terms Act 1977**, which applies to clauses covering business liability, divides exclusion clauses into two types; those which are **void** and those which are **valid only as far as they are reasonable**.

Under s2, **liability for personal injury or death due to negligence may never be excluded**. An exemption for loss due to negligence in other circumstances will be valid only insofar as it is **reasonable**. Reasonableness is to be considered with reference to the parties' obligations of skill and care.

Andy's injury

Taking into account s2 of UCTA 1977, **Bash Ltd would not be able to rely on the exclusion clause** to avoid liability for the injuries to Andy which arose from its **negligence** due to the actions of the towing vehicle's driver.

Damage to Andy's car

The exclusion clause seeking to exempt Bash Ltd from liability for the damage to Andy's car will only be valid if it is **reasonable**. Courts will take into account all the circumstances which were known, or ought to have been known by the parties when the contract was made and it will be up to Bash Ltd to prove that the clause was reasonable: *St Albans City and District Council v International Computers Ltd 1994.*

The company would be **unlikely** to succeed in avoiding liability for damage to Andy's car since it is reasonable to expect its driver not to be negligent in operating such a tow truck.

32 Breach of contract

Text reference. Chapter 7.

Top tips. Be careful to read the question carefully as you are not just required to give a general explanation of breach of contract. Your answer must pay particular attention to anticipatory breach.

Easy marks. Defining breach of contract and anticipatory breach.

Examiner's comments. This question required candidates to show understanding of what is meant by breach of contract paying particular attention to anticipatory breach. On the whole the question was answered well. Many candidates were able to explain breach and the consequences according to the status of the term broken – either warranty, condition or innominate term, although some candidates did take this as an opportunity to answer a question on terms rather than breach. In this question it is pleasing to note that explanations were very often supported by accurate references to relevant case law.

Anticipatory breach was dealt with equally well on the whole, with many candidates drawing the distinction between express/implied anticipatory breach. Once again the relevant case law was cited in support of the explanations.

However, in spite of the question generally being well done there was considerable room for improvement, not just in terms of being better prepared to answer the question but also in terms of examination technique. Too many candidates spent an inordinate amount of time and effort in producing an introduction to their answer by explaining in considerable detail the essential elements of legally binding contracts, when in fact the question assumed the existence of the same. Such an approach not only wasted valuable time but also produced unfocused answers that gained fewer marks that they might otherwise have gained had they limited their time and effort to the essential matter of the question.

Marking scheme

This question requires candidates to show understanding of what is meant by anticipatory breach. In demonstrating such understanding candidates should mention the consequences of such a breach of contract, but answers should not focus too much on remedies.

8–10 marks:	A thorough explanation of the concept of breach providing cases or examples by way of explanation.
5–7 marks:	A clear understanding of what is meant by breach but perhaps lacking in the detail expected of the very best answers.
2–4 marks:	Some understanding of the breach, but confused or lacking in explanation as to meaning or effect.
0–1 mark:	No real understanding of the meaning of the term.

Breach of contract

A party is said to be in **breach of contract** where, without lawful excuse, they do not perform their contractual obligations precisely.

A person sometimes has a lawful excuse not to perform contractual obligations, if:

- Performance is **impossible**, perhaps because of some unforeseeable event.
- They have tendered performance but this has been **rejected.**
- The **other party** has made it **impossible** for them to perform.
- The contract has been discharged through **frustration**.
- The parties have by **agreement** permitted **non-performance.**

Breach of contract gives rise to a **secondary obligation** to **pay damages** to the other party. However, the primary obligation to perform the contract's terms remains, unless the party in default has **repudiated** the contract. This may be before performance is due, or before it has been completed, and repudiation has been accepted by the injured party.

Anticipatory breach

Anticipatory breach occurs before the time of performance arrives and can occur in two ways.

Explicit (express) anticipatory breach

This is where one party **declares in advance** that they will not perform their side of the bargain when the time for performance arrives. For example, in *Hochster v De La Tour 1853* , an agreement to act as a courier from 1st June was cancelled by letter on 11th May. The court held that action for breach of contract could commence straight away rather than waiting for actual breach on 1st June as there had been express anticipatory breach.

Implicit (implied) anticipatory breach

This is where some **action** occurs which makes **future performance impossible**. For example, where a person has a contract to sell their car, but before the buyer pays, they sell it to someone else.

Remedies

As a **consequence** of anticipatory breach, the wronged party may **treat the contract as discharged** and **sue for damages immediately**, or **continue with their obligations until actual breach occurs**. Their claim for **damages** will then depend upon what they have **actually lost**. For example, in *White & Carter (Councils) v McGregor 1961* there was a contract to supply adverts on litter bins. Before the claimant performed their side of the bargain, the defendant wrote to cancel the contract. However, the claimant continued to provide the adverts anyway and then sued the defendants to claim the agreed price. This was upheld by the court.

33 Arti

Text reference. Chapter 7.

Top tips. Although the solution to this question may seem obvious, don't make the mistake of leaping straight into the conclusion – most of the marks are for explaining the law, not for the conclusion.

Easy marks. Stating the law on breach of contract and the various remedies.

Examiner's comments. This question required candidates to analyse a problem scenario from the perspective of contract law and apply the appropriate legal rules, specifically relating to anticipatory breach of contract and the remedies subsequent to any such action.

On the whole the question was dealt with fairly well, with the majority of candidates recognising that the issue involved anticipatory breach and providing appropriate case authority to support their analysis. A number, however, spent a largely wasted time considering the distinction between conditions and warranties and citing the cases in that area. A smaller group suggested that there was no real problem in any case as Arti might still produce the material, so they didn't write anything about the law relating to the problem scenario.

The remedies issue was done less well, with the majority failing to pursue it with the necessary detail and a surprising minority suggesting that specific performance could be awarded.

Marking scheme

This question requires candidates to analyse a problem scenario from the perspective of contract law and apply the appropriate legal rules.

8–10 marks	Clear analysis of the problem scenario – recognition of the contract law issues raised and a convincing application of the legal principles to the facts. Appropriate case authorities are likely to be cited.
6–7 marks	Sound analysis of the problem – recognition of the major principles involved and a fair attempt at applying them. Perhaps sound in knowledge but lacking in analysis and application.
3–5 marks	Unbalanced answer perhaps showing some appropriate knowledge but weak in analysis or application.
0–2 marks	Very weak answer showing little analysis, appropriate knowledge or application.

Issue

From the facts it is clear that there is a contract between Arti and Bee Ltd for Arti to write a study manual that will be ready by 30 June 20X8. As of 31 May 20X8, Arti had not commenced work on the study text, he has also written to Bee Ltd stating that he is too busy to write it. The issue at hand is the apparent breach of contract by Arti, and Bee Ltd needs to know what remedies are available to it.

The law

A party is said to be in **breach of contract** where, without lawful excuse, they do not perform their contractual obligations precisely. Breach of contract often occurs at the time the contract is performed. However in Arti's case, breach has occurred before the date of performance.

Where a party breaks a condition of the contract by declaring in advance that they will not perform it, the other party may treat this as **anticipatory breach**. This allows them to either treat the contract as discharged immediately (*Hochster v De La Tour 1853*), or allow the contract to continue until there is an actual breach (*White & Carter (Councils) v McGregor 1961*).

If the innocent party elects to treat the contract as still in force, they may continue their preparations for performance and **recover the agreed price** for their services. Any claim for damages will be assessed on the basis of what the claimant has really lost.

Remedies

Two remedies for breach of contract which may be relevant are specific performance and damages.

Specific performance

This involves the party in breach being compelled to perform their obligations by the court. No compensation is paid to the injured party – the benefit to them is that the contract is fulfilled. This remedy is not available in employment contracts or contracts for personal services.

Damages

Damages is a remedy which is available where any contract is breached. It is a monetary payment from the party in breach to the innocent party. However, a party can only be sued for damages if the loss **arises naturally from the breach in a manner which the parties may reasonably be supposed to have contemplated, in making the contract, as the probable result of the breach of it** (*Hadley v Baxendale 1854*).

As a general rule, the amount awarded as damages is what is needed to **put the claimant in the position they would have achieved if the contract had been performed**. Punishing the party in breach is not the aim. Loss of profit can be claimed if it is deemed normal (*Victoria Laundry (Windsor) v Newman Industries 1949*). Preliminary expenses can also be claimed if they are in the ordinary course of business and not excessive (*Anglia Television Ltd v Reed 1972*).

In assessing the amount of damages it is assumed that the claimant will take any reasonable steps to reduce or **mitigate** their loss (*Payzu Ltd v Saunders 1919*). The burden of proof is on the defendant to show that the claimant failed to take a reasonable opportunity of mitigation. However, this does not appear necessary in cases of anticipatory breach, as the *White and Carter* case allows the injured party to continue to make preparations as if the other party will fulfil the contract.

The injured party is not required to take **discreditable** or **risky measures** to reduce their loss since these are not 'reasonable'.

Application and conclusion

Applying the law to the facts it would appear that Arti is in **anticipatory breach** of his contract with Bee Ltd.

Bee Ltd has the option to **continue** as if the contract will be performed and claim damages when Arti fails to supply the study text, or it may treat the contract as **discharged** and seek a remedy immediately.

Bee Ltd may wish to force Arti to fulfil his part of the deal since time is running out for them to find another author who can write the material at short notice. This unfortunately is not an option as **specific performance** is not a remedy in contracts for personal service.

If another author is sought in **mitigation** then Arti would be liable for any damages where the **cost of the new author** is greater than what Bee Ltd would have paid Arti. Arti would be liable for any extra author costs.

If no author can be found then Bee Ltd could claim **loss of profit** as a consequence of it not being able to supply the text to the accountancy body but only if the profit is normal profit. Arti would not be liable for profits which are outside what was expected when the contract was signed. Bee Ltd could also claim its **preliminary expenses** which appear to be reasonable in the circumstances.

34 Astride

Text reference. Chapter 7

Top tips. Contract law questions are often based on one issue – in this case breach of contract and remedies. Don't waste time discussing formation of contracts as it is not relevant and you will not earn any marks. If you applied the ISAC approach to this question then you would not have made this mistake (I = identify the issue).

Easy marks. Setting out the basic principles of law relevant to the issues in the question.

Examiner's comments. Overall, candidates acknowledged that there had been a breach of contract and displayed a good understanding of the various remedies available and the better answers recognised that the estimation of damages in relation to construction contracts was difficult. A sound understanding of relevant case law was displayed with many candidates referring to Ruxley Electronics and Construction Ltd v Forsyth (1995) and acknowledging that the cost of remedying defects has to be proportionate to the difference between the services ordered and those supplied.

Marking scheme

This question requires candidates to analyse a situation from the perspective of contract law. In particular it requires an understanding, explanation and application of the law relating to the remedies available for breach of contract. Marks will be allocated as follows:

8–10 marks	Full and thorough explanation of the law relating to remedies for breach of contract, with case authorities or examples. Good and accurate application of the law to the particular issues raised in the problem.
5–7 marks	Good treatment of the topic but perhaps not dealing with all the issues raised or lacking in some knowledge or application. Perhaps lacking balance.
3–4 marks	Lacking in detail in some or all aspects or lacking in application.
0–2 marks	Some but little knowledge of the topic with little appropriate application.

Issue

Astride has made legally enforceable contracts with Bild Ltd and Chris so the issue appears to be **breach of contract** and what **remedies** are available to her.

Breach of contract

Breach of contract may occur **before** the time of performance (**anticipatory breach**) or at the time of performance (**repudiatory breach**). Astride's dispute with Bild Ltd is therefore repudiatory breach; her dispute with Chris is anticipatory breach.

Repudiatory breach allows the injured party to either seek a remedy or affirm the contract. Astride is clearly not going to affirm the contract so she will seek a remedy.

Where **anticipatory breach** occurs, the injured party has a choice. They can either treat the contract as repudiated immediately and seek a remedy (*Hochster v De La Tour 1853*), or continue with their preparations for the contract and sue the defendant for the full amount of their losses (*White & Carter (Councils) v McGregor 1961*).

Remedies

One common law and one equitable remedy have been identified as potentially relevant to the situation.

Common law remedy – Damages

Under **common law**, a breach of contract automatically gives the right of monetary compensation (damages) to the injured party. **Damages** are intended to restore them to the same position they would have been in if the contract had been performed. Payment of damages is subject to two tests; **remoteness of damage** and **measure of damages.**

Remoteness of damage

Under the **remoteness of damage** test, losses must be **natural consequences** of the breach. As this is obviously the case in Astride's dispute with Bild Ltd and Chris, it will not be discussed any further. The key issue to the case is the measure of damages.

Measure of damage

The **measure of damage** is what is required to compensate for the loss incurred. It is not intended that the injured party should profit from a claim. Damages may be awarded for financial and non-financial loss.

Building contract disputes are particularly difficult to resolve. Problems can occur if the work is not up to a **particular standard** or does not meet a **certain specification**. The usual measure of damages is the cost of rectifying the work. However, where the **cost** of such work is **out of proportion** with the **benefit** to the claimant, compensation will be granted instead. This is the difference between the value of the work done and what was contracted.

This was highlighted in *Ruxley Electronics and Construction Ltd v Forsyth 1995* where a swimming pool was constructed slightly shallower than was agreed. Correcting the defect required demolishing the shallower (but otherwise perfectly serviceable) pool and constructing a new one. The court held that the cost of such remedial work was disproportionate to its benefit and that loss of value based damages should be paid.

Where a building contractor **fails to perform** the work, damages will be awarded which represent the cost of another party performing the work instead.

Equitable remedy – specific performance

The court may at its **discretion** give an equitable remedy by ordering the defendant to perform their part of the contract instead of letting them 'buy themselves out of it' by paying damages for breach.

The order will **not** be made if it would require performance over a period of time and the court could not ensure that the defendant complied fully with the order. Therefore specific performance is not ordered for contracts of **employment** or **personal service** nor usually for building contracts.

Applying the law to Astride's case.

(a) **Specific performance** is not available as a remedy in building contracts therefore Astride can only claim **damages**. Her case is different to the *Ruxley* case as all that is required is for the wall height to be increased to the contracted height. The court will award her damages for this **extra cost**.

(b) Astride cannot get an order of specific performance against Chris but she has the choice to sue for **damages** either before, or at the time of performance. In either case she will be awarded damages to cover the **additional cost** of another person performing the work (**£500**).

35 Remedies for breach

Text reference. Chapter 7.

Top tips. Before you start to write, take a minute or two to run through the different remedies for breach of contract in your head. Do not restrict yourself purely to damages.

Easy marks. For each remedy that you discuss make sure that you cite a case or an illustration in support.

Examiner's comments. This was a very popular question and was answered well by most candidates. However some students restricted themselves to damages and no matter how good their answers, they could not earn full marks. Some candidates fell into the trap of discussing breach of contract and anticipatory breach, neither of which was relevant to this question. This could have been a result of students rote learning the answers to past papers and then not appreciating that the question was actually a little different.

Marking scheme

This question requires candidates to examine the various remedies that may be available to innocent parties when they suffer as a consequence of a breach of contract.

8-10 marks	Thorough to complete answers, showing a detailed understanding of all or certainly most of the remedies available, perhaps with examples or cases.
5-7 marks	A clear understanding of the topic perhaps lacking in detail.
2-4 marks	Some knowledge, although perhaps not clearly expressed, or very limited in its knowledge and understanding of the various remedies.
0-1 marks	Little or no knowledge of the topic.

Breach of contract

A party is said to be in **breach of contract** where they **fail to perform their contractual obligations fully and precisely** without lawful excuse. Breach of contract always gives rise to an obligation to **compensate** the other party for losses sustained. In certain cases, the breach may also entitle the innocent party to treat the contract as discharged.

The **remedies** available are as follows:

Damages

Damages are a **common law remedy** primarily intended to restore the person who has suffered loss to the same position they would have been in had the contract been performed. Where there is no contractual provision for liquidated damages, the courts will determine the damages payable with reference to the following factors:

- The remoteness of damage
- The measure of damages

Remoteness of damages

With regard to **remoteness**, the courts consider how far down the chain of cause and effect the consequences of breach should be traced before they become so remote that no compensation should be awarded in respect of them.

Under the rule in *Hadley v Baxendale 1854*, damages may be awarded in respect of losses which **arise naturally**, according to the **usual course** of things or which arise in a manner which the parties may **reasonably be deemed to have contemplated** as the probable result of breach of contract.

If the resulting loss is of an **unusual type**, that is, outside the natural course of events, it may be claimed only if the defendant was aware of the unusual circumstances which might give rise to that abnormal loss *(Victoria Laundry (Windsor) v Newman Industries 1949).*

Measure of damage

In assessing the **measure of damages**, it should be noted that damages are intended to **restore** the wronged party to the position they would have been in if the contract had been performed but not to put them in a better or more profitable position nor to be punitive. Measurement of financial loss is usually made with reference to the available market rule.

Action for the price

If the breach of contract is one party's **failure to pay the contractually agreed sum**, the other party should bring a personal action for the price against the party in breach. This is subject to the proviso that the property in the goods has passed to them unless the price has been agreed to be paid on a specific date.

Quantum meruit

A 'quantum meruit' award may be sought as an **alternative to damages** where, for example, one party has already performed part of their obligations and the other party then repudiates the contract. Provided the injured party elects to treat the contract as terminated, they may claim a reasonable sum in respect of the work done *(De Bernardy v Harding 1853)*. A quantum meruit award, unlike damages which is a compensatory award, is a restitutory award and aims to restore the claimant to the position they would have been in if the contract had never been made.

Specific performance

An order of specific performance is an **equitable remedy** and is an order to the party in breach to **perform their part of the contract**. It is at the discretion of the court and will only be awarded where damages would not be an adequate remedy. It will not be awarded where performance would be required over a period of time and the court could not properly supervise the performance. For example in a contract for employment or personal services or building contracts.

Injunction

An injunction, like specific performance, is an **equitable remedy** at the discretion of the court. The court can require the defendant to **observe terms** in the contract which are in substance negative restraints. The court may award an injunction in cases where specific performance would be refused. For example in a contract of personal service *(Warner Bros Pictures Inc v Nelson 1937* and *Metropolitan Electric Supply Co v Ginder 1901)*. An injunction will not be granted merely to restrain the defendant from acts inconsistent with their positive obligations *(Whitwood Chemical Co v Hardman 1891)*.

Rescission

Rescission entails **setting the contract aside** as if it had never been made. Rescission is an equitable remedy which seeks to ensure that the parties should be restored to their position before the contract was made. The right to rescind is lost where:

- The misled person affirms the contract after discovering the true facts
- The parties can no longer be restored to their original positions
- The rights of third parties would be prejudiced by rescission
- So much time has elapsed that allowing rescission would be inequitable.

36 Remoteness and measure of damages

Text reference. Chapter 7.

Top tips. This questions asks you to 'describe the rules'. Spend a minute or two when you start the question clarifying in your own mind what the rules are and jot them down so that you don't miss anything out. Then decide in what order to present them in your answer. Make sure that you divide your time on this question equally between the two parts.

Easy marks. As you discuss each rule make sure that you support your point with a decided case, and if you can't remember a case try to make up an example or illustration which will add authority to your answer.

Examiner's comments. Some candidates were confused as to the difference between remoteness and measure of damages and could not produce separate answers for parts (a) and (b). The examiner noted that some candidates who did badly on this question did reasonably well on their other questions, indicating that they had insufficient knowledge to tackle all questions competently. Candidates should make sure that they have adequate knowledge across the syllabus.

Marking scheme

This questions is divided into two parts, each worth 5 marks each. Each part should be marked independently on its own merits although candidates may well run the two parts together.

6-10 marks	The best answers will provide a clear explanation of the test for deciding remoteness of damage and the various rules relating to fixing the amount of damages to be paid and reference will be made to cases.
0-5 marks	Weaker answers may show little understanding of the rules. Alternatively they may be unbalanced or deal only with one aspect of the question.

Damages

Damages are a **common law remedy** primarily intended to restore the person who has suffered loss to the same position they would have been in **had the contract been performed**. Where there is no contractual provision for liquidated damages, the courts will determine the damages payable with reference to the following factors: the remoteness of damage and the measure of damages.

(a) **Remoteness of damage**

Damages for breach of contract will not be awarded to the extent that they are considered too remote. In considering remoteness, the court is asking how far down the **sequence of cause and effect** the consequences should be traced before they become so indirect or remote that they should not be compensated for.

In contract, the **remoteness of damage test** (otherwise known as the rule in *Hadley v Baxendale 1854*) is in two parts. It provides:

- That damages may be awarded only in respect of losses which **arise naturally**, according to the usual course of things, from the breach or in a manner which the parties may reasonably be deemed to have contemplated as the probable result of breach of contract.
- That if the resulting loss is of an **unusual type**, that is, outside the natural course of events, it may be claimed only if the defendant had **actual or constructive knowledge** of the unusual circumstances which might give rise to that abnormal loss.

Defendant's knowledge

Both parts of the rule are concerned with **what the defendant must have known**. Under the first head of the rule, they are **deemed to accept any normal consequence** which any other person might expect. Under the second head, if the consequence of breach is abnormal, or not what one would ordinarily expect, they are liable only if, in making the contract, they **knew of the special circumstances** from which the abnormal consequence of breach could arise.

In *Victoria Laundry (Windsor) v Newman Industries 1949*, the defendant was in breach of contract for failing to deliver goods on time. As a result, the claimant lost profits on **regular contracts** and on abnormally lucrative contracts which would have been performed had the goods been delivered on time. It was held that damages for loss of the normal profits were recoverable, but not for the **abnormal profits** since the defendant had no knowledge of these special contracts. The second head of the rule was not satisfied in respect of these lost profits.

In *The Heron II 1969* on the other hand, the defendant was held liable for damages when they failed to deliver a cargo of sugar on time and the claimant lost potential profits on resale due to a drop in the market value of sugar during the period of delay. The defendant argued that they were unaware that the claimant intended to sell the cargo immediately. The court held that it is a matter of **common knowledge** that commodities fluctuate in value, which means that delay can cause loss and that the defendant should reasonably have expected that the claimant intended to resell the cargo.

(b) **Measure of damages**

Damages are intended to restore the wronged party to the position they would have been in if the contract had been performed but **not to put them in a better or more profitable position**. This is sometimes referred to as protecting the **expectation interest** of the claimant. The claimant's expectation loss may be defined as the loss of what the claimant would have received had the contract been properly performed.

A claimant may alternatively seek to have their **reliance interest** protected; this refers to the position they would have been in had they not relied on the contract. Because they compensate for wasted expenditure, damages for reliance loss cannot be awarded if they would put the claimant in a better position than they would attain under protection of their expectation interest.

Market rule

Measurement of financial loss may be made with reference to the **available market rule**. If a buyer refuses to take delivery of goods which they have contracted to buy, and the seller sues for loss of profit on the transaction, the existence of a market in which there is an excess of supply over demand will lead to a successful claim *(Thompson Ltd v Robinson (Gunmakers) Ltd 1955)*. Whereas if there is an excess of demand over supply, only nominal damages will be payable *(Charter v Sullivan 1957)*. Damages will be awarded only in respect of reasonably foreseeable loss, which is not too remote *(Hadley v Baxendale 1854)*.

Financial loss

Financial loss is usually based on the actual loss suffered, although some types of non-financial loss are recoverable (*Jarvis v Swan Tours 1973*).

Mitigation

The claimant must, however, take reasonable steps to **mitigate** their loss. This means that they must take reasonable steps to put themselves in as good a position as if the contract had been performed. For example, where goods are not delivered the buyer must take steps to buy the same goods from elsewhere as cheaply as possible *(Payzu v Saunders 1919)*.

Liquidated damages

The parties to a contract may seek to avoid complicated calculations of loss and disputes as to damages by providing a formula for the calculation of damages in the contract itself. For example a daily rate of payment in the event of late completion or late delivery of goods. A **liquidated damages** clause will be upheld by the court in the event of breach provided it is a genuine attempt to anticipate the appropriate level of damages *(Ford Motor Co (England) Ltd v Armstrong 1915)*.

Penalty clauses

Any term which amounts to a **penalty clause** will be void. In determining whether the clause in question is a penalty clause or a liquidated damages provision the courts will look to see if the clause represents a genuine pre-estimate of loss *(Dunlop Pneumatic Tyre Co Ltd v New Garage & Motor Co Ltd 1915)*. If so, the clause will be upheld, even if the actual loss is greater or smaller.

37 Liquidated damages, penalty clauses and mitigation

Text reference. Chapter 7.

Top tips. Note the unequal mark scheme and make sure that you give the appropriate amount of time to the two halves of this question. You cannot earn good marks if you devote all your energies to part (b) but don't make a proper attempt at part (a).

Easy marks. Explain what liquidated damages, penalty clauses and mitigation are, and try to quote a case as an illustration of each. By doing that you should earn more than half marks on the question.

Examiner's comments. Part (a) required an explanation of the difference between liquidated damages and penalty clauses and on the whole it was dealt with well, but it has to be said that candidates either performed very well or completely missed the point of the question. Some candidates clearly explained what both liquidated damages and penalty clauses were and consequently distinguished between them. Some candidates provided good supporting case authority. Some candidates tended to provide a general answer on the topic of damages without sufficiently focusing on the core issue. A number of candidates ran the two categories together and did not distinguish them and some thought that penalty clauses were actually provisions for liquidated damages. Those with even less knowledge took the word liquidated to refer to consequences of liquidation and consequently went completely off the point.

Part (b) referred to the duty to mitigate losses and some candidates picked up full marks by explaining the general concept and the operation of the market rule, with supporting authority. The main weakness in relation to this part of the question was that a number of candidates simply offered a tautological explanation of the duty to mitigate losses, i.e. it means that parties have to mitigate losses. This gained no credit.

Marking scheme

This question requires an explanation of two aspects the law relating to damages for breach of contract. It is split into two parts with 7 marks being available for part (a) and 3 marks for part (b).

(a)	5–7 marks	A good explanation of the difference between liquidated damages and penalty clauses with perhaps some examples or cases.
	3–4 marks	Some, but limited, understanding of the topic, or clear understanding of only one aspect.
	0–2 marks	Little knowledge of either element of the question or unbalanced in only dealing with one of the elements.
(b)	2–3 marks	A thorough explanation of the duty to mitigate losses with examples or cases.
	0–1 mark	Some, if little, knowledge of the duty but not clear or lacking in detail.

(a) **Liquidated damages**

Liquidated damages are a fixed or ascertainable sum agreed by the parties which is payable in the event of a breach of contract. The parties to a contract may seek to avoid complicated calculations of loss and disputes as to damages by providing a **formula for the calculation** of such damages in the contract itself, for example a daily rate of payment in the event of late completion or late delivery of goods. A **liquidated damages clause** will be upheld by the court in the event of breach provided it is a genuine to anticipate the appropriate level of damages (*Ford Motor Co (England) Ltd v Armstrong 1915*).

Penalty clauses

A **Penalty clause** is a sum payable in the event of a breach of contract to deter the breach occurring.

Any term which amounts to a **penalty clause** will be **void**. In determining whether the clause in question is a penalty clause or a liquidated damages provision the courts will look to see if the clause represents a **genuine pre-estimate of loss** *(Dunlop Pneumatic Tyre Co Ltd v New Garage & Motor Co Ltd 1915)*. If so, the clause will be upheld, even if the actual loss is greater or smaller. In the Dunlop case, the garage sold tyres at below a minimum retail price, arguing that the £5 per tyre which the manufacturer was entitled to under the contract was in fact a penalty rather then a genuine pre-estimate of loss. Although the court stated that, generally, when a fixed amount is payable for breaches of different kinds, some more serious than others in their consequences, the clause would be void as a penalty clause, it held that here the formula was a genuine attempt to agree on liquidated damages.

In *Bridge v Cambell Discount Co 1962*, a clause in a hire purchase contract required the debtor to pay on termination both arrears of payments due before termination and an amount which, together with payments made and due, amounted to two-thirds of the total hire purchase price, and to return the goods. It was held that this was a penalty clause – and therefore void. In most circumstances, the creditor would receive on termination more than 100% of the value of the goods.

The difference

Under the common law, an injured party should not benefit from claiming damages – the award should cover their **actual losses**. Liquidated damages attempt to achieve this by setting out in advance what a party's losses will be in given circumstances and are therefore acceptable under common law. Penalty clauses on the other hand are designed to **penalise** one party, and by definition the other party will benefit. This is why they are not enforceable.

(b) **Mitigation**

In the event of a breach of contract, the inured party must take reasonable steps to **mitigate their loss** or they may not receive their full losses. This means that they must take reasonable steps to put themselves in **as good a position as if the contract had been performed**. For example, where goods are not delivered the buyer must take steps to buy the same goods from elsewhere as cheaply as possible. Equally, if the seller of goods does not receive payment, they are required to obtain as good a price as possible for them elsewhere.

In *Payzu v Sanders 1919*, the buyer in a contract for delivery of goods by instalments failed to pay for the first instalment within the agreed credit period. The seller refused to make any further deliveries unless the buyer paid cash in advance on the remaining instalments. The buyer refused to accept delivery on those terms, the price of the goods rose and the buyer sued for breach of contract. It was held, first, that the seller had no right to repudiate the original contract and, secondly, that the buyer should have mitigated its loss by accepting the seller's offer of delivery against cash payment. Damages were therefore limited to the amount that the buyer would have lost if they had paid in advance, which amounted to the interest that would have been foregone over the period of any pre-payment.

The **injured party** does not have to take discreditable or risky measures to mitigate their loss *(Pilkington v Wood 1953)*. In this case, which involved negligence by a solicitor in checking title of a property, the buyer of the property sued the solicitor, claiming the difference between the valuations with good and defective title respectively. The solicitor argued that the buyer should have mitigated their loss by claiming against the previous owner of the property, but it was held that the claimant was under no duty to embark upon complicated litigation which might well not have succeeded.

BPP LEARNING MEDIA

38 Roger and Lulu

Text reference. Chapter 8

Top tips. Maximise your marks by identifying the issues, stating the relevant law and then applying it to the scenario.

Easy marks. There are few easy marks unless you revised this area of law well. Stating what contributory negligence and *volenti non fit injuria* are will earn you some basic marks.

Issue

The issue at hand is whether or not the fight organisers or the train station can claim any **defences** that reduce or eliminate their liabilities to Roger and Lulu.

There are two defences to a claim in **negligence**: **contributory negligence** and ***volenti non fit injuria***.

Contributory negligence

Contributory negligence does not exonerate the defendant from their negligence completely, but their liability to pay compensation may be reduced by the courts if the injured party is proved to have contributed to the loss they suffered in some way.

In the case of *Sayers v Harlow UDC 1958*, a lady was injured while trying to climb out of a public toilet cubicle which had a defective lock. The court held that she had **contributed** to her injuries by the method by which she had tried to climb out.

Courts will **reduce damages** awarded to the claimant on a percentage basis which is just and reasonable. This is typically in the range of 10% to 75%, however it is possible to reduce the claim by up to 100%.

Volenti non fit injuria

Volenti non fit injuria is voluntary acceptance of the risk of injury. This defence is available to the defendant where both parties have **expressly consented** to the risk (such as on waiver forms signed by those taking part in dangerous sports), or it may be implied by the conduct of the claimant. This could be the case, for example, where it is reasonable for the parties to expect a high degree of risk and to accept it.

In *ICI v Shatwell 1965* the two injured parties disregarded safety instructions whilst handling detonators. It was upheld that their reckless action was enough to establish acceptance of the risk of injury.

This defence will **exonerate** the party that caused the injuries from liability in negligence as the injured party accepted the risk when they undertook the activity.

Roger and Lulu

Whilst it is not clear that Roger and Jack **expressly agreed** to the risk, it is reasonable for them to expect and accept it. Roger has taken part in many fights so he cannot argue that he was not aware of the risk – therefore on the grounds of volenti non fit injuria Jack and the organisers are likely to be exonerated from any liability under negligence for the injuries caused to Roger.

Lulu's case is very similar to the case of *Sayers v Harlow UDC* mentioned above. If she had heeded the warning notice then she would **not have** received the injuries that she did. Therefore the court is likely to find that she contributed to her own injuries and will reduce her claim against the train station accordingly. This does not exonerate the train station from liability but merely reduces the damages owed to Lulu because of her own actions.

39 Remoteness of damage

Text reference. Chapter 8

Top tips. Do not dump everything you know about negligence when answering this question! It is explicitly about remoteness of damage so keep your answer focused on this area.

Easy marks. Stating the basic rules on remoteness of damage.

Examiner's comments. The vast majority of candidates simply ignored the reference to tort and answered the question on the basis of contract law and consequently got very few if indeed any marks, depending on whether they gave a sufficiently general explanation of remoteness that could be applied to tort. Even those candidates who did recognise that the question related to tort rather than contract still tended to produce overly general answers, treating the questions as an invitation to write all they knew about tort law.

Marking scheme

	Marks
A thorough understanding of the issues involved. It is likely that the best answers will focus on the cases, although examples might be used.	8–10
A clear understanding of the topics but perhaps lacking in detail.	5–7
Some, but limited, understanding of the issue, perhaps not referring to any cases to support the explanation.	2–4
Little or no knowledge of the topic.	0–1

Remoteness of damage

Even where it is proved that a **defendant's negligence** caused damage to a claimant, a **negligence claim** can still **fail** if the damage caused is **'too remote'**. This rule, which is comparable to remoteness of damage in contract cases, is important as it **restricts a defendant's liability** for damage to those losses which they should **reasonably have foreseen**. It would be unfair for a party to be held liable for **damage** which, although they may have caused it, was unforeseeable and therefore in theory impossible to prevent.

The **test** of **reasonable foresight** developed out of *The Wagon Mound 1961*. Liability is limited to **damage** that a **reasonable man could have foreseen**. This does not mean the exact event must be foreseeable in detail, just that the eventual outcome is foreseeable.

Case law

In the case of *The Wagon Mound 1961* a ship was taking on oil in Sydney harbour. Oil was spilled onto the water and it drifted to a wharf 200 yards away where welding equipment was in use. The owner of the wharf carried on working because they were advised that the sparks were unlikely to set fire to furnace oil. Safety precautions were taken. A spark fell onto a piece of cotton waste floating in the oil, thereby starting a fire which damaged the wharf. The owners of the wharf sued the charterers of the Wagon Mound. The court decided that the claim must fail. Pollution was the foreseeable risk: fire was not.

The test has since developed further. In *Jolley v London Borough of Sutton 2000* it was held that the remoteness test can be passed if some **harm is foreseeable** even if the exact nature of the injuries could not be. In this case the defendants should have removed a boat which had been dumped two years previously. A teenage boy was injured while attempting to repair it. The court decided that even though the precise incident was not foreseeable, the authority should have foreseen that some harm could be caused since they knew children regularly played on the abandoned boat.

Invariably it **is up to the court** concerned to decide what damage is foreseeable given all the **circumstances** and **facts** available to it.

40 Duty of care

Text reference. Chapter 8

Top tips. Keep your answer focussed on the meaning of duty of care and avoid becoming sidetracked onto other areas of the tort which are not being examined (breach of duty and defences for example).

Easy marks. Quoting the main cases (see the examiner's comments) will earn you good marks quickly.

ACCA examiner's answers. The ACCA examiner's answer to this question can be found at the back of this kit.

Examiner's comments. Candidates seem unable to be able to distinguish between the different areas within the law of tort and are not comfortable in answering questions in this area very well. However, a number of candidates did produce good answers which focussed on the correct area and were able to describe the tort of negligence, the relevance of the duty of care, the fact that there did not have to be a contractual duty to demonstrate liability, and a good description of *Donoghue v Stevenson* and the neighbour principle. Some answers described the extent of the duty of care and what the claimant had to prove and quoted relevant principles from *Caparo v Dickman, Hedley Byrne v Heller.*

Marking scheme

This question requires candidates to explain the meaning of the concept duty of care in the tort of negligence.

8–10 marks:	Thorough explanation of the meaning of duty of care with appropriate references to cases.
5–7 marks:	Reasonable on duty of care but perhaps lacking in detail or cases authority.
3–4 marks:	Unbalanced answer, lacking in detailed understanding.
0–2 marks:	Very unbalanced answer, demonstrating very little understanding.

Duty of care

In the tort of negligence an individual is not liable for every action they take, only to those whom they owe a duty of care. Whether or not a duty of care exists in any situation is generally decided by the courts on a **case by case basis**, with each new case setting a precedent based on its own particular facts.

Donoghue v Stevenson 1932

In the landmark case of *Donoghue v Stevenson 1932,* the House of Lords ruled that a person might owe a duty of care to another with whom they had **no** contractual relationship at all.

In this case, the claimant purchased a bottle of **ginger beer** for consumption by another person. This other person drank part of the contents, which contained the remains of a decomposed snail, and became ill. The manufacturer argued that as there was no contract between themselves and the person who drank the ginger beer, they owed them no duty of care and so was not liable.

The House of Lords refuted this and laid down the general principle that **every person** owes a duty of care to his 'neighbour', to 'persons so closely and directly affected by my act that I ought reasonably to have them in contemplation as being so affected'.

Hedley Byrne & Co Ltd v Heller and Partners Ltd 1964

In *Hedley Byrne & Co Ltd v Heller and Partners Ltd 1964* the principle of a duty was **extended** from physical damage to also include **financial loss** as well. In this regard it was held that a duty can be owed in respect of negligent misstatement made by a party to another whom they have a special relationship with.

Anns v Merton London Borough Council 1977

Anns v Merton London Borough Council 1977 established a **two-stage test** to determine whether one party owes another a duty of care.

Two questions should be asked:

- Is there **sufficient proximity** between the parties, such that the harm suffered was reasonably foreseeable?
- **Should the duty be restricted** or limited for reasons of economic, social or public policy?

Caparo

The law on duty of care was further refined in the case of *Caparo Industries plc v Dickman and Others 1990* which established a three stage test for establishing a duty of care that still stands:

- Was the harm **reasonably foreseeable**?
- Was there a **relationship of proximity** between the parties?
- Considering the circumstances, is it **fair, just and reasonable** to impose a duty of care?

By meeting this test, a claimant will have established that they are owed a duty of care by the defendant.

41 An auditor's duty of care

Text reference. Chapters 8 and 9 .

Top tips. It is advisable to begin your answer with a brief explanation of duty of care generally before leaping into an explanation of the cases that are relevant to auditors.

Easy marks. Stating the basic rules of duty of care and the *Caparo* case. Use other cases to illustrate the other rules relating to auditors.

Examiner's comments. Some answers, and there was a disappointingly large number of these, tended to provide descriptions/explanations of tort law generally, or negligence specifically, while ignoring its application to auditors. Other answers focussed on the role and accountancy duties of auditors within companies to the exclusion of their duty of care in negligence. Such a result could only be the result of a misreading, whether wilful or otherwise, of the question, which was quite explicit in what was required. This is the first example of a significant number of candidates ignoring the actual question, which they might not know the answer to, in order to provide an answer that they did know. Such tactics are not to be recommended as they never work.

Marking scheme

This question requires candidates to explain the extent of a company auditor's duty of care and to whom such a duty is owed.

8–10 marks	A thorough understanding of how professional negligence applies to auditors demonstrated by references to cases or examples.
5–7 marks	A clear understanding of the topic, perhaps lacking in detail. Alternatively an unbalanced answer showing good understanding of one part but less in the others.
2–4 marks	Some, but limited, understanding of the topic, or clear understanding of only one aspect.
0–1 mark	Little or no knowledge of the topic.

Duty of care

The concept of duty of care is central to the tort of **negligence**. To succeed in a claim the claimant must prove that:

- The defendant had a **duty of care** to avoid causing injury, damage or loss
- There was a **breach** of that duty by the defendant
- In consequence the claimant **suffered** injury, damage or loss

In the landmark case of *Donoghue v Stevenson 1932*, the House of Lords ruled that a person might owe a duty of care to another with whom they had **no** contractual relationship at all. It stated that **every person** owes a duty of care to his 'neighbour', to 'persons so closely and directly affected by my act that I ought reasonably to have them in contemplation as being so affected'.

Duty of care and auditors

The first hurdle that a claimant must overcome when attempting to prove that an auditor is liable to them for negligence is that the auditor owed them a **duty of care**. The courts generally decide whether a duty is owed on a case by case basis, with each new case setting a precedent based on its own particular facts.

The starting point for an auditor's duty of care is the **common law position** for negligence in general. This states that the actions of persons who hold themselves out to possess a particular skill shall be judged against another reasonable person who posses the same skill. Professions (such as auditors) can set their own standards that their members should meet.

Over the years there has been much case law concerning **auditors**. Most of it has concerned whether or not an auditor should owe a duty of care to a person that they do not know, especially if they had no idea of the purpose that person would use, say, their audit report for.

The following cases are important in determining the duty of care owned by an auditor.

Caparo Industries plc v Dickman and Others 1990

This case made considerable changes to the tort of negligence as a whole, and the **negligence of professionals** in particular, and set a precedent which now forms the basis for courts when considering the liability of professional advisers.

It was decided in this case that auditors only owe a duty of care to the **shareholders as a body** to allow them to exercise proper control over the management of the company. They do not owe a duty to potential investors or those increasing their stakes.

The case centred on a takeover bid by Caparo to buy Fidelity plc. The last audited accounts showed a profit of £1.3m, but after the takeover Caparo claimed that it should have shown a £400,000 loss. It claimed that Fidelity plc's auditors owed a duty of care to **investors and potential investors** in respect of the audit. They also should have been aware that a press release stating that profits would fall significantly had made Fidelity vulnerable to a takeover bid and that bidders might well rely upon the accounts.

The House of Lords decided that there were **two different** circumstances that may face a person giving professional advice.

Firstly, that they are preparing information in the knowledge that a particular person was **contemplating a transaction** and would rely on the information in deciding whether or not to proceed with the transaction. Secondly, that they prepare a statement for **general circulation**, which could foreseeably be relied upon by persons unknown to the professional for a variety of different purposes.

It was held therefore that a public company's auditors owed no duty of care to the **public at large** who relied on the audit report in deciding to invest – and, in purchasing additional shares, an existing shareholder was in no different position to the public at large.

Morgan Crucible Co plc v Hill Samuel Bank Ltd and Others 1990

In this case the court held that the duty of care of accountants is **higher** when advising on takeovers than when auditing. The directors and financial advisors of the target company in a contested takeover bid were held to owe a duty of care to a known takeover bidder in respect of financial statements prepared for the purpose of contesting the bid.

ADT Ltd v BDO Binder Hamlyn 1995

In this case, auditors were held liable for a statement made by an audit partner. A meeting was arranged between the auditors and ADT Ltd who were considering a takeover of one of the auditor's clients. This meeting was described by the judge as the '**final hurdle**' before ADT finalised its bid and the partner confirmed that they stood by the results of the audit.

The audit was found to have carried out negligently and as a result greatly overvalued the target. ADT lost a large amount of money in the deal and sued Binder Hamlyn for damages. The judge found in ADT's favour as Binder Hamlyn **assumed responsibility** for the statement made by the audit partner and so a 'special relationship' was established.

42 Standard of care

Text reference. Chapter 8

Top tips. There are not many knowledge-based questions that can be written on the standard of care in the tort of negligence and this one covers just about everything. Note how the answer is broken down into short paragraphs with headers. This makes it easier for markers to award you marks as points stand out clearly.

Easy marks. Stating that individuals have a duty to act as a reasonable man would and the six factors used in deciding whether a duty of care has been breached.

Examiner's comments. The majority of candidates did not answer the question asked and produced general explanation of the law of tort or the duty of care, rather than the specific issue of standard of care.

Marking scheme

This question requires candidates to explain the standard of care owed by one person to another in relation to the tort of negligence.

8–10 marks	Full understanding and explanation of the topic. It is likely that cases will be cited as authority although examples will be acceptable as an alternative.
5–7 marks	Lacking in detail in some or all aspects of the topic. Unbalanced answer that only focuses on some particular issues.
3–4 marks	Some, but little, knowledge of the topic.
0–2 marks	Little if any knowledge of the topic.

Duty of care

To succeed in an action for **negligence** the claimant must prove that; the defendant had a **duty of care** to avoid causing injury, damage or loss, there was a **breach of that duty** by the defendant and in **consequence** the claimant suffered **injury, damage** or **loss**.

The **standard of reasonable care** requires that the person concerned should do what a **reasonable man** would do. This also means the reasonable **employer**, or the reasonable **adviser**.

The following factors should be considered when deciding if a duty of care has been breached.

Probability of injury

It is presumed that a reasonable man takes **greater precautions** when the risk of injury is high. Therefore when the risk is higher the defendant must do more to meet their duty. In *Glasgow Corporation v Taylor 1992* a local authority was held to be negligent when children ate poisonous berries in a park. A warning notice was not considered to be sufficient to protect children.

Seriousness of the risk

The young, old or disabled may be prone to more serious injury than a fit able-bodied person. The **'egg-shell skull'** rule means that you must take your victim as they are. Where the risk to the vulnerable is high, the level of care required is raised. In *Paris v Stepney Borough Council 1951* an employer was found to owe a higher standard of care to an employee who only had one eye when the other eye was blinded at work.

Practicality and cost

It is not always reasonable to ensure all possible precautions are taken. Where the **cost** or **disruption** caused to eliminate the danger far **exceeds the risk** of it occurring it is likely that defendants will be found not to have breached their duty if they do not implement them.

In *Latimer v AEC Ltd 1952* an employer was held not liable for an injury to an employee who slipped over at work. The factory was flooded and the employer did all they could to make the floor safe using sawdust. However, not all the floor could be protected and the employee was injured on one of the few areas not treated. The only other option, closing the factory, would have outweighed the risk to the employees.

Common practice and custom

Where an individual can prove their actions were in line with **common practice** or **custom** it is likely that they would have met their duty of care. This is unless the common practice itself is found to be negligent.

Social benefit

Where an action is of **some benefit** to society, defendants may be **protected** from liability even if their actions create risk. For example, a fire engine that speeds to a major disaster provides a social benefit that may outweigh the greater risk to the public.

Professions and skill

Persons who hold themselves out to possess a particular skill should be judged on what a **reasonable person possessing the same skill** would do in the situation rather than that of a reasonable man. Professions are able to set their own standards of care for their members to meet and therefore members should be judged against these standards rather than those laid down by the courts.

Res ipsa loquitur

In some circumstances the claimant may argue that the **facts speak for themselves** (*res ipsa loquitur*). Want of care being the only possible explanation for what happened, negligence on the part of the defendant must be presumed.

The claimant must demonstrate, firstly, that the thing which caused the injury was under the **management and control** of the defendant. Secondly they must prove that the accident would not have occurred if the defendant used **proper care**. In *Mahon v Osborne 1939* a surgeon was required to prove that leaving a swab inside a patient after an operation was not negligent.

Where **res ipsa loquitur** is established, the standard of care and its breach becomes irrelevant, the defendant is automatically liable unless they can prove they were not negligent.

43 Defences

Text reference. Chapter 8

Top tips. This is a straightforward question, but to pass it you must ensure your answer is complete and contains sufficient examples that show how the defences are applied in practice. Your opening paragraph should explain what tort is. This was not asked for directly in the question but is required to give context to the rest of your answer.

Easy marks. There are few easy marks unless you revised this area of law well. Your definitions of contributory negligence and *volenti non fit injuria* will earn you the basic marks.

Examiner's comments. Answers varied in standard although on the whole, this question was answered very unsatisfactorily. It was apparent that candidates were not comfortable with this area of law. They tended to either write hardly anything at all, or wrote everything they knew on the area starting with the neighbour principle, regularly citing *Donoghue v Stevenson* and going on to write in detail about the consequences of negligent advice. *Hedley Byrne v Heller* featured very frequently in answers. There was also discussion of remoteness of damage and the quantum of damages, which would be awarded in cases of personal injury.

Marking scheme

8–10 marks:	Thorough explanation of the meaning and effect of both elements of the question. Cases or examples will be expected to gain full marks.
5–7 marks:	Reasonable explanation of both concepts but perhaps lacking in detail or cases authority.
3–4 marks	Some but limited knowledge of both elements or only dealing with one of them.
0–2 marks:	Very unbalanced answer, lacking in detailed understanding.

Tort

Tort is different from other legal wrongs. Firstly, it is **not a breach of contract**, where the obligation which is alleged to have been breached arose under an agreement between two parties. Secondly, it is **not a crime**, where the object of the proceedings is to punish the offender rather than to compensate the victim.

Instead, torts **are civil wrongs** and the person wronged **sues in a civil court** for **compensation** or an **injunction**. The claimant's claim generally is that they have suffered a loss, such as personal injury, at the hands of the defendant who should pay them damages.

No **previous transaction** or **contractual relationship** need exist between the parties. Claims are based on the principle that people owe **duties of care** to each another. A **liability** will exist if it is proved that a **duty of care** is **breached**, that the **breach caused the damage** suffered by the claimant, and that the **damage is not too remote**.

However, two defences are available to a defendant who would otherwise be liable under tort. These are **contributory negligence** and ***volenti non fit injuria***.

(a) **Contributory negligence**

Contributory negligence does not exonerate the guilty party completely, but their **liability** to pay compensation may be **reduced** by the courts if the injured party is proved to have contributed to their loss or damage.

In *Sayers v Harlow UDC 1958*, a lady was injured whilst trying to climb out of a public toilet cubicle which had a defective lock. The court held that she had **contributed** to her injuries by the method she had tried to climb out.

Courts will **reduce damages** awarded to the claimant on a percentage basis which is just and reasonable. This is typically in the range of 10% to 75%, however it is possible to reduce the claim by up to 100%.

(b) **Volenti non fit injuria**

Volenti non fit injuria is the voluntary acceptance of the risk of injury. This defence is available to the defendant where both parties have **expressly consented** to the risk (such as on waiver forms signed by those taking part in dangerous sports), or it may be implied by the conduct of the claimant. This could be the case, for example, where the injured party was involved in stealing and joyriding a car which crashes.

In *ICI v Shatwell 1965* the two injured parties disregarded safety instructions whilst handling detonators. It was upheld that their reckless action was enough to establish acceptance of the risk of injury.

This defence will **exonerate** the party that caused the injuries from a liability in negligence as the injured party accepted the risk when they undertook the activity.

44 Accountants4U

Text Reference. Chapter 9

Top tips. Remember, in scenario questions such as this the key is to **identify** the law at issue, **state** the law, **apply** the law and form a **conclusion**.

Easy marks. Setting out the requirements for liability not only forms a solid base for your answer, but will also attract some easy marks for demonstrating knowledge.

Issue

Accountants4U would be liable to GWZ Ltd for **negligence** if GWZ Ltd can prove:

- Accountants4U **owed** them a **duty of care**
- It **breached** that **duty of care**
- As a **natural consequence** of the breach they suffered **damage**

Duty of care

In the case of *Caparo Industries plc v Dickman and Others 1990* it was decided that auditors owe a duty of care to the shareholders of a company in respect of their audit work. This duty does not extend to the world at large or to shareholders increasing their stakes in the company.

This means that GWZ Ltd is not owed any duty in respect of its reliance on the accounts for making its investment decision. However, the company could argue that a '**special relationship**' had been established. Firstly, since Accountants4U provided information in the knowledge that GWZ was contemplating an investment and secondly, that GWZ would rely on the information provided by the senior partner when deciding whether or not to proceed.

Similar facts occurred in *ADT Ltd v BDO Binder Hamlyn 1995*. In this case, similar comments were made by an audit partner in respect of a proposed takeover. The court decided that the auditors assumed responsibility for the comments made and held that a duty was owed.

It is therefore **likely** that **GWZ Ltd is owed a duty of care by Accountants4U**.

Breach of duty

Where auditors provide information that is to be used in important business transactions, a higher standard of care is required, *Morgan Crucible Co plc v Hill Samuel Bank Ltd and others 1990*. On the facts of the case it is likely that Accountants4U will be found to have breached this duty as they did not carry out any extra work to support the advice given by Sally.

Causality

It is clear that the negligent advice caused the loss to GWZ Ltd – had they been advised that the figures were inaccurate then it is unlikely that the takeover would have gone ahead.

Defences

Volenti non fit injuria does not apply in this case and the actions of GWZ Ltd seem reasonable in the circumstances. Therefore Accountants4U would not have a defence to a claim against them.

Conclusion

On the facts of the case and that of *ADT Ltd v BDO Binder Hamlyn 1995*, it is likely that GWZ Ltd could recover damages from Accountants4U for the loss they suffered.

45 Employed v self-employed

Text reference. Chapter 10

Top tips. You may be tempted to 'waffle' if you are not quite sure what to write when answering this question. Avoid this at all costs. If you are really stuck then a shorter answer containing everything that you know is almost certainly better than a longer answer that has been spun out. Save your time for a question that you are happier with.

Easy marks. This is a difficult question as you may struggle to come up with enough facts to answer it. This said, you could obtain several marks quickly by distinguishing between contracts of and for service and giving some examples of the consequences of being an employee or independent contractor. Stating the three tests would also earn you a mark or two.

Examiner's comments. ... this was clearly a topic that many candidates had prepared for well. On the whole this question was well done and in some instances done very well indeed, with the well prepared candidates providing good case authority to support their explanations. Of those who did not do well in their answers, the major shortcoming was a tendency to focus just on one of the tests and not to consider the others.

Marking scheme

This question asks candidates to explain the common law rules used to distinguish contracts of service from contracts for services.

8–10 marks	A thorough treatment of all of the rules, perhaps placing them in their historical context but certainly providing case support and providing a good application of the law to the scenario.
5–7 marks	Good analysis and case support, although perhaps limited in appreciation.
3–4 marks	Recognition of the areas covered by the question, but lacking in detailed analysis.
0–2 marks	Little or no analysis or knowledge of the subject of the question.

(a) **Contracts of service and for services**

A general rule is that an employee is someone who is employed under a **contract of service**, for example, a person working as an administrator for a large insurance company. An independent contractor is someone who works under a **contract for services**, for example, a plumber whom you hire to do some work in your home.

It is important to distinguish between them as each has **different rules** concerning the legal rights and obligations of the person concerned.

Examples of the different rules include:

Employment protection

Employment law confers protection and benefits upon employees under a contract of service, for example regarding unfair dismissal and notice periods. Such protection is not available to independent contractors.

Liability

Employers are generally vicariously liable for tortious acts of employees, committed in the course of employment. Independent contractors are liable for their own actions.

Taxation

Employees pay tax and national insurance through the PAYE scheme via their employers. Independent contractors are taxed differently and must administer it themselves.

(b) **The courts**

In practice, the distinction between employees and independent contractors depends on many factors. The **courts** will primarily look at the **reality of the situation** rather than accept the form of the arrangement on face value.

Initially, they will look at the **relationship** between the parties and any **agreement** between them. Where the 'employee's' status is still unclear, a series of tests will be applied; the **control, integration** and **economic reality (multiple)** tests.

The control test

The court will consider whether the employer has **control** over the way in which the employee performs their duties. Where it appears that the 'employer' may control how the 'employee's' duties are performed, then they will be treated as an employee; *Mersey Docks & Harbour Board v Coggins & Griffiths (Liverpool) 1947.*

The integration test

The courts consider whether the employee is so skilled that they cannot be controlled in the performance of their duties. Lack of control indicates that an 'employee' is **not integrated** into the employer's organisation, and is therefore not employed. In *Cassidy v Ministry of Health 1951* a doctor was held to be an employee as they were selected for a particular task and integrated into the organisation to perform certain surgical operations. If patients had the right to choose the doctor, this would indicate that the doctor was not so integrated and they would have been treated as an independent contractor.

The control and integration tests are important, but **no longer decisive** in determining whether a person is an employee.

The economic reality (multiple) test

Courts now focus on whether the 'employee' was **working on their own account** and this requires numerous factors to be considered.

In *Ready Mixed Concrete (South East) v Ministry of Pensions & National Insurance 1968* it was held that a contract of service existed where:

- There is **agreement** from the worker that they will provide work for their master in exchange for remuneration.
- The worker agrees either expressly or impliedly that their master can exercise **control** over their performance.
- There are other **factors** included in the contract that make it **consistent** with a contract for service.

Other factors that can be considered include:

- Does the 'employee' use their **own tools and equipment** or does the 'employer' provide them?
- Does the 'employer' have the power to **select or appoint** its 'employees', and may they dismiss them?
- **Payment of salary** is a fair indication of there being a contract of employment.
- **Working for a number of different people** is not necessarily a sign of being an independent contractor. A number of assignments may be construed as 'a series of employments'.

The decision whether to classify an individual as an employee or not is also influenced by **policy considerations**. For example, an employment tribunal might regard a person as an employee for the purpose of unfair dismissal despite the fact that the tax authorities treated them as self-employed.

46 Employment contracts

Text reference. Chapter 10.

Top tips. Reference to each of the three tests should be supported by a case example.

Easy marks. Explaining the three tests for employment status should be lodged firmly in your memory by now and will earn you good marks if you can repeat them.

ACCA examiner's answers. The ACCA examiner's answer to this question can be found at the back of this kit.

Examiner's comments. Some answers described in detail, with examples and the reference to the relevant case law, the tests which are applied in determining the employment status of an individual. Some were extremely thorough and even went on to consider the particular position of part-time workers. However, as has the case in past sittings, candidates often overlooked the key tests and instead described the various taxation implications of being employed as against being self-employed, including reference to sole trader as against limited company liability, Class 1 as against Class 2 NICs and due dates for payment of income tax. Clearly answers to these sorts of questions need to be more tailored to law rather than accounting/tax to gain good marks.

Even where candidates were able to cite the three tests there tended to be some confusion about the integration test in particular, with a number of candidates confusing the actual outcome and relevance of *Cassidy v Ministry of Health.*

Marking scheme

This question asks candidates to explain the common law rules used to distinguish contracts of service from contracts for services.

8–10 marks: A thorough treatment of all of the rules, perhaps placing them in their historical context but certainly providing case support.

5–7 marks: Good analysis and case support, although perhaps limited in appreciation.

3–4 marks: Recognition of the areas covered by the question, but lacking in detailed analysis.

0–2 marks: Little or no analysis or knowledge of the subject of the question.

Contracts of service and for services

An **employee** is someone employed by an employer under the terms of a formal contract of employment (a '**contract of service**').

An **independent contractor** is a self-employed person who contracts to provide services for another party (a '**contract for services**') but who does not enter into a contract of employment. Sometimes the distinction between the two is very obvious – such as where the employer deducts PAYE and NI from the worker's gross pay – but often it is not. The expressed intentions of the parties will not necessarily be conclusive (*Ferguson v John Dawson & Partners 1976*).

The distinction

The courts will look at the **reality of the situation** rather than at the expressed intentions of the parties. The courts have generally applied one or more of three tests – of **control, integration** and **economic reality**.

Control test

The **control test** asks whether the employer has control over the way in which the employee performs their duties. In the past, this has been quite a good indication of the existence of an employee relationship, but working practices are changing.

An example of this test is in *Walker v Crystal Palace FC 1910* where it was held that a **professional footballer** was employed because he was subject to the control of his club the form of training, discipline and method of pay.

The control test is **less definitive now**, at a time where many employees have a degree of skill which makes the relationship difficult to define.

Integration test

The **integration test** was developed to overcome this difficulty, and applies where the employee has such a degree of skill that they cannot be 'controlled' in the performance of their duties. Applying this test, the court asks whether they became an **integral part of the employer's business organisation**, or did their work remain outside of and merely accessory to it? Therefore, in *Cassidy v Ministry of Health 1951*, it was held that a skilled surgeon was the employee of the Ministry of Health since, although the Ministry could not possibly control the doctor in their medical work, it (not the patient) had selected them and integrated them into the organisation.

Economic reality

The **economic reality** or '**multiple**' **test** is a further development and asks whether the employee is **working on their own account**. Here the court will consider all relevant factors including the employer's right to appoint and dismiss, the basis on which payment is made, whether tax and NI is deducted, and who provides the tools and equipment (*Ready Mixed Concrete (South East) v Ministry of Pensions and National Insurance 1968*). The courts will also consider whether the employee is entitled to delegate all their obligations (in which case there is no contract of employment), whether they are restricted in their place of work, whether they are obliged to work and whether holidays and hours of work are agreed (*O'Kelly v Trusthouse Forte plc 1983*).

47 Employer and employee duties

Text reference. Chapter 10.

Top tips. Notice that this question is asking for the common law duties, not duties in general. Make sure that you don't waste your time by listing all of the duties you can think of from whatever sources: focus your answer on what the question requires.

Easy marks. Stating the duties of employee and employer

Examiner's comments. Candidates should read the words of the question and only deal with what was asked and not waste time on unnecessary material. The question specifically stated that it referred to the 'common law', but so many candidates, who had prepared another topic, focused on statutory rights. Some even claimed that the common law rights were themselves a result of legislation, specifically the Employment Act 1996.

Candidates should allocate time and words in relation to the mark allocation. Once again, many ignored this advice and even compounded the problem by dealing with part (b) first, so that they would have more time to deal with it.

Nonetheless, all that being said, this question tended to be answered well.

Marking scheme

This question requires an explanation of the common law duties owed by both employers and employees.

(a)	5–6 marks	Good awareness of the implied duties imposed on employers. Examples used to highlight answers.
	3–4 marks	Sound understanding but perhaps no examples.
	0–2 marks	Limited knowledge only about the topic.
(b)	3–4 marks	Good awareness of the implied duties imposed on employees.
	0–2 marks	Limited knowledge about the topic.

(a) **Employer's duties**

Common law duties of the employer include:

Mutual trust and confidence

The overriding duty of the employer at common law is a duty of **mutual trust and confidence**. The employer should not act in a manner which could damage their relationship with the employee. For example, a director calling his secretary 'an intolerable bitch on a Monday morning' was held to breach their relationship: *Isle of Wight Tourist Board v Coombes 1976*.

To indemnify the employee

An employer should **indemnify the employee** against expenses and losses incurred in the course of employment.

Reasonable care

An employer has a duty to take **reasonable care for the safety** of the worker. Therefore, they must provide competent staff, safe premises and equipment and a 'safe system of work'. The employer could be liable in negligence if this is not done.

Remuneration

In the unlikely circumstances of there being no agreement as to remuneration, the rate of **remuneration** must be reasonable. However, statute largely governs the method and rate of payment (including the Equal Pay Act 1970 and the National Minimum Wage Act 1998).

Provide work

In certain circumstances, the common law will imply **a duty to provide work**. Employees protected include those paid on a piecework or commission basis and those whose earning power and reputation is founded on active occupation, for example actors and journalists. If there is in fact no work available, the duty will not be breached as long as the employee continues to receive remuneration, unless the employee is skilled and needs relevant work in order to prevent the skills falling into disuse.

(b) **Employee duties**

At common law, employees owe duties to their employer.

Reasonable competence, skill and care

Employees are expected to show **reasonable competence, skill and care** when performing their job: *Lister v Romford Ice and Cold Storage Co 1957*.

Obey lawful instructions

Employees are expected to **obey their employer's** instructions unless they require them to do an unlawful act or to expose themselves to personal danger or are instructions outside the employee's contract. For example, in *Pepper v Webb 1969* a gardener failed to follow his employer's instructions and swore at them.

Account for all money and property

Employees have a duty to **account for all money and property** received during the course of their employment. For example, in *Boston Deep Sea Fishing and Ice Co v Ansell 1888* a company was justified in dismissing an employee who accepted personal commissions from suppliers on orders which he place with them for goods supplied to the company.

Faithful and personal service

Faithful service means that the employee should not pass on **confidential information**, such as trade secrets, to third parties as in *Faccenda Chicken Ltd v Fowler 1986*, or work for a competitor in their spare time as in *Hivac Ltd v Park Royal Scientific Instruments Ltd 1946*.

Personal service means that the employee may not delegate their duties without the employer's express or implied consent.

48 Redundancy

Text reference. Chapter 11.

Top tips. Although the requirement of this question is set out in just one sentence, you must notice that there are actually two requirements: explain the meaning redundancy (what it is) and explain the rules which govern it. You must try to address both issues.

Easy marks. Setting out what redundancy is and the compensation available to qualifying employees.

Examiner's comments. This question required candidates to explain the meaning of the term redundancy and the legal rules relating to it.

The question enabled candidates who knew the law on redundancy to perform well since there are marks available for a large number of legal points/range of relevant legal information e.g. the definition of redundancy; the meaning of 'dismissal'; qualification; the effect of offers of alternative employment and trial periods; remedies and so on. Candidates who could clearly and accurately state these points with reference to some case-law examples scored well.

Candidates also were able to score by referring to the collective provisions on trade union consultation and particularly if they were able to identify the relationship of the individual redundancy payment with individual claims for unfair dismissal arising out of unfair selection.

Many candidates were able to accurately state the basic rules and some to describe the relationship with other rules such as dismissal and trade union consultation.

However, there were common basic errors in that candidates were unable to correctly state e.g. the length of the qualifying periods or time limits for claims. Others seemed unable to comprehend the distinction between a claim for a redundancy payment and other claims (e.g. common law for wrongful dismissal) or statutory (notice entitlement and unfair dismissal).

Thus some scripts made no distinction between the statutory rules on notice and those on redundancy. A significant number seemed to have no awareness that unfair dismissal and redundancy provide separate remedies e.g. some stated that an employee would only be redundant if the selection was unfair, or that an employee would be redundant if they e.g. lacked qualification or competence for the job. The remedy, it seems to some, for redundancy is re-instatement, re-engagement or a compensatory award. Others thought that the employee could claim 'damages' for loss or earnings. In other cases redundancy was described as a wrongful dismissal.

Marking scheme

This question requires candidates to explain redundancy and the legal rules relating to it.

8–10 marks:	Thorough to complete answers, showing a detailed understanding of the concept of redundancy, the rules for calculating payment and probably making references to the legislation.
5–7 marks:	A clear understanding of the topic, but perhaps lacking in detail. Alternatively an unbalanced answer showing good understanding of one part but less in the other.
2–4 marks:	Some knowledge, although perhaps not clearly expressed, or very limited in its knowledge and understanding of the topic.
0–1 mark:	Little or no knowledge of the topic.

Redundancy

The law relating to **redundancy** is set out in the **Employment Rights Act 1996**.

A dismissal is treated as caused by **redundancy** where the only or main reason for the dismissal is that:

- The employer has **ceased** or **intends to cease** carrying on the business in which the employee has been employed or at the local establishment where the employee has been employed
- The **requirements of that business** for employees to carry on the work done by the employee have **ceased** or **diminished**.

The business

The businesses of **associated employers** are usually **treated as one business** for this purpose. If the employee's contract requires them to work at places other than their present place of employment, and the employer under the terms of the contract requires them to move to a different place of work because there is no longer work at their present place of employment, that is not a case of redundancy.

Job loss

In considering whether the **requirements of the business** for staff have diminished, it is the **overall position** which must be considered. If for example A's job is abolished and A is moved into B's job and B is dismissed, that is a case of redundancy although B's job continues. If the employer reorganises their business or alters their methods so that the same work has to be done by different means which are beyond the capacity of the employee, that is not redundancy. The test is whether the job still exists *(North Riding Garages v Butterwick 1967* and *Vaux and Associated Breweries v Ward 1969)*.

Alternative employment

The employer may offer a redundant employee **alternative employment** for the future. If the employee then **unreasonably refuses** the offer, they lose their entitlement to redundancy pay. The offer need not be in writing but must be made before the end of the old employment, to take effect within not more than four weeks after it will end. The offer must be of alternative employment in the **same capacity**, at the **same place** and on the **same terms** and **conditions** as the **previous employment**. If it differs in any such respect, it must be suitable employment in relation to the employee. The alternative employment must not be perceived as being lower in status *(Cambridge District Co-operative Society v Russell 1993)*. These matters are questions of fact.

Trial period

The employee is entitled to a **4 week trial period** in the alternative employment and if either party terminates the new contract during this trial period, it is treated as a case of redundancy at the expiry date of the old employment. If the employee accepts and continues in the new employment, their service is treated as continuing from the old employment.

Redundancy payment

An employee has a right to a **redundancy payment** if they are dismissed because of redundancy. The employee must show that they were dismissed. It is then for the employer to rebut the presumption that they were dismissed for redundancy. An employee is not entitled to redundancy pay if they resign voluntarily or if they accept suitable alternative employment or if they are dismissed for misconduct.

The employee must **qualify** for redundancy by:

- Having been **continuously employed** for **at least two years**,
- Having been **dismissed** (or laid off or put on short time),
- The **reason** for their **dismissal being redundancy**.

Redundancy pay is calculated as follows:

- 1.5 weeks pay for each such year of employment consisting wholly of weeks in which the employee was aged 40 or more;
- 1 week's pay for each such year consisting wholly of weeks in which they were aged between 22 and 40;
- 0.5 week's pay for each year where they were aged between 18 and 22.
- A week's pay (subject to a statutory maximum, currently set at £380 per week) is taken as pay of the final week of employment.

Disputes are heard by an **employment tribunal** and, on appeal, by the **Employment Appeal Tribunal**. The employer is expected to act reasonably and to follow the ACAS Code of Practice on Disciplinary Practice and Procedures in Employment.

49 Constructive and unfair dismissal

Text reference. Chapter 11

Top tips. Part (a) is a good opportunity to explain the law on constructive dismissal by using case law. If you can state the points of law from at least four cases then you will be well on your way to a good answer. If you got stuck in Part (b) try to think in terms of the real world. If you were unfairly dismissed what remedies would you want?

Easy marks. Describing constructive dismissal in Part (a) and listing the remedies for unfair dismissal in Part (b).

Examiner's comments. There were still candidates who appeared not to recognise any distinction between wrongful and unfair dismissal or between unfair dismissal or redundancy or between unfair dismissal and rights to minimum periods of notice. For these candidates, such errors appeared on both parts of the question. In relation to part (b) especially, some simply listed broad and unspecific grounds for dismissal - fighting, pregnancy, discrimination with no reference at all to the question being asked. Part (b) did not ask for the test of fairness of the dismissal, but for an explanation of the remedies.

Marking scheme

		Marks
(a)	Requires candidates to explain what is meant by constructive dismissal.	
	A clear concise explanation perhaps citing cases or examples.	4–5
	A clear understanding, but perhaps lacking authority or examples.	2–3
	Unbalanced, or may not deal with all of the required aspects of the topic. Alternatively the answer will demonstrate very little understanding of what is actually meant by constructive dismissal.	0–1
(b)	Thorough to complete answers, showing a detailed understanding of all or certainly most of the remedies available.	4–5
	A clear understanding of the remedies, but perhaps lacking in detail.	2–3
	Little or no knowledge of the topic.	0–1

(a) **Constructive dismissal**

Constructive dismissal occurs where the **employee terminates** their **employment contract** either with or without notice **due to the behaviour of their employer**. Outwardly the employer will often appear willing to continue the employment, but through their actions they **repudiate some essential term** of the contract. If the effect of this repudiation is that the employee resigns then the employer is potentially liable for breach of contract as a result of constructive dismissal.

Case law

Examples of breaches of contract which have lead to claims of constructive dismissal include **reduction in pay** (*Industrial Rubber Products v Gillon 1977*), **a complete change in the nature of the job** (*Ford v Milthorn Toleman Ltd 1980*), **failure to follow the prescribed disciplinary procedure** (*Post Office v Strange 1981*), **failure to provide a suitable working environment** (*Waltons and Morse v Dorrington 1997*) and **failure to implement a proper procedure** (*WA Goold (Pearmak) Ltd v McConnell & Another 1995*).

Breach of contract

To establish constructive dismissal, the **employee** must show that their employer has committed a serious breach of contract (a repudiatory breach), that they left because of the breach and that they did not 'waive' the breach, thereby affirming the contract.

Conduct

Courts will therefore look carefully at the **conduct of both parties** involved in a constructive dismissal claim. In *Western Excavating (ECC) Ltd v Sharp 1978* the employee was suspended without pay for misconduct. This caused them financial difficulties, and so they applied for an advance against holiday pay but this was refused. They then left and claimed for constructive dismissal. In this case the court found that the employer had not repudiated the contract and so there had been no dismissal.

(b) **Remedies for unfair dismissal**

Remedies for a successful claim for unfair dismissal include **reinstatement**, **re-engagement** and **compensation**.

Reinstatement

Reinstatement is return to the same job without any break of continuity by order of the employment tribunal.

Re-engagement

Re-engagement occurs when the employment tribunal orders that the employee is given new employment with the employer on terms specified in the order.

When deciding whether to exercise powers of **reinstatement** and **re-engagement**, the tribunal must take into account whether the complainant wishes to return to work for their employer and whether it is practicable and just for the employer to comply. **Such orders are in fact very infrequent**.

Compensation

If the tribunal does not order reinstatement or re-engagement the tribunal may award **compensation**, which may be made in three stages.

- **Basic award**

  A **basic award** calculated as follows. Those aged 41 and over receive one and a half weeks' pay (up to a maximum of £380 gross per week) for each year of service up to a maximum of 20 years. In other age groups the same provisions apply, except that the 22-40 age group receives one week's pay per year and the under 22 age group receives half a week's pay.

- **Compensatory award**

  A **compensatory award** for any additional loss of earnings, expenses and benefits on common law principles of damages for breach of contract. This is limited to £66,200 by the Employment Rights Act 1996.

- **Punitive award**

  If the employer does not comply with an order for reinstatement or re-engagement and does not show that it was impracticable to do so a **punitive additional award** is made of between 26 and 52 weeks' pay (again subject to the £380 per week maximum).

- **Reduced award**

  The employment tribunal may reduce the amount of the award if the employee **contributed** in some way to their own dismissal, if they **unreasonably refused** an offer of reinstatement, or if it is **just and equitable** to reduce the basic award by reason of some matter which occurred before dismissal.

50 Fair and constructive dismissal

Text reference. Chapter 11.

Top tips. Read this question carefully. For example in part (a), it would be easy to discuss unfair reasons for dismissal by mistake.

Easy marks. Defining fair and constructive dismissal.

Examiner's comments. This question was one of the few, it has to be said, where candidates performed most satisfactorily. Sound answers to (a) precisely identified the statutory grounds covering fair dismissal under Employment Rights Act 1996, viz. capability or qualification, misconduct, redundancy, breach of statutory provision and other substantial reasons. The very best also referred to dismissal upon retirement. All too frequently, however, candidates listed a range of possible fair dismissal scenarios without tying them into the statutory headings, e.g. theft, fraud, violence, making secret profits, failing professional qualifications, absenteeism and a range of other possibilities. Many of these overlapped and could have been cited as instances of one of the general headings. Marks awarded depended on the comprehensive nature of these instances, but a number merely cited examples of misconduct and consequently did not gain the level of marks available.

The answers to part (b) were well done. Many candidates were able to adequately define constructive dismissal and to offer one or two case examples.

Simmos v Dowty Seals Ltd (1978) was often referred to. The best answers went on to discuss the contractual basis of constructive dismissal, citing *Western Excavating v Sharp* (1978) and went on to mention possible remedies.

Some answers completely misinterpreted the concept of constructive dismissal, often portraying it as an extra weapon in the employer's armoury in the defence of an unfair dismissal claim. A number of candidates adequately defined constructive dismissal but appeared to believe that it only related to redundancy dismissals.

Marking scheme

This question relating to issues in employment law is divided into two parts and the marks will be allocated equally.

(a) Requires candidates to explain the provisions of the Employment Rights Act 1996 relating to the statutory grounds covering fair dismissal.

3–5 marks: A good explanation of the grounds upon which dismissal may be fair.
0–2 marks: Some awareness of the area but lacking in detailed knowledge.

(b) 3–5 marks: Candidates must show an understanding of what is meant by constructive dismissal, perhaps citing cases or examples.

0–2 marks: Unbalanced, or may not deal with all of the required aspects of the topic. Alternatively the answer will demonstrate very little understanding of what is actually meant by constructive dismissal.

(a) **Fair grounds for dismissal**

Under the **Employment Rights Act 1996**, employers wishing to justify the dismissal of an employee as fair must prove their **principal reason** relates to:

Capability or qualifications of the employee

Capability is assessed by reference to skills, aptitude, health or any other physical or mental quality. **Qualification** means any academic or technical qualifications relevant to the position that the employee holds': s 98(3). In addition to the lack of capability or qualification, employers must also show that they acted reasonably before dismissing the employee.

Conduct

To dismiss on grounds of **misconduct**, the employer must prove that the employee's actions can be categorised as **gross misconduct**, which justifies summary dismissal on the first occasion, rather than **ordinary misconduct**, which is not usually sufficient grounds for dismissal unless it is persistent. Gross misconduct may include theft or drunkenness at work.

Redundancy

Redundancy is always a fair reason for dismissal providing it fulfils the **legal criteria** for redundancy and the employee was **fairly selected** for it.

Legal prohibition or restriction

Dismissal on the grounds of a **statutory prohibition** or **restriction** that prevents the employee from **lawfully working** in the position which they are employed for is a fair reason for dismissal. For example, where a doctor is struck off the relevant professional register and so is ineligible to practise.

Some other substantial reason which justifies dismissal

The category of **other substantial reason** permits the employer to rely on some factor which is unusual and likely to affect them adversely. For example, an employer has justified dismissal where:

- The employee was married to one of their competitors.
- The employee refused to accept a reorganisation. For example, a change of shift working made in the interests of the business and with the agreement of a large majority of other employees.

(b) **Constructive dismissal**

Constructive dismissal occurs where the **employee terminates** their **employment contract** either with or without notice **due to the behaviour of their employer**. Outwardly the employer will often appear willing to continue the employment, but through their actions they **repudiate some essential term** of the contract. If the effect of this repudiation is that the employee resigns then the employer is potentially liable for breach of contract as a result of constructive dismissal.

Examples of breaches of contract which have lead to claims of constructive dismissal include; **reduction in pay** (*Industrial Rubber Products v Gillon 1977), **a complete change in the nature of the job** (*Ford v Milthorn Toleman Ltd 1980), **failure to follow the prescribed disciplinary procedure** (*Post Office v Strange 1981), **failure to provide a suitable working environment** (*Waltons and Morse v Dorrington 1997*) and **failure to implement a proper procedure** (*WA Goold (Pearmak) Ltd v McConnell & Another 1995*).

To **establish constructive dismissal**, the **employee** must show that their employer has committed a **serious breach of contract** (a repudiatory breach), that they left because of the breach and that they did not 'waive' the breach, thereby affirming the contract.

Courts will therefore look carefully at the **conduct of both parties** involved in a constructive dismissal claim. In *Western Excavating (ECC) Ltd v Sharp 1978* the employee was suspended without pay for misconduct. This caused them financial difficulties, and so they applied for an advance against holiday pay but they were refused. They then left and claimed for constructive dismissal. In this case the court found that the employer had not repudiated the contract and so there had been no dismissal.

51 Fine Ltd

Text reference. Chapter 11.

Top tips. Read questions like this very carefully, at least twice. Although there is not much information, it is all relevant and you need to pick it all up. Notice the split of the mark allocation, and make sure that you give the appropriate amount of time to each part.

Easy marks. Explaining that this may be a case of unfair dismissal.

Examiner's comments. The examiner expressed surprise that some candidates did not recognise the issue of unfair dismissal in the question. In part (a) some candidates provided general essays on unfair dismissal, which was not what was required, while others wrote about redundancy, which was not relevant and earned no marks. Part (b) was generally well-answered.

Marking scheme

The question is divided into two distinct elements; part (a) for six marks requiring an explanation of unfair dismissal and an application of the general law to the particular situation of the scenario, and part (b) carrying four marks which required an explanation of the remedies that are available for a successful claimant for unfair dismissal. Marks will be allocated as indicated in the exam paper.

(a)	4-6 marks	Full understanding of the concept of unfair dismissal, locating constructive dismissal within it, together with a thorough explanation of the law relating to it.
	1-3 marks	Lacking in detail in some or all aspects of the concept of unfair dismissal or lack of application.
(b)	3-4 marks	Full understanding of the remedies for unfair dismissal.
	1-2 marks	Lacking in detail in some or all aspects of the remedies available for unfair dismissal.

(a) **Constructive dismissal**

Constructive dismissal takes place where the **employer repudiates some vital term of the employment contract** and, despite the employer's willingness to continue the employment, the **employee resigns** because of it. No notice of termination is served on either party. In such cases, the employer is liable for breach of contract. Provided the breach is sufficiently serious, the employee may make a claim for unfair dismissal.

The employee must show that the **employer has committed a serious breach of contract**, that they left because of it and that they have not waived the breach, thereby affirming the contract. If the employee waits for too long before resigning, for example, they may be taken to have accepted the breach and waived their rights in respect of it. However, delaying for a reasonable period while they find alternative employment may be acceptable.

Case law

The breach must be **serious** and amount to a **repudiatory breach** *(Western Excavating (ECC) Ltd v Sharp 1978)*. In this case, the employee was suspended without pay for misconduct. This caused them financial difficulties and so they applied for an advance of holiday pay. This was refused, as was a subsequent request for a loan, so they left and claimed constructive dismissal. On appeal, it was held that the employer's actions did not amount to a breach of contract.

Unilaterally imposing a complete change in the employee's duties *(Ford v Milthorn Toleman Ltd 1980)* or **reducing the employee's pay** *(Industrial Rubber Products v Gillon 1977)* have been held to be sufficiently serious to entitle the employee to claim breach of contract and claim for constructive dismissal.

Similarly, a **failure to provide a suitable working environment** *(Waltons and Morse v Dorrington 1997)* and a **failure to follow the prescribed disciplinary procedure** *(Post Office v Strange 1981)* have also been held to be sufficient grounds for constructive dismissal.

Gus

Applying this to the scenario given it is suggested that, unless Gus's contract includes an **express mobility clause**, the actions of the employer could amount to constructive dismissal. Gus will therefore have grounds for an unfair dismissal claim.

(b) **Unfair dismissal remedies**

Where unfair dismissal is shown, three remedies are available:

- **Reinstatement to the same job** without any break in the continuity of employment;
- **Re-engagement in a different but comparable and suitable job** with the same employer or their successor or associate;
- **Compensation**.

In considering **reinstatement** and **re-engagement** all factors, including the employee's wishes and the practicality and overall fairness of such an award, will be taken into account. An order for re-engagement will not be made where there has been a breakdown in confidence between the parties *(Wood Group Heavy Industrial Turbines Ltd v Crossan 1998)*.

Compensation is the most usual award. This consists of a basic award, calculated on age, length of service and weekly wage. Therefore, employees aged 41 and over receive 1.5 weeks pay (to a maximum £380 gross pay per week) for each year of service (to a maximum of 20 years). For employees between 22 and 40, the base figure is 1 week's pay and, for those aged 21 and under, 0.5 weeks pay.

There may also be a **compensatory award** for additional losses of earnings, expenses and benefits, calculated on ordinary common law principles of damages for breach of contract and up to a maximum of £66,200.

52 Grace and Fawn Ltd

Text reference. Chapter 11.

Top tips. Even in relatively short questions like this, follow our suggested approach: **identify** the issue, **state** the law, **apply** the law and **conclude**.

Easy marks. Stating the criteria for redundancy and calculating redundancy pay would earn you pass marks.

Marking scheme

	Marks
Redundancy	
Criteria for redundancy	3
Qualification for redundancy pay	2
Calculation of redundancy pay	2
Redundancy selection procedure	2
Grace qualifies for redundancy	1
	10

Redundancy

The law relating to redundancy is found in the Employment Rights Act 1996.

Qualifying employee

A **qualifying employee** has a right to a redundancy payment (as compensation) in the event that they are dismissed because of redundancy, that is (s 139) 'where the only or main reason for the dismissal is that:

- The employer has **ceased** or **intends to cease** carrying on the business in which the employee has been employed or at the local establishment where the employee has been employed or
- The **requirements of that business** for employees to carry on the work done by the employee have **ceased or diminished'**.

If the employer requires the employee to move to a **different place of work** and that is within the terms of the contract of employment, then there is no redundancy.

Dismissal

The onus is on the employee to show that they were **dismissed** and then on the employer to show that the dismissal was for some reason other than redundancy, such as:

- Dismissal by the **employer bringing the contract** to an end, with or without notice;
- Dismissal where a **fixed term contract ends** and is not renewed (although protection may be lost if the contract is for more than one year's duration);
- When the **conduct of the employer is sufficiently serious** that it amounts to a repudiation of the employment contract and the employee resigns as a result, lawfully terminating the contract without notice by reason of the employer's conduct. If the employee is dismissed for misconduct, they will not be entitled to a redundancy payment (*Sanders v Neale 1974*). Similarly if they resign voluntarily there is no entitlement.

Alternative employment

The employer may choose to offer a redundant employee **alternative employment** (s 141). If the employee unreasonably refuses the offer, they lose their entitlement to a redundancy payment. Broadly speaking, the alternative employment must be in the **same capacity**, at the **same place** and on the **same terms** and **conditions** as the old employment. It should not be perceived as being lower in status (*Cambridge District Co-operative Society v Russell 1993*).

An employee **qualifies** for redundancy pay if (s 109) they have been **continually employed for 2 years** or more.

Redundancy pay

Redundancy pay is calculated as follows: 1.5 weeks pay for each complete year of employment during which the employee was aged 40 or more, 1 week's pay for each year where they were aged between 22 and 40 and 0.5 week's pay for each year where they were aged between 18 and 22. A week's pay is capped at £380.

The entitlement to a redundancy payment is lost if the **employee does not claim** a payment within **6 months** of the relevant date (such as the expiry of the dismissal notice). If the employer disputes their claim, the employee should refer it to an Employment Tribunal. A right of appeal lies to the Employment Appeals Tribunal.

Selection

The employer should have a **redundancy selection procedure** which conforms to good industrial relations practice (*Williams v Compair Maxam Ltd 1982*). They should give as much warning as possible of impending redundancies, consult with the relevant trade union, make the selection fairly and consider whether offers of alternative employment can be made. Protective awards may be made against an employer who fails to consult trade unions or to give notice of impending redundancies to the government.

Conclusion

As **Grace's part of the business** (the shop) is being **closed** she is being made redundant. She has been employed for over two years and is 33 years old and is therefore entitled to **redundancy pay** of 1 week's pay per complete year of employment subject to a maximum of £380 per week.

We are not told Grace's salary, but her **maximum entitlement** to redundancy pay **is £1,140** (3 x £380).

53 Impact College

Text reference. Chapter 11.

Top tips. When reading through the question, make sure that you pick up all the details that might be relevant to your answer. For example, you are told that all the staff members have been employed for six years, so you do not need to discuss factors such as the time requirements for actions for unfair dismissal

Easy marks. Making sure that you advise Fred, Gale and Hilda, as required by the question.

Marking scheme

8-10 marks	A full and detailed treatment of all elements of the question.
6-7 marks	Less complete answer, or lacking in some detail. Perhaps slightly unbalanced in not dealing with all of the elements of the question.
4-5 marks	Unbalanced answers evidencing knowledge of only some of the elements in the question, or lacking of detail in relation to the answers provided.
0-3 marks	Very unbalanced to the extent of dealing with only one or two of the elements, or evidencing little or no knowledge of any aspect of the question.

Unfair dismissal

Every employee who qualifies has the right not to be unfairly dismissed from that employment. When a case comes before an employment tribunal it is for the employer to prove that the **dismissal was for a fair reason** (capability, conduct, redundancy, legal prohibition or another substantial reason). However, in addition to this, some grounds put forward for dismissal will be **automatically unfair**. These are as follows.

Pregnancy

Regardless of the length of service, a dismissal on grounds of **pregnancy** or a pregnancy-related illness, or any matter related to **childbirth**, is automatically unfair.

Trade Union membership or activities

A dismissal on the grounds of an employee's actual or proposed membership of an independent **trade union** or their taking part at an appropriate time in the activities of such a trade union or their refusal to be a member of a trade union is automatically unfair. However, it is fair to dismiss employees involved in an unofficial strike, lockout or other industrial action.

Spent conviction

An employee dismissed on the basis of a **conviction** which is actually spent under the Rehabilitation of Offenders Act 1974 has been dismissed for an automatically unfair reason.

Health and safety

Dismissal is automatically unfair if it is for the reason that an employee took steps to carry out **health and safety related activities** as requested by their employer, or brought health and safety risks or dangers to the employer's attention, or left work reasonably believing themselves to be in danger.

Enforcing statutory rights

Where an employee takes action against an employer to **enforce statutory rights and duties** and the employer dismisses them as a result (s.104 ERA), this is an automatically unfair reason for dismissal.

Conclusion

If Fred, Gale and Hilda can show that their dismissals are **automatically unfair** under the above categories then their employer will be liable for unfair dismissal.

Fred and Hilda

Both Fred and Hilda feel that their **confrontations with Jack**, which are both related to automatically unfair reasons for dismissal (trade union membership and health and safety), are the reasons why they were dismissed. However they will need to prove this to any employment tribunal.

Gale

Gale's position is a little more straightforward. She is **pregnant** and she has been **dismissed**. Therefore it is likely that she will succeed in proving that she was dismissed for an automatically unfair reason.

54 Types of authority

Text reference. Chapter 12.

Top tips. This was another reasonably straightforward 'explain' requirement, although some students find the authority of the agent a tricky area.

Even if you had scored full marks on part (a), you would have failed the question if you had not been able to answer parts (b) and (c).

This illustrates the importance of reading through and getting to grips with the key terms and definitions given in the Study Text. You can then build on your understanding of these by seeing the law in practice – in the case examples given in the Text.

Easy marks. Defining the types of authority.

Examiner's comments. Candidates generally did not do well on this question, possibly because agency was a new topic in the syllabus at the time the question was set. However many candidates did not seem to have grasped the essential principles, especially of implied authority.

Many candidates failed to answer part (c) of the question despite the fact that it was worth 4 marks. The candidates who did attempt part (c) often repeated material that they already produced for part (a).

Marking scheme

			Marks
(a)	Definition of express authority	1	
	Depends on terms of agency agreement	1	
	Breach of warranty of authority	1	
			3
(b)	Implied incidental authority	1	
	Implied customary authority	1	
	Implied usual authority	1	
			3
(c)	Explanation	1	
	Case or example	1	
	Agency by estoppel requirements	2	
			4
			10

Authority of an agent

As a general rule, in order to be valid and binding on the principal and third party, a contract entered into by an agent must be entered into within the bounds of the agent's authority. However, that authority need not be express for the contract entered into by the agent to bind the principal. It may be implied actual authority or apparent authority.

(a) **Express authority**

Express authority is the extent of authority which it is agreed (between the principal and agent) the agent shall have to enter into contracts on the principal's behalf. The precise scope and extent of 'express actual authority' will depend on the construction of the written document in which the appointment or conferring of authority is contained or on the evidence supporting an oral giving of actual express authority. If the **agent** acts outside their express authority, they will be **liable** to the **principal** for breach of contract and to the **third party** for breach of warranty of authority.

(b) **Implied authority**

Actual authority may be implied rather than express:

- '**Implied incidental authority**' will be deemed to exist where it is reasonable to suppose that the principal also gave the agent authority to enter into transactions which are necessarily incidental or subordinate to the matter of the express authority. For example, the authority to advertise goods when the agent is expressly authorised to sell them.
- '**Implied customary authority**' is that which an agent shall be deemed to have by reason of their operating in a particular market or business, for example an estate agent may have implied authority to show potential buyers round a house.
- '**Implied usual authority**' is that which an agent shall be deemed to have by reason of their occupying a particular position or engaging in a particular trade.

In cases of **implied actual authority**, the **third party** who contracts with the agent is entitled to assume that the agent has implied authority unless they know to the contrary.

In *Watteau v Fenwick 1893*, the principal was held to be bound by a contract entered into by their agent with implied usual authority (as a hotel manager, they bought cigars on credit) even though the third party did not know that the agent, as the other contracting party, was the agent of the principal. As between the agent and the principal, however, the agent is not entitled to contravene the principal's express authority or instructions by claiming implied authority.

(c) **Apparent authority**

'**Apparent**' or '**ostensible**' **authority** is that which the **principal represents** to other parties they have given their agent. Although matters of apparent authority and implied usual authority often appear to be co-extensive, it is the conduct of the principal which creates apparent authority. It also arises where the principal is aware that an agent is claiming to be their appointed agent and yet does nothing to correct that impression. In either case, the principal will be bound by the actions of the ostensible agent.

In *Freeman & Lockyer v Buckhurst Park Properties (Mangal) Ltd 1964*, a company was bound by the acts of one of its directors who acted like a managing director even though they had not been appointed formally to that position. By its mere acquiescence, the company had led the third party to believe that they were the managing director and the third party had relied on that impression.

Pre-existing relationships

There need not be a pre-existing agency relationship. Apparent or ostensible authority (or 'agency by estoppel') requires a **representation which is relied upon** thereby causing an alteration in the position of the representee. The representation may be express or implied from previous dealings or implied from conduct.

Revocation

Where the principal has **subsequently revoked** an agent's authority, they will continue to be bound by acts entered into by that agent within their former authority with third parties who dealt with them previously, until they inform those third parties that the agent is no longer so authorised (*Willis Faber and Co Ltd v Joyce 1911*).

Representation

The **representation** must be made either by the **principal** or by **another agent** acting on their behalf (*Armagas Ltd v Mundogas SA, The Ocean Frost 1986*) but not by the agent claiming to have the authority. It must be one of fact and not of law and it must be made to the third party. If the third party knew that the agent had no authority or did not believe them to have, they cannot claim **agency by estoppel**. Unless the alteration of position also causes damage or detriment, any damages awarded will be nominal although, strictly speaking, it is not necessary to show that reliance resulted in such damage or detriment.

55 Unlimited and limited partnerships

Text reference. Chapter 13.

Top tips. This is a straightforward factual question and is nicely broken down so that you should be able to gain good marks on each part. Notice that part (c) is asking specifically about limited liability partnerships, so you should restrict your answer to consideration of those.

Easy marks. There is half a mark available for each valid point in part (a). Try to think of a range of ideas to demonstrate the breadth of your knowledge. In part (b) there are two marks for an explanation of apparent authority and a further mark for an example. In part (c) assume a mark and a half for each of the two requirements.

Marking scheme

			Marks
(a)	PA 1890 definition	1	
	Person	1	
	Carrying on a business	1	
	View of profit	1	4
(b)	Definition in PA 1890	1	
	Example, case or illustration	1	
	Purpose the protection of third parties	1	3
(c)	Definition	1	
	Examples of filing requirements	1	
	Examples of publicity	1	
			3
			10

(a) **Unlimited partnerships**

Unlimited partnerships are governed by the **Partnership Act 1890**, which defines a partnership as 'the relations which exist between persons carrying on a business with a view of profit.'

Person

A person can include a **registered company** as well as **individual** living people. There must be at least **two** parties for partnership to exist.

Carrying on a business

Business can include any **form of activity** that must have a beginning and an end. It can consist of a single transaction such as a joint venture.

View of profit

The partners must **intend** to make a profit, if they intend to trade just to gain experience there is no partnership: *Davies v Newman 2000*. A partnership will still exist even if losses are made – it is the partners' intention that is key.

(b) **Partners' authority**

Partners in a firm are regarded as having both **actual** and **apparent authority** to bind the firm. Their actual authority is the authority given to them by the partnership agreement to carry out certain acts.

Apparent authority

Their **apparent authority** is defined by the Partnership Act 1890. This states that every partner is an agent of the firm and the other partners for the purpose of the business of the partnership.

The partner's actions in the **normal course of business**, of a sort that the firm would normally be expected to do, **bind the firm** and the other partners, so that they too are liable to the third party. However, if the partner does not have the authority to make the contract, and the **third party knows that to be the case or does not know or believe them to be a partner**, then the firm will not be bound.

Example

For example, X is a partner in a firm that runs a garage buying and selling second hand cars, but the partnership agreement states that the firm is not to trade in new cars. If X enters a contract for the purchase of a new car from a third party who is not aware of the prohibition in the partnership agreement, then the firm as a whole would be bound by that contract, as X had apparent authority to enter into it.

Purpose

The **purpose** of the law is the **protection of third parties**, and the nature of the authority often depends on the perception of the third party involved. If the third party genuinely believes that the partner has authority, the firm is likely to be bound by the partner's actions.

(c) **Limited liability partnership**

A **limited liability partnership** (LLP) formed under the Limited Liability Partnership Act 2000 is a corporate body with separate legal personality from its members, but it retains some of the features of a partnership.

In order to be incorporated, the subscribers must **file details** with the Registrar of Companies:

- The **name** of the LLP
- The **location** of its **registered office** (ie England and Wales, Wales or Scotland)
- The **address** of the **registered office**
- The **name** and **address** of **all the members** of the LLP
- Which members are to be **designated members**, who take responsibility for the publicity requirements of the LLP.

The **designated members** of a LLP are required to:

- **File notices** with the Registrar of Companies, for example when a member leaves
- **Sign** and **file accounts**
- **Appoint auditors** if appropriate

56 Ham, Sam and Tam

Text reference. Chapter 13.

Top tips. You need to consider the authority of partners and the liability they have for the firm's debts. Avoid the temptation in to discuss all you know about agency law – keep your answer focused on partnerships.

Easy marks. Stating the basic rule of partnership authority.

Examiner's comments. This question required candidates to consider key issues relating to the powers, authority and liability of partners. Candidates were required to exhibit a thorough knowledge of partnership law together with the ability to analyse the problems contained in the question and apply the law accurately. While there were many decent answers to the question, with candidates demonstrating a reasonable understanding of partnership law, once again it has to be said that some candidates simply did not recognise the issues involved in the problem scenario. As has been said a small number of candidates appeared to take the fact that the business of the partnership was limited to the sale of petrol as an indication that it was a limited partnership and produced answers explaining that business form. Others presented general answers on the different possible partnership forms without making any real attempt to deal with the question, a clear indication that they prepared an answer and were going to reproduce it whether it was relevant or not.

Marking scheme

This question refers to key issues relating to the powers, authority and liability of partners.

8–10 marks: Candidates will exhibit a thorough knowledge of partnership law together with the ability to analyse the problems contained in the question.

5–7 marks: Candidates will exhibit a sound knowledge of partnership law together with the ability to recognise the issues contained in the question. Knowledge may be less detailed or analysis less focused.

3–4 marks: Identification of some of the central issues in the question and an attempt to apply the appropriate law. Towards the bottom of this range of marks there will be major shortcomings in analysis or application of law.

0–2 marks: Very weak answers which might recognise what the question is about but show no ability to analyse or answer the problem as set out.

Issue

Ham, Sam and Tam have set up in partnership together. They have a partnership agreement and debts in the name of the partnership amounting to over £25,000.

Partners' relationships with third parties

Each partner is the agent of the firm and when a third party contracts with a partner, they contract with all the partners.

There are **exceptions** to this third party principle. One is that the partners are bound to an act which a partner has carried out in the normal course of business, unless the partner acting had **no authority** to do so, **and** the **third party was aware** that the partner did not have authority to do so.

Another exception is that if one partner **pledges the credit of the firm** for a **purpose apparently not connected with the firm's business**, the firm is not bound unless the partner is specifically authorised to undertake that transaction.

However, as a general rule, the **firm** (that is, all the individual partners) is **liable** to third parties for actions of a partner where they have **apparent** or **actual** authority.

The bank loan

Sam has taken money from the **firm's bank account** to use for a personal holiday. However, as a partner, and in the absence of any specific mention to the contrary in the agreement, **he has authority** to withdraw money from the bank account.

His action has therefore **incurred a debt** to a third party that is owed by all three partners, not just himself, and if he cannot repay the money to the bank, the bank is entitled to **sue the other partners** for the balance.

The debt for the cars

Tam has entered into a **contract to buy cars** in the name of the partnership. The **partnership agreement** specifies that the partnership should **only sell petrol**, so Tam does not have authority to undertake this contract. However, the **third party** is not privy to the partnership agreement so is not aware that the contract is beyond the scope of the partnership. Tam has **apparent authority** to undertake the contract on behalf of the other partners.

However, as the trade of the partners is to **sell petrol**, it is possible that this contract might fall into the other exception to the authority rule, because the sale of cars is **not connected** to their business. It is a moot point whether selling cars is connected to selling petrol and a court might well rule that the two were connected, in which case, all three partners would be liable for this debt.

The debt for the petrol

Purchasing petrol is a **normal** part of business for this partnership. Whoever made the contract would have had **authority** to do so and bound the other partners to the contract. They are all liable for the petrol bill.

57 Clare, Dan and Eve

Text reference. Chapter 13

Top tips. This question requires you to advise three people who have slightly different circumstances. It is often quicker to answer such questions by taking each person in turn and applying the ISAC approach to each.

Easy marks. There are few easy marks here. If you know partnership law well, the easiest marks are in its application to the scenario.

Examiner's comments. On the whole the majority of candidates recognised the specific underlying issues within the general context of partnership law, although the manner in which they applied the law to the issues differed significantly depending on their knowledge of partnership law. The question concerned three distinct characters; Clare, Dan and Eve and most candidates dealt with each in turn although not always appropriately.

Marking scheme

This question requires candidates to analyse a problem scenario that raises issues relating mainly to partnerships but which also involves agency law.

8–10 marks	Clear analysis of the problem scenario – recognition of the issues raised and a convincing application of the legal principles to the facts. Appropriate case authorities may be cited, but are not necessary if the principles are understood.
5–7 marks	Sound analysis of the problem – recognition of the major principles involved and a fair attempt at applying them. Perhaps sound in knowledge but lacking in analysis and application.
3–4 marks	Unbalanced answer perhaps showing some appropriate knowledge but weak in analysis or application.
0–2 marks	Very weak answer showing little analysis, appropriate knowledge or application.

Assumption

In answering this question it is assumed that Clare, Dan and Eve are involved in a **traditional partnership**. This is because no mention is made of a Limited Partnership under the Limited Partnerships Act 1907 or a Limited Liability Partnership under the Limited Liability Partnerships Act 2000.

Therefore, partners are **jointly liable** for all partnership debts that result from contracts made by other partners which bind the firm.

Clare

A **sleeping partner** is a common term used to describe a partner who puts capital into the partnership but has no day-to-day involvement in the running of the business. They are distinct from limited partners in limited partnerships as they do not have limited liability.

Clare was unwise not to become involved in the firm as she would have had an equal say in how it was run and maybe could have prevented the financial problems. Unfortunately, as the firm does not have limited liability, she is **fully liable** for the debts of the firm.

Dan

Partners are liable for debts incurred **during their time** as partners, but when they retire special rules apply.

Retiring partners are still liable for any **outstanding debts** incurred while they were a partner, unless creditors agree to **release** them from liability.

They are also **liable** for debts of the firm incurred after their retirement if the creditor knew them to be a partner (before retirement) and has not had **notice** of their retirement.

They are **not liable** for debts incurred with **new customers** after they retire providing the new customer was not aware of them as a partner or they knew them but were also aware of their retirement.

It would appear that **Dan is liable** for the debt with **Greg** as it does not appear that Greg had notice of Dan's retirement, nor did he agree to release him from liability.

Hugh was aware of Dan's capacity as a partner so Dan **will be liable** for the debt with Hugh unless Hugh was aware of his retirement.

Eve

Like the others, Eve is **liable** for the debts of the partnership. The partners have **joint liability**. This usually means that debts are shared equally, but if one partner cannot afford to pay their full share, the others have to make up the shortfall. If Dan is not liable on the debt with Hugh, then this debt will be **shared equally** between Clare and Eve.

58 Chi, Di and Fi

Text reference. Chapter 13.

Top tips. The facts of this question are almost identical to a question set in December 2008 and therefore students who have attempted this question already should find this one very easy indeed. This demonstrates the benefit of practising as many questions as you can before your exam.

Easy marks. Identifying the authority and liability of partners.

ACCA examiner's answers. The ACCA examiner's answer to this question can be found at the back of this kit.

Examiner's comments. Whilst there were many sound answers, it has to be said that on the whole it was not done as well as might have been expected. There was a lot of repetition of the facts from the scenario. Whilst this is sometimes relevant to demonstrate application skills, there was not often a link between the scenario and the law identified. Most candidates were good at dealing with the general law of partnership and they set it out, sometimes in great detail before going on to apply it to the three parties in the scenario. However, it was in the application that a significant number of candidates let themselves down by not applying the law they had actually stated and in many instances actually contradicting what they had written previously.

Marking scheme

This question refers to key issues relating to the powers, authority and liability of partners.

8–10 marks:	Candidates will exhibit a thorough knowledge of partnership law together with the ability to analyse the problems contained in the question.
5–7 marks:	Candidates will exhibit a sound knowledge of partnership law together with the ability to recognise the issues contained in the question. Knowledge may be less detailed or analysis less focused.
3–4 marks:	Identification of some of the central issues in the question and an attempt to apply the appropriate law. Towards the bottom of this range of marks there will be major shortcomings in analysis or application of law.
0–2 marks:	Very weak answers which might recognise what the question is about but show no ability to analyse or answer the problem as set out.

Issue

Chi, Di and Fi have set up in partnership together. They have a **partnership agreement** and debts in the name of the partnership.

From the facts of the scenario it appears that neither a **limited** or **limited liability partnership** was established and therefore under a **traditional or ordinary partnership** all the partners are jointly liable for the debts of the partnership.

The law

In a partnership **each partner is the agent of the firm** and when a third party contracts with a partner, they contract with all the partners.

There are **exceptions** to this third party principle. One is that the partners are bound to an act which a partner has carried out in the normal course of business, unless the partner acting had **no authority** to do so, **and** the **third party was aware** that the partner did not have authority to do so.

Another exception is that if one partner **pledges the credit of the firm** for a **purpose apparently not connected with the firm's business**, the firm is not bound unless the partner is specifically authorised to undertake that transaction.

However, as a general rule, the **firm** (that is, all the individual partners) is **liable** to third parties for actions of a partner where they have **apparent** or **actual** authority.

The **Civil Liability Act 1978** provides that judgement against one partner does not prevent subsequent actions against other partners.

Application of the law

The bank overdraft

Chi has taken money from the **firm's bank account** to use for a personal holiday. However, as a partner, and in the absence of any specific mention to the contrary in the agreement, **she has authority** to withdraw money from the bank account.

Her action has therefore **incurred a debt** to a third party that is owed by all three partners, not just herself.

The debt for the books

Di has entered into a **contract to buy books** in the name of the partnership. The **partnership agreement** specifies that the partnership should **only sell paintings, sculptures and other works of art**, so Di does not have authority to undertake this contract.

However, the **third party** is not privy to the partnership agreement so is not aware that the contract is beyond the scope of the partnership. Di has **apparent authority** to undertake the contract on behalf of the other partners.

However, as the trade of the partners is to **sell art**, it is possible that this contract might fall into the other exception to the authority rule, because the sale of books is **not connected** to their business.

It is a moot point whether selling books is **connected** to selling art but it is likely that a court might well rule that the two are connected, in which case all three partners would be liable for this debt.

Conclusion

As both the overdraft and contract for the books are binding on the partnership all three partners are personally liable if the partnership does not have sufficient funds to pay them.

Chi

In addition to being liable for her share of the partnership debts, Chi may also be liable to the other partners in respect of her breach of the partnership agreement in using the overdraft for a non-business purpose.

Di

In addition to being liable for her share of the partnership debts, Di may also be liable to the other partners in respect of her breach of the partnership agreement for the book contract as it is for a non-business purpose.

Fi

Fi is jointly liable for the debts of the partnership to the third parties. However as the partnership agreement limits her liability to £100,000 she will be able to claim any amount over this from Chi and Di.

59 Partnership liability

Text reference. Chapter 13

Top tips. Part (a) is only worth two marks so do not spend long on it. Ensure your answer clearly states what liability is in each type of partnership.

Easy marks. A description of each type of partnership and a statement of liability would be enough to pass this question.

Marking scheme

			Marks
(a)	Definition of partnership	1	
	Jointly liable	1	
			2
(b)	Description of limited partnership	1	
	One limited, one unlimited partner	1	
	Limited partner cannot participate	1	
	Limited partner cannot bind the firm	1	
			4
(c)	Description of limited liability partnership	1	
	Limited liability	1	
	Legal status of partnership	1	
	Partners' authority	1	
			4
			10

(a) **Traditional partnership**

A **traditional partnership** is the relationship which subsists between persons carrying on a business in common with the intention of making a profit (s1 Partnership Act 1890). A partnership does not have a separate legal identity distinct from the partners. One of the consequences of this is that the partners are jointly and severally liable for all debts and liabilities arising under any contracts made which bind the partnership to the full extent of each partner's wealth.

(b) **Limited partnership**

A limited partnership under the **Limited Partnership Act 1907** is also known as a **limited liability partnership**. They are formed when one or more of the partners invest capital into the business but do not participate in running and managing the business. These partners therefore have limited liability as they can only lose the amount of money that they initially invested into the business.

In a limited partnership, the law states that there must be at least one partner who has unlimited liability (a **general partner**). The general partner has control of the management of the business. However, none of the limited partners is permitted to participate in the management of the business. If they do, their limited liability is lost. A limited partner cannot bind the partnership. Only the general partner can do that.

In order to take advantage of the protection afforded by limited liability, an organisation which constitutes itself as a limited partnership must comply with the requirements of the Limited Partnership Act 1907. In particular, the partnership must be registered at Companies House giving details of the partners and the extent of their liability.

(c) **Limited liability partnerships**

Limited liability partnerships (**LLPs**) are a relatively new form of business structure, following the enactment of the **Limited Liability Partnership Act 2000**. An LLP combines the features of a partnership along with the limited liability and creation of a legal personality more usually associated with limited companies. An LLP is not dissolved on a change of membership. At the end of the life of a partnership, it is wound up rather like a company.

An LLP is a body corporate and therefore an **artificial legal person** with its own property and liabilities, separate from its members. Every member-partner is treated as an agent of the LLP and therefore (usually) has **authority to bind the LLP** by their actions.

Since the LLP is a **separate legal entity** the members are not jointly liable for contracts entered into by the LLP and/or jointly and severally liable for any wrong-doings committed by the LLP. However, members will be liable for their own acts of negligence or wrong-doing much in the same way as company directors are. The rules on fraudulent and wrongful trading apply to an LLP in much the same way as they do to a limited company, as do the Companies Act provisions regarding the disqualification of directors, insolvency and winding up procedures.

LLPs are incorporated by **registration** at **Companies House** and are required to file accounts there. An **incorporation document** to which the initial members have subscribed must be submitted to the **Registrar of Companies**. This document will set out the name of the LLP along with its registered office, the name and address of each member and which members are to be '**designated members**' (who are responsible for compliance with the filing and administrative requirements).

60 Partnership v company

Text reference. Chapter 13.

Top tips. This is a straightforward question on the benefits of incorporation against a partnership. Commit the table in Study Text Chapter 13 to memory and use the points to answer any similar question that may arise in future.

Easy marks. Stating the differences will earn you quick marks – remember to use a separate paragraph for each.

Marking scheme

	Marks
Separate legal personality	1
Contrast with partnership	1
Limited liability	1
Contrast with partnership	1
Perpetual succession	1
Contrast with partnership	1
Transferability of interest	1
Contrast with partnership	1
Capital	1
Security	1
	10

Advantages of incorporation

There are a number of advantages offered by incorporating the business into a private limited company:

Legal entity

Probably the most important factor which distinguishes a company from other forms of organisation is that a company is a distinct legal entity separate from its members whereas in a partnership there is no separate legal person as distinct from the partners. This means that the assets and liabilities of the business belong to the company itself.

Limited liability

If the company becomes insolvent, the shareholders are not liable for the company's debts which belong to the company. They are liable only to the company for that amount, if any, which remains unpaid on their shares. In contrast, a partner is normally jointly and severally liable for all the debts of the firm to the extent of their personal wealth. However, directors of private companies are often required to give personal guarantees to lenders so the distinction is not always so great.

Perpetual succession

In the case of companies, there is no cessation brought about by a change in the membership, but any change of partners in a partnership (by death, bankruptcy or resignation) operates as a termination of the old partnership and the beginning of a new one. In practice, a partnership agreement will often provide that for so long as there are two or more surviving partners on the death of one partner the partnership shall continue between them. Dissolution of the partnership can be effected by the agreement of the partners or according to the terms of the partnership agreement. A company is 'dissolved' by liquidation.

Transferability

Subject to any restrictions imposed by the company's constitution, a company member's shares constitute a form of property and are freely transferable. Although a partner can assign their interest, the assignee of it will not as a result become a partner in the partnership (whereas a transferee of a member's shares thereby becomes a member of the company).

Capital and security

A company may find it easier to raise capital for the expansion of the business than a partnership since the liability of potential investors is limited as described above and a company can borrow by debentures and loan stock. Furthermore, a company can raise capital by providing a fixed or floating charge as security but a partnership cannot provide security by way of a floating charge. There are, for the benefit of shareholders, various rules and regulations, contained in the Companies Act and the company's constitution, which are stringently applied relating to the reduction or distribution of a company's capital whereas in the case of a partnership partners may, by mutual agreement, withdraw capital from the partnership as they wish.

61 Termination of partnerships

Text reference. Chapter 13.

Top tips. Think carefully before attempting a question like this: it requires detailed knowledge of a fairly narrow area of the law on partnership and you must keep your answer focused on the requirement.

Easy marks. Stating each ground for termination.

Examiner's comments. This was a popular question and was relatively well-answered. The main criticism is that some candidates just listed the grounds as bullet points, and did not explain how the circumstances would arise. Many candidates did not make the point that the dissolution can occur at the volition of either the partners or in some instances the court.

Marking scheme

	Marks
Dissolution by agreement of partners	2
Partnership Act 1890 grounds:	
Specific venture/fixed period ends	2
Death or bankruptcy of one of the partners	1
Supervening illegality	1
Notice by a partner	1
By agreement	1
By court order	2
	10

Dissolution

Dissolution is the term used to describe when a **partnership comes to an end**. A partnership can always be dissolved by **agreement** of the partners. In addition the Partnership Act 1890 provides that a partnership will be dissolved in the **following circumstances**.

Fixed time/specific venture

Where the partnership was entered into for a **specific venture or a fixed time period** and that venture or fixed period comes to an end. If in fact the partners decide to continue even after such time, the partnership is thereafter referred to as a 'partnership at will' and like any other partnership can be brought to an end by the partners' wishes.

Death or bankruptcy

On the **death or bankruptcy of one of the partners**. Since a partnership has no separate legal personality but is the relationship that subsists between its partners, it follows that the death or bankruptcy of one of its partners will bring the partnership to an end (this is not the case with partnerships created under the Limited Liability Partnerships Act 2000). In practice, however, a partnership agreement will usually provide for the partnership business to continue under the control of the remaining partners who automatically constitute a new partnership.

Illegality

In the case of **supervening illegality**. Where the business of the partnership becomes illegal, it is automatically dissolved. For example where the outbreak of war means that the partnership is thereafter trading with the enemy or if a solicitor in a partnership fails to renew their practice certificate, as required by law.

Notice

Where one partner gives **notice of dissolution** to the remaining partners, provided the partnership is for an unlimited duration.

Agreement

By **agreement** between the partners that the partnership should be dissolved.

Court order

By order of the **court**. The court may order dissolution of a partnership.

62 Limited liability and types of company

Text reference. Chapter 13.

Top tips. At first sight this looks like a gift of a question, but do make sure that you write sufficient worthwhile points about each type of company to maximise your mark.

Easy marks. Explaining how member liability is different in each type of company.

Examiner's comments. Once again it should be noted that the question was clearly couched in the terms of company law and company formation. However, a significant number of candidates approached the question from the perspective of partnership law. Some candidates thought that the underlying unifying aspect of the question was separate personality, which led them to conclude that only limited companies had such separate personality.

Marking scheme

This question is likely to be answered in a global way and marks will be awarded inline with points made.

(a) Up to 3 marks for a general explanation of limited liability.

(b) (i) Up to 2 marks for an explanation of unlimited liability and why it might be used.

(ii) Up to 2 marks for knowledge of companies limited by guarantee. What they are, where they are used and the nature of liability.

(iii) Up to 3 marks for a thorough explanation of liability limited by reference to the amount unpaid on shares and how it operates.

(a) **Limited liability**

The **Companies Act** provides that an incorporated company may have either (a) no limit to the members' liability ('an **unlimited company**'), (b) the liability of its members limited to the amount unpaid on the shares respectively held by them ('a **company limited by shares**'), or (c) the members' liability limited to such amount as the members undertake to contribute to the assets in the event of a winding up ('a **company limited by guarantee**').

(b) (i) **Unlimited companies**

An **unlimited company's** constitution makes no reference to members' liability as there is **no limit to their liability**. In the event of a liquidation, all members can be required to contribute as much as necessary in order to pay the company's debts in full. An unlimited company has the advantages of not being required to file copies of its annual accounts and reports (save in certain cases) and it may purchase its shares from its own members without following any formal processes.

(ii) **Companies limited by guarantee**

In a **company limited by guarantee**, each shareholder is liable to contribute to the company the amount specified in the **company's constitution** in the event of the company going into liquidation but not before. Creditors have no direct claim on members since the guarantee is between the member and the company only.

(iii) **Companies limited by shares**

In a **company limited by shares**, the fixed amount of each share will be specified in the company's constitution and that amount fixes the maximum liability of each shareholder which they agree to pay in money or money's worth either in one sum or by instalments. In the event of a winding up, the **members can be required to contribute any part of their stated liability which remains unpaid at that date** but not more. As above, creditors are owed debts by the company and have no claim against the members save in the event of liquidation.

63 Separate personality

Text reference. Chapter 13

Top tips. Notice how our answer is broken down into short paragraphs with headers. Always present your answers this way as it draws the marker's attention to your points and enables them to award you marks quickly and easily.

Easy marks. Defining legal personality and explaining its consequences.

Examiner's comments. Once again it has to be stated that a significant number of candidates did not even attempt this question on one of the most fundamental principles of company law.

Marking scheme

This question asks candidates to consider the doctrine of separate personality, one of the key concepts of company law. It also requires some consideration of the occasions when the doctrine will be ignored, and the veil of incorporation pulled aside. This latter part will demand consideration of both statute and common law provisions. The question is divided into two parts to indicate to candidates the weighting they should apply in answering the question, although the answers can be answered as a whole.

(a) Carries 6 marks

5–6 marks	A thorough to complete answer explaining the meaning and effect of separate personality. It is likely that cases will be cited as authority although examples will be acceptable as an alternative.
2–4 marks	Some but limited knowledge of the topic. Perhaps uncertain as to meaning or lacking in detailed explanation or authority.
0–1 mark	Very little or no understanding whatsoever.

(b) Carries 4 marks

3–4 marks	A thorough to full explanation detailing the situations under which separate personality will be ignored.
1–2 marks	Some understanding perhaps lacking in explanation or examples of when the doctrine will be ignored.
0 marks	No understanding whatsoever.

(a) **Legal personality of companies**

Corporate personality is a common law principle that grants a company a legal identity, separate from the members who comprise it.

The case of *Salomon v Salomon & Co Ltd 1897* is considered the key case that established the above principle. Salomon ran a non-incorporated business for 30 years but decided to convert it into a limited liability company where he would hold 20,001 shares and his family would hold 6 shares.

After incorporation, the business ran into financial difficulties and went into **liquidation**. Several creditors could not be paid out of the assets of the business and Salomon was taken to court to recover the debts.

The claimant argued that since Salomon held most of the shares the business was **still in effect his own** and therefore he was liable for the business' debts.

However, the court held that the **assets** and **liabilities** of the **business** were that of the company as it was a **separate legal entity** in it own right. Therefore Salomon was not liable.

The **consequences of separate legal personality** are:

Limited liability

The **company** itself is **liable without limit for its own debts**. If the company buys goods from another company it owes the other company money.

Limited liability is a benefit to members. They own the business, so might be the people whom the creditors logically ask to pay the debts of the company if the company is unable to pay them itself.

Limited liability prevents this by stipulating the **creditors** of a limited company **cannot demand payment of the company's debts** from members of the company.

The only liability members have is to repay any amount unpaid on the nominal value of the shares that they hold.

Legal capacity

The company may enter into **agreements** and **contracts** in its own name and **sue** and be **sued** in matters of contract law, criminal law and tort. This means that where the company has suffered damage, it is the only proper claimant to demand compensation. This decision is taken by the members collectively under majority rule. Individual members are not permitted to take action themselves for wrongs suffered by the company.

Perpetual existence

Unlike partnerships which dissolve when partners leave or die, companies continue to exist despite changes in membership. Companies cannot die and can only cease when liquidated and removed from the companies register.

Assets

All assets transferred to the company become the property of the company. This means that although members collectively own the company, they do not have a direct claim on specific assets. As a result of this, companies may issue fixed and floating charges over their assets - chargeholders are safe in the knowledge that members cannot claim the assets for themselves.

(b) **The veil of incorporation**

Because companies have **separate legal personality** people can look at them and not know who or what owns or runs them. The fact that members are 'hidden' in this way is sometimes referred to as the '**veil of incorporation**'. Literally, the members are 'veiled' from view.

However, under the **circumstances** below, the veil may be lifted and the doctrine of separate legal personality set aside.

Lifting the veil by statute to enforce the law

A public company must obtain a **trading certificate** from the Registrar before it may commence trading. Failure to do so leads to **personal liability** of the directors for any loss or damage suffered by a third party resulting from a transaction made in contravention of the trading certificate requirement.

Persons (usually the directors) who are knowingly parties to **fraudulent or wrongful trading** shall be **personally responsible** under civil law for the debts and other liabilities of the company: s 213 and 214 Insolvency Act 1986.

Directors who participate in the management of a company in contravention of an order under the Company Directors Disqualification Act 1986 will be **jointly** or **severally liable** along with the company for the company's debts.

The Insolvency Act 1986 (s 217) makes it a criminal offence and the directors personally liable where they are a director of a company that goes into insolvent liquidation and they become involved with the directing, managing or promoting of a business which has an **identical name** to the original company, or a **name similar** enough to suggest a connection.

Lifting the veil to prevent evasion of obligations

A company may be identified with those who control it, for instance to determine its residency. The courts may also ignore the distinction between a company and its members and directors if the latter use that distinction to **evade** their **existing legal obligations**; *Gilford Motor Co Ltd v Horne 1933*.

In time of war a company is not permitted to trade with '**enemy aliens**'. The courts may draw aside the veil if, despite a company being registered in the UK, it is suspected that it is controlled by aliens.

The veil may also be lifted where directors **ignore** the separate legal personality of two companies and transfer assets from one to the other in disregard of their duties in order to avoid an existing liability *Re H and Others 1996*.

An application to wind up a company on the '**just and equitable**' ground under the Insolvency Act 1986 may involve the court lifting the veil to reveal the company as a **quasi-partnership**. This may happen where the company only has a few members, all of whom are actively involved in its affairs. Typically the individuals have operated contentedly as a company for years but then fall out, and one or more of them seeks to remove the others *Ebrahimi v Westbourne Galleries Ltd 1973*.

Lifting the veil in group situations

The principle of the veil of incorporation extends to the holding (parent) company/subsidiary relationship. Although holding companies and subsidiaries are part of a group under company law, they retain their **separate legal personalities**; *Adams v Cape Industries plc 1990*.

64 Mick

Text reference. Chapters 13 and 14.

Top tips Do not fall into the trap of devoting your efforts to the part that you think you will be best at, therefore denying or limiting yourself many of the marks available for the question as a whole.

Easy marks. This is a very straightforward question and you need to go into as much depth as possible in your answers to maximise the marks available to you. Notice in part (b) that you are asked for both the **procedures** and **documentation** needed to register the company. Notice also that the question is asking you about private limited companies, so you will gain no marks from discussing issues such as trading certificates.

Marking scheme

(a)	4-5 marks	A clear explanation of corporate personality with reference to case authority.
	2-3 marks	Some, but limited explanation of the concept, perhaps only reference to Salomon with no explanation.
	0-1 marks	Very little explanation of the concept.
(b)	4-5 marks	A good answer setting out most of the documents required.
	2-3 marks	Some knowledge but lacking in explanation, or perhaps an unbalanced answer focusing on only some of the documents.
	0–1 marks	Very limited knowledge or explanation.

(a) A legal 'person' possesses **legal rights** and is subject to **legal obligations**. The term 'person' is used to mean both individual human beings (natural persons) and other bodies, including registered companies.

Corporate personality

A company is **distinct** as a separate legal person from its owners or members and hence a 'veil of incorporation' exists between them. The distinction between a company and its members was clearly set out in *Salomon v Salomon & Co Ltd 1897*.

In this landmark case, the court held that Salomon, although he owned 20,001 out of 20,007 shares in Salomon & Co Ltd, was under **no personal liability** to the failed company or to its creditors. Additionally, the court held that debentures issued to him by the company created a valid security over the company's assets which ranked before the claims of unsecured creditors of the company.

Since then, the distinction has been developed in both case law and statute. In limited circumstances the metaphorical **veil will be lifted by statute or common law** in order to avoid the inequitable consequences of adhering strictly to the rule of law in Salomon's case.

Consequences of separate personality

As a result of having separate personality, a corporation can enter into **contracts** in its own right and will be liable for breach of contract and may have to pay **damages** or suffer some other remedy awarded against it. Conversely, it may sue on a contract, it being the proper person to bring an action, not the members. The fact that a company has limited legal liability means that the shareholders of the company cannot be required to contribute more than the amount outstanding (if any) on their shares. A company's assets and liabilities are its own, and members do not have an insurable interest.

(b) **Company registration**

Most companies are formed by **incorporation** under the Companies Act. Under this Act, an application should be completed and the following documents should be prepared and delivered to the Companies Registry to obtain registration of a company and a certificate of incorporation:

Memorandum of association

The memorandum is a simple document which states that the subscriber(s) wish to form a company and agree to become members of it, each taking at least one share. It is signed by each of them.

Articles of association

The articles will govern the procedures for the daily running of the company, including the voting rights attached to shares and the calling and conduct of meetings. They only need to be submitted if the company does not need model articles or if the model articles are to be amended.

Statement of proposed officers

This gives particulars of the company's first directors and secretary with their signed consent to act.

Statement of compliance

This confirms that the requirements of the Companies Act on company formation have been fully complied with.

Statement of capital and initial shareholdings

This is required from all companies with share capital. It contains details of the company's share capital and the initial shareholdings of the subscribers.

Fee

A registration fee.

Certificate of incorporation

Once these have been checked and found to be in order by the Registrar of Companies, a **certificate of incorporation** is issued under the Companies Act. This is conclusive evidence that the formalities of registration have been complied with. Alternatively, a company may be bought 'off the shelf' from an appropriate enterprise which has already incorporated a range of companies for sale. In such cases, the name of the company and the directors will need to be changed (as a minimum).

65 Public companies

Text reference. Chapter 14.

Top tips. This question from June 2010 is almost identical to a Pilot Paper question. The only difference is that the Pilot Paper question also required an explanation of the extra information which is required to be sent to the Registrar before a registered Public Limited Company can start trading. This extra information is provided at the end of the answer.

This is a straightforward question as it does not require much application of the law. Given that students traditionally tend to find the application questions more difficult, it is a good opportunity to gain much needed marks.

Easy marks. Stating and explaining all the required documents that should be sent to Companies House would earn you enough marks to pass this question.

ACCA examiner's answers. The ACCA examiner's answer to this question can be found at the back of this kit.

Examiner's comments. This question was answered well by all candidates. It was encouraging to see that candidates understood the documents needed and the procedures which need to be followed to set up a PLC. Full marks were frequently awarded. However, one point that has to be made is that a number of candidates still made use of the old, pre 2006 law, especially in relation to the memorandum of association. As a result they tended to overemphasise the importance of the memorandum and correspondingly to play down the importance of the application, which of course is now the most important document.

Marking scheme

This question requires candidates to list and explain the documents required to be submitted to the companies' registry in order to register a company.

8–10 marks:	Thorough explanation of the documents and procedure.
5–7 marks:	Reasonable treatment but perhaps lacking in detail.
3–4 marks:	Unbalanced answer, perhaps not dealing with all elements of the question or lacking in detailed knowledge of those elements.
0–2 marks:	Very weak answer demonstrating little understanding of the documents or procedure.

Registered companies

A registered company is a commercial concern which is incorporated and registered under the **Companies Act 2006**. A registered company always has a written constitution comprising its **articles of association** and any other **resolutions** or **agreements** that it may make. Any company not registered as a public company is a private company.

Registration

To register a new company, s9 requires an **application for registration** to be made and submitted, together with a fee, to the Registrar. The application must contain: the company's **proposed name,** the **location** of its **registered office** (England and Wales, Wales, Scotland or Northern Ireland), a statement that the **liability of members** is to be **limited** by **shares** or **guarantee** and a statement of the **intended address** of the **registered office**.

Additionally, the following documents should be prepared and accompany the application.

Memorandum of association

The memorandum is a simple document which states that the subscriber(s) wish to form a company and agree to become members of it, each taking at least one share. It is signed by each of them.

Articles of association

The articles will govern the procedures for the daily running of the company, including the voting rights attached to shares and the calling and conduct of meetings. They only need to be actually submitted if the company does not need the default model articles or if the model articles are to be amended.

Statement of proposed officers

This gives particulars of the company's first directors and secretary with their signed consent to act.

Statement of compliance

This is a statement which confirms that the requirements of the Companies Act on company formation have been fully complied with.

Statement of capital and initial shareholdings

This statement is required from all companies with share capital. It contains details of the company's share capital and the initial shareholdings of the subscribers.

Incorporation

Once the documents have been checked and found to be in order by the Registrar of Companies, a **certificate of incorporation** is issued. This is conclusive evidence that the formalities of registration have been complied with.

Additional information

Before a **public limited company** can trade, the directors must obtain a **trading certificate** by submitting a form signed by a director or secretary to the Registrar of Companies. The submission should include a **statement of compliance** that the nominal value of the **allotted share capital** is at least **£50,000,** plus details of any **preliminary expenses** and **payments** or **benefits** to **promoters**.

66 Company registers and accounting records

Text reference. Chapter 14.

Top tips. Another straightforward question that does not require application of the law. Jot down all the points you need to make before writing your answer to ensure your answer is complete.

Easy marks. Learn all the company registers, if you can state and explain them well you would earn almost enough marks to pass.

Marking scheme

			Marks
(a)	Register of members	2	
	Register of charges	1	
	Register of directors	1	
	Records of directors' service contracts	1	
			5
(b)	Sufficient to show company's transactions	2	
	Daily entries of cash	1	
	Record of assets and liabilities	1	
	Statement of stocks	1	
			5
			10

(a) **Company registers**

Under the Companies Act, companies are bound to keep a number of **statutory registers** available for public inspection and normally held at the company's registered office (although companies can nominate a single alternative inspection location).

- A **register of members** containing the name and address of each member and the class to which they belong, the number of shares held by them and the date on which they became and (when appropriate) ceased to be a member;
- A **register of charges** containing details of all fixed and floating charges affecting the company property or undertaking, setting out brief descriptions of property charged, the amount secured and the name of the chargee.
- A **register of directors** containing details of each individual's name and address (usually a service address), nationality, business occupation, and date of birth;
- **Records of service contracts**. Copies or written memoranda of all service contracts for directors, including contracts for services other than as the capacity of director.

(b) **Accounting records**

A company is required to keep accounting records **sufficient to show and explain the company's transactions**, so that it is possible at any time to determine the company's financial position and to ascertain that any balance sheet or profit and loss account complies with the Act.

The records must contain **daily entries of sums paid** and **received** (describing the nature and source of the transactions), and a **record of assets and liabilities**. Where the company deals in goods, the accounts must also contain **statements of stocktaking** and the stock held at the end of each financial year and **statements of goods bought and sold** (except retail sales).

67 Eden plc

Text reference. Chapter 14.

Top tips. Make sure that you address all three of the issues (with a clear sub-heading for each) and get the easy marks by identifying what the point of law is, eg in part (i) it is the personal liability of promoters etc. Even if you cannot say much about it, identifying the issue will earn you marks.

Easy marks. Don't forget to have a go at advising the parties involved in this question. Marks will be available as long as you base your advice on the conclusions you have reached.

Marking scheme

This question requires candidates to explain the law relating to company promoters. Marks will be allocated as follows:

8-10 marks	Full and thorough explanation of the law relating to promoters with good and accurate application of the law to the particular issues raised in the problem.
6-7 marks	Good treatment of the topic but perhaps not dealing with all the issues raised or lacking in some knowledge or application. Perhaps lacking balance in that it only deals with some of the elements of the question.
4-5 marks	Lacking in detail in some or all aspects or lacking in application.
0-3 marks	Some but little knowledge of the topic with little appropriate application.

Promoters

In the scenario described, Don has taken on the legal role of '**promoter**' to Eden plc. A promoter is 'one who undertakes to form a company with reference to a given project and to set it going and who takes the necessary steps to accomplish that purpose' *(Twycross v Grant 1877).*

The term promoter also includes anyone who makes any **business preparations** for the company. They will normally require the company to agree to reimburse their expenses incurred in the promotion and formation once the company has been incorporated.

A solicitor, accountant or other professional who acts in their **professional capacity** in connection with the formation of a company is not a promoter on that basis. Whether someone is a promoter is a question of fact.

(a) **Computer equipment**

The general rule is that a **promoter is personally liable** on any **completed pre-incorporation contract** entered into with a third party. A pre-incorporation contract is a contract purported to be made by a company or its agent at a time before the company has received its certificate of incorporation.

Since the **company does not exist** at the time the contract is made, it cannot be held liable in respect of its terms, nor can it ratify it or enforce it.

Section 51(1) CA 2006 provides that the person purporting to act for the company shall be **personally liable** on the contract subject to any agreement to the contrary.

It is irrelevant whether the **other party** knew that the company did not exist or whether the contract is made in the company's name or in the agent's name.

In the situation described involving Don and Eden plc, the **directors are not legally bound** to honour the purported contract with the computer equipment supplier. The supplier will have to take action against Don for breach of contract.

(b) **Patent**

A company may however enter into a **new contract** (a '**novation**') on similar terms after incorporation. Mere recognition of the pre-incorporation contract by **performing** it or **accepting** benefits under it is not sufficient to constitute a new contract. However, this new contract will of course require the third party to be willing to enter into it on the same terms.

In the situation described involving Don and Eden plc, there is simply **no contract involving the company**. If the other party does not wish to proceed, the directors will be unable to show any legal obligation for them to do so.

(c) **Equipment**

In order to overcome the difficulties posed by the law relating to pre-incorporation contracts, the promoter might seek to avoid liability by **postponing completion** of the contract until after incorporation of the company or by providing that their liability shall cease as and when the newly incorporated company enters a new contract on identical terms.

In the situation described involving Don and Eden plc, there is **no contract** since Eden plc does not wish to pursue the arrangements with Fad Ltd. Fad Ltd therefore has no cause of action against either Don (since the condition has not been fulfilled and therefore the contract has not come into existence) or the company.

68 Objects clause

Text reference. Chapter 15.

Top tips. Notice the different requirements of the parts of the question. Part (a) is asking just for the extent of the company objects, while part (b) asks for the meaning of *ultra vires* and also its effect.

Easy marks. Defining what *ultra vires* is.

Marking scheme

This question requires candidates to explain the extent of a company's objects clause, and in particular to explain the current operation of the doctrine of ultra vires.

8–10 marks	Thorough to complete answers, showing a detailed understanding of both elements of the question.
5–7 marks	A clear understanding of the topic, but perhaps lacking in detail. Alternatively an unbalanced answer showing good understanding of one part but less in the other.
2–4 marks	Some knowledge, although perhaps not clearly expressed, or very limited in its knowledge and understanding of the topic.
0–1 mark	Little or no knowledge of the topic.

(a) **Company objects**

A company's **constitution**, and in particular its **articles of association**, contains its **objects**. Under the Companies Act 1985, every company was required to state its objects so defining the **purpose of the company** and its capacity to act. Companies could **not** enter into agreements that were not consistent with their objects.

The **Companies Act 2006** changed matters and now all companies with model articles are **automatically** deemed to have completely **unrestricted objects** and so may enter into any contract so long as it is legal. However companies are permitted to **restrict** their objects by **special resolution**. Therefore should the members wish to prevent directors entering into certain types of contract they can do so.

(b) **Ultra vires**

The contractual capacity of a registered company is **defined by its objects clause** and this is usually unrestricted. Any contract entered into which is subject to a restriction under that clause is in theory *ultra vires* (and void). However, given that the validity of a company's acts cannot be questioned on the grounds of it having lacked legal capacity (s.39 CA 2006), the *ultra vires* rule is of very limited effect in so far as third parties are concerned.

Internal ultra vires

Internally, the *ultra vires* rule is still relevant. The **directors** owe a duty to act in **accordance** with the company's **constitution** and only to exercise powers for the purposes for which they were conferred. A member can obtain an injunction to restrain the doing of an *ultra vires* act before it is done. However, in the event that the directors are in breach of this duty, the action can be ratified by **ordinary resolution**.

External ultra vires

Externally, s.39 CA 2006 provides that *'the validity of an act done by a company shall not be called into question on the ground of lack of capacity by reason of anything in the company's constitution'*. Neither the company nor the third party can plead *ultra vires* to escape their obligations and there is no requirement for good faith. Therefore, the *ultra vires* rule has effectively been abolished in relation to acts done between a company and a third party unless the third party acts in bad faith and the directors exceed their authority. Now almost all such acts will be capable of validation at the instance of either party.

S.39 is supported by s.40 which states that *'in favour of a person dealing with a company in good faith, the power of the directors to bind the company, or authorise others to do so, shall be deemed to be free of any limitation under the company's constitution.'* This means that providing the **third party** acts in **good faith**, they can **assume that the directors have the authority to bind the company**. Third parties do not need to check the articles for any restrictions.

Any *ultra vires* transaction between a company and a director will be **voidable** at the instance of the company unless ratified or third party rights intervene or where restitution can no longer be made.

69 Articles

Text reference. Chapter 15.

Top tips. Make sure that you give the correct amount of time to the three parts of this question. The two mark section should only be allocated about 3½ minutes. Don't over-run on any one part as that means that you will deny yourself the opportunity for the easy marks on the later parts of the question. Notice that part (b) is effectively asking you two things, as it requires the contractual effect on both members and non-members.

Easy marks. When you state a point of law in an answer the easy way to double your marks is to cite a case or two in support. The law on articles includes a lot of straightforward quotable cases, so include as many of them as you can.

Examiner's comments. This was a popular question on this paper and it was relatively well done. The worst done part was part (c) where many candidates merely talked about the requirement for a special resolution and did not consider the issue of whether alterations were *bona fide* and in the interests of the company as a whole.

Marking scheme

6-10 marks	Thorough treatment of both the content and effect of articles of association. Answers towards the top end will provide cases to exemplify the operation of the articles and will be rewarded accordingly.
0-5 marks	Weak understanding of the articles generally. Perhaps unbalanced in that there is knowledge of some cases but little in other important areas.

(a) **Model articles**

A company's articles of association deal mainly with matters affecting the **internal conduct of the company's affairs** including the issue and transfer of shares and class rights, dividends and alterations of capital structure, the convening and conduct of general meetings, the appointment, powers and proceedings of directors and company accounts.

A company may have its own full-length special articles or it may adopt **model articles**. Model articles are deemed to apply to the extent that the company does not submit its own articles in substitution on registration. The provisions of the Companies Act override a company's articles where they prohibit something which, on the face of it, is permitted by the articles or where the Companies Act require a special procedure to be followed.

(b) **Effect of the articles of association**

A company's **articles of association**, bind:

- Its members to the company,
- The company to its members, and
- Its members to each other (s.33 CA 2006).

This contractual effect **does not bind the company** to **third parties** and it applies only to rights and obligations which affect members in their capacity as members *(Hickman v Kent or Romney Marsh Sheepbreeders Association 1915)*. Therefore in *Eley v Positive Government Security Life Assurance Co 1876* when Eley, although a member of the company, brought a claim in his capacity as solicitor and not as member, the contractual effect of s.33 could not be relied upon.

The **members are contractually bound** by the articles in their **dealings with one another** as if each had separately agreed to be bound by them *(Rayfield v Hands 1958)*. If an outsider enters into a contract with a company which is silent on a particular point but that same point is covered by the articles, then the contract is deemed to incorporate the articles to that extent *(Re New British Iron Co, ex parte Beckwith 1898)*. Essentially in such cases the articles operate to supply a missing term in a contract made with the company.

(c) **Altering the articles of association**

A company's **articles of association** may be **altered** by the company by passing a **special resolution** to that effect in general meeting. The articles once properly altered are binding on the company and its members in the same way as the original articles.

Restrictions

An article **cannot be made unalterable** by declaring it to be unalterable in the articles or by requiring a greater majority vote than 75% or by means of a separate contract under which the company undertakes not to alter it.

An alteration will be void if it **conflicts with the Companies Act**. Equally it will be void if it compels any member to subscribe for additional shares or if the majority who approve it are not acting **bona fide** in what they deem to be the **interests of the company as a whole**.

An alteration **cannot have retrospective effect**. Any alteration which varies class rights must be made according to the correct rights variation procedure. An alteration purporting to give the majority the right to buy the shares of the minority will not be valid *(Brown v British Abrasive Wheel Co 1919).*

In *Greenhalgh v Arderne Cinemas Ltd 1950* the Court of Appeal made it clear that the **'bona fide** for the **benefit of the company as a whole**' test referred to above is a **single test** and also a **subjective test** (ie what did the majority believe?). The company as a whole in this context means the **general body of shareholders**. The test is whether every 'individual hypothetical member' would in the honest opinion of the majority benefit from the alteration.

Provided the purpose is to benefit the company as a whole, the alteration does not become invalid by reason of the **minority suffering special detriment** or some members escaping loss *(Allen v Gold Reefs of West Africa Ltd 1900).*

A company **cannot be prevented** from **altering its articles of association** where such an alteration causes a breach of a contract entered into by the company although it may be liable for damages if that is the result *(Southern Foundries (1926) Ltd v Shirlaw 1940).*

70 Fred

Text reference. Chapter 15.

Top tips. This is a short scenario so it should be easy for you to identify the issue. Make sure you state what it is at the start of your answer. You must then state the relevant law and apply it to Fred's case before coming to a conclusion.

Easy marks. Stating the rules of amending the articles of association.

Examiner's comments. This question required candidates to examine the law relating to the power of companies to change their articles of association. As the substantive law, either in the statute or case law relating to this area has not been changed this question allowed even those candidates who were unaware of the Companies Act 2006 an opportunity to do well. Unfortunately it was an opportunity not taken by many candidates, as the question tended to be done inadequately. A number of candidates wilfully misinterpreted the question as relating to directors' duties and wasted a lot of time and effort in pursuing that path. The majority of candidates recognised that the issue was about the alteration of articles, and recognised that it required the passing of a special resolution with a 75% majority. However very few were able to explain the tests for deciding whether the alteration could be challenged in court. Even those who were aware of the bona fide '*interest of the company as whole*' test tended not to explain it further, with only a small number considering the situation of the '*hypothetical individual*' member.

As a result although many concluded that the alteration could be challenged in the courts, no legal principle or authority was cited in support, or irrelevant law relating to directors or indeed partnerships was cited.

Marking scheme

This question requires candidates to examine the law relating to the power of companies to change their articles of association.

8–10 marks:	Candidates will exhibit a thorough knowledge of the relevant law together with the ability to analyse the problems contained in the question.
5–7 marks:	Candidates will exhibit a sound knowledge of the relevant law together with the ability to recognise the issues contained in the question. Knowledge may be less detailed or analysis less focused.
3-4 marks:	Identification of some of the central issues in the question and an attempt to apply the appropriate law. Towards the bottom of this range of marks there will be major shortcomings in analysis or application of law.
0–2 marks:	Very weak answers which might recognise what the question is about but show no ability to analyse or answer the problem as set out.

Issue

The members of Glad Ltd wish to **amend the company's articles of association** to force Fred to sell them his shares in order to remove him from being a member of the company. The question that must be answered is **can** the articles be amended for this, and if so, will the amendment be **legally binding**?

Articles of association

S.33 CA2006 provides that a company's **articles of association bind a company to its members, the members to the company and members to members**. Members are deemed to have separately covenanted with each other and the company to observe the provisions of the articles.

Altering articles of association

A company's articles of association may be altered by the company by passing a special resolution to that effect in general meeting. The articles once properly altered are binding on the company and its members in the same way as the original articles.

However, such alterations will be **void** if they compel any member to **subscribe for additional shares** or if the **majority** who approve them are not acting **bona fide** in what they deem to be the **interests of the company as a whole**.

In *Greenhalgh v Arderne Cinemas Ltd 1950* the Court of Appeal made it clear that 'the company as a whole' in this context means the **general body of shareholders**. The test is partly subjective and partly objective, ie whether every 'individual hypothetical member' would in the honest opinion of the majority benefit from the alteration.

Provided the purpose is to benefit the company as a whole, the alteration does not become invalid by reason of the **minority suffering special detriment** or some members escaping loss (*Allen v Gold Reefs of West Africa Ltd 1900*).

Case law

The following cases are relevant to Fred's situation.

In *Brown v British Abrasive Wheel Co 1919*, the 98% majority was prepared to inject more capital into the company, but only if they could acquire the shares of the 2% minority, who refused to sell. The majority purported to alter the articles to provide for **compulsory acquisition** of the shares on a fair value basis. The minority objected and the alteration was held to be invalid.

In *Sidebottom v Kershaw, Leese & Co Ltd 1920* a new article permitted the acquisition of the shares of minority shareholders who carried on a competing business. The validity of such an alternation was upheld by the court.

However, in *Dafen Tinplate Co Ltd v Llanelly Steel Co (1907) Ltd 1920* a similar amendment was held to be invalid because it permitted the company to acquire the shares of any member, even if there were no specific grounds to show that it would benefit the company.

Fred

Following the principles set out it above, it appears that a new article that requires the acquisition of a member's shares would be valid if it would be of **benefit to the company**, and this certainly appears to apply in Fred's case (he is in direct competition with Glad Ltd). However, the **resolution actually proposed by Glad Ltd** would allow the company to acquire the shares of **any member** for a fair price. Therefore it is likely to be held as invalid under the facts of the *Dafen* case.

71 Company names

Text reference. Chapter 15.

Top tips. Before you start to write your answer, take a minute to go through in your head and jot down on a piece of paper the main points that you need to make – in parts (a) and (b) this means at least four good company name rules and facts about passing off.

Easy marks. Get the basic marks for each part by explaining the importance of a company's name, the tort of passing off and the role of the company names adjudicators.

Examiner's comments. This question, divided into three parts, required candidates to explain the limitations on the use of company names, the tort of 'passing off' and finally the role of the company names adjudicators under the Companies Act 2006.

It has to be said that this question, and in particular part (a) was extremely well done. The great majority of candidates were well able to cite most of the rules governing what names can and can't be used by companies. Part (b) was also done fairly well with many candidates able to cite cases in support of their explanation of the law. Part (c), which introduced the new concept of the company names adjudicator was also done fairly well. It is pleasing to see that candidates are now coming to terms with the 'new' companies legislation.

Marking scheme

(a)	3–4 marks	Good explanation of the rules relating to company names.
	0–2 marks	Some but limited knowledge of the control over company names.
(b)	3–4 marks	Good explanation of the tort of 'passing off' with case authority to support the explanation.
	0–2 marks	Some but limited knowledge of 'passing off'.
(c)	2 marks	Good explanation of the role of the company names adjudicators and why they are necessary.
	0–1 mark	Little if any knowledge of the concept.

(a) **Company name**

The **name of a company** must be specified in the company's **constitution** and serves to **identify the company**, distinguishing it from any other company. The Registrar of Companies has statutory powers of control over the choice of names in order to ensure that they comply with both statutory and common law restrictions and requirements. These apply both on the initial registration of a company by its promoters and on any subsequent change of name by the company.

Public and private companies

If the company is a **public company**, the name must end with the words 'public limited company' or 'plc'. If it is a **private limited company**, the name must end with the word 'limited' or 'ltd'. This is except in the case of private companies limited by guarantee and companies licensed before 25 February 1982 where the word 'limited' may be omitted if certain conditions are satisfied. Appropriate Welsh wording may be used by companies having a registered office in Wales.

Restrictions on names

A company **cannot share the name of any existing company** which appears in the statutory index at the Companies Registry. Nor can a company bear a name which, in the Secretary of State's opinion, is **offensive, sensitive** or constitutes **a criminal offence** or suggests a connection with the **government** or a **local authority**. Words such as 'British' or 'National' will only be permitted if the nature and size of the company is appropriate. A name which suggests some **professional expertise** will be permitted only if that expertise exists in the company and appropriate professional bodies have no objection.

Under the Companies Act 2006, the **Secretary of State** may order a company to change its name where it is the same or 'too like' another on the register.

(b) **Passing off**

Under the common law, a company can be prevented from using its registered name if the use of that name causes the company's goods or services to be confused with those of another company. The court may grant an injunction in a **'passing-off'** tort action brought by that other company and may also force the defendant company to change its name (*Ewing v Buttercup Margarine Co Ltd 1917*).

In this case, a sole trader was prevented from using the business name 'The Buttercup Dairy Co' in the north of England because of confusion with the business in the London area of Buttercup Margarine Co Ltd.

If, however, the two companies' businesses are different, confusion is unlikely to occur, and hence the courts will refuse to grant an injunction: *Dunlop Pneumatic Tyre Co Ltd v Dunlop Motor Co Ltd 1907*

The complaint will also not succeed if the claimant lays claim to the exclusive use of a word which has a general use: *Aerators Ltd v Tollit 1902.*

(c) **Company Names Adjudicators**

Under the Companies Act 2006, companies have the right to appeal to the **Company Names Adjudicators** if they feel that another company's name is too similar. The Adjudicators will look into the case and make a decision which is binding on both parties. This decision may be to **compel a name change** (including in some cases the determination of what the new name will be) or to do nothing. If a party is unhappy with the decision they may appeal it in court.

72 Various terms

Text reference. Chapter 13.

Top tips. Read this sort of question very carefully before launching yourself into the answer. Make sure that you have clearly distinguished between the various terms in your own mind. The examiner noted that in part (c) some candidates thought that plc meant private limited company. This must have been as a result of their not stopping to think properly before they wrote their answer, as private companies had already been covered in part (b).

Easy marks. As with many questions of this type, the easy marks are for defining the terms.

Examiner's comments. This was another very popular question with the majority of candidates attempting it. Usually, it was answered well. The majority observed that the question was in parts and structured their answers accordingly: only a small minority grouped everything together and produced a confused answer.

In part (a) on limited liability partnerships, some candidates based their answers around the 1907 Act and did not mention the 2000 Act, and hence did not score very good marks. Part (b) on private limited companies was generally well-attempted. In part (c) on plcs, a minority of candidates thought that the term stood for private (instead of public) limited companies

Marking scheme

8-10 marks	Good to complete answer which shows a knowledge of the meaning and effect of the three terms.
5-7 marks	Some basic knowledge of what is meant by the terms, but no real depth of understanding. Perhaps an unbalanced answer that only deals with one or two parts of the question.
0-4 marks	Little knowledge or knowledge of only one of the forms.

(a) **LLP**

LLP stands for **limited liability partnership**. This is a form of partnership created under the **Limited Liability Partnership Act 2000**, which is actually a **corporate body with a separate legal personality.** This differentiates it from a traditional partnership, which has no separate legal personality and in which the partners' liability is unlimited. The limited liability partnership, which is denoted by the suffix LLP, therefore has some of the attributes of a limited company.

To **incorporate** a limited liability partnership, the subscribers must lodge a document with the **Registrar of Companies**. This must include the **name** of the partnership, the **location of its registered office** (eg England and Wales), the **address of the registered office**, the **names** and **addresses of all the members** of the LLP, the identities of those members who are going to be '**designated**' **members** and the registration fee. Designated members are responsible for the publicity requirements of the LLP including signing and delivering the accounts.

Every member of the LLP is an agent of the partnership and as such, provided the member has authority to act**, the LLP will be bound by its members' acts**. An LLP does not dissolve on a member leaving it, but, like a company, continues in existence. A formal winding up is required if the members decide to dissolve an LLP.

(b) **Ltd**

'**Ltd**' shows that the business organisation is a limited company, and, in particular, **a private limited company** as opposed to a public limited company. The essential characteristic of a company is the distinction between the corporation and its members (*Salomon v Salomon & Co Ltd 1897*) which means that the company's assets and liabilities are its own and a company can enter into and enforce contracts in its own right. Likewise, a company is liable for breach of contract and may have to pay damages or suffer some other remedy against it.

The significance of the word 'limited' is that the **liability of the company's members is limited to such amount as is unpaid on their shares.** Once shares are fully paid up, the owners of those shares have no further liability in respect of the debts of the company. A company will not cease to exist on a change in its membership.

The **name** of a private limited company must end with the word '**limited**' or '**ltd**', save where a specific exception applies, in order to publicise to parties dealing with the company the fact of its members' limited liability. Appropriate Welsh wording may be used by companies having a registered office in Wales.

(c) **plc**

'**plc**' denotes a **public limited company** which is also a separate legal entity distinct from its members. As with a private limited company, **the members' liability is limited to the amount outstanding on their shares**. A public company must **state in its constitution that it is a public company** and its **name** must end with the words '**public limited company**' or '**PLC**' or '**plc**' or its Welsh equivalent. A public company is one registered as such under the Companies Act.

Unlike a private company**, a public company can raise capital by offering its shares and debentures to the public.** Only a public company can be listed on the Stock Exchange or other investment exchange. Generally speaking, a public limited company is subject to more stringent accounting and other regulations than a private limited company.

73 Discount and premium

Text reference. Chapter 18.

Top tips. Notice that the requirement in this question falls into two parts. It asks you to explain both 'the meaning' and 'the effect' of the two issues. This should help you build up marks in your answer by making sure that you address both of these requirements. For example, in part (a), to explain the **meaning** of the concept, you really have to answer the question 'discount to what?' In other words, you have to explain that shares have a **nominal value** attached and that they cannot be issued at a discount to that. The basic **effect** of the concept is that if shares are issued at a discount to nominal value, this is illegal. This means that any money due to make the payment up to nominal value could be called in event of liquidation. This is similar to the effect of having partly paid shares.

Easy marks. There are no easy marks unless you can explain the various rules that are required.

Marking scheme

			Marks
(a)	Explanation of nominal value	2	
	Protection of creditors needed	1	
	Explanation of issue at discount	1	
	Valuation of non cash consideration by plcs	1	
	Other exceptions	1	
			6
(b)	Explanation of share premium	2	
	Examples of uses	2	
			4
			10

(a) **Issuing shares at a discount**

A company may issue shares within the **authority granted to directors**. Every share has a **nominal value** and **cannot be allotted at a discount** to that value s580. In order to protect the company's creditors, a company must obtain in money or money's worth consideration of a value at least equal to the nominal value of the shares allotted. The **uncalled capital** passes as a debt on a transfer of the shares so that it is payable by the holder at the time payment is demanded (s588).

If shares are allotted at a **discount**, the allottee is still **liable to pay the full nominal value** together with interest at the appropriate rate. The issue of shares at a price which is less than the **market value** (but equal to or more than the nominal value) of existing shares does not contravene the provision.

In the case of **private companies**, shares may be allotted for **inadequate consideration** by the acceptance of **goods** or **services at an over value**. A blatant and unjustified overvaluation will not, however, be upheld. Any non-cash consideration must be valued in the case of public companies.

It is not a contravention of s580 to issue shares at par but to pay an **underwriting fee** or other **commission** which reduces the net amount received below par value provided the company's articles permit it to do so.

(b) **The share premium account**

A company may issue shares for a price in **excess** of the **nominal value** of those shares. The excess is called the **'share premium'** and must be credited to a **share premium account**. Where the shares are issued for a non-cash consideration in excess of the shares' nominal value, the excess should still be credited to the share premium account, since the statutory rule applies to issues of shares 'at a premium whether for cash or otherwise'.

The general rule is that reduction of the share premium account is subject to the same restrictions as reduction of share capital. **No part of the account can be distributed as dividend**. The account can be used to pay up fully paid shares under a **bonus issue** since this operation simply converts one form of fixed capital into another.

It can also be used to pay **issue expenses** and **commission** in respect of a **new share issue**.

Furthermore, the share premium account is included in the **'undistributable reserves'** when determining whether a dividend can lawfully be declared by a public company.

74 Capital terms I

Text reference. Chapter 16.

Top tips. Notice the mark allocations for the four separate parts of this question and make sure that you stick to the associated timings. You should only be spending about 3½ minutes on a 2 mark part.

Easy marks. Make sure that in each part of the question you focus on the specific subject of that part, eg issued capital, and explain it in as much depth as you can.

Marking scheme

This question seeks an explanation of the nominal value of shares and their market value together with an explanation of the two types of share capital listed.

8-10 marks	Thorough explanation of all the elements in the question.
5-7 marks	Thorough treatment of some of the elements, or a less complete treatment of all of them.
0-4 marks	Unbalanced to very unbalanced answer, focusing on only one element and ignoring the others, or one which shows little understanding of the subject mater of the question.

Shares

A **share** is **the interest** of a **shareholder** in the company measured by a **sum of money**, for the purpose of liability in the first place, and of investment in the second, but also consisting of a series of mutual covenants entered into by all the shareholders inter se *(Borland's Trustees v Steel Bros & Co Ltd 1901)*. It is a transferable form of property carrying rights and obligations.

(a) **Nominal value**

The **nominal value** of a share is the **fixed monetary amount specified** in the **constitution** and does not usually change. The nominal value indicates how much the company raised when the shares were first issued (assuming they were fully paid up) and forms the company's capital which is subsequently used for investment in the operation of the company. For example, a company may issue 100,000 shares at £1 nominal value. If the shares are fully paid, the shareholders will pay a total of £100,000 to the company.

(b) **Market value**

Shares of a public company, once issued, may be traded – publicly or privately – so that the identity of some or all shareholders changes. In trading these shares, the shareholders may, subject to certain constraints, agree **a price for the shares that does not necessarily match the nominal value**. This is known as its **market value**. If the company is performing well and its prospects are good, the market value may be higher than the nominal value. Alternatively, the market value may fall below the nominal value.

(c) **Issued capital**

A company's **issued share capital** is the type, class, number and amount of shares actually held by its shareholders. A company may issue ordinary shares for cash provided it has the **authority** to do so. The authority to issue – or allot – shares is normally given to the directors by the company's articles of association. Alternatively, an ordinary resolution can be passed which gives the directors authority. A company may only allot shares within this authority but need not issue as many shares as it is authorised to.

In the case of a **public limited company**, the **issued share capital must be at least £50,000** of which at least one quarter plus the full amount of any share premium must be paid up.

(c) **Paid-up capital**

Paid-up capital is the amount of a company's issued share capital for which the company has actually **received payment** from the shareholders. If a company's shares have a nominal value of £1, it is usual, although not necessary, for the whole amount to be paid immediately. The company may for example request a first payment of 50p per share, in which case the shares are said to be part-paid. Until the full nominal value of the shares is paid, the shareholders will retain liability for the unpaid element. This element is referred to as **uncalled capital**.

75 Shares and debentures

Text reference. Chapters 16 and 17

Top tips. You may be tempted to write more than you need to when answering this question. Remember that only ten marks are on offer for all three parts - that means three or four marks per part. Nothing elaborate is needed, just make enough points in each part and then move on.

The marking scheme indicates that you would be awarded marks for the standard of your overall answer, rather than per part.

Easy marks. All marks in this question are easy – you only need to state simple facts about each source of capital.

Examiner's comments. The majority of candidates dealt with the question well, indeed it was the best answered question in the paper, but [in] some answers there was a tendency to define [the investments] in terms of each other and hence effectively to repeat information. Surprisingly candidates were less successful at defining the ordinary share, although those who made use of the definition in Borland's Trustees v Steel (1901) invariably produced reasonable answers.

Marking scheme

This question requires candidates to consider the various investment mechanisms available to investors.

8–10 marks	Full understanding and explanation of the various forms of investment.
5–7 marks	Lacking in detail in some or all aspects of the possible investment forms. Unbalanced answer that only focuses on some of the forms.
3–4 marks	Some, but little, knowledge of the topic.
0–2 marks	Little if any knowledge of the topic.

(a) **Ordinary shares**

According to the decision in *Borland's Trustee v Steel Bros & Co Ltd 1901* a **share** is; 'the interest of a shareholder in the company measured by a sum of money, for the purpose of a liability in the first place, and of interest in the second, but also consisting of a series of mutual covenants entered into by all the shareholders *inter se*'.

There are three consequences of this definition.

- The share must be **paid for** ('liability'). The nominal value of the share fixes this liability; it is the base price of the share eg a £1 ordinary share.
- It gives a **proportionate entitlement** to dividends, votes and any return of capital ('interest').
- It is a form of **bargain** ('mutual covenants') between shareholders which underlies such principles as majority control and minority protection.

A share's **nominal value** is its face value. So a £1 ordinary share for instance, has a nominal value of £1. No share can be issued at a value below its nominal value. However, the company may allow shareholders to pay less than the full nominal value when then shares are purchased.

Any **outstanding liability** can be called upon at a later date and this amount represents the shareholder's only liability should the company be liquidated.

Possible **drawbacks** of ordinary shares include the possibility that no dividends are paid and/or their market value will fall if the company is not profitable.

(b) **Preference shares**

Preference shares are regarded as a slightly safer investment than ordinary shares since they carry one or more rights. By default they are deemed to have **identical rights** to ordinary shares. However, a company's articles or resolutions may create differences between them.

Common differences include:

- A **preference share** may carry a **prior right** to receive an **annual dividend of fixed amount**, say a dividend of 6% of the share's nominal value. Dividends are usually **cumulative** – if they are not paid one year they rollover to the next.
- A **preference share does not usually carry a right to vote, or voting is permitted only in specified circumstances**. For example, failure to pay the preference dividend, variation of their rights or a resolution to wind up.
- **Preference shares** may carry a **priority right** to **return** of **capital**. Essentially this means that the amount paid up on the preference shares is to be repaid in liquidation **before** anything is repaid to **ordinary shareholders**. However this right has a price. Usually holders of the preference shares are not entitled to share in **surplus assets** when the ordinary share capital has been repaid.

(c) **Debentures**

A **debenture** is the written acknowledgement of a debt by a company, normally containing provisions as to payment of interest and the terms of repayment of capital.

A debenture is usually a printed legal document. There are three main types.

- **Single debentures**. These are one-off debentures issued to individual lenders such as banks in return for a secured loan or overdraft.
- **Debentures issued as a series**. These are used when finance is raised from a number of different lenders who provide different amounts on different dates and the intention is that they should rank equally in their right to repayment.
- **Debenture stock subscribed to by a large number of lenders**. This type of debenture is used when a company wishes to publicly raise funds from a number of lenders at the same time. Only public companies may use this method as it constitutes a prospectus.

Whatever the type of debenture, holders are **creditors** of the company. Unlike shareholders they are entitled to receive **interest payments** even if the company is not profitable.

A debenture may create a **charge** over the company's assets as security for the debt.

Fixed charges attach to the asset as soon as the charge is created. If the company disposes of the charged asset it will either **repay the secured debt** out of the proceeds of sale, or **pass the asset over to the purchaser** still subject to the charge.

Floating charges attach to the asset on **crystallisation** (specific circumstances which cause a floating charge to convert into a fixed charge), rather than on creation. This means floating charges rank after fixed charges for payment if both types of charge are secured on the same asset. Floating charges are usually secured on assets such as **receivables** or **inventory**.

76 Capital terms II

Text reference. Chapters 13 and 16.

Top tips. Notice the mark allocations for the four separate parts of this question and make sure that you stick to the associated timings. You should only be spending about 3½ minutes on a 2 mark part.

Easy marks. Make sure that in each part of the question you focus on the specific subject of that part, eg paid-up capital, and explain it in as much depth as you can.

Examiner's comments. This was the first question that required an understanding of the provision in the Companies Act 2006 and unfortunately the majority of candidates were simply unaware of the changes introduced by that piece of legislation. As a result part (a) was very inadequately done. Answers also indicated that many candidates still are of the opinion that the memorandum of association is still the most important constitutional document for companies and that it contains the company's 'authorised capital', a concept completely removed by the 2006 Act.

Marking scheme

This question seeks an explanation of the different types of share capital listed together with an explanation of the difference between the nominal value of shares and their market value.

8–10 marks: Thorough explanation of all of the elements in the question.

5–7 marks: Thorough treatment of some of the elements, or a less complete treatment of all of them.

0–4 marks: Unbalanced to very unbalanced answer, focusing on only one element and ignoring the others, or one which shows little understanding of the subject matter of the question.

Shares

A **share** is **the interest** of a **shareholder** in the company measured by a **sum of money**, for the purpose of liability in the first place, and of investment in the second, but also consisting of a series of mutual covenants entered into by all the shareholders inter se *(Borland's Trustees v Steel Bros & Co Ltd 1901).* It is a transferable form of property carrying rights and obligations.

(a) **Statement of capital and initial shareholdings**

As part of the process of forming a company, a return known as a **statement of capital and initial shareholdings** is required to be made to the **Registrar of Companies**.

This statement provides a **public record** of the following details in respect of the **share capital** of the company and is **up to date** as of the statement date.

- The **total number** of shares of the company
- The **aggregate nominal value** of the shares
- For each **class of share**, the **prescribed particulars** of any rights attached, the **total number** of shares in the class and the **aggregate nominal value** of shares in the class
- The **amount paid up** and the amount (if any) **unpaid** on each share, either on account of the nominal value of the share or by way of premium.

There should be **sufficient information** to **identify each subscriber** to the Memorandum of Association with the **number**, **nominal value** and **class of share** taken by them on **formation** as well as **amounts paid** and **unpaid** on the **nominal value** and any **share premium**. This information must be provided for **each class of share** the subscriber will hold on formation.

(b) **Authorised minimum issued capital in a public company**

A company's **issued share capital** is the **type**, **class**, **number** and **amount of shares** actually held by its shareholders. In the case of a **public limited company**, the **issued share capital must be at least £50,000** or the prescribed **Euro** equivalent.

(c) **Paid-up capital**

Paid-up capital is the amount of a company's **issued share capital** for which the company has actually **received payment** from the shareholders. If a company's shares have a nominal value of £1, it is usual, although not necessary, for the whole amount to be paid immediately. The company may for example request a first payment of 50p per share, in which case the shares are said to be **part-paid**. Until the full nominal value of the shares is paid, the **shareholders** will **retain liability** for the unpaid element. This element is referred to as **uncalled capital**. Shares in a public company must be one quarter paid up.

(d) **Nominal and market value**

The **nominal value** of a share is the **fixed monetary amount** specified in the constitution and does not usually change.

Shares of a **public company** may be traded on a stock market. As part of the deal, the parties may agree **a price for the shares that does not necessarily match the nominal value**. This is known as its **market value**. For example, if the company is performing well and its prospects are good, the market value may be higher than the nominal value. Alternatively, the market value may fall below the nominal value.

77 Capital maintenance and reducing share capital

Text reference. Chapter 18.

Top tips. The use of examples to illustrate the types of reduction available to companies is a quick and easy method of demonstrating your knowledge.

Easy marks. Defining the principle of capital maintenance and stating the three methods of capital reduction will get you the basic marks. However, you need to provide some explanation of the reduction methods and outline the procedure to pass.

Examiner's comments. Part (a) required candidates to comment on their understanding of the doctrine of capital maintenance. A majority of candidates correctly identified that the capital should be maintained as a buffer for creditors and should not be used to pay dividends to shareholders. A number of candidates went on to explain that shares should not be issued below nominal value, the rules relating to the payment of dividends and that public companies are required to have £50,000 minimum share capital. A minority of candidates struggled to clearly explain the doctrine and as a result spent a lot of time discussing the different types of shares and debt (fixed and floating charges) for which no marks were awarded.

Part (b) required candidates to discuss when a company may want to reduce its capital and the procedure to be adopted by both public and private companies. A vast majority of candidates correctly identified when a reduction in capital would be appropriate, a few also mentioned share buyback for which credit was given.

With regard to the procedural aspects there appeared to be some confusion. A number correctly distinguished the procedural differences, however, many candidates went off tangent by either writing a substantial amount of text regarding share buyback or a combination of company law points, which were not directly related to the question.

Overall, this was very well attempted question. It appears that candidates are gradually becoming more familiar with the technical aspects of the Companies Act 2006.

Marking scheme

(a)	3–4 marks	Thorough explanation of the doctrine of capital maintenance perhaps with some examples of its application.
	0–2 marks	Some knowledge but lacking in detail.
(b)	4–6 marks	Good to full consideration of the procedure for reducing capital. Reference must be made to the 2006 Act procedure and the difference between public and private companies should be mentioned specifically.
	2–3 marks	Some general knowledge but lacking in detail as regards to the process or not mentioning the difference between the two company forms.
	0–1 mark	Little or no understanding of the process.

(a) **Capital maintenance**

Capital maintenance is a fundamental principle of company law. It states that limited companies should not be allowed to make payments out of capital except in certain limited circumstances.

The Companies Act contains many examples of control upon **capital payments**. These include provisions restricting dividend payments, and capital reduction schemes.

Another rule of capital maintenance is that **shares** cannot be **issued at a discount**.

The principle **ensures a minimum amount of capital** is left in the company to protect creditors. However, it is often also in the shareholders' best interests too since it acts as a guard against the business running out of capital and potentially becoming insolvent.

(b) **Reducing share capital**

A limited company is permitted without restriction to cancel **unissued shares** as that change does not alter its financial position.

There are **three basic methods of reducing issued share capital** specified in s 641 of the Companies Act 2006.

Extinguish or reduce liability on partly paid shares

For example, a company has shares with a nominal value of £1 which are 75p paid up and it chooses to reduce the nominal value to 75p or to a figure between 75p and £1. Nothing is repaid to the shareholders; it is their potential future liability on the shares which is reduced.

Pay off part of paid-up share capital out of surplus assets

For example, a company has shares with a nominal value of £1 which are fully paid and it chooses to reduce the nominal value from £1 to 70p and repays 30p in the pound to shareholders.

Cancel paid-up share capital which has been lost or which is no longer represented by available assets

For example, a company has shares with a nominal value of £1 which are fully paid, but its net assets are only worth 50p per share. Therefore it has a debit balance on its reserves and is unable to pay dividends to its shareholders. By reducing the nominal value to 50p per share, it is able to write off the debit balance, and if it is profitable, it can pay dividends to the shareholders immediately without having to wait for future profits to clear the debt.

Procedure

A limited company may reduce its issued share capital if:

- It has **power** to do so in its articles. If it does not have power in the articles, these may be amended by a **special resolution.**
- It passes a **special resolution**. If the articles have been amended, this is another special resolution.
- It obtains **confirmation** of the reduction **from the court** (public companies only), or makes a **statement of solvency** (private companies only).

Court approval

When the court receives an application for reduction of capital its **first concern** is the effect of the reduction on the company's ability to pay its debts, that is, that the creditors are protected.

If the reduction is by extinguishing liability or paying off part of paid-up share capital, the court requires that **creditors** shall be **invited** by advertisement to state their objections (if any) to the reduction. Where paid-up share capital is cancelled, the court **may** require an invitation to creditors.

Normally the company persuades the court to dispense with advertising for creditors' objections (which can be commercially damaging to the company). This may be achieved by **paying off the creditors** before application is made to the court, or it may produce to the court a **guarantee**, say from the company's bank, that its existing debts will be paid in full.

The **second** concern of the court, where there is more than one class of share, is whether the reduction is fair in its effect on different classes of shareholder.

If the reduction is, **in the circumstances**, a **variation of class rights** the **consent** of the class must be obtained under the variation of class rights procedure.

Within each class of share it is usual to make a **uniform reduction** of every share by the same amount per share, though this is **not** obligatory.

The court may also be concerned that the **reduction should not confuse or mislead people who may deal with the company in future**. It may insist that the company add 'and reduced' to its name or publish explanations of the reduction.

If the court is satisfied that the reduction is in order, it confirms the reduction by making an order to that effect. A **copy of the court order** and a **statement of capital**, approved by the court, to show the altered share capital is delivered to the Registrar who issues a certificate of registration.

Solvency statement

A private company need not apply to the court if it supports its special resolution with a solvency statement. A **solvency statement** is a **declaration** by the directors, provided **15 days** in advance of the meeting where the special resolution is to be voted on. It states there is **no ground** to suspect the company is currently **unable** or will be **unlikely to be able** to pay its debts for the next **twelve months**. All possible liabilities must be taken into account and the statement should be in the prescribed form, naming all the directors. Copies of the special resolution and solvency statement must be sent within 15 days of being passed to the Registrar.

78 Class rights

Text reference. Chapter 16.

Top tips. Class rights and their variation are often thought of as a difficult technical subject, but the law is relatively straightforward. Remember the rights of the existing shareholders are paramount and must be protected.

Easy marks. Describing what class rights are.

Examiner's comments. Most candidates had a reasonable attempt at part (a), although many only discussed voting rights and did not mention rights for return of capital. Part (b) was poorly answered as candidates did not know enough about the statutory provisions for variation of class rights. Candidates did well when explaining minority objection rights.

Marking scheme

			Marks
(a)	Tend to be decided by Articles	1	
	Examples: ordinary and preference shares	1	
	Rights to receive dividends	2	
	Rights to and return on capital	2	
			6
(b)	Special resolution; ¾ majority	1	
	Rights in articles	1	
	Other: 75% majority	1	
	Minority objection rights	1	
			4
			10

(a) **Class rights**

There are no statutory definitions of what particular rights are enjoyed by particular classes of shares. Rather, **class rights are those provided by the company's articles of association** and on the issue of the relevant shares. If no differences between shares are expressly provided then it is assumed that they all carry the same rights. A company may choose to **specify particular rights** and attach them to particular classes of shares. Such rights will deal with matters concerning **dividends**, **return of capital**, **voting** and the **right to appoint directors**.

All shares carrying **identical rights** are **grouped together into a class of shares**. The most common instances of different classes are **ordinary shares** and **preference shares** but a company may also have ordinary shares with voting rights and ordinary shares without voting rights, for example.

The main difference between ordinary shares and preference shares is the implied right attaching to preference shares to receive an annual dividend of a fixed amount.

Examples of rights

The **right to receive a preference dividend is deemed to be cumulative unless the contrary is stated**. The preference shareholders cease to be entitled to arrears however, where the company goes into liquidation unless the dividend was declared at the time liquidation commenced or unless there is express provision in the articles or other terms of issue. Preference shareholders are not entitled to participate in any additional dividend over and above their specified rate. In other respects, preference shareholders carry the same rights as ordinary shareholders unless otherwise stated.

The **holders of ordinary shares will be entitled to the surplus profits** once other commitments have been met whereas preference shares carry no such right beyond payment of the fixed dividend.

Similarly, holders of ordinary shares will be entitled to a share of the **surplus assets on a winding up** whereas other types of shareholder will normally only be entitled to a return of their capital.

Preference shares will normally be expressed **not to carry voting rights** or only limited voting rights, unlike ordinary shares.

Shareholders may have some class **rights which attach to them as members** even though those rights are not attached to particular classes of shares.

(b) **Variation of class rights**

A **variation of class rights** is an alteration in the position of shareholders with regard to those benefits or duties which they have by virtue of their shares.

Consent

The rights vested in the holders of a class of shares can only be varied by the company with the **consent of all the holders** or with such consent of a majority as is prescribed (usually) by the articles.

Special resolution

Normally the procedure is that a **special resolution** be passed giving approval for a proposed variation by a three-quarters majority cast either at a separate meeting of a class or by written consent (s 630). If the rights are set by the constitution or otherwise and there is a **variation procedure** laid down then that procedure must be followed.

Appeal

Whenever class rights are varied in pursuance of a procedure laid down by the company's constitution, holders of at least **15%** of the issued shares of the relevant class **who have not themselves consented** to or voted in favour of the variation may **apply to the court** within **21 days** of the class consent being given for an order cancelling the variation (s 633).

They must satisfy the court that the variation is '**unfairly prejudicial**' to the class, usually by showing that the majority who voted in favour were seeking some advantage to themselves as members of a different class instead of considering the interests of the class in which they were then voting. The court can either **approve** or **cancel** the variation but cannot modify its terms or give conditional approval.

Not a variation

It might be noted that the **subdivision of shares** in one class with the effect of increasing that class's voting strength is not strictly a variation of class rights (*Greenhalgh v Arderne Cinemas Ltd 1946*), even though the effect is prejudicial to members of another class by reducing the value of their rights.

Similarly, **issuing shares of the same class to allottees** who are **not already members** of the class, is not a variation of class rights (*White v Bristol Aeroplane Co Ltd 1953*).

79 Flop Ltd

Text reference. Chapters 16 and 18.

Top tips. This is a very practical question and we shall probably see many more like this in the F4 exams. A careful reading of the question should show you that the first purchase by Gus was within the rules on share capital, as the shares were issued but an amount was left unpaid. As Flop Ltd was in financial difficulties you should then have been alert to the possibility that there was a problem with the second issue. As with all scenario questions you need to be careful to **identify** the issues at stake, then **state** the law applying to those issues, then **apply** the law to the facts of the case and **conclude**.

Easy marks. State that companies issue shares of a designated and fixed monetary amount (their nominal value), and that they can be issued at a premium but never at a discount to that nominal value.

Marking scheme

8–10 marks	A complete answer, highlighting and dealing with all of the issues presented in the problem scenario. It is most likely that cases and statutory provisions will be referred to, and they will be credited.
5–7 marks	An accurate recognition of the problems inherent in the question, together with an attempt to apply the appropriate legal rules to the situation.
2–4 marks	An ability to recognise some, although not all, of the key issues and suggest appropriate legal responses to them. A recognition of the area of law but no attempt to apply that law.
0–1 mark	Very weak answer showing no, or very little, understanding of the question.

Shares

A **company share** was defined in *Borland's Trustee v Steel Bros & Co Ltd 1901* as the interest of a shareholder in the company measured by a sum of money for the purpose of a liability. This means that the share must be paid for by the shareholder.

Issued and allotted capital

Issued and **allotted share capital** is the **type**, **class**, **number** and **amount** of the **shares issued** and **allotted** to **specific shareholders**, including shares taken on **formation** by the **subscribers to the memorandum**. These totals are divided into shares of fixed nominal amount, a figure such as 50p or £1 which is chosen by the company but which has no direct correlation with either their value to the shareholder or the assets of the company.

Shares may be issued to shareholders in return for the **full nominal value** of each share, in which case it is called '**issued and fully paid**', but the company need not necessarily require full payment immediately for the share, in which case there is an amount left unpaid. This amount remains a **liability** of the shareholder to the company. Once a share is **fully paid**, the shareholder has **no remaining liability** to the company, even if it goes into insolvent liquidation.

Issue at a discount

The rules on leaving amounts unpaid as a call on shareholders are not contradicted by the rule that every share with a **nominal value may be issued at a premium** to that value **but may not be issued at a discount** to it: s580 and *Ooregum Gold Mining Co of India v Roper 1892.*

Flop Ltd made the **first issue** of shares to Gus at their **nominal value**, that is **without a discount**, although it was prepared to wait for 25% of the issue price to be paid. Furthermore, in allotting shares the company should receive **money** or **money's worth**; this Flop Ltd did by accepting 75p per share and a promise to pay 25p per share when called on to do so.

A company may resolve to **write off** any unpaid capital but if it subsequently becomes insolvent this resolution is ineffective and the shareholder is still liable.

Gus

Applying these rules to the scenario, it is clear that Flop Ltd had a **remaining call** on Gus after the first issue for the amount left **unpaid** on his shares, that is £2,500. When a company does **issue shares at a discount to their nominal value** it is effectively saying that the shareholder has a £1 share, say, but only needs to pay 75p in total for it. This is **prohibited**: the shareholder must nonetheless pay the full nominal value plus interest at the appropriate rate. Any person to whom the shareholder transfers the shares and who knew of the underpayment is similarly liable s588.

Applying these rules to the scenario, when it makes the second issue to Gus, Flop Ltd is trying to do so at a 50p discount to their nominal value. This is **disallowed** under s580 and **Gus is still liable** for the balance (10,000 x 50p = £5,000) plus interest.

80 Lux Ltd

Text reference. Chapters 15 and 16

Top tips. The question does not explicitly require a discussion on the articles of association or how minorities can oppose a variation of class rights, but to answer it in sufficient detail you need to discuss these first – make sure that you keep your explanation focussed on the issues in the scenario.

Easy marks. Stating the nature of the articles as a contract, the nature of class rights and how each can be amended.

Articles of Association

A company's **articles,** together with any **resolutions or agreements** that it makes, forms its **constitution**. Under s33 Companies Act 2006 a company's **constitution binds** the **members to the company**, the **company to its members** and **members to other members**. The constitution does **not** bind the company to third parties and it only applies to rights and obligations that affect members **in their capacity as members**: *Eley v Positive Government Security Life Assurance Co 1876.*

Alteration of articles

All companies have a statutory power to alter their articles by **special resolution**, or in the case of a private company, by **written resolution** with a 75% majority. Therefore the consent of each individual member is not required for alteration of the articles, just the requisite majority.

For an alteration to be valid the majority must **honestly believe** that it is in the **interest of the company** as a whole (a subjective test) and that it would be in the interests of a **hypothetical individual member** (an objective test): *Greenhalgh v Arderne Cinemas Ltd 1950.* Where a person has a **contract** contained in the articles, they cannot obtain an injunction to prevent the articles being altered: *Southern Foundries (1926) Ltd v Shirlaw 1940.*

Class rights

A company's shares confer certain **rights** on the members who own them. Where only one type of share exists the rights are normally the same, however different types of share will often confer different rights. For example **preference shares** usually entitle the member to a **fixed dividend** with **priority** of payment over ordinary shares and priority over the **repayment of capital** (ahead of ordinary shares) in the event of a winding up. Other class rights may attach regarding voting or the right to remove a director. Any share that has **different rights** from others is grouped with the other shares carrying identical rights to form a **class**.

Altering class rights

Alteration of the rights that attach to a particular class of share requires the **consent of the members** of that class. Members are not entitled to **vote on a resolution** that affects the rights of a class of share that they do not own.

The **standard procedure** for a variation of class rights is contained in s630 Companies Act 2006. This states that a **special resolution** should be passed by a **three quarters majority** cast either at a **separate meeting** of the class, or by **written consent**. If the company's articles impose any other requirements then these must be followed instead.

Appeal

Whenever class rights are varied a **minority** of holders of shares of that class may apply to the court to have the variation cancelled. Under s633 Companies Act 2006, the objectors together must:

- Hold **not less** than **15%** of the **issued shares** of the class in question
- **Not** themselves have **consented** to or voted in favour of the variation
- **Apply** to the court within **21 days** of the consent being given by the class

The court can either approve the variation as made or cancel it as **'unfairly prejudicial'**. It cannot, however, modify the terms of the variation.

To establish that a variation is 'unfairly prejudicial' to the class, the minority must normally show that the **majority** who voted in favour was seeking **some advantage** to themselves as **members** of a **different class** instead of considering the interests of the class in which they were then voting.

Removal of Matt from his position of editor of the Lux paper

Matt has a **separate employment contract** that is not affected by changes in the articles. Employment is not a **right of membership** so the articles themselves cannot form a contract of employment between Matt and the company (*Eley v Positive Government Security Life Assurance Co 1876).* If the courts were to establish an **outside contract** with the terms contained within the articles (*Re New British Iron Co, ex parte Beckwith 1898)*, Matt **could not prevent** the company from altering its articles and terminating his employment, but he would have the right to sue for breach of contract (*Southern Foundries (1926) Ltd v Shirlaw 1940).*

Reduction of preference share dividend from 10% to 5%

The **reduction of dividends** is clearly a **variation of a class right** that under the variation procedure requires a **75% majority** by **special** or **written resolution**. Kudos Ltd is likely to want to prevent this variation but as it only holds 20% of the shares in the class it cannot prevent the variation by itself. However, Kudos Ltd does hold over 15% of the shares in the class so it could **apply to the court** for the variation to be cancelled. As the effect on Kudos Ltd is relatively minor and as it affects all shareholders equally it is likely that the court would uphold the variation.

81 Gilt Ltd

Text reference. Chapter 19.

Top tips. Read this question very carefully so that you correctly identify the two issues at hand. These are (1) whether the shares were validly allotted and (2) whether Harry breached any of his duties as a director.

Easy marks. Stating cases and statute which address the issues at hand will gain you the basic marks. However you will not score well with just a general discussion on directors' duties and the allotment of shares. Your statement of the law must be relevant to the question.

ACCA examiner's answers. The ACCA examiner's answer to this question can be found at the back of this kit.

Examiner's comments. This question essentially was divided into two distinct parts, one requiring candidates to consider the issue of directors' duties with an element raising the issue of share allotment. It has to be stated at the outset that it was by far and away the worst done question on the paper. A surprising number of candidates simply did not recognise the issues raised in the problem scenario and attempted to apply various aspects of company law such insider dealing, money laundering, fraudulent trading and wrongful trading, and sometimes all of these together.

Marking scheme

This question refers to issues relating to the directors' duties and in particular the duty not to accept personal benefits and what is referred to as the 'improper purpose rule'.

8–10 marks: Candidates will exhibit a thorough knowledge of the law as set out in the Companies Act 2006 together with the ability to analyse the problems contained in the question. It is likely, but not necessary, for candidates to make reference to the previous non-statutory rules. It is likely that reference will be made to case authorities.

5–7 marks: Candidates will exhibit a sound knowledge of the law together with the ability to recognise the issues contained in the question. Knowledge may be less detailed or analysis less focused.

3–4 marks: Identification of some of the central issues in the question and an attempt to apply the appropriate law. Towards the bottom of this range of marks there will be major shortcomings in analysis or application of law.

0–2 marks: Very weak answers that might recognise what the question is about but show no ability to analyse or answer the problem as set out.

Issue

There are **two issues at hand**, both of which concern Itt plc's takeover of Gilt Ltd.

The first issue is the £50,000 **'facility fee'** paid to Harry for ensuring the takeover is successful.

The second issue is the **allotment of Gilt Ltd shares to Itt plc**. The allotment appears to have been made purely to out-manoeuvre Gilt Ltd's shareholders who were opposed to the takeover.

The law

Under the Companies Act 2006 directors of companies owe **statutory duties** to their companies which are in addition to their common law fiduciary duties.

Facility fee issue

Directors have long had a **fiduciary duty** as agents of the company to avoid circumstances where their personal interests conflict, or may possibly conflict, with the company's interests. This is unless they made the company aware of the conflict and the members ratified the directors' actions: *Regal (Hastings) Ltd v Gulliver 1942*.

This fiduciary duty was given a statutory footing under **s175** of the Companies Act 2006 – directors have a **duty to avoid a conflict of interest**.

Also, under **s176** of the Companies Act 2006, directors have a **duty not to accept benefits from third parties**.

Share allotment issue

Under **s171** of the Companies Act 2006, directors owe a **duty to act within their powers**, in other words, in accordance with the company's constitution. They should also exercise their powers for the purposes they were conferred: *Bamford v Bamford 1969*.

Directors also have a fiduciary duty to the company to **exercise their powers** bona fide in what they honestly consider to be the interests of the company: *Re Smith v Fawcett Ltd 1942*.

If the irregular use of directors' powers is in the **allotment of shares** the votes attached to the new shares may not be used in reaching a decision in general meeting to sanction it: *Howard Smith Ltd v Ampol Petroleum Ltd 1974*.

However, **members can ratify the actions of directors** where they have exceeded their powers.

Application

Facility fee issue

Harry clearly had a **conflict of interest** when he was offered the facility fee which he should have declared to the company. As the £50,000 is a **benefit from a third party,** which he should not have accepted, Harry is in breach of his s175 and s176 duties under the Companies Act.

The other directors of Gilt Ltd are not implicated in this.

Share allotment issue

The correct **purpose for issuing shares is for the company to raise capital** – not to enable a takeover bid to succeed: *Howard Smith Ltd v Ampol Petroleum Ltd 1974.*

Therefore all the directors of Gilt Ltd are in breach of their s171 **duty to act within their powers.** As a consequence of this, the shares allotted to Itt plc should not be counted in the resolution concerning whether to accept or reject the takeover.

Conclusion

May could apply to the court to have the **share allotment to Itt plc ruled invalid** – this would also mean that the resolution of the company accepting the takeover would also be invalid. However, another resolution could be taken on the issue, although Itt plc would not be permitted to vote.

Regarding **Harry**, the members could vote to **remove him from office** by ordinary resolution. He could also **be liable to pay the money** he received from Itt plc to Gilt ltd.

82 Dividends

Text reference. Chapter 18.

Top tips. This question provides you with a good structure to work with as it could quite easily have been written with one single requirement asking you to explain the rules on dividends, so take advantage of this and organise your answer well. Be quick as you have just about six minutes on each part to get down all your facts. This is no time to waffle so stick to the point!

Easy marks. The calculation of distributable profits. Learn it if you don't know it.

Examiner's comments. Too many candidates focused their answers on the different type of shares that companies can issue and the order in which the holders of these different types of share receive their dividend. Secondly, and in a similar vein, too many candidates focused on the procedure for declaring dividends rather than on the rules relating to what can actually be paid

Marking scheme

	Marks
A thorough understanding of law relating to dividends as it applies to both public and private companies. Cases may well be cited and will be credited.	8–10
A clear understanding of the general law but perhaps lacking in detail or unbalanced in only dealing with one of the types of company.	5–7
Some, but limited, understanding of the law.	2–4
Little or no knowledge of the clauses.	0–1

(a) **Dividends**

All companies have the power to **declare dividends**. This is the return given to members for their investment in the company. The directors may authorise the payment of **interim dividends** during the financial year but the **final dividend** must be **approved by the members**, usually by **ordinary resolution** with a simple majority at a public company's AGM or by **written resolution** of private companies. Members cannot declare a dividend themselves or increase the amount of a dividend above that recommended by directors, but they may resolve to take a smaller one.

Dividends are **usually declared payable** on the **paid up amount of share capital** and are usually paid in **cash**. They may however be paid wholly or partly by the distribution of non-cash assets.

Funding of dividends

The **general rule** applicable to all companies is that **dividends may not be paid out of capital.** The Companies Act 2006 sets out specific rules that must be followed which essentially mean that dividends must be paid out of profits that they have available for that purpose, in other words **distributable profit**.

'Distributable profit' is defined in the Companies Act as 'accumulated realised profits, so far as not previously utilised by distribution or capitalisation, less accumulated realised losses, so far as not previously written off in a reduction or reorganisation of capital duly made'. Only profits realised at the balance sheet date shall be included in the calculation.

'Accumulated' means that any losses of previous years must be included in reckoning the current distributable surplus. In order to be treated as 'realised', a profit or loss must be deemed to be realised in accordance with generally accepted accounting principles prevailing when the accounts are prepared.

(b) **Public company dividends**

In addition to the rules stated above, a **public company** can only make a distribution if its **net assets**, at the time, are **equal** to or **greater** than the **aggregate of its called up share capital and undistributable reserves**. The amount of any dividend cannot exceed such amount as would leave its net assets at not less than that aggregate amount.

Undistributable reserves comprise the **share premium account**, the **capital redemption reserve**, the **revaluation reserve** and any reserve which the company is prohibited from distributing by statute or its own constitution. This means that a **public company** can only make a **distribution** from its profits **after depreciating fixed assets**.

(c) **Consequences of breach of dividend rules**

If a dividend is paid otherwise than out of distributable profits the **company**, the **directors and** the **shareholders** may be involved in making good the unlawful distribution.

The directors are held **responsible** since either they recommended to members in general meeting that a dividend should be declared or they declared interim dividends.

The directors may however **honestly** rely on proper accounts which disclose an apparent distributable profit out of which the dividend can properly be paid. They are not liable if it later appears that the assumptions or estimates used in preparing the accounts, although reasonable at the time, were in fact unsound.

The company can **recover from members** an **unlawful dividend** if the **members knew** or had **reasonable grounds** to believe that it was unlawful: s847. If the directors have to make good to the company an unlawful dividend they may claim **indemnity from members** who at the time of receipt knew of the irregularity.

83 Debentures and charges

Text reference. Chapter 17.

Top tips. Keep the three parts of the question separate. Do not be tempted to start discussing charges in part (a) on the nature of debentures, as you will then duplicate your answers for parts (b) and (c).

Easy marks. Defining the three terms will provide you with the basic marks on offer.

ACCA examiner's answers. The ACCA examiner's answer to this question can be found at the back of this kit.

Examiner's comments. Some candidates thought that debentures were actually shares and/or a share of profit granted by the company. The majority of answers were of a high standard, recognising that a debenture was a written acknowledgement of indebtedness, that the debenture holder was a creditor and that there were no voting rights attached, just an entitlement to interest. Full marks were quite often awarded.

In part (b) candidates again either readily described the features of both fixed and floating charges, or made the mistake of assuming that a fixed charge merely meant that a fixed rate of interest would be charged on the loan and that a floating charge related to a variable rate of interest. Unfortunately this is always a common mistake by candidates.

Marking scheme

This question requires candidates to consider how companies may raise loan capital and how they secure such loans against their assets. Marks will be allocated as indicated in the paper.

8–10 marks: A good to full answer providing a clear explanation of each of the elements of the question.

5–7 marks: Sound understanding of the concepts but perhaps lacking detail or slightly unbalanced.

3–4 marks: Weak answer lacking in detailed knowledge.

0–2 marks: Very weak answer demonstrating little understanding of the topic.

(a) **Debentures**

A **debenture** is a **written acknowledgement of debt**, which may be any document which states the terms on which a company has borrowed money. A debenture may create a **charge** over the company's assets as security for the loan. It entitles the debentureholder to **payment of interest** as a creditor but to no other rights, such as voting at a general meeting.

A debenture is usually a **formal printed legal document**. A **single debenture** is issued to a single lender but debentures may be issued as **a series to different lenders**. In this case each lender receives a debenture in identical form in respect of their loan and the lenders' rights rank pari passu in their right to repayment and in any security given to them. Public companies only may issue debenture stock to members of the public by means of a prospectus.

Secured debentureholders may enforce their security by taking possession of the charged assets and selling them (in the case of a legal charge) or appointing a **receiver**. These rights will normally arise from the express provisions of the relevant charge or, in certain circumstances, may be awarded by court order.

(b) **Fixed charges**

A **fixed** or specific **charge attaches** to the relevant asset as soon as the charge is **created**, for example a charge over named property given as security for a loan to the owner of the property. If the company needs to dispose of the charged asset, it will either repay the secured debt out of the sale proceeds so that the charge is discharged or dispose of the asset still subject to the charge.

Any type of charge gives to the holder a **priority claim** to payment of what is owing to them out of the value of the property which is subject to that charge. The ranking of that priority will depend on the types and times of creation of all relevant charges.

(c) **Floating charges**

Where a charge is created over certain assets but the company retains the right to deal with those assets during the ordinary course of business until the charge **crystallises**, that charge is a 'floating charge'. On crystallisation, a floating charge is converted into a fixed charge on the assets owned by the company at the time of crystallisation. Crystallisation will occur on the happening of any of the events specified in the charge, such as the **liquidation of the company** or the **cessation of its business**

Whether or not the parties label a charge as 'fixed' or 'floating' will not be conclusive but the general rule will be applied. For example a charge which covers present and future **book debts**, whatever it is called by the parties, will be floating if the company is allowed to deal with money collected from debtors without notifying the chargee and fixed if the money must be paid to the chargee, for example in reduction of an overdraft *(Siebe Gorman & Co Ltd v Barclays Bank Ltd 1979).*

The main advantage enjoyed by a holder of a fixed charge as opposed to a floating charge is that a fixed charge confers **immediate rights over identified assets**. It is therefore more certain as to which of the chargor's assets are subject to the charge and gives an immediate right of sale over them.

A fixed charge will **rank in priority** to a floating charge even if it was created after the floating charge since it attaches to the property at the time of creation rather than at the time of crystallisation.

The one exception to this general rule is where a **floating charge** contains an express prohibition on the creation of subsequent fixed charges (**a negative pledge clause**) and a subsequent chargee has actual notice of such prohibition.

84 Resolutions

Text reference. Chapter 20.

Top tips. You should be familiar with all the types of resolution a company can pass. This question should therefore hold no fear, as it is an ideal opportunity to earn easy marks.

Easy marks. Defining each type of resolution.

Examiner's comments. This question required candidates to explain the meaning of and procedure for the passing of (a) an ordinary and a special resolution and (b) a written resolution. Once again although the terms were continued from the previous companies Act, the 2006 Act made significant changes to them.

As a whole, candidates performed well on part (a) with the majority of candidates identifying that resolutions were decisions by members, usually held by a poll or a show of hands at a meeting (either AGM or GM) and that a simple majority is required for the passing of the ordinary resolution and 75% for a special resolution. Some candidates went further and provided examples of when the two types of resolutions would be used. It has to be noted, however, that a number of candidates thought that such decisions were taken by directors rather than members. Part (b) relating to written resolutions was inadequately answered. Most candidates worked out from the question that this procedure applied only to private companies, but only a few went on to develop their answers. While some candidates were aware that these resolutions were available when such companies did not hold general meetings, some insisted that they were passed at general meetings. As has been said very few candidates were aware of the changes introduced by the 2006 Companies Act.

Marking scheme

This question requires candidates to consider the way in which resolutions are voted on in companies.

(a) Requires candidates to explain the rules relating to ordinary and special resolutions.

3–5 marks: A good explanation of the difference between the two types of resolution.
0–2 marks: Some awareness of the area but lacking in detailed knowledge.

(b) 3–5 marks: Candidates must not only show an understanding of what is meant by a written resolution but also the rules relating to them.

0–2 marks: Unbalanced, or may not deal with all of the required aspects of the topic. Alternatively the answer will demonstrate very little understanding of what is actually meant by a written resolution.

(a) **Ordinary and special resolutions**

Resolutions voted on at **private company** meetings are either classed as **ordinary** or **special resolutions**.

Requisitioning resolutions

The **directors** normally decide which resolutions shall be voted on in a meeting. However, members can also take the initiative to requisition certain resolutions be considered at as well.

In order for **members** to put forward a resolution, they must represent **5% of the voting rights**, or be at least **100 in number** with an average paid up capital of £100 per member and must deliver the resolution to the company at least **6 weeks in advance** of the meeting. They may also request a **statement** of less than 1,000 words regarding the resolution be circulated to all members. Members requisitioning a resolution are **liable** to pay any **incidental expenses** unless the company agrees otherwise.

Passing ordinary resolutions

An **ordinary resolution** is one carried by **a simple majority of over 50%** of votes cast. This is in terms of number of hands in the case of a vote on a show of hands or voting rights where a poll is called. A **14 days' notice** period applies to **meetings** where an ordinary resolution is to be considered.

Ordinary resolutions are commonly used for **non-contentious issues** such as the approval of a dividend, but are also used on issues such as the removal of a director.

Passing special resolutions

A **special resolution** requires **a majority of 75%** or more to pass it and it also requires a **notice period of 14 days**. They are required for a **change of name**, **reduction of share capital**, **restriction of the objects** or **amendments to the articles** and are therefore used where major or contentious decisions need to be made.

Filing procedure

A **signed copy** of all **special resolutions** must be **delivered to the Registrar of Companies** for filing, usually within 15 days of their being passed. Also their **text** must be **set out in full in the notice convening the meeting** and they must be described as special resolutions. No such procedure applies in respect of ordinary resolutions.

(b) **Written resolutions**

A **written resolution** is one which may be passed only by a **private company**. They are available to them because **private companies** are **not required** to hold **general meetings** and therefore they are the easiest method to make decisions without having to hold one. They can be used to pass almost any type of decision, **however they cannot be used to remove a director or auditor** from office since both have a right to attend and speak at a meeting where any proposal for removal is to be discussed.

Procedure

Copies of the resolution must be sent to **all members** eligible to vote as a **hard copy**, **email** or through a **website**. Alternatively, the **same copy** may be sent to each member in turn. The resolution should be accompanied by a statement informing the member, how to **signify their agreement** to the resolution and the **date** the resolution must be passed by.

The required **majority** to pass the resolution will **depend on the nature of the business** being considered. Where a three quarters majority would have been required if the vote took place in a meeting then the same majority is required for an identical written resolution.

As with **ordinary** and **special resolutions**, **members holding 5%** of the **voting rights** may request a written resolution providing it **would be effective** (not prevented by the articles or law) and is **not defamatory, frivolous** or **vexatious**. A **statement** containing no more than **1,000 words** on the subject of the resolution may accompany it. Members requisitioning such resolutions are **liable** for **any incidental costs** unless the company decides otherwise.

85 Meetings

Text reference. Chapter 20.

Top tips At first sight this looks a gift of a question, but beware! You can probably rustle up a few marks worth of comment on AGMs, but do you know enough about other general meetings and class meetings? Although you may feel comfortable with the first part of the question, there is a risk that you will score few marks on the other parts unless you are confident with the subject matter.

Our answer to part (b) contains much more detail than you would need for 2 marks. The list of who can call a general meeting is included as a valid answer could have covered them. To get the marks you would have needed to cover the material in the first paragraph and give a couple of examples of who can call a meeting.

Easy marks. To make the most of the marks available here, notice the allocation of the marks to each of the three parts of the question and allocate your own time accordingly. You need to go into as much detail as possible on AGMs as that part attracts half of the marks for the question.

Marking scheme

8–10 marks	A good treatment of all three types of meeting, probably, although not necessarily, with reference to statutory provisions
5–7 marks	A sound understanding of this area, although perhaps lacking in detail.
2–4 marks	Some understanding of the area but lacking in detail, perhaps failing to deal with one type of meeting
0–1 mark	Little or no knowledge of the area.

(a) **Annual general meetings**

Every **public company** must hold an **annual general meeting** ('**AGM**') in each calendar year within **six months** of the company's year end. Private companies are not required to hold an AGM. At least **21 days' written notice** must be given for each AGM unless all members entitled to attend agree to shorter notice. The notice must specify the meeting as an AGM.

Ordinary business to be transacted at an AGM includes the consideration of the **directors'** and **auditors' reports** and the **company accounts**, the **election of directors** and **appointment of auditors**, the fixing of **auditors' remuneration** and the **declaration of dividends**. The full text of any proposed resolution concerning special business is set out in the notice which may be provided as a hard copy or electronically.

(b) **General meetings**

Other meetings of the company are **general meetings**. A minimum of **14 days' written notice** must be given. The meeting may be called in any of the following ways:

- By the **directors** whenever they see fit;
- By the directors on the **requisition of members** holding at least 10% of the paid up share capital carrying voting rights or (if there is no share capital) 10% of the voting rights, in which case the meeting must be called within 28 days of the requisition being deposited. The required percentage is reduced to 5% for private companies that have not held a meeting for 12 months;
- By the **court**, on the application of a director or member, usually in the case of deadlock (for example where one member of two refuses to attend and so provide a quorum);
- By an **auditor** who gives a statement detailing the circumstances for their **resignation** or other loss of office and requires their explanation to be considered by the company;
- Compulsorily, by the directors of a public company where the **net assets fall to half or less of the amount of its called up share capital** (s656).

(c) **Class meetings**

A **class meeting** may be called by the directors or other competent person or authority for the **holders** of **one class of shares** to approve a **proposed variation** of the rights attached to those shares. Alternatively under a scheme of arrangement the holders of shares in one class may be divided into separate classes, for whom separate meetings are required, where the scheme proposed affects each group differently.

The **standard general meeting rules** on issuing notices and on voting apply to a class meeting. The quorum for a class meeting is two persons who hold at least one third in nominal value of the issued shares of the class except that a quorum of one is permissible where all the shares are held by one member.

86 Company secretary

Text reference. Chapter 19.

Top tips. Use the question to provide a structure for your answer and attempt all three elements.

Easy marks. Marks are available for addressing each of the question's three requirements.

ACCA examiner's answers. The ACCA examiner's answer to this question can be found at the back of this kit.

Examiner's comments. This was not answered particularly well. Whilst most candidates stated that a company secretary was an administrative officer of a company, there was then a tendency to describe directors' duties. The better-prepared candidates recognised the qualifications needed to be appointed as a company secretary.

Marking scheme

This question requires candidates to consider the company secretary in the context of the idea of corporate governance.

8–10 marks: Thorough treatment of all three aspects of the question including at least some consideration of corporate governance itself.

5–7 marks: Thorough treatment of some aspects of the question or a reasonable, but less than full, treatment of some aspects.

3–4 marks: Unbalanced answer, merely dealing with a limited number of aspects of the question.

0–2 marks: Demonstrating little or no understanding of the nature of the question.

Role in corporate governance

Corporate governance concerns how **companies are directed and controlled.** The company secretary is an officer of the company and has an important role to play in how the organisation is run. The **UK Corporate Governance Code** states that along with the chairman, the secretary should ensure **good information flows** to the directors. It also states that the company secretary is responsible for **advising the chairman** on **all governance matters,** and for assisting in the **induction and professional development of directors**

Appointment

Every public company must have a secretary. A corporation can fulfil the role of secretary to a company. A company may also have two or more joint secretaries.

The **directors of a public company must take all reasonable steps to ensure that the secretary is suitably qualified** for the post by their knowledge and experience. A public company secretary may be anyone who:

- Has been a public company secretary for at **least three out of the five years prior to their appointment**
- **Is a member of the ACCA or one of a number of other professional bodies**: CIMA, ICAEW, ICAS, ICAI or CIPFA
- Is a **barrister, advocate or solicitor** in the UK
- **Is a person who**, by virtue of holding or having held any other position or being a member of any other body, **appears to the directors to be capable of the post.**

Duties

The **duties of the secretary** are not defined by the Companies Act but are **laid down by the company's board of directors**, therefore they vary according to the size and nature of the company. Generally, the company secretary is seen as the person who is charged with ensuring that the company and its officers comply with statutory and regulatory requirements. More specifically, the secretary's duties will include the following:

- **Convening meetings** and **making all arrangements incidental to meetings of the Board of Directors.** This will include matters such as issuing the agenda, collating or preparing papers to be submitted to the meeting, attending the meeting, taking minutes of the meeting and communicating decisions of the meeting as appropriate to persons inside and outside the company.
- **Signing forms and returns** as required
- **Maintaining the register of members**, recording transfers of shares and issuing share certificates to members
- Maintaining the **other statutory registers** and ensuring that all necessary **documents, returns and notices** are delivered to the **Registrar of Companies**
- Ensuring that **accounts are kept** in accordance with the requirements of the Companies Act (unless the company has an accountant or a finance department)

Powers

Under the general principle of the law of agency, a **company secretary may be treated as having apparent authority to bind the company** by their actions on its behalf, unless the company has denied them that authority and the other party has notice of the restriction.

In *Panorama Developments (Guildford) Ltd v Fidelis Furnishing Fabrics Ltd 1971*, the Court of Appeal recognised that it is the normal function of the company secretary to enter into contracts **connected with the administration of a company** (in this case ordering cars from a car hire firm purportedly for the company's business).

87 Implied authority and company secretary

Text reference. Chapters 12 and 19.

Top tips. Not all questions require you to explain the facts of a case, but when you are required to explain an area of law it may be a very good idea to refer to cases in detail. However you would have also scored marks if you illustrated your answer with a hypothetical situation instead.

Easy marks. Defining implied authority in Part (a) and remembering the cases in Part (b). There are very few cases on company secretaries so you should try to remember them all.

(a) **Implied authority**

Where there is no express authority, authority may be **implied** from the **nature** of an agent's activities or from what is **usual** or **customary** in the **circumstances** or in the person's position. Where a person has implied authority they may enter into contracts on behalf of their principal, binding them to a third party.

As far as **third parties** to contracts made by agents are concerned, they are entitled to assume that the agent has all the usual powers that they would be expected to have. They may also assume that the agent has all the usual authority that goes with their position, unless they are aware of anything to the contrary.

For example, in *Watteau v Fenwick 1893* the owner of a hotel employed the previous owner to manage it. The previous owner was **forbidden to buy cigars** on credit but did so anyway. When the cigar seller was not paid it sued the new owner who argued that they were not bound by the contract, since the manager had no actual authority to make it.

However, it was decided that **purchasing cigars** on credit was within the **usual authority** of a manager of a hotel and therefore the new owner was bound by the contract as the restriction of usual authority had not been communicated to the cigar seller.

All **employees** and **directors** have **different levels of implied authority** that are relevant to their position. For example a managing director has implied authority to enter into commercial contracts.

(b) **Company secretary**

As mentioned in Part (a), all employees and directors have some level of **implied authority** brought about by their position and the company secretary, as an officer of the company, is no different. The powers of the company secretary have historically been very limited, but the common law increasingly recognises that they may be able to act as agents in some circumstances. Specifically, they may enter the company into contracts connected with the **administrative side** of the company: *Panorama Developments (Guildford) Ltd v Fidelis Furnishing Fabrics Ltd 1971*.

88 Appointment and removal

Text reference. Chapter 19.

Top tips. For part (b) of this question, which is worth 7 marks, make sure that you think through the various possibilities while planning your answer. It is not enough just to talk about removal under S168 CA2006; you must think about the other forms of removal of directors, for example under the terms of the Company Directors Disqualification Act.

Easy marks. Maximise the marks you can get for part (a) by discussing all the ways in which a director can be appointed, not just by the members on an ongoing basis. For example, what happens when a company is formed: how are the directors appointed then? What happens if there is a casual vacancy?

Examiner's comments. Candidates generally answered part (a) well, although not many were able to discuss appointment to fill a casual vacancy. It was worrying that some candidates thought that directors are elected by their fellow directors. In part (b) a surprising number of candidates did not deal with the s168 procedure or were unsure as to the type of resolution required. A surprising number thought that directors had the power to dismiss other directors.

Marking scheme

This question requires candidates to explain the ways in which company directors can be appointed and also the ways in which they can be removed from office. Part (a) carries three marks and part (b) carries seven marks reflecting the amount required in each answer.

8-10 marks	Thorough explanation of both aspects of the question.
5-7 marks	Thorough treatment of one of the elements, or a less complete treatment of both of them.
0-4 marks	Unbalanced to very unbalanced answer, focusing on only one element and ignoring the other, or one which shows little understanding of the subject matter of the question.

(a) **Appointment**

The **first directors** of a company will be those named in the particulars delivered to the Registrar of Companies on incorporation. Subsequent directors will be appointed as provided for by the **articles**. Most companies adopt model articles which provides for the co-option of new directors by existing ones and for the election of directors by the company in general meeting.

The directors themselves may fill a **casual vacancy** by co-option, with such an appointee being required to stand at the next election of directors. A company may also elect new directors in general meeting by passing an ordinary resolution to that effect. A director is normally a shareholder in the company but this is not required by law; however the Articles may require that the directors hold shares in the company.

A **public company** must have at least **two directors**, but a **private company** need only have **one**.

(b) **Removal**

A director may **leave office** by removal under **s 168**, by **disqualification**, by **resignation**, by **not offering themselves for re-election**, on **death**, on **dissolution** of the company or in accordance with **provisions of the articles** (for example, for no longer holding the necessary number of qualification shares).

Model articles set out a procedure for the **retirement and re-election ('rotation')** of directors whereby, one third of the directors retire by rotation annually, but all retiring directors are eligible for re-election.

S168 CA 2006 provides that a director may be **removed** from office at any time by **ordinary resolution** of which **special notice** (28 days) has been given to the company by the person proposing it.

On receipt of the special notice, the company must **send a copy to the relevant director** who may require that a memorandum of reasonable length be issued to the members. They also have the right to address the meeting at which the resolution is considered.

Section 168 cannot be overridden by the articles or by any service agreement although the articles can provide for **weighted voting rights** (*Bushell v Faith 1970)* or permit an easier procedure, for example a resolution of the board of directors.

Model articles provide that a director must vacate office if they are **disqualified by statute** or become **bankrupt** or enters into an arrangement with their creditors or if they become of **unsound mind** or **resign by written notice** or if they are **absent for three consecutive months** from board meetings **without leave** from the other directors who resolve that they should therefore vacate office.

An **undischarged bankrupt** cannot act as a director nor be concerned directly or indirectly in the management of a company except with leave of the court that adjudged him bankrupt. The Company Directors Disqualification Act (CDDA) provides that a director may be disqualified (for up to 15 years) for persistent **breaches** of companies legislation, **fraudulent or wrongful trading** or **insider dealing**.

A director may **retire** at any time.

89 Statutory grounds for disqualifying directors

Text reference. Chapter 19.

Top tips. If you could not remember the statutory grounds for disqualification, you could have thought about why a court would want to ban a person from acting as a director. In this case, fraud, failing to provide statutory returns, or being generally unfit for the position may have occurred to you.

Easy marks. There are no easy marks here unless you know the law. If you did, stating the statutory reasons for disqualification will get you quick and easy marks.

Examiner's comments. This question required candidates to explain the operation of the Company Directors Disqualification Act 1986. Performance in relation to the question was patchy, with some candidates providing thorough answers, but a large number mistaking the whole import of the question and delivering an answer, either on directors' duties, or the removal of directors, or a mixture of both. Unfortunately these issues overlapped and even then marks had to be awarded generously. Not only did this confusion not allow candidates to do well in this particular question but it indicated an overall confusion about the nature of directors' duties and their control. In the final analysis, if the candidate cannot refer to the appropriate legislation they are not going to get many marks.

Marking scheme

This question requires candidates to explain the operation of the Company Directors Disqualification Act 1986.

8–10 marks	Thorough to complete answers, showing a detailed understanding of the legislation.
5–7 marks	A clear understanding of the topic, but perhaps lacking in detail. Alternatively an unbalanced answer showing good understanding of one part but less in the other.
2–4 marks	Some knowledge, although perhaps not clearly expressed, or very limited in its knowledge and understanding of the topic.
0–1 mark	Little or no knowledge of the topic.

Vacation of office

Directors may be required to **vacate office** because they have been disqualified on grounds dictated by the articles. They may also be disqualified from a wider range of company involvements under the **Company Directors Disqualification Act 1986 (CDDA)**.

Disqualification under statute

The **Company Directors Disqualification Act 1986** provides that a **court may** formally **disqualify a person from being a director** or in any way directly or indirectly being concerned or taking part in the promotion, formation or management of a company: s1.

Therefore the terms of the disqualification order are very wide, and include acting as a consultant to a company. The Act, despite its title, is not limited to the disqualification of people who have been directors. Any person may be disqualified if they fall within the following grounds.

Where a person is convicted of an indictable offence in connection with the promotion, formation, management or liquidation of a company or with the receivership or management of a company's property (s 2)

An indictable offence is an offence which may be tried at a Crown Court; it is therefore a serious offence. It need not actually have been tried on indictment but if it was the maximum period for which the court can disqualify is fifteen years, compared with only five years if the offence was dealt with summarily (at the Magistrates Court).

Where it appears that a person has been persistently in default in relation to provisions of company legislation (s 3)

This legislation requires any return, account or other document to be filed with, delivered or sent or notice of any matter to be given to the Registrar. Three defaults in five years are conclusive evidence of persistent default.

The maximum period of disqualification under this section is five years.

Where it appears that a person has been guilty of fraudulent trading (s 4)

This means the director has been found guilty of an offence under s993 of the Companies Act 2006. It generally means that they carried on a business with intent to defraud creditors or for any fraudulent purpose. It applies whether or not the company has been, or is in the course of being, wound-up.

The person does not actually have to have been convicted of fraudulent trading. The legislation also applies to anyone who has otherwise been guilty of any fraud in relation to the company or of any breach of their duty as an officer.

The maximum period of disqualification under this section is fifteen years.

Where the Secretary of State acting on a report made by the inspectors or from information or documents obtained under the Companies Act, applies to the court for an order believing it to be expedient in the public interest (s 8)

If the court is satisfied that the person's conduct in relation to the company makes that person unfit to be concerned in the management of a company, then it may make a disqualification order. Again the maximum period of imprisonment is fifteen years.

Unfitness (s 6)

A court **must** make a disqualification order where a person has been a director of a company which has at any time become **insolvent** and **their conduct** as a director of that company makes them **unfit to be concerned in the management of a company**. The courts may also take into account their conduct as a director of other companies, whether or not these other companies are insolvent. Directors can be disqualified under this section even if they take no active part in the running of the business.

In such cases the **minimum** period of disqualification is two years – the maximum period is fifteen years.

Other situations

Other, less common situations (amongst others) where a director can be disqualified include:

- **Where a director was involved in certain competition violations** – (maximum period fifteen years).
- **Where a director of an insolvent company has participated in wrongful trading** - (maximum period fifteen years).

90 Statutory duties

Text reference. Chapter 19.

Top tips. You have been asked for a brief explanation of five of the duties. Therefore you must limit the amount of time you spend on each to about three and a half minutes otherwise you will go over the time allocation for the question. Although you are only required to explain five duties our answer covers seven for completeness.

Easy marks. Stating each duty and the relevant section number.

The Companies Act 2006 introduced **seven statutory duties** that directors must meet.

(1) **Duty to act within powers (s 171)**

This duty requires directors not to exceed the powers given to them by the company. In particular they must only exercise powers for the purpose for which they were conferred.

(2) **Duty to promote the success of the company (s 172)**

The principle of 'enlightened shareholder value' requires directors to act in a way which is most likely to promote the success of the company for the benefit of the members as a whole.

(3) **Duty to exercise independent judgement (s 173)**

Directors must exercise independent judgement. They must not delegate their powers or be swayed by the influence of others.

(4) **Duty to exercise reasonable skill, care and diligence (s 174)**

Directors have a duty to exercise the same standard of care, skill and diligence that would reasonably be expected of a reasonably diligent person with:

- The knowledge, skill and experience which may be reasonably expected of a person in their position and
- The knowledge, skill and experience they actually have.

(5) **Duty to avoid conflicts of interest (s 175)**

The Act suggests a number of circumstances where a director's personal interests may conflict with the company's interests. Directors have a duty to avoid such circumstances.

(6) **Duty not to accept benefits from third parties (s 176)**

This duty prevents directors from accepting benefits from parties outside the company (usually bribes). It supports the duty under s 175 by preventing a potential conflict of interest.

(7) **Duty to declare an interest in proposed transactions or arrangements (s 177)**

Directors must declare the nature and extent of any proposed arrangement or transaction they may be involved in with the company either personally or through a third party. Disclosure may be given by written or general notice or at a board meeting, but must be made to the directors, as disclosure to the members is not sufficient to discharge the duty.

91 Promoting success

Text reference. Chapter 19.

Top tips. Directors' duties were put into a statutory basis under the Companies Act 2006. The duty to promote the success of the company attracted significant press attention, so don't be afraid to bring in any knowledge from your wider reading on this area.

Easy marks. There are no easy marks unless you have read and understood the issues surrounding this duty.

Examiner's comments. This question required candidates to explain the duty of directors to promote the success of the company and to whom such a duty is owed. This question required specific reference to section 172 of the Companies Act 2006, but only a small minority of candidates appeared to be aware of that Act let alone the detail of section 172. Very few produced satisfactory answers to this question. They were clearly up to speed on the Companies Act 2006 and exhibited a sound knowledge and understanding of directors' duties and, specifically, the duty to promote the success of the company. The others either used the out of date 1985 Act or relied on a general description of directors' duties

Marking scheme

This question requires candidates to explain the duty of directors to promote the success of the company and to whom such a duty is owed.

8–10 marks:	A very good answer revealing a thorough to complete understanding of both elements of the question.
4–7 marks:	A good answer but perhaps unfocused or lacking in detail as to the specific duties applied under s.172.
0–3 marks:	Weak answer, not fully explaining the law or issues involved.

Duty to promote the success of the company

An overriding theme of the Companies Act 2006 is the principle that the **purpose of the legal framework** surrounding companies should be **to help companies do business**. Their main purpose is to create wealth for the shareholders.

This theme is evident in the **duty of directors to promote the success of a company** under Section 172 of the Act. During the Act's development, the independent Company Law Review recommended that company law should consider the interests of those who companies are run for. It decided that the new Act should embrace the principle of **'enlightened shareholder value'**.

In essence, this principle means that the law should encourage **longtermism** and **regard for all stakeholders** by directors and that **stakeholder interests** should be **pursued** in an **enlightened** and **inclusive** way.

To achieve this, a duty of directors to act in a way, which, in **good faith**, promotes the success of the company for the benefit of the members as a whole, was created.

Requirements of the duty

The requirements of this duty are difficult to define and possibly problematic to apply, so the Act provides directors with a **non-exhaustive list** of issues to keep in mind.

When **exercising this duty** directors should consider:

- The **consequences of their decisions** in the long term.
- The **interests of** their **employees**.
- The need to **develop good relationships** with **customers** and **suppliers**.
- The **impact of the company** on the **local community** and the **environment**.
- The desirability of **maintaining high standards of business conduct** and a **good reputation**.
- The need to **act fairly as between all members** of the company.

The list identifies areas of **particular importance** and **modern day expectations** of **responsible business behaviour**. For example the interests of the company's employees and the impact of the company's operations on the community and the environment.

The **Act does not define** what should be regarded as the **success of a company**. This is down to a director's judgement in good faith. This is important as it ensures that business decisions are for the directors rather than the courts.

No guidance is given for what the **correct course of action** would be where the various s172 **duties are in conflict**. For example a decision to shut down an office may be in the long term best interests of the company but it is certainly not in the interests of the employees affected, nor the local community in which they live. Conflicts such as this are inevitable and could potentially leave directors open to breach of duty claims by a wide range of stakeholders if they do not deal with them carefully.

To whom the duty is owed

Section 170 of the Act makes it clear that directors owe their duties to the company, **not** the members. This means that the **only company itself can take action against a director** who breaches them. This puts the common law position set out in *Percival v Wright 1902* onto a statutory footing. However, it is possible for a member to bring a derivative claim against the director on behalf of the company.

92 Caz

Text reference. Chapter 19.

Top tips. Read the question carefully at least twice so that you appreciate exactly what the scenario involves and make a note of the points you need to make before starting to write your answer.

Easy marks. For each of the two parts of the question, make sure that you:

- **Identify** the law
- **State** the law
- **Apply** the law
- **Conclude** on the situation in the question

Examiner's comments. Unfortunately, it has become repetitive to say that candidates provided the right answer to the wrong question, but in this instance too, some candidates seemed to recognise this as a question about insider dealing rather than what it was actually about. Perhaps, in this instance, the rubric did not mention directors' duties specifically, but to see the question as being about insider dealing is not only to misunderstand the question, but also to completely misunderstand insider dealing.
Some answers recognised that the question was about directors' duties in relation to their companies, but once again many candidates wasted time and effort by dealing with the full amount of directors' duties, rather than focusing on the key duties involved in the question. Such a response indicates a lack of analytical skill in relation to the scenario questions.

Marking scheme

This question requires candidates to analyse a problem scenario and explain and apply the law relating to directors' contracts with their companies.

8–10 marks	A good analysis of the scenario with a clear explanation of the law relating to contracts between directors and their companies, both at common law and under statute. Cases and/or references to the Companies Act will be provided.
5–7 marks	Some understanding of the situation but perhaps lacking in detail or reference to the statute.
3–4 marks	Weak answer lacking in knowledge or application, with little or no reference to the Companies Act.
0–2 marks	Little if any knowledge of the appropriate legal principles.

Directors' duties

Since they make contracts as agents of the company and have control of its property, **directors** are said to be akin to trustees and therefore owe **fiduciary duties** to the company in the same way that trustees owe fiduciary duties to the trust. Therefore a director must act *bona fide* and honestly and not seek any personal advantage. Under the Companies Act 2006 they also owe a number of **statutory duties**.

Under s 175 a director must avoid any **conflict of duty and personal interest** and must not obtain any **personal advantage** from their position as director without the consent of the company. In *Regal (Hastings) v Gulliver 1942* the directors funded the creation of a subsidiary company in order to purchase two more cinemas. This resulted in profits on a later sale of the company. It was held that they had only made the profits because of their position as directors of the parent company and they were therefore required to account for the profits.

It is not necessary to prove an actual conflict, nor that the company has been **prejudiced** in any way by any such conflict.

A statutory and common law framework exists enabling directors to be interested in contracts with the company but only subject to certain safeguards, the **principal common law condition** being that a director **cannot obtain personal advantage** from their position as director unless permitted by the company. Without such consent, the contract would be voidable at the instance of the company.

Under s177 of the Act, directors must always disclose the **nature** and **extent of any interest, direct** or **indirect**, that they have in a **contract** or **proposed contract** with the company.

The disclosure must be made **before** the company enters into the transaction and should be made to the directors by **general** or **written notice** or **verbally** at a board meeting. Disclosure just to the members is not sufficient and should the disclosure become void or out of date then a fresh one should be made.

Under s182 of the Act, directors must disclose an interest in an **existing contract**. This duty is identical to the s177 duty except it applies to transactions which have already occurred.

Caz

Turning to the case in question, it appears that Caz has not disclosed either her **interest** in Era Ltd or her interest in this particular contract. Under s177 of the Companies Act 2006 the interest should have been stated at the board meeting that Caz attended which approved the contract. It was not. It should also have been declared under s182 once it had occurred – but it was not either. She will therefore have to account to Dull plc for any **profit** that she makes on the transaction and she may also be subject to a **fine**. Had she dealt honestly with Dull plc by declaring her interest and obtaining company approval, she would have been permitted to retain any profit which is made.

93 Directors

Text reference. Chapter 19

Top tips. This question is not technically difficult, but having to answer three parts may have caused you to spend too long answering it. Watch your time and aim to write for five or six minutes on each part before moving on. Jotting down bullet points as an answer plan is always a good idea as it helps focus the mind on the task in hand and prevents you straying off target.

Easy marks. Defining each type of director.

Examiner's comments. Most candidates made a reasonable attempt at explaining the role of the executive directors and gave comprehensive explanations about the role they play in the day-to-day management of the company. There was also a reasonable effort shown in tackling part (b) of the question about the role of the NED. Many made good reference to the importance of corporate governance and the need for some sort of 'check' on the powers of the executive directors.

Marking scheme

This question raises issues relating to the important topic of corporate governance. It requires a consideration of the role of directors generally together with an explanation of the distinction between executive or non-executive directors and an explanation of the meaning of the term 'shadow director'.

8–10 marks	Full understanding and explanation of all three elements of the question.
5–7 marks	Lacking in detail in some or all elements of the question. Unbalanced answer that only focuses on two of the elements.
3–4 marks	Some, but limited knowledge of the nature of the three elements, or unbalanced in dealing with only one or two aspects of the question.
0–2 marks	Little if any knowledge of the topic or very unbalanced in its treatment of the question.

(a) **Executive directors**

An **executive director** is a director who performs a specific role in a company under a **service contract** which requires a regular, possibly daily, involvement in management.

Such a director may also be an **employee** of the company. This fact may create a potential conflict of interest which in principle a director is required to avoid. To allow an individual to be both a **director and employee** the articles usually make express provision for it, but prohibit the director from voting at a board meeting on the terms of their own employment.

Directors who have additional management duties as employees may be distinguished by **special titles**, such as 'Finance Director'. However (except in the case of a managing director) **any such title does not affect their personal legal position**.

They have two distinct positions as:

- A **member of the board** of directors; and
- A manager with management responsibilities as an **employee**

(b) **Non-executive directors**

A **non-executive director** does not have a function to perform in a company's management but is involved in its governance. They are subject to the same legal duties as executive directors

In **listed companies**, corporate governance codes state that boards of directors are more likely to be fully effective if they comprise both **executive directors** and strong, independent **non-executive directors**.

The **main tasks** of Non-executive directors are as follows:

- **Contribute** an **independent view** to the board's deliberations
- **Help the board provide** the company with **effective leadership**
- **Ensure** the **continuing effectiveness** of the **executive directors** and management
- **Ensure high standards** of **financial probity** on the part of the company

(c) **Shadow directors**

According to company law, a **director** is a person who is responsible for the overall direction of the company's affairs. This means any person occupying the position of director, by whatever name they are called.

A **shadow director** has also been defined as any person in accordance with whose instructions the directors are accustomed to act. However this does not include professionals such as accountants or solicitors.

A person might seek to **control** a company as a **director** but **avoid the legal responsibilities of being a director**. The law seeks to prevent this by extending several statutory rules to **shadow directors**. Shadow directors are directors for legal purposes if the board of directors are accustomed to act in **accordance with their directions** and **instructions**.

An example of a shadow director would be a **major shareholder** who uses their power to **manipulate** the **board of directors**.

Shadow directors are subject to the **same legal duties** as executive directors.

94 Auditors I

Text reference. Chapter 19.

Top tips. The important thing to notice in this question is that it is asking you for four specific things (appointment, removal, rights and duties), on top of the basic requirement for an explanation of the role of the auditor. The best way to structure your answer would be to have a heading for each of these, so that you can show the marker clearly that you have addressed all of them.

Easy marks. Make at least one or two, and hopefully more, points about each of the four topics specifically mentioned in the question.

Examiner's comments. Most candidates dealt adequately with the appointment, role and duties of auditors, although there was some uncertainty over appointment. The best answers also considered the duty of care of auditors and cited cases such as *Caparo*.

Marking scheme

This question requires candidates to consider the role of the auditor in relation to companies and the precise way in which this relationship is regulated by company law.

6-10 marks	A thorough understanding of the role of the auditor explaining their rights and duties. Mention will also be made of their qualifications for office and the manner in which they are appointed and may be removed.
0-5 marks	Some knowledge of the role of auditors but lacking in detail or unbalanced in the detail provided.

Auditors

Every public company is required to appoint auditors. Auditors are appointed to ensure that the **interests of a company's shareholders** are being protected and to make certain **reports to the shareholders**.

The Companies Act 2006 provides that an auditor must be a member of a **recognised supervisory body** and hold an appropriate qualification. Certain types of person are **ineligible** for appointment as a company auditor.

These include officers and employees of the company, anyone employed by or in partnership with such a person or anyone who holds such a position in respect of an associated company. An auditor may be an individual or a body corporate or a partnership.

Appointment

Appointment is usually made in the first instance by the **directors of a new company**. They are appointed to hold office until the conclusion of the first meeting at which the accounts are considered. The directors or the company in general meeting may also appoint an auditor to fill a **casual vacancy**.

In normal circumstances, the **members** appoint the auditors at each general meeting at which the accounts are considered, to hold office until the next such meeting, that is, to audit and report on the accounts to be prepared for that subsequent meeting. If the members fail to appoint auditors at the general meeting at which the accounts are considered, the company must, within 28 days of the meeting, give notice to the **Secretary of State**, who has the power to appoint auditors.

Removal

An auditor may **resign** by giving notice in writing to the company's registered office. The auditor must deposit at the registered office a **statement** that states that there are **no circumstances** connected to their resignation that should be brought to the attention of the members and creditors. If there are such circumstances then a statement to that effect should be deposited instead.

The company must send a **copy of the notice of resignation** to the Registrar and, if there is a statement of circumstances, a copy of this statement to every member entitled to receive accounts.

If a statement has been circulated, the **auditor** is **entitled** to **circulate an explanatory statement of reasonable length to the members**, **requisition a general meeting** to explain the reasons for the resignation and attend and speak at any meeting where the appointment of successors is discussed. Similarly, if an auditor declines to accept reappointment, a statement of circumstances – or that there are none – is required.

An auditor may be **removed from office** before expiry of their appointment by the passing of an **ordinary resolution** in general meeting. **Special notice** is required and members and auditors must be notified. Similarly where an auditor is not re-elected when their term of office expires, special notice must be given of any resolution to appoint different auditors. Special notice means that a copy of the proposed resolution is given to the auditor who has the statutory right to defend themselves by issuing a statement or addressing the meeting in person.

Duties

The statutory duty of auditors is to **report to the members of the company** on whether the accounts which they have audited

- Give a **true and fair view** of the result for the year and the state of affairs of the company (and, if applicable, the group of companies) and
- Have been **properly prepared** in accordance with the Companies Act.

This report covers the profit and loss account and balance sheet of the company. They must also report on whether the information given in the **directors' report** is **consistent** with the accounts.

In reaching the opinion expressed in these reports, the auditors must form an opinion:

- As to whether **proper accounting records** have been kept,
- Whether proper **returns** adequate for the audit have been received from **branches**,
- Whether the accounts are in **agreement** with the underlying accounting records and
- Whether the company has complied with the requirements of the Companies Act regarding **disclosure of directors' emoluments and other benefits**.

Under the principles of the law of tort, an auditor has a **duty of care**. This duty of care is owed to the company rather than to individual shareholders or potential investors *(Caparo Industries plc v Dickman and Others 1990)*. The duty of care means that an auditor must perform the audit with **reasonable care and skill**. If a breach of the duty of care is shown, the auditor may be sued for damages. Under the Companies Act 2006 auditors have the right to agree with their client a **limitation of liability** for negligence. This should be prepared annually.

Rights

The auditors are given certain **legal rights** to enable them to carry out their duties:

- A right at all times of **access to the books and records of the company**
- A right to require such **information and explanations** from the company's officers as they consider necessary for the performance of their duties
- A right to **attend any general meetings** of the company and to receive all notices of, and communications relating to, such meetings
- A right to be **heard at general meetings** which they attend on any part of the business that concerns them as auditors
- A right to **receive notice** of any written resolution proposed

95 Auditors II

Text reference. Chapter 19.

Top tips. Don't let the length of this answer put you off. There is a very wide scope for answering this question and therefore the answer reflects almost everything that you could have written. A good answer would have explained at least three or four points in a fair degree of detail for each of the three aspects in the question. An explanation of auditor liability was not explicitly required by the question but it is included here as the examiner's answer covered it and marks would have been awarded if your answer included this material.

Easy marks. Listing the duties of auditors in Part (c).

Examiner's comments. There was a significant tendency for candidates to overstate the powers of auditors, even to the extent of suggesting that they could take over the running of the company or dismissing the board of directors. Perhaps of more importance in this regard, and certainly from the accountancy point of view, was the almost general tendency to assert that the auditors had to ensure that the accounts provided a true and fair view, rather than the correct approach that the auditors reported on whether the accounts presented actually portrayed a true and fair view. The difference is subtle but important.

Marking scheme

	Marks
A thorough understanding of the role of the auditor explaining their rights and duties. Mention will also be made of their qualifications for office and the manner in which they are appointed and may be removed.	8–10
A clear understanding of the general law but perhaps lacking in detail or unbalanced in only dealing with some issues.	5–7
Some knowledge of the role of auditors but lacking in detail or unbalanced in the detail provided.	2–4
Little or no knowledge of the topic.	0–1

Auditors

The general role of **auditors** is to support the concept of **good corporate governance** by providing **independent reports** that confirm or deny the accuracy and reliability of financial information produced by the company. Such reports protect the interests of the shareholders since they involve an independent assessment of the financial controls and results of the company that they have invested in.

All **public companies** must have an auditor but private companies that meet the requirements of the Companies Act Small Companies Regime are exempt from an audit. These companies are often run and owned by the same small group of people and therefore an audit is not required to safeguard their interests.

(a) **Qualification of auditors**

Membership of a **Recognised Supervisory Body** is the main prerequisite for eligibility as an auditor. The Act requires an auditor to hold an **'appropriate qualification'**. This means that they must satisfy **criteria** for appointment as an auditor, such as holding a **recognised qualification**.

Under the Companies Act 2006, a person may be ineligible on the grounds of **'lack of independence'**. This means that a person is ineligible for appointment as a company auditor if for example they are an **officer** or **employee** of the company being audited, or a **partner** or **employee** of such a person.

The legislation does **not** disqualify a shareholder, a debtor, a creditor or a close relative of an officer or employee of the company from being its auditor.

Appointment and removal of auditors

The **first auditors** are usually appointed by the directors, to hold office until the **first general meeting** at which their appointment is considered. Members usually subsequently appoint auditors, in general meeting with an ordinary resolution. **Subsequent auditors** may not take office until the previous auditor has ceased to hold office. The auditors will hold office from 28 days after the meeting at which accounts are laid until the end of the corresponding period next year (public companies). **Casual vacancies** in the post of auditor are usually filled by either the directors or the members.

Auditors of **private companies** are deemed **automatically re-appointed** unless the auditor was **appointed by the directors**, the **articles require formal re-appointment**, **members holding 5% of the voting rights** serve notice that the auditor should not be re-appointed, a resolution has been passed that prevents re-appointment or the **directors have resolved that auditors should not be appointed** for the forthcoming year as the company is likely to be exempt from audit.

To **leave office** auditors may **resign** their appointment or they may **decline re-appointment**. They may be **removed from office** before the expiry of their appointment by the passing of an **ordinary resolution with special notice** in general meeting or simply by **not being re-appointed** when their term of office expires. **Special notice** must be given of any resolution to appoint auditors who were not appointed on the last occasion of the resolution

(b) **Powers of auditors**

Statutory rights

The Companies Act provides **statutory rights** for auditors to enable them to carry out their duties.

Access to records

Auditors have a right of access at all times to the books, accounts and vouchers of the company: s499(1).

Information and explanations

Auditors have a right to require from the company's officers, employees or any other relevant person such information and explanations as they think necessary for the performance of their duties: s499(1)

Attendance at/notices of general meetings

Auditors have a right to attend any general meetings of the company and to receive all notices of and communications relating to such meetings which any member of the company is entitled to receive: s502(2)

Right to speak at general meetings

Auditors have a right to be heard at general meetings which they attend on any part of the business that concerns them as auditors: s502 (2)

Rights in relation to written resolutions

Auditors have a right to receive a copy of any written resolution proposed: s502(1)

(c) **Duties of auditors**

The **statutory duty** of auditors is to report to the members whether the accounts give a **true and fair view** and have been properly prepared in accordance with the Companies Act.

They must also **state** whether or not the **directors' report** is **consistent** with the **accounts**. For **quoted companies**, they must **report** to the members on the **auditable** part of the **directors' remuneration report** including whether or not it has been properly prepared in accordance with the Act.

To fulfil their statutory duties, the auditors **must carry out such investigations as are necessary** to form an opinion as to whether:

- **Proper accounting records** have been kept and **proper returns** that are adequate for the audit have been received from branches
- **Accounts** are in **agreement** with the **accounting records**
- **Information** in the **directors' remuneration report** is consistent with the **accounts.**

Auditors' liability

Professional negligence cases such as *Caparo* have resulted in an increase in litigation against auditors for breach of duty and negligence. The **Companies Act 2006** has provisions which permit auditors to agree **limited liability** with their clients.

Under s532 any **agreement** between an auditor and a company that seeks to **indemnify the auditor** for their own negligence, default or breach of duty or trust is **void**. However under s534, an agreement can be made which **limits the auditor's liability** to the company. Such **liability limitation agreements** can only stand for **one financial year** and must therefore be replaced annually.

Liability can only be **limited** to what is **fair and reasonable** having regard to the auditor's responsibilities, their contractual obligations and the professional standards expected of them. Such agreements must be approved by the members and **publicly disclosed** in the **accounts** or **directors' report**.

96 Katch Ltd

Text reference. Chapters 12 and 19.

Top tips. Although you may recognise the facts of the *Freeman & Lockyer* case in the scenario and therefore have a good idea of what the answer is, you must explain all the types of authority so that you can eliminate them. Stating that the company is liable due to the *Freeman* case might be the right answer but it would not earn you enough marks to pass.

Easy marks. Quoting the *Hely* and *Freeman* cases and using them to explain implied and apparent authority.

Examiner's comments. While the majority of candidates grasped the essence of this question, a fairly substantial minority failed to see what was required and based their answers on topics which were not central to the question.

Marking scheme

	Marks
A thorough analysis of the scenario focusing on the appropriate rules of law and Applying them accurately. It is extremely likely that cases will be cited in support of the analysis and/or application.	8–10
A clear understanding of the general law but perhaps lacking in detail or unbalanced in only dealing with some issues.	5–7
Some, but limited, understanding of the law or completely lacking in application.	2–4
Little or no knowledge of the relevant law.	0–1

Directors' powers

The powers of the directors are **defined by the articles**. The directors are usually authorised 'to manage the company's business' and 'to exercise all the powers of the company for any purpose connected with the company's business'. As **agents of the company**, directors may have **express**, **implied** or **apparent** authority to enter the company into binding contracts.

Express authority

Express authority to enter into a **particular contract** can be granted by the board of directors to one or more of their number. Where such express authority is given, the company will be bound by the agreement.

Implied authority

Where there is no express authority, authority may be **implied** from the director's position within the company. A company's articles usually provide for one or more directors to be appointed as managing director. **Managing directors** usually have authority to make commercial contracts on behalf of the company and therefore those appointed as such are permitted to exercise this authority as they see fit, their actions binding the company. As far as **third parties** are concerned, they are entitled to assume that a person appointed as managing director has this implied authority unless they know to the contrary.

In *Hely-Hutchinson v Brayhead Ltd 1968* it was held that implied authority can be **extended to directors** who, although **never formally appointed** as managing director, nonetheless act as if they were (they are known as *de facto* managing directors).

Apparent authority

Where an individual has neither express nor implied authority they may still be able to bind the company in contracts if they have apparent authority. This authority arises where they are **'held out'** by members of the board **as having authority** to enter into contracts. The company will be **estopped** from denying this if a third party acts on the representation.

In *Freeman & Lockyer v Buckhurst Park Properties (Mangal) Ltd 1964* a company carried on a business as a property developer. The articles contained a power to appoint a managing director but this was never done. One of the directors of the company, to the knowledge but without the express authority of the remainder of the board, acted as if they were managing director. They found a purchaser for an estate and also engaged a firm of architects to make a planning application. The company later refused to pay the architect's fees on the grounds that the director had no actual or apparent authority.

The court found the company liable since, by its acquiescence, it had **represented** that the director was a managing director with the authority therefore to enter into contracts that were normal commercial arrangements in that sector, and which the board itself would have been able to enter.

Len

From the facts of the case it is clear that **Len did not have express authority** from the company to enter into the contract and therefore from this point of view the company is not liable.

As **Len is not a director he cannot have implied authority** to bind the company; the *Hely-Hutchinson* case makes it clear that implied authority can only be extended to directors, not employees.

The circumstances in which Katch Ltd finds itself are very similar to that of the *Freeman & Lockyer* case**. Len has been allowed by the board to act as if he were managing director** and therefore as a third party Mo is entitled to assume that he has the **implied authority** of one. This authority permits him to bind the company in **commercial contracts**, so the company will be bound by the advertising contract entered into by Len. Katch Ltd therefore has a liability to pay Mo or be sued for breach of contract.

97 Clean Ltd

Text reference. Chapter 19.

Top tips. Following the ISAC approach as our solution does gives your answer a ready-made structure and takes you through a logical process to come to your conclusion.

Easy marks. Identifying the issue, stating and applying the law, and coming to a reasonable conclusion.

Examiner's comments. This question required an analysis of the doctrine of corporate opportunity and the rules relating to directors' duties. It has to be said it was the least popular question on the paper and was not attempted by a considerable minority of candidates, and those who did tackle it, did not do particularly well in it.

There were essentially two core issues in the question, relating to conflict of interest, corporate opportunities and the much less essential corporate personality issue.

The majority of candidates recognised that the question related to directors' duties in some way, but apart from citing those generally, could get no further than that. Very few candidates even considered the corporate opportunities issue, preferring to go down the road of patent law, which is not even part of the syllabus of this paper.

As for the corporate personality issue, although not central to the question a number of candidates saw it as the key issue and spent all their time dealing with that –perhaps it would not be too cynical to suggest that this was in response to their lack of knowledge relating to any other aspect of the question.

Marking scheme

This question requires a consideration of the statutory duties placed on company directors under the Companies Act 2006.

8–10 marks	Thorough to complete answers, showing a detailed understanding of the rules relating to conflict of interest.
5–7 marks	A clear understanding of the topic but perhaps lacking in detail or application.
2–4 marks	Some knowledge, although perhaps not clearly expressed, or very limited in its application.
0–1 mark	Little or no knowledge of the topic.

Issue

The issue at hand is the actions of Des in setting up a rival company (Flush Ltd) and taking a major customer away from the company of which he was a director (Clean Ltd). Flush Ltd also manufactures a profitable product which Clean Ltd employees discovered.

The law

The Companies Act 2006 sets out the **principal duties** that directors owe to their company. Many of these duties developed over time through the operation of **common law** and **equity,** or are **fiduciary duties** which have now been codified to make the law clearer and more accessible.

A **fiduciary duty** is imposed upon certain persons because of the position of trust and confidence in which they stand in relation to another.

Broadly speaking directors must be **honest** and **not allow their personal interests to conflict with their duties as directors.** The directors are said to hold a **fiduciary position** since they make contracts as **agents** of the company and have control of its property.

The duties which are relevant to the situation with Des are:

Promote the success of the company (s 172)

Under this duty, directors must act in a way which, in **good faith**, promotes the success of the company for the benefit of the members as a whole. However, as it is a new duty created by the Companies Act 2006 it is as yet unclear how it will be interpreted and applied.

Avoid conflicts of interest (s 175)

Directors have a **duty to avoid circumstances** where their **personal interests conflict**, or may possibly conflict, **with the company's interests**. This may occur when a director makes personal use of corporate opportunities, information or property belonging to the company, whether or not the company was able to take advantage of them at the time (*Regal (Hastings) Ltd v Gulliver 1942).*

Directors will not be liable for a breach of this duty if:

- The **members** of the company **authorised** their actions
- The **situation cannot reasonably be regarded** as likely to give rise to a conflict of interest
- The **actions have been authorised by the other directors**. This only applies if they are genuinely independent from the transaction and:
  - If the company is private - the articles do not restrict such authorisation, or
  - If it is public - the articles expressly permit it.

Declare interests in transactions or arrangements (s 177 and 182)

Directors are required to **disclose to the other directors** the nature and extent of any interest, direct or indirect, that they have in relation to a **proposed transaction** or **arrangement** with the **company**.

Disclosure to the **members** is **not** sufficient to discharge the duty. Directors must declare the **nature** and **extent** of their interest to the **other directors** as well.

Directors also have a statutory obligation to declare any direct or indirect interest in an **existing transaction** entered into by the company.

The case of *Industrial Development Consultants Ltd v Cooley 1972* indicates that a director's duties can also apply after they leave the service of the company that they are a director of.

Remedies

Breach of duty comes under the **civil law** rather than criminal law. Section 170 makes it clear that directors owe their duties to the company, **not** the members. This means that **only the company itself can take action against a director** who breaches them. This usually means the other directors starting proceedings.

Consequences of breach include:

- **Damages** payable to the company where it has suffered loss.
- **Restoration** of company property
- **Repayment of any profits** made by the director
- **Rescission of contract** (where the director did not disclose an interest)

Application and conclusion

By creating Flush Ltd as a rival to Clean Ltd, Des set up a situation where he has a **conflict of interest**. He has a personal interest in Flush Ltd and a professional duty to Clean Ltd. A further conflict was created where Dank plc sought to move its business from Clean Ltd to Flush Ltd. The result was Clean Ltd losing its major customer.

Des also had a duty to **declare an interest in the proposed transaction** of Dank plc contracting with Flush Ltd rather than Clean Ltd.

Des is clearly in breach of his duties under s 175 and 177 of the Companies Act 2006.

Additionally, by creating a rival in Flush Ltd, it could be argued that Des is also in **breach of his duty** under s 172 – **to promote the success of Clean Ltd**. This duty is likely to also be broken by Flush Plc selling the new glue which was developed by Clean Ltd.

Clean Ltd will have suffered loss in two areas. Firstly the loss of Dank plc as its major customer, and secondly loss of profits on the new glue being sold by Flush Ltd. The court could order Des pay Clean Ltd **damages** and **repay any profits** earned by Flush Ltd from Dank plc and on the sale of the glue. He will not be protected by the corporate veil of Flush Ltd as the court will simply lift it.

98 Liquidation

Text reference. Chapter 21.

Top tips. In part (a) notice that the question asks you to 'state and explain' the grounds. This means that you must say what they are, and then give as much further information as you can. For example, what does 'just and equitable' mean? How does a court decide that a company cannot pay its debts – how much does it have to owe?

In part (b) do not confuse members' and creditors' winding up on one hand and compulsory and voluntary winding up on the other.

Easy marks. In questions like this which are very technical, marks are available for just stating the law and require little application. You should be able to pass the question by repeating book knowledge.

Examiner's comments. The question was not popular and was very poorly done. The majority of candidates did not actually address the issue of S122, but merely discussed the winding up of companies in general terms. Many candidates only seemed able to address one of the grounds in any depth; this limited mark-earning potential.

Marking scheme

This question requires candidates to explain the grounds under which a company may be wound up under s 122 of the Insolvency Act 1986.

8-10 marks	Thorough to complete answers, showing an understanding of all or certainly most of the grounds for winding up.
5-7 marks	A clear understanding of the topic, perhaps lacking in detail.
2-4 marks	Some knowledge, although perhaps not clearly expressed, or very limited knowledge in its understanding of the topic.
0-1 mark	Little or no knowledge of the topic.

(a) **Compulsory winding-up**

A **compulsory winding-up** is one ordered by the court under s.122 IA on one or more of seven specified grounds. The most important of these grounds are:

- That the company is **unable to pay its debts**; and
- That it is **just and equitable** to wind up the company.

Unable to pay its debts

Where a creditor is owed more than **£750** and makes a written demand for payment and the company fails to pay the debt, or offer reasonable security for it, within **three weeks**, the company is deemed unable to pay its debts. The creditor may persuade the court of the company's inability to settle its debts in other ways, for example by proving that the company's assets are less than its liabilities.

Just and equitable ground

The **just and equitable** ground is usually relied on by a **member** who is **dissatisfied** with the directors' or controlling shareholders' **management** of the company, provided they can show that no other remedy is available and satisfactory.

A member who is dissatisfied with the directors or controlling shareholders over the management of the company may **petition the court** for a winding up on the basis that to do so is **just and equitable**. Such winding up orders have been made where the **substratum** (the only main object) of the company **no longer exists** *(Re German Date Coffee Co 1882)*, where the company was formed for an **illegal or fraudulent purpose**, where there is a **complete deadlock in the management** of the company's affairs *(Re Yenidje Tobacco Co Ltd 1916)* and where the **trust and confidence** between both **directors** and **shareholders** in a small company have **broken down** *(Ebrahimi v Westbourne Galleries Ltd 1973)*.

(b) **Creditors' voluntary winding-up**

The winding up is instigated by a **special resolution** of the company in general meeting, by which the company states that it cannot continue to trade because of its liabilities. Private companies may pass a **written resolution** with a three quarters majority.

Creditors' meeting

The company must call a **meeting of creditors** for a day not later than the 14th day after the day on which the special resolution was passed. The creditors must receive at least 7 days notice of the meeting.

The **notice** must state either:

- The name and address of an **insolvency practitioner** who will furnish creditors free of charge with such information as they reasonably require, or
- A place in the locality where on the two days before the meeting of creditors is held, a list of the names and addresses of the **company's creditors** will be available for inspection free of charge.

Notice of the creditors' meeting must be **advertised** in the *Gazette* and in at least two newspapers circulating in the locality in which the company's principal place of business was situated.

Liquidator

During the period before the creditors' meeting but after the resolution for winding-up the **members' nominee** will act as **provisional liquidator**. They will have restricted powers to act during this period, subject to application to the court. This restriction is necessitated by the practice of 'centrebinding', whereby the assets are fraudulently disposed of before the creditors' meeting.

At the creditors' meeting the **creditors may appoint their own nominee** to act as liquidator. The **creditors' choice will prevail** over the members' choice if there is a conflict; usually there is not.

Statement of affairs

The **directors** of the company must prepare and lay before the creditors' meeting a **statement of affairs** of the company but, importantly, they do not have to make a statutory declaration of solvency.

99 Compulsory winding up

Text reference. Chapter 21.

Top tips. Note that the question relates to compulsory winding up: do not get side tracked into other types of liquidation.

Easy marks. Explaining what compulsory liquidation is and its effects.

Compulsory winding-up

The statutory provisions on **compulsory winding up** are in the Insolvency Act 1986, to which all section references in this question refer.

The two **general effects** of compulsory liquidation are:

- That the management of the company passes to a liquidator and the **directors' powers cease**, and
- **Dispositions** of the company's **property** or **shares**, and **actions** against the company, are **restrained.**

There is **no** automatic cancellation of company contracts, but many commercial contracts provide for cancellation at the option of the other party if the company goes into liquidation.

Commencement

Compulsory winding up is deemed to commence from the date on which the petition was presented, unless the company was then already in voluntary liquidation. In effect the order for compulsory liquidation is retrospective.

Effects

The more **specific effects** of compulsory liquidation are as follows.

- The **Official Receiver** becomes **liquidator** from the making of the order, and they continue until some other liquidator, who must be an insolvency practitioner, is appointed: s 136.

- The **powers of the directors are terminated** and they are **dismissed.**

- Any **disposition of the company's property** from the commencement of the liquidation **is void** unless approved by the court.

  The court may give approval with **retrospective effect** but it is safer to apply for it in advance, when the petition has been represented. The court will only give its approval if it considers that it is in the interests of the company and its creditors that the company should continue to carry on its business pending a decision on the petition.

- Any **transfer of the company's shares is void** unless approved by the court: s 127.
- **No creditor may commence or continue legal action** against the company except with the leave of the court: s 126.

- The **employment of the company's staff ceases** unless the liquidator retains them to carry on the business.

- **Floating charges crystallise.**

100 Lazy Days

Text reference. Chapter 21.

Top tips. At all times remember the purpose of administration. It is not a winding up, but an attempt to save the business. Do not stray off the subject matter or you will lose marks and waste time.

Easy marks. If you set out the law in parts (a) and (b) then applying it is very straightforward and will earn you the easy marks here.

(a) **Administration**

An **administration order** is an order of the court which puts an insolvency practitioner in control of the company with a defined programme for rescuing the company from insolvency as a going concern.

Its effect is to insulate the company from its creditors while it seeks:

- To **save itself**, or failing that
- To achieve a **better result** for creditors than an immediate winding up would secure, or failing that
- To **realise property** so as to make a distribution to creditors.

During the process, the company is **protected** as follows:

- Voluntary and compulsory **liquidation** cannot be applied for
- Company **property cannot be seized** as payment of debts
- Goods on **lease** or **hire purchase** cannot be seized
- **Legal proceedings** against the company cannot be instigated

Administration orders and **liquidation** are **mutually exclusive**. Once an administration order has been passed by the court, it is no longer possible to petition the court for a winding up order against the company. Similarly, however, once an order for winding up has been made, an administration order cannot usually be granted.

(b) **Procedure**

A company or its directors may **appoint an administrator** if (subject to the articles of association):

- They have not done so in the last **12 months** or been subject to a moratorium as a result of a voluntary arrangement with its creditors in the last 12 months
- The company is, or is likely to be, **unable to pay its debts**
- **No petition** for winding up nor any administration petition in respect of the company has been presented to the court and is outstanding
- The **company is not in liquidation**
- **No administrator** is already in office

The company or its directors must give notice to any **floating chargeholders** entitled to appoint an administrative receiver or an administrator. This means that the floating chargeholders may appoint their own administrator within this time period, and so block the company's choice of administrator.

Once the notice period is over, the company or its directors must, as soon as **reasonably practicable**, file at court:

- The **notice** in the **prescribed form** identifying the proposed administrator
- A **statutory declaration** that:
  - (i) The company **is**, or is **likely to be**, **unable to pay** its **debts**
  - (ii) The company is **not in liquidation**
  - (iii) As far as ascertainable there is **no restriction** in making the appointment

(c) **Granting an order**

The court will grant the **administration order** if it is satisfied that:

- The company is, or is likely to be, **unable to pay its debts**, and
- The administration order is **reasonably likely** to achieve the purpose of administration

Lazy Days

In Lazy Days Ltd's case the issue is not whether the company is unlikely to be **able to pay its debts**, but whether or not the **purpose** of administration will be achieved. The company is currently running at a £7,000 loss per month and this must be **solvable** for the order to be granted. If the company can argue that it has a good chance of increasing trip sales from 50% to nearer 80% to 90% and that these extra sales will make up the shortfall in revenue then it would have a good chance of obtaining the order.

101 Compulsory winding up and administration

Text reference. Chapter 21.

Top tips. Note that the question relates to compulsory winding up and administration only. Do not get side tracked into other types of liquidation. This question has quite a wide scope and the ACCA model answer indicated marks would also be awarded for describing the role of the Official Receiver or Liquidator.

Easy marks. Explaining what compulsory liquidation and administration are (definitions) and their effects.

Examiner's comments. Some of the less well-prepared candidates, at least as regards administration, spent far too much time on compulsory winding up – far more than the allocated 4 marks could ever justify. This raises two related points: the first.... that.... candidates had prepared a full winding up answer and were going to deliver, no matter what the question might ask and consequently reward; the second point is that candidates must use the mark breakdown as an indication of how much time they should spend on a question, that is why the have been broken down that way in the first place. As a final point in this regard, and again one that reflects/repeats what has been said previously, those who had prepared the general winding up question tended to explain 'voluntary' winding up, which was specifically excluded from the question. Candidates must read the actual words not what they want to see.

Marking scheme

This question, in two parts, carrying 4 marks for part (a) and 6 marks for part (b), requires candidates to explain the meaning of the terms 'compulsory winding up' and 'administration'.

(a)	3–4 marks	A good explanation of the meaning and effect of winding up generally and compulsory winding up in particular.
	0–2 marks	Some, if little knowledge of winding up, or perhaps too general or unbalanced in not dealing specifically with compulsory winding up.
(b)	4–6 marks	A good explanation of the meaning and effect of administration generally and contrasting its purpose with that of compulsory winding up.
	2–3 marks	Some, if little, explanation of administration, but perhaps too general or lacking in detail.
	0–1 mark	Little or no knowledge of the topic.

(a) **Compulsory winding-up**

Compulsory winding up involves the termination of a company's life under one of seven grounds, however only two are common. The statutory provisions on **compulsory winding up** are in the Insolvency Act 1986, to which all section references in this question refer.

The first main ground is under s122(1)(f) – the company is **unable to pay its debts**. This can be brought by a creditor who is owed £750 or more, where the company has failed to pay the debt within 21 days of receiving a formal written demand.

The second main ground is under s122(1)(g) – it is **just and equitable to wind the company up**. This can be brought by any company member but the court will need strong evidence that it is the right thing to do as closing an otherwise healthy company is a drastic step.

Compulsory winding up is deemed to commence from the date on which a petition was presented, unless the company was then already in voluntary liquidation. In effect the order for compulsory liquidation is retrospective.

Effects

Some **specific effects** of compulsory liquidation are as follows.

- The **Official Receiver** becomes **liquidator** from the making of the order, and they continue until some other liquidator, who must be an insolvency practitioner, is appointed: s 136.
- The **powers of the directors are terminated** and they are **dismissed**.
- Any **disposition of the company's property** from the commencement of the liquidation **is void** unless approved by the court.
- Any **transfer of the company's shares is void** unless approved by the court: s 127.
- **No creditor may commence or continue legal action** against the company except with the leave of the court: s 126.
- The **employment of the company's staff ceases** unless the liquidator retains them to carry on the business.
- **Floating charges crystallise**.

(b) **Administration**

Administration puts an insolvency practitioner in control of a company with a defined programme for rescuing it from insolvency as a going concern.

Its effect is to insulate the company from its creditors while it seeks:

- To **save itself**, or failing that
- To achieve a **better result** for creditors than an immediate winding up would secure, or failing that
- To **realise property** so as to make a distribution to creditors.

During the process, the company is **protected** as follows:

- Voluntary and compulsory **liquidation** cannot be applied for
- Company **property cannot be seized** as payment of debts
- Goods on **lease** or **hire purchase** cannot be seized
- **Legal proceedings** against the company cannot be instigated

Administration orders and **liquidation** are **mutually exclusive**. Once an administration is in place it is no longer possible to petition the court for a winding up order against the company. Similarly, however, once an order for winding up has been made, an administration order cannot usually be granted.

A company, its directors and floating chargeholders may **appoint an administrator** either with or without a court order. Fixed chargeholders can only put the company into administration through the courts.

The administrator of a company may do **anything necessarily expedient** for the management of the affairs, business and property of the company.

This usually means that they **take on the powers previously enjoyed by the directors** and they therefore have the following specific powers to:

- Remove or appoint a **director**
- Call a **meeting of members or creditors**
- **Apply to court for directions** regarding the carrying out of his functions
- Make payments to **secured or preferential creditors**
- With the permission of the court, **make payments to unsecured creditors**

The administration period **ends** when:

- The administration has been **successful**
- **12 months** have elapsed from the date of the appointment of administrator
- The **administrator applies to the court** to end the appointment
- A **creditor applies to the court** to end the appointment
- An **improper motive of the applicant** for applying for the administration is discovered.

The administrator automatically vacates office after **12 months of his appointment.** This time period can be extended by court order or by consent from the appropriate creditors.

Alternatively, the administrator may **apply to the court** when he thinks:

- The **purpose** of administration **cannot be achieved**
- The **company should not have entered into administration**
- The **administration has been successful** (if appointed by the court)

102 Earl

Text reference. Chapters 10, 16, 17 and 21

Top tips. You must be prepared to answer questions such as this which cross syllabus areas. It is not just about insolvency but also has elements of share capital, borrowing and company charges. Establishing from the start that there are three distinct issues will give structure to your answer and will show the examiner that you have a good understanding of the law.

Easy marks. The calculation of the amount outstanding on Earl's shares in Part (b).

Examiner's comments. The skill, in this question, was to identify the relevant areas of law and apply that law to the facts stated in the problem. Explanations of the meaning and procedures involved in voluntary and compulsory liquidations were not relevant to this question. The focus should be on Earl and the legal issues raised by his concurrent relationships with Flash Ltd.

Marking scheme

		Marks
(a)	A good to thorough explanation of the situation of employees as preferred creditors.	2–3
	Little or no knowledge of the relevant law.	0–1
(b)	A good general knowledge of the liability of holders of unpaid shares.	2–3
	Little or no knowledge of the relevant law.	0–1
(c)	A good explanation of fixed charges together with accurate application of the law.	2–4
	Some knowledge, but lacking in detail or application.	0–1

Issues

Earl has **three relationships** with **Flash Ltd**: as an **employee**, a **shareholder** and a **debentureholder**. The liquidation of the company has raised issues concerning his unpaid salary, the loss in value of his partly- paid shares and the repayment of his secured loan. Each issue is subject to different rules which we consider below.

(a) **Unpaid wages**

Earl will become an **unsecured creditor** in respect of his **unpaid wages** and as such he will only have a claim to have the debt paid to him after the secured creditors have been repaid in full. He will be in a slightly better position than other unsecured creditors (such as suppliers) since in law he will be treated as a preferential unsecured creditor for payment of his unpaid salary and any redundancy payments to which he is entitled. This protection is up to a statutory limit.

(b) **Shareholding**

The **nominal value of a share** (plus any premium on issue) represents the total amount of a shareholder's interest in the company.

Any **amount** of **nominal value** that is **unpaid must be contributed to a company in the event of a winding up**. Once all the creditors have been repaid the balance is then distributed among the shareholders. In cases of insolvent liquidation there is often no money left for the shareholders who therefore lose the whole amount that they invested.

Earl's shares were only **75% paid up** and therefore he has a **liability** for the **25% balance**:

25% × £5,000 = £1,250

He must pay this money over to the liquidator.

(c) **Debentures**

Earl's debentures are secured by a **fixed charge** on the land that the factory is built on and he is therefore a **secured creditor** of the company. Should the company fail to repay the loan or any interest due, the debentureholders may appoint a receiver for the asset who will sell it to realise cash to repay them. As the company is being liquidated the asset will be sold anyway.

Earl and the other **debentureholders** will be **repaid** their **debentures from the sale of the land**; any balance left over will be available to repay the company's other creditors. Should the asset realise less than the total debt secured by the fixed charge then each debentureholder will receive proportionately less. The good news is that as land is such a valuable asset it is likely that Earl's loan will be repaid in full.

103 Directors and corporate governance

Text reference. Chapters 19 and 22.

Top tips. This question needs you to explain the concept of corporate governance. In part (b) you need to look at the different roles that the different directors have. Do not just explain what they do, however. You need to link back their duties and tasks to the concept of corporate governance.

Easy marks. State what is meant by (a) corporate governance and (b) the two types of director.

Marking scheme

8–10 marks	A good explanation of the meaning of corporate governance generally and the roles of the two types of directors in particular. Reference might well be made to the OECD or the UK Corporate Governance Code.
5–7 marks	A sound understanding of this area, although perhaps lacking in detail.
2–4 marks	Some understanding of the area, but lacking in detail, perhaps failing to deal with the relationship of the two groups of directors.
0–1 mark	Little or no knowledge of the area.

(a) **Corporate governance**

Corporate governance is the **system by which companies** (bodies corporate) **are directed and controlled** (governed). It is important that companies are governed well because companies are often directed and controlled by different people from those who have an interest in the company.

It is therefore **important** to each of these parties that the **company is well run** and is not run into financial difficulties. The leadership of the company (**directors**) is in a position by their policies to seek to prevent such problems. Bad corporate governance can open the company up to all sorts of problems.

(b) **Executive directors**

An **executive director** is a director who performs a **specific role** in a company under a **service contract** which involves a regular, possibly daily, involvement in management. A director may also be an employee (usually a member of management) of their company.

Directors who have additional **management duties** as employees may be distinguished by special titles such as **'finance director'**. Such titles do not affect their personal legal position.

Non-executive directors

A **non-executive director**, on the other hand, acts only as a member of the board of directors. Their usual involvement is to attend board meetings. They are not involved in the day to day management of the company. In a public limited company, the role of the non-executive director has become more important in recent years with the increasing emphasis on, and regulation of, **good corporate governance**.

The **tasks** of the non-executive director include the following:

- To contribute an **independent** view to the board's deliberations;
- To help the board provide the company with effective **leadership**;
- To ensure the continuing **effectiveness of the executive directors and management**;
- To ensure **high standards of financial probity** on the part of the company.

Non-executive and executive directors are subject to the same statutory and fiduciary duties.

104 UK Corporate Governance Code

Text reference. Chapter 22.

Top tips. This question, whilst specifically on the UK Corporate Governance Code, is actually quite wide in scope as there are a number of areas that you could bring into your answer. However, don't fall into the trap of thinking that you have to explain the history behind the Code as that will not earn you any marks – your answer must stay focused on how it affects a board of directors.

To earn full marks you should have come up with ten points, each with a brief explanation. You may have come up with other points from our model answer and providing they are based on the UK Corporate Governance Code then you should award yourself marks. Examples of other areas you might have covered are given at the end of the answer.

Easy marks. There is a large number of possible points you can make and so you should be looking to score highly. Easy marks are available for stating how the Code affects the board. Needless to say there are no easy marks if you failed to study the material on the Code in any depth.

The UK Corporate Governance Code

The UK Corporate Governance Code is a **non-legal code** designed to promote good and effective governance in all business organisations, although only major listed companies have to follow it as part of their listing obligations. Many of its principles and provisions are designed to control the behaviour and performance of a board of directors and include the following.

Role of an effective board

The Code makes a board of directors **responsible for the success or failure of an organisation**. It does this by stating that all listed companies should be led by an **effective board** which is **collectively responsible** for the **long-term success of the company**. It makes it clear that a board's role is to provide **entrepreneurial leadership** and is responsible for setting **strategic aims**, ensuring sufficient financial and human resources are available, reviewing management performance, setting values and standards and ensuring obligations to shareholders are met.

Actions of directors

The Code reinforces the Companies Act, and makes directors **responsible for their own actions**, by stating clearly that all directors must act in what they consider to be the **best interests of the company**, consistent with their statutory duties.

Chairman and chief executive

Many corporate governance problems are caused by one person having too much power within an organisation. To prevent this, the Code requires that a **clear division of responsibilities** should exist at the head of the company between running the board (the chairman's role) and running the business (the chief executive officer's role). There should be a balance of power, with no one person having unfettered powers of decision. The roles of **chairman** and **chief executive** should not be exercised by one person and a **chief executive should not go on to become chairman of the same company**.

Composition of the board

The Code appreciates that to be effective, a board should consist of a **balance of personalities**, **skills** and **knowledge**. To achieve this aim, the Code states that a board and its committees should have a balance of **skills, experience, independence and knowledge** and should be of **sufficient size** to **operate effectively**, but not so large as to be **unwieldy.** It should have a **balance** of **executive and non-executive directors** so that no individual or small group is dominant. At least half the board of FTSE 350 companies should be **independent non-executive directors**. Smaller listed companies should have at least **two independent non-executive directors.**

Non-executive directors

Non-executive directors play an important role on the board by acting as a **check on executive directors** and **voicing concerns** shareholders may have. The Code states that they should **constructively challenge strategy** and help develop proposals on it.

They should **monitor the reporting of performance**, scrutinise the performance of management against agreed goals and objectives, and obtain assurance about the integrity of financial information and that financial controls and risk management systems are **robust** and **defensible**.

Evaluation

Under the Code, there should be a **vigorous annual performance evaluation** of the board as a whole, individual directors and board committees. This enables there to be some regulation or check over the performance of the board.

Re-election

Under the Code, all directors should submit themselves for **re-election regularly**, and at least once every three years. Directors of **FTSE 350** companies should be subject to **annual election by shareholders.** Requiring directors to be subject to regular re-election means that unpopular or ineffective directors can be removed within a fixed period of time.

Financial and business reporting

The board is required to present shareholders with a **review of corporate performance** to help them judge its effectiveness. This should include a **balanced and understandable assessment** of the **company's position and prospects** in the annual accounts and other reports such as interim reports and reports to regulators.

Risk management and internal control

The Code aims to prevent (or at least make shareholders aware of) risk taking by the board. It does this by stating that the board is responsible for determining the **nature and extent of the significant risks** it is willing to take to achieve objectives. To counter any risks, sound systems of **risk management and control** should be maintained and directors should **review effectiveness** annually, and report to shareholders that they have done so.

Additional information

Other areas that you may have mentioned in your answer include:

Appointments to the board
Time commitment
Training and development of directors
Supply of information to the board and access to professional advice and the company secretary
Director remuneration
Dialogue with shareholders
Use of the AGM

105 Huge plc

Text reference. Chapter 23.

Top tips. Insider dealing questions tend to encompass more than one of the offences being committed, and this is no exception. While Slye's guilt is very clear, you have to look a little harder to decide on Mate and Tim.

Easy marks. State what is meant by insider dealing, dealing, inside information, insider and money laundering (definitions).

Marking scheme

8–10 marks	A good analysis of the scenario with a clear explanation of the law relating to the insider dealing, with detailed reference to statutory provisions.
5–7 marks	Some understanding of the situation but perhaps lacking in detail or reference to the statutes.
0–4 marks	Weak answer lacking in knowledge or application, with little or no reference to the statute.

Insider dealing

The law attempts to prevent people '**in the know**' from making a profit or avoiding a loss in buying or selling shares or other securities on the back of their **inside knowledge** and at the expense of open dealings in the market.

Significant inside knowledge – of a takeover, an oil strike or a massive fall in profits – will affect the share price when it becomes known, so it is not right that insiders should benefit from dealing in advance of the knowledge becoming generally known.

Criminal Justice Act 1993

In the context of the **Criminal Justice Act 1993, insider dealing is dealing in securities while in possession of inside information as an insider, the securities being price-affected by the information**. An offence is also committed if an individual, in possession of information as an insider, **encourages another person to deal** in the price-affected securities, knowing or having reasonable cause to believe that dealing would take place. Finally, it is also an offence for an insider to **disclose the information to another person** otherwise than in the proper performance of the functions of their employment, office or profession.

Slye and others

At the time of the chain of events that is described, the information that Huge plc is to make a takeover bid for Large plc is not in the **public domain** and could therefore be considered to be **inside information**, since it is **price sensitive** in respect of both Huge plc and Large plc.

Slye is a director of Huge plc and the fact that the company has decided to make the bid (as stated at its board meeting) **qualifies** as **inside information** since it relates to particular issuers of securities that will be **price-affected** (Huge plc and Large plc), it has not been made public and it will, once made public, have a significant effect on price. It is **specific information** on the making of the takeover bid rather than precise information.

Slye

Slye has **inside information as an insider** as a director and employee of Huge plc. Slye knows that the information is inside information. He then buys shares in Large plc, which constitutes **dealing** because he is 'acquiring securities'. He has therefore dealt in price-affected securities while in possession of inside information as an insider, and has **committed the offence of insider dealing.**

Mate

As an insider, in telling Mate about the takeover bid without any justification of it being by way of employment etc, Slye has committed the **further offence of disclosing the inside information**.

Mate has knowingly received inside information from a person whom he knows to be an insider (Slye), so he has **become an insider** and in dealing he too has **committed the primary offence of insider dealing**.

Tim

In advising Tim to buy shares in Large plc, **Slye** has committed the third possible insider dealing offence: an insider **encouraging another person to deal in price-affected securities**, knowing or having reasonable cause to believe that Tim would take his advice and do so. However, **Tim did not receive inside information** as what Slye told him was neither precise nor specific, so he has **committed no offence**.

106 Sid and Vic

Text reference. Chapter 23.

Top tips. There are some areas of the syllabus that you just have to learn and be able to repeat in an exam. The rules on insider dealing are one of them. Make sure you understand the three offences.

Easy marks. There are no easy marks unless you can remember the rules.

Examiner's comments. There seemed to be a general lack of detailed knowledge about the meaning of insider dealing and contents of the Criminal Justice Act 1993 and those who did have such knowledge tended not to apply it properly. There was a general misunderstanding that insider dealing was simply having 'secret' information without explaining the specific, price-sensitive, nature of that information and the need to deal in shares on the basis of that information.

Marking scheme

This question requires candidates to consider the criminal offence of insider dealing. However, it also requires some understanding of the practical nature of the activity together with an ability to apply that knowledge to the facts contained in the problem.

8–10 marks	A thorough understanding of the legislation together with an accurate application of it to the individuals in the question is to be expected for the very highest marks.
5–7 marks	Good but limited analysis, or perhaps unbalanced in not dealing equally well with the application of the law.
3–4 marks	Some, but limited, knowledge of what the question is about, or a recognition of what it is about but lacking in any analysis.
0–2 marks	Little if any understanding of what the question is about.

(a) **Insider dealing**

The **Criminal Justice Act 1993** (CJA) contains rules on **insider dealing** which is a crime. To convict it must be proved that the possessor of inside information (under s 52 CJA):

Dealt in price-affected securities on a regulated market

Dealing is acquiring or disposing of or agreeing to acquire or dispose of relevant securities whether directly or indirectly: s 55 CJA.

Encouraged another to deal in price-affected securities on a regulated market

This occurs where an individual, having information as an insider, encourages another person to deal in price-affected securities in relation to that information. They must know or have reasonable cause to believe that dealing would take place.

It is **irrelevant** whether:

- The person encouraged **realises** that the securities are price-affected securities
- The **inside information** is **given** to that person.
- Any **dealing takes place**, the offence being committed at the time of encouragement

Disclosed the information other than in the proper performance of their employment, office or profession

This would occur for instance where a finance director provides inside information to a friend and not as part of their professional duties.

Inside information

Inside information must be likely to have a **significant effect on price** and it must be **specific or precise**.

CJA defines **inside information** as:

- Relating to **particular securities**
- Being **specific** or **precise**
- **Not made public**
- Likely to have a **significant effect** on the **price of securities**

Under s 57 a person has information as a **primary insider** if it is (*and* they **know** it is) inside information, and if they have it (*and* **know** they have) from an inside source:

- Through being a **director**, **employee** or **shareholder** of an issuer of securities
- Through access because of **employment**, **office** or **profession**

Defences to dealing and encouraging others to deal

Under s 53, an individual has a **defence** if they prove that:

- They **did not expect** there to be a **profit** or **avoidance of loss**
- They had **reasonable grounds** to believe that the **information** had been **disclosed widely enough** to ensure that those taking part in the dealing would be prejudiced by having the information
- They **would have done what they did even if they did not have the information**

Defences to disclosure of information by an individual

An individual has a defence to this offence if:

- They **did not expect** any person to deal
- Although dealing was expected, **profit** or **avoidance of loss** was **not expected**

Application to Sid

Under s57, Sid is an **insider** by virtue of his position as **director** in Trend plc and Umber plc. The information he holds is **price-sensitive** as it concerns large profits and large losses. Therefore, it would appear that he is **liable** under s52 for **dealing in price-affected securities.** None of the **defences** would apply to him as he clearly expected to make a profit in one transaction and to avoid a loss in the other.

He also becomes liable for the offence of **encouraging another to deal in price-affected securities** when he advises his brother to buy shares in Umber plc. This is even though we are not told whether the brother actually brought the shares and that no inside information was passed. Sid's offence is merely for encouraging.

No **specific information** was passed to the brother which means he has committed no offence.

(b) **Vic**

Vic's position is **wholly unrelated** to Sid. He sold his shares **willingly** and it is unfortunate for him that the share price subsequently may have risen. It may be possible for the company to take action against Sid for breach of his duties as a director although this would not be open to Vic as an individual shareholder.

107 Wrongful trading

Text reference. Chapter 23.

Top tips You need to have a detailed knowledge of S214 IA86 to score anything approaching a pass mark.

Easy marks. Notice that the question is asking you for both the **meaning** and the **effect** of wrongful trading. Try to define the term in as much depth as you can, and then explain the effect, for example on directors who cause a company to engage in wrongful trading.

Examiner's comments. Although this was quite a popular question, it was not one that was generally done very well. It required a detailed analysis of S214 IA86, but rather than focus on that, candidates tended to introduce irrelevant material. For example many candidates concentrated on breach of directors' duties and even insider dealing. Many others cited every instance of wrongdoing and acting as director whilst disqualified.

Some of the better candidates referred to the fact that the duty directors owe to their companies has increased as a consequence of S214.

Marking scheme

6-10 marks	A good to full answer explaining both the provision of section 214 of the Insolvency Act and the effect of that provision. The very best answers will provide reasons for the introduction of the section.
0-5 marks	Some knowledge of the concept behind the section but perhaps lacking in detailed knowledge of its content or its effect

Wrongful trading

Under s.214 Insolvency Act 1986, where a company has gone into insolvent liquidation and where the liquidator can show that a director **knew, or should have known**, that there was no reasonable prospect that the company could have avoided going into insolvent liquidation, the director may be liable for **wrongful trading**.

The element of real dishonesty needed for liability for **fraudulent trading** under s.213 need not be shown. The offence of wrongful trading was introduced to make it easier for creditors to make negligent directors liable for company debts owing to the difficulties in proving the necessary fraudulent intent. The assets available for distribution in a winding up may be significantly increased by **directors' contributions** ordered under this statutory provision.

s.1157 Companies Act 2006, which provides **relief** from court in proceedings for **negligence** or **breach of duty** or **trust** to directors who acted **honestly** and **reasonably**, is not available as a defence to proceedings under s.214 (*Halls v David and Another 1989*). A director may **avoid** or **lessen liability** however, by showing that they took **all steps to minimise the potential loss** to the company's creditors after the time at which they knew or ought to have known that insolvent liquidation was inevitable.

Objective test

An **objective test** will be applied, namely whether a **reasonably diligent person** with the **general knowledge**, **skill** and **experience** that might **reasonably be expected** of a **person carrying out that particular director's duties** would have concluded that the company could not avoid insolvent liquidation. A director cannot claim lack of knowledge where it results from failing to comply with Companies Acts requirements, such as preparation of accounts (*Re Produce Marketing Consortium 1989*). In addition, a director's liability can even be **increased** by applying a subjective test based on the director's particular knowledge, skill and experience.

Effect

In the event of **liability**, the court can require a director to **contribute to the assets of the company** in an amount determined by the court. The extent of liability will be assessed in the light of all relevant circumstances of the case, but will not be low or nominal merely because there is no fraud.

A director found guilty of fraudulent or wrongful trading is **liable to disqualification** under the Company Directors Disqualification Act 1986 (CDDA). The court has a discretion to make such an order where a person is convicted of an indictable offence in connection with the promotion, formation, management or liquidation of a company or with the receivership or management of a company's property. The maximum period of disqualification is 15 years.

108 Fran, Gram and Hen

Text reference. Chapter 23.

Top tips. Application of the rules on fraudulent and wrongful trading should not pose you any problems providing you know them. Remember intention must be proved in fraudulent trading cases. In wrongful trading cases liability will be established if it is proved that the defendant knew or should have known about the impending insolvency – directors are deemed to know or should know about the financial position of their company.

Easy marks. Stating the fraudulent and wrongful trading rules.

Examiner's comments. Again this was not answered well by a significant minority of candidates. The problem stemmed from a general lack of knowledge. Many candidates tended to rewrite the problem scenario as an answer without being able to refer to the detailed law relating to fraudulent trading, only a tiny minority made any reference to s.993 and few were able to explain s.214. That being said the small minority produced some very thorough answers, using the historical problems with fraudulent trading, as expressed through the case law, to explain the development of wrongful trading in s.214.

Marking scheme

This question requires candidates to consider fraudulent trading both under s.993 of the Companies Act 2006 and s.213 of the Insolvency Act 1986, and wrongful trading under s.214 of the Insolvency Act 1986.

(a)	4–5 marks	Clear explanation of operation of the law relating to fraudulent trading, under both criminal and civil law, but with the emphasis on the Insolvency Act provisions.
	2–3 marks	Some to good understanding but lacking detail.
	0–1 mark	Little or no knowledge.
(b)	4–5 marks	Clear explanation of the law relating to wrongful trading, probably, but not necessarily referring to case law.
	2–3 marks	Some to fair understanding but lacking detail.
	0–1 mark	Little if any knowledge.

(a) **Fraudulent trading**

If a court finds that the business of a company in liquidation has been carried on with **intent to defraud creditors** or for any fraudulent purpose it may declare that **any persons** who were knowingly parties to carrying on the business in this fashion shall be liable for the debts of the company as the court may decide: **s213 Insolvency Act 1986**. This is a civil penalty.

There is also a criminal offence of **fraudulent trading** under **s993 of the Companies Act 2006** which applies to anyone who has been party to carrying on a business with the intention to defraud creditors, other persons or for any other fraudulent purpose.

Various rules have been established to determine **what is fraudulent trading**:

- Only persons who **take the decision** to carry on the company's business in this way or play some active part are liable.
- **'Carrying on business'** can include a single transaction and also the mere payment of debts as distinct from making trading contracts.

If a liquidator considers that there has been fraudulent trading they should apply to the court for an order that those responsible are liable to make good to the company all or some specified part of the **company's debts**.

The liquidator should also report the facts to the Crown Prosecution Service and Director of Public Prosecutions so that **criminal proceedings** may be instituted under the Companies Act.

The **burden of proof** for liability for fraudulent trading is **high**, as the liquidator must **prove intention** to defraud.

Fran, Gram and Hen

As Gram and Hen both actively **falsified the company's accounts**, they are likely to be guilty of intention to defraud under both civil and criminal law. As a consequence they may be imprisoned and made to contribute towards the company's debts.

There is not enough evidence to prove Fran is guilty – the prosecution is unlikely to be able to prove he **intended** to defraud the creditors or others.

(b) **Wrongful trading**

The problem of proving intention to defraud in cases of alleged fraudulent trading resulted in a further civil liability of '**wrongful trading**' being introduced. Like s 213, s 214 Insolvency Act 1986 applies to companies in **liquidation** but **no dishonesty or intention to defraud need be proved**.

A director will be liable for **wrongful trading** if the liquidator proves that they:

- **Knew**, or **should have known**, that there was **no reasonable prospect** that the **company** could **have avoided going into insolvent liquidation**. This means that directors cannot claim they lacked knowledge if their lack of knowledge was a result of failing to comply with Companies Act requirements: *Re Produce Marketing Consortium 1989*.
- Did not take **sufficient steps** to minimise the potential loss to creditors.

The section goes on to provide that the **directors** will be **deemed to know** that the company could not avoid insolvent liquidation if that would have been the conclusion of a **reasonably diligent person** with the **general knowledge**, **skill and experience** that might reasonably be expected of a person carrying out that particular director's duties (ie a reasonable occupant of a similar post). If the director has greater than usual skill then they will be judged with reference to their own capacity.

Fran, Gram and Hen

Gram and Hen will be **personally liable** under s 214 for the increase in the company's debts since it is already established that they are likely to be liable for fraudulent trading which carries a higher burden of proof. **Fran** will **also be liable** for the company's debts since as a director of a company he should have been aware of the situation.

109 Money laundering

Text reference. Chapter 23.

Top tips. Make sure that you allocate your time equally to the two halves of the question, ie allow nine minutes for each. Try to be as detailed as possible in your answer, as the question is on quite a narrow area.

Easy marks. To earn the easy marks on both parts of this question, try to ensure that you do not duplicate your effort on the two parts. You do not need to go into any detail about the Proceeds of Crime Act in part (a) as you are specifically asked about it in part (b). You won't get extra marks in part (b) for repeating what you have already said in part (a).

Examiner's comments. Although this question covered a subject area that is relatively new to the syllabus, it was generally well tackled by students. A good proportion of answers contained a high level of detail particularly in relation to the offences where knowledge of the statutory sources extended to the levels of punishment. Not all students were able to name the specific processes within money laundering, but they could earn marks by describing them.

Poorer answers showed little or no knowledge of the Proceeds of Crime Act 2002 but did make an attempt to define money laundering. The weakest answers merely linked money laundering to organised crime and terrorism in a generalised manner without reference to the actual processes involved.

Marking scheme

8-10 marks	Good explanation of both the meaning of the concept and offences under the Act.
5-7 marks	Fair explanation of the general concept but lacking in detail in relation to the Act.
0-4 marks	Very unbalanced answer or lacking any detail.

(a) **Money laundering**

Money laundering is the term given to **attempts to make the proceeds of crime appear respectable**. It can refer to any process by which criminals seek to hide the source and ownership of the proceeds of criminal activities, enabling them to keep control over such proceeds and, ultimately, to provide an apparently legitimate cover for their sources of income.

The **money laundering process** aims to disguise the source of the proceeds so that the criminal can remain free from suspicion as to its source. The process usually involves three phases:

Placement

This is the actual disposal of the proceeds of the initial illegal activity, usually into an apparently legitimate activity.

Layering

This involves the transfer of money from business to business, or one geographical location to another, in order to conceal the original source.

Integration

Having been layered, the money takes on the appearance of coming from a legitimate source and, therefore, of being legitimate funds.

Money laundering was recognised as a criminal offence in the UK under the **Drug Trafficking Offences Act 1986**. It is now regulated by the **Proceeds of Crime Act 2002** and the **Money Laundering Regulations 2007**. Other relevant legislation includes certain **anti-terrorist legislation**, in particular the Terrorism Act 2000 andAnti-Terrorism, Crime and Security Act 2001.

(b) The **Proceeds of Crime Act 2002** identifies three categories of criminal offence: laundering, failure to report, and tipping off.

Laundering

This involves the **acquisition**, **possession** or **use of the proceeds of criminal conduct**, or assisting another to retain the proceeds of criminal conduct, and concealing the proceeds of criminal activity. Under the Act, it is an offence to conceal, disguise, convert, transfer or remove criminal property from the UK. 'Concealing or disguising criminal property includes concealing or disguising its nature, source, location, disposition, movement or ownership or any rights with respect to it.'

Criminal property is defined as property which the alleged offender knows (or suspects) to constitute or represent benefit from any criminal conduct. It includes, by way of example, proceeds of tax evasion, any benefit obtained through bribery and corruption and benefits obtained through the operation of a criminal cartel.

The offence of **knowingly assisting** in the laundering of criminal funds is punishable by imprisonment up to a maximum of fourteen years and/or a fine.

Failure to report

This is failure to disclose knowledge or suspicion of money laundering. Under the Act it is an offence for a person who 'knows or suspects … that another person is engaged in money laundering, where the information or other matter on which his knowledge or suspicion is based … came to him in the course of a business in the regulated sector' not to report the fact to the appropriate authority.

The offence only relates to **individuals**, such as accountants who are acting in the course of business. Any individual who is covered by the section is required to make disclosure to the nominated money laundering reporting officer within their organisation. Alternatively, disclosure may be made directly to the **Serious Organised Crime Agency** (SOCA).

The offence of failure to report is punishable by imprisonment up to a maximum of five years and/or a fine.

Tipping off

This involves **disclosing information** to any person if disclosure may prejudice an investigation into drug trafficking, drug money laundering, terrorist-related activities or laundering the proceeds of criminal conduct. It therefore covers the situation where an accountant informs a client that a report has been submitted to the SOCA.

The offence of **tipping off** is punishable by imprisonment up to a maximum of five years and/or a fine.

110 Greg

Text reference. Chapter 23.

Top tips. This question is a little unusual because it is a scenario question which is broken down into two parts. However, don't let this put you off from applying the ISAC approach to each.

Easy marks. Stating the basic points of law concerning insider dealing and money laundering.

Examiner's comments. This question required candidates to explain the meaning and regulation of the two criminal offences of insider dealing and money laundering and apply that law to a problem scenario.

This question tended to be sufficiently well done.

The money laundering aspect of the problem was particularly well done, with candidates explaining in very full terms what was involved in the process and the details of its legal regulation. However, there was some concern as to the insider dealing part of the problem, which raised some concerns and which suggest that a full question on that area would have met with much less success. The essential problem was that candidates seemed to think that insider dealing was just using or revealing information gained from inside a company. That, of course, is completely incorrect and it is not insider dealing unless the purchase or sale of securities is involved.

Marking scheme

This question requires candidates to explain the meaning and regulation of the two criminal offences of insider dealing and money laundering and apply that law to a problem scenario. Candidates may mention market abuse as an alternative to insider dealing in which case they should be credited for their knowledge.

8–10 marks	Clear analysis of the problem scenario – recognition of both the criminal law issues raised and a convincing application of the legal principles to the facts.
6–7 marks	Sound analysis of the problem – recognition of the major principles involved and a fair attempt at applying them. Perhaps sound in knowledge but lacking in analysis and application.
3–5 marks	Unbalanced answer perhaps showing some appropriate knowledge but weak in analysis or application.
0–2 marks	Very weak answer showing little analysis, appropriate knowledge or application.

(a) **Insider dealing**

Issue

The issue here is whether or not Greg's activity in arranging for Jet Plc to buy Kop Plc shares ahead of its takeover constitutes **insider dealing**.

The law

The **Criminal Justice Act 1993** (CJA) contains the rules on **insider dealing** and states that it involves **dealing in securities** while in possession of **inside information as an insider**, the securities being **price-affected** by the information.

Dealing

According to s 55 CJA, dealing is **acquiring or disposing** of or **agreeing** to **acquire** or **dispose** of relevant securities whether **directly** or **through an agent** or nominee or a person acting according to direction.

Insider

Under s 57 a person has information as a **primary insider** if it is (*and* they **know** it is) inside information, and if they have it (*and* **know** they have) from an inside source:

- Through being a **director**, **employee** or **shareholder** of an issuer of securities
- Through access because of **employment**, **office** or **profession**

Price-affected

Inside information must, if made public, be likely to have a **significant effect on price** and it must be **specific or precise**. Specific would, for example, mean information that a takeover bid would be made for a specific company; precise information would be details of how much would be offered for shares.

Defence

Under s 53, the individual has a **defence** regarding dealing if they prove that:

- They did **not expect** there to be a **profit** or avoidance of loss
- They had **reasonable grounds** to **believe** that the information had been **disclosed widely** enough to ensure that those taking part in the dealing would be prejudiced by having the information
- They would have **done** what they did **even** if they did not have the **information**, for example, where securities are sold to pay a pressing debt

Application and conclusion

On the facts, Greg's position as a director of Huge plc makes him an insider, the takeover information is clearly inside information and by instructing Jet plc to buy Kop plc shares he was involved in dealing. Therefore he has committed the offence of insider dealing and is liable for **imprisonment** and/or a **fine**. It is unlikely that any of the three defences available to him will be acceptable to the court.

(b) **Money laundering**

Issue

The issue here is whether or not by arranging the transfer of the profit on the sale of the Kop plc shares to Imp plc, and then to himself via a dividend transfer, Greg committed the offence of **money laundering**.

The law

Under the **Proceeds of Crime Act 2002**, money laundering is defined as the acquisition, possession or use of the proceeds of criminal conduct, or assisting another to retain the proceeds of criminal conduct and concealing, disguising, converting, transferring or removing criminal property. This relates to its nature, source, location, disposition, movement or ownership of the property.

For the purposes of laundering, '**criminal property**' is defined by s 3 CJA as a property which the alleged offender knows (or suspects) constitutes or represents being related to any criminal conduct. This is any conduct that constitutes or would constitute an offence in the UK.

Application and conclusion

It has already been established that the profit on the sale of the Kop plc shares was created as a result of insider dealing – a criminal offence. Greg has sought to disguise the profit by transferring it as a consultancy fee to Imp plc and as a dividend to himself. Therefore he has also committed the offence of money laundering under the Proceeds of Crime Act 2002 and is liable for imprisonment and/or a fine.

Mock exams

ACCA Fundamentals Level
Paper F4
Corporate and Business Law
(Eng)

Mock Examination 1

Question Paper	
Time allowed	
Reading and Planning Writing	**15 minutes** **3 hours**
ALL TEN questions are compulsory and MUST be attempted	
During reading and planning time only the question paper may be annotated	

DO NOT OPEN THIS PAPER UNTIL YOU ARE READY TO START UNDER EXAMINATION CONDITIONS

All TEN questions are compulsory and MUST be attempted

Question 1

(a) Explain the powers of the courts in interpreting legislation, paying particular regard to the rules they use in so doing. **(7 marks)**

(b) How has the Human Rights Act 1998 affected this process? **(3 marks)**

(Total = 10 marks)

Question 2

Explain the ways in which a contractual offer can come to an end. **(10 marks)**

Question 3

In relation to the law contract explain:

(a) The doctrine of privity **(3 marks)**

(b) How the doctrine can be avoided at common law **(4 marks)**

(c) How the doctrine is avoided under statute **(3 marks)**

(Total = 10 marks)

Question 4

Explain the following in the context of the law of negligence:

(a) Duty of care **(3 marks)**

(b) Breach of duty of care **(2 marks)**

(c) The chain of causality **(3 marks)**

(d) Remoteness of damage **(2 marks)**

(Total = 10 marks)

Question 5

Explain in relation to the formation of a company what is meant by the terms:

(a) Promoter **(5 marks)**

(b) Pre-incorporation contract **(5 marks)**

(Total = 10 marks)

Question 6

Explain the following within the context of company general meetings:

(a) Who has the power to call meetings? **(6 marks)**

(b) How are votes taken? **(4 marks)**

(Total = 10 marks)

Question 7

(a) Explain what is involved in the criminal offence of insider dealing. **(4 marks)**

(b) In particular explain the meaning of the following terms:

(i) Dealing **(2 marks)**
(ii) Inside information **(2 marks)**
(iii) Insider **(2 marks)**

(Total = 10 marks)

Question 8

Adam, who operates an accountancy practice, charges £1,000 per year for producing business accounts for tax purposes. Unfortunately he has had some difficulty in recovering his fees from two clients as follows.

1 Bob, a car mechanic, told Adam that he could only raise cash to pay half of his fees but that he would service Adam's car for the coming year. Adam reluctantly agreed to this proposal.

2 Dawn, a not very successful musician, also told Adam that she could only pay half the money she owed him as she needed to use the other half to finance her new recording. Once again Adam agreed to accept the half payment. Dawn's recording subsequently became a major hit and she made £100,000 profit from it.

Adam himself is now in financial difficulty and needs cash to pay his own tax bill.

Required

Advise Adam whether he can recover any of the outstanding money from the above clients. **(10 marks)**

Question 9

Mat is considering setting up a new internet café as a private limited company. He has been told that in order to register the company he should submit appropriate articles of association and a memorandum of association. He has also been informed that he can borrow money from a bank but only if the company provides the bank with a fixed charge against its assets.

He also thinks that as there is an existing business called Netscape Ltd it would be a good idea to call his new company Netscope Ltd based on the chance that he could transfer some of its business to his new company.

Explain:

(a) The difference between the articles of association and the memorandum of association. **(4 marks)**

Do not describe the contents of the articles and memorandum.

(b) The meaning and effect of a fixed charge. **(3 marks)**

(c) The meaning and effect of an action for 'passing off', advising Mat as to whether he may be liable for an action under it **(3 marks)**

(Total = 10 marks)

Question 10

Five years ago Kim, Liz and Meg formed Orb Ltd in which Kim and Liz each hold 40% of the shares and Meg owns the remaining 20%. They are the only directors. The objects of Orb Ltd contained in its articles are restricted to research, production and marketing environmentally-friendly cleaning products.

In the course of a research project for Orb Ltd, Kim discovered a new highly powerful industrial cleaner, but unfortunately it was extremely toxic and not at all environmentally-friendly. She has persuaded Liz that Orb Ltd should market the new product but Meg maintains that to do so would be contrary to the restrictions stated in Orb Ltd's articles. Nonetheless Kim and Liz insist that they will use their majority power to make and market the new cleaner.

Required

Advise as to the rules relating to the doctrine of *ultra vires* and whether Meg can take any action against Kim and Liz for ignoring the objects of Orb Ltd. **(10 marks)**

(Total = 100 marks)

Answers

DO NOT TURN THIS PAGE UNTIL YOU HAVE COMPLETED THE MOCK EXAM

A plan of attack

If this were the real Corporate and Business Law exam and you had been told to turn over and begin, what would be going through your mind?

Perhaps you're having a panic. Stop that now! What you should do is spend a good five minutes looking through the paper in detail, thinking about the topics and working out the order in which to attempt the questions. So turn back to the paper and let's sort out a plan of attack.

Looking through the paper

You have no choices in this paper and must attempt all questions. During reading and planning time you should decide the order that you will attempt them.

The questions in this paper are as follows.

- Question 1 requires you to talk about the interpretation of legislation, with three marks on the Human Rights Act.
- Question 2 asks for an explanation of how a contractual offer ends.
- Question 3 asks for an explanation of privity of contract.
- Question 4 is a test of what is needed to prove a claim under the law of negligence.
- Question 5 is on promoters and pre-incorporation contracts.
- Question 6 examines the rules on convening company meetings and conducting voting.
- Question 7 is on one of the examiner's favourite subjects: insider dealing.
- Question 8 is a scenario-based contract law question on consideration.
- Question 9 is a scenario-based question which examines the meaning of various key terms in company law.
- Question 10 is a scenario-based question on restrictions on company objects and *ultra vires*.

Tackling the paper

You can answer the questions in any order, but we would advise you to **take the first seven questions first**. This is because the questions are more straightforward than the last three scenario questions and you can build up marks quickly, by ensuring that you get the simple marks in each of the questions you undertake. Also, if you do miscalculate your time apportionment and you have done the scenario questions first, you run the risk of missing a knowledge-based question out, and consequently losing the straightforward marks in that question, in favour of marks which are harder to get in other questions.

Here are some points to note:

- It is not wise to ignore a syllabus area when revising, as you reduce your potential score by 10% for each question you cannot answer in the exam.
- If you think that there are any questions that you cannot do, look through them all carefully. Do any of the questions have parts that you think you can attempt? At least attempt the parts that you can answer.

The last three scenario questions are longer than the seven knowledge-based questions and usually require you to apply legal principles to situations. We suggest that you tackle them second when you have 'warmed up' by answering the knowledge-based questions.

A key skill is to be able to break down the larger questions into the components within them, to see where you will build up your marks.

Allocating your time

BPP's advice is always allocate your time according to the marks for the question in total and for the parts of the question. That means for paper F4 that you should spend 18 minutes on each question. However, use your common sense. If you are doing a question but know you can't answer part (c), allocate those minutes to another question, where you may be able to pick up more marks.

Forget about it!

And don't worry if you found the paper difficult. More than likely other candidates will too. If this were the real thing you would need to forget the exam the minute you left the exam hall and think about the next one. Or, if it is the last one, celebrate!

Question 1

Text reference. Chapters 2 and 3.

Top tips. Notice what the examiner says (below) about the depth of answers given. To pass this exam, you are required to demonstrate an understanding of the law and legal process, not just list the facts or rules you have read in your Study Text. This is why making reference to case law can assist your answers as cases illustrate the law in practice. This is not to say you will fail if you don't refer to cases. Just make sure you explain how the law works in practice; using cases is one way of doing that.

Although the answer focuses on the main three rules on statutory interpretation, you would also be awarded a mark if you mentioned the golden and mischief rules.

Part (b) may have seemed more difficult if the Human Rights Act seems daunting. You should have been able to make reference to the requirements to interpret English law in a way that is compatible with the convention. Revise this area using the suggested answer if not.

Easy marks. The question is specifically testing the rules of statutory interpretation, so be sure to mention them.

Examiner's comments.

(a) Although most candidates could identify the three main rules of interpretation used by the courts, there were wide differences in the level of understanding of them and the ability to do any more than merely naming them. Where candidates mentioned the other rules of and aids to interpretation, they were given credit. Most candidates appreciated the fact that although in principle Parliament is the supreme source of law, judges continue to play an important part in the interpretation of legislation to solve problems of ambiguity and uncertainty.

(b) Not many candidates were able to demonstrate other than a basic knowledge of the Human Rights Act 1998. Very few could explain the effect that the Act has on the role of the UK courts in their capacity as interpreters of legislation.

Marking scheme

			Marks
(a)	Explanation of interpretation	1	
	Literal rule (1 for explanation; ½ for example)	$1^1/_2$	
	Purposive rule (1 for explanation; ½ for example)	$1^1/_2$	
	Contextual rule (1 for explanation; ½ for example)	$1^1/_2$	
	Presumptions	$1^1/_2$	
			7
(b)	Background to HRA	1	
	UK interpretation to be compatible	1	
	Declaration of incompatibility	1	
			3
			10

(a) **Need for statutory interpretation**

Although the wording of a **piece of legislation is carefully scrutinised** at all stages of its development, from its initial drafting through to the various stages of its passage through the two Houses of Parliament, **difficulties may nonetheless be encountered in its application**.

When the statute comes to be applied in the courts, there may be uncertainty over the **precise meaning** of a word or whether a particular term applies to the circumstances of the case. The applicability of legislative provisions may be uncertain when **unforeseeable or unforeseen developments** have occurred since the legislation was enacted.

It is the **role of the judiciary to apply the law made by Parliament as legislation**. The courts are therefore required to determine the meaning of such legislation. In doing so, they will apply a number of well-established rules and principles to interpret the statute.

Rules of statutory interpretation

The following rules of statutory interpretation have been developed by the courts:

(i) **The literal rule**

The most important guide to the purpose of the statute is the wording of that statute. Under the literal rule, words are to be given their literal, or plain and ordinary, meaning and should be interpreted in the same way throughout the statute. This means that if the words used are clear, the courts must apply them even if they find the consequences distasteful. Therefore in *Whitely v Chapell 1868*, a statute made it an offence to impersonate any person entitled to vote at an election. The accused was acquitted because they impersonated a dead person (who clearly was not entitled to vote).

(ii) **The purposive rule**

The words of a statute are interpreted not only in their ordinary, literal and grammatical sense, but also bearing in mind the purpose of the legislation: what is it trying to achieve? An example is seen in *Gardiner v Sevenoaks RDC 1950* when it was held that the term 'premises' should include a cave where film was stored, as the purpose of the Act concerned was the safety of people in premises.

(iii) **The contextual rule**

Under the contextual rule, a word in a statute should be construed in its context. The court can look at the statute as a whole to ascertain the meaning of a word within it. Increasingly it is thought that the courts should apply the law for the purpose that Parliament intended.

Presumptions of statutory interpretation

In addition to these main rules of statutory interpretation, the courts will also apply a number of other **principles and maxims**, for example the *eiusdem generis* rule, which provides that where a statute appends general terms to a list of specific words, the general words are to be limited in their meaning to other things of the same type as the preceding specific word (*Evans v Cross 1938*).

(b) **The Human Rights Act 1998**

The Human Rights Act 1998 incorporates the **European Convention for Human Rights and Fundamental Freedoms** into UK domestic law. The extent of the impact of the legislation will become clearer as case law develops.

The effect that this Act has on statutory interpretation is that UK courts are now required to **interpret UK law in a way compatible with the Convention so far as it is possible to do so** (s3). They must also take into account previous decisions, judgments, declarations and adverse opinions of the European Court of Human Rights.

Where a court considers that any legislative provision is incompatible with the Convention, it cannot disregard it but may make a **declaration of that incompatibility**. The provision remains valid in domestic law until amended by legislation or statutory instrument.

Question 2

Text reference. Chapter 4.

Top tips. This is a straightforward question. Any introductory material must be kept brief. Remember to write about all the different aspects of end of offer instead of putting too much detail about one area. Refer to the marking guide: only a limited number of marks are available for each reason for termination.

Easy marks. Lots of marks are available for quoting cases in this sort of question.

Marking scheme

	Marks
Lapse within a fixed or reasonable time	1
Rejection	1
Counter-offer	1
Revocation at any time up to acceptance	1
Unless an option granted	1
Express revocation	1
Or via a reliable third party	1
Revocation by post	1
Death	1
Failure of condition	1
	10

Offers

An **offer may be accepted** so as to form a binding contract **only for so long as it remains open**. It is therefore important to be able to identify the point at which an offer is terminated. The most **common reasons** for the termination of an offer are **lapse of the offer**, **rejection** of the offer by the offeree or **revocation** of the offer by the offeror.

Lapse

An offer may be **expressed to remain open** (or the parties may agree that it shall remain open) for a **specified length of time**, in which case it will **terminate upon expiry of that time**. It cannot be accepted thereafter.

If no express time limit is set, it will be deemed to **expire after a reasonable time**. What is reasonable depends upon the circumstances of each individual case *(Ramsgate Victoria Hotel Co v Montefiore 1866).*

Rejection

A **clear rejection** of an offer **will terminate the offer**. A request for further information is not a clear rejection of the offer, as in *Stevenson v McLean 1880*, where one of the parties asked if the other would accept payment by instalments.

Counter-offer

However, an offer is terminated where a **response introduces a new term**. This is known as **counter-offer** (for example, if one party is asking for £1,000, the other saying 'I'll give you £950). A **counter offer always terminates the original offer** (*Hyde v Wrench 1840*).

Revocation

The general rule regarding revocation or cancellation is that the **offeror may revoke** the offer **at any time up to acceptance** (*Payne v Cave 1789*). However, this is not true if they have granted a separate option agreement to keep the offer open for a period of time, for which consideration has been given (*Routledge v Grant 1828*). **Once accepted, an offer cannot be revoked**.

Revocation may be an **express statement** to that effect. It may also be an **act of the offeror** indicating that the offer is no longer in force (for example sale of the goods to a third party). Whatever form it takes, it is **essential that the revocation is communicated** to the offeree in order to be effective. Revocation of an offer may be communicated **by the offeror or by any third party who is a sufficiently reliable informant** (*Dickinson v Dodds 1876*).

While a postal acceptance of an offer is usually effective from the time of posting, a **postal revocation of an offer does not take effect until received by the offeree** (that is, it has actually been communicated to the offeree). Therefore, where a letter of revocation of offer crosses in the post with a letter of acceptance, a legally binding contract will have been formed from the time the letter of acceptance was posted (*Byrne v Van Tienhoven 1880*).

Where an **offer is intended to be accepted by conduct** (a unilateral contract), it has been held that the **offer cannot be revoked once the offeree has begun to perform the necessary act** required to accept the contract.

Death

An offer will terminate in the event of death of the offeree. Death of the offeror normally has the same effect, although if the offeree accepts the offer in ignorance of the offeror's death and the offer is not of a personal nature, a valid contract may still result (*Bradbury v Morgan 1862*).

Failure of condition

In the case of a **conditional offer**, **if the stated condition fails or is not satisfied**, then the offer cannot be accepted (*Financings Ltd v Stimson 1962*).

Question 3

Text reference. Chapter 5.

Top tips. Allocate the time available in proportion to the marks available for the different parts of the question. Try not to discuss points relevant to the next part of the question in the part that you are dealing with, for example when explaining the doctrine in part (a) do not embark on a discussion of how it can be avoided.

Easy marks. In each part of the question clearly address the precise requirement of the question and cite cases in support as much as possible.

Examiner's comments. A significant number of candidates ran their answers to parts (b) and (c) on common law and statutory exceptions to the doctrine together, rather than keeping them separate. This meant that they tended to focus on common law rather than statutory exceptions and therefore did not gain the marks available for the latter. Very few candidates mentioned collateral contracts or the Contracts (Rights of Third Parties) Act 1999.

Marking scheme

This question is divided into three parts although the marks are indicative of how candidates should allocate their time and answers will most likely be done as one.

8-10 marks	A thorough understanding of privity demonstrated by references to cases or examples.
5-7 marks	A clear understanding of the topic perhaps lacking in detail. Alternatively an unbalanced answer showing good understanding of one part but less in others.
2-4 marks	Some, but limited, understanding of the topic or clear understanding of only one aspect.
0-1 marks	Little or no knowledge of the topic.

(a) **Privity of contract**

The doctrine of **privity of contract** provides that only a **party to the contract** has **enforceable rights** and **obligations** under it and a person who is not party to the contract cannot enforce it, even if the promises are given for their benefit.

In the leading case in this area, *Dunlop v Selfridge 1915*, Dunlop supplied tyres to a distributor, for resale, and the distributor sold them to Selfridge. The contract between Selfridge and the distributor provided for payments to Dunlop if Selfridge sold the tyres at less than a fixed price. Although Selfridge failed to observe this clause and sold the tyres at a lower price, Dunlop was unable to enforce the promise. It was held that this was part of the contract between Selfridge and the distributor, to which Dunlop was not a party.

There are some **exceptions** to the general rule of privity of contract, both at **common law** and under **statute**, where a third party may be allowed to enforce a contract.

(b) **Common law**

Where the beneficiary may sue in some other capacity

In *Beswick v Beswick 1968* a widow sued for specific performance in her capacity as her husband's administratrix (rather than simply as his widow) to enforce a contract between her husband and the successor to his business. The contract provided for payment of an annuity to the widow. In her capacity as administratrix, she was able to enforce the contract for her own benefit as third party to the contract. In her personal capacity as recipient, she had no right of action.

Where there is a collateral contract

In *Shanklin Pier Ltd v Detel Products Ltd 1951*, the claimant entered into a contract to have their pier repainted. The painters used a particular paint produced by the defendant as required by the claimant. The paint was unsatisfactory. The defendant fought an action by the claimant on the basis that they had only entered into a contract of supply with the painters and since the claimant was not a party to that contract they could not enforce it. The court held that there was a collateral contract between the claimant and the defendant by which the defendant guaranteed the suitability of the paint in return for the claimant requiring the painters to use it.

Where a party validly assigns the rights contained in a contract

A party may not assign the burden of their contractual obligations without the other party's consent.

Where breach of contract results in loss or damage to a third party which was clearly foreseeable

In *Linden Gardens Trust Ltd v Lenesta Sludge Disposals Ltd 1994*, a contract for works was entered into with the likelihood that the property would subsequently be transferred to a third party. Although no formal assignment was made, the House of Lords held that the original promisee should be able to claim full damages on behalf of the third party for breach of contract. The commercial nature of the contract and the circumstances which made the subsequent transfer so likely were relevant factors.

Where equity provides that an implied trust has been created

In *Gregory and Parker v Williams 1817*, Parker owed money to Gregory and Williams and agreed to transfer his property to Williams if Williams paid Parker's debt to Gregory. When the property was transferred, Williams refused to pay Gregory who was clearly not a party to the contract between Parker and Williams. Nonetheless, the court held that Parker could be regarded as a trustee for Gregory under an implied trust and so Gregory could bring an action jointly with Parker.

Where there is an agency relationship

If an agent enters into a contract with a third party apparently on their own behalf but in fact on behalf of an undisclosed principal, the agent may sue the third party (since they are treated as the other party to the contract) until such time as the principal intervenes and enforces the contract on their own behalf. Where the principal is disclosed, the contract is treated as one between the principal (and therefore enforceable by the principal) and third party even though made by the agent.

Restrictive covenants

A **restrictive covenant** can be attached to land which binds future owners (for example preventing them from building on the land). A third party may be granted a right of action against a future owner who breaches the covenant *(Tulk v Moxhay 1848).*

(c) **Statutory exceptions**

Under the **Road Traffic Act 1972**, accident victims can claim from the other party's insurers and the **Married Woman's Property Act 1882** allows a beneficiary spouse to enforce life insurance taken out by their partner.

The principal statutory exception is contained in the **Contracts (Rights of Third Parties) Act 1999** which sets out the circumstances in which a third party can enforce a contract in the event of breach, or have it varied or rescinded. These are either (a) where the contract expressly so provides or (b) where the term confers a benefit on the third party (unless it appears that the contracting parties did not intend them to have the right to enforce it). The **third party must be identified** in the contract by name, class or description but need not be in existence when the contract is made. The Act does not confer third party rights in relation to a **company's constitution** or **employment contracts**.

Question 4

Text reference. Chapter 8.

Top tips. Like many similar questions, pay close attention to the marks on offer and do not spend too long on each part. It is better to have a short description on all parts than a long description on one or two.

Easy marks. Stating the three tests for a duty of care from the *Caparo* case.

Marking scheme

This question tests the candidate's understanding of certain concepts involved in bringing a claim for negligence. Parts (a) to (d) – one mark for each valid point up to a maximum available for question part.

(a) **Duty of care**

In the landmark case of *Donoghue v Stevenson 1932* the House of Lords ruled that a person might owe a duty of care to another with whom they had no **contractual relationship** at all.

In that case the House of Lords laid down the **general principle** that every person owes a duty of care to their 'neighbour', to 'persons so closely and directly affected by my act that I ought reasonably to have them in contemplation as being so affected'. If a person breaks this duty they may be liable in negligence.

Over time the principle has developed and now a claimant must prove the following for a duty of care to exist: *Caparo Industries plc v Dickman and Others 1990.*

- Was the harm **reasonably foreseeable**?
- Was there a **relationship of proximity** between the parties?
- Considering the circumstances, is it **fair, just and reasonable** to impose a duty of care?

(b) **Breach of duty of care**

Breach of duty of care is the second issue to be considered in a negligence claim. The **standard of reasonable care** requires that the person concerned should do what a **reasonable man** would do. If a person did not act in the manner of a reasonable man, taking into account the probability of injury and the seriousness of the risk, then they may be found to have breached their duty of care.

(c) **The chain of causality**

To satisfy the requirement that harm must be caused by another's actions, the **'But for'** test is applied. The claimant must prove that 'but for' the defendant's actions they would not have **suffered damage**. Therefore claimants are unable to claim for any harm that would have happened to them anyway irrespective of the defendant's actions.

Certain events may break the chain of causality, and therefore prevent a defendant from becoming liable. Where there are **multiple possible causes** of an injury, the claimant must prove it is most likely to have been caused by the negligence of the defendant. **Acts of the defendant**, **claimant** and **natural events** may also break the chain. It is up to the claimant to prove that they do not.

(d) **Remoteness of damage**

Even where causation is proved, a negligence claim can still fail if the damage caused is 'too remote'. The test of **reasonable foresight** developed out of *The Wagon Mound 1961*. Liability is limited to damage that a **reasonable man** could have foreseen. This does not mean the exact event must be foreseeable in detail, just that the eventual outcome is foreseeable. If the claimant cannot prove that the damage is not too remote then the claim will fail.

Question 5

Text reference. Chapter 14.

Top tips. Take a minute or two to plan how you are going to tackle a question like this. The risk otherwise is that you will confuse the two parts and waste time by repeating points in both.

Easy marks. Try to expand your definitions as much as possible, or try to produce more than one definition, for example, for the term promoter. Easy marks will be available for cases too, so bring in as many as you can.

Examiner's comments. Some candidates did not use the guidance of the structure of the question and included points in part (a) which should really have been in part (b). They did not lose marks because of this, but it probably meant that they wasted time.

Marking scheme

			Marks
(a)	Definition, eg *Twycross v Grant*	2	
	Not solicitors/accountants	1	
	Duty of skill and care	1	
	Duty not to benefit secretly	1	
			5
(b)	Definition/explanation	2	
	Co. not bound	1	
	Promoter personally liable	1	
	Novation possible	1	
			5
			10

(a) **Promoters**

A **promoter** is 'one who undertakes to form a company with reference to a given project and to set it going and who takes the necessary steps to accomplish that purpose' (*Twycross v Grant 1877*). The term promoter also includes anyone who makes any **business preparations** for the company. They will normally require the company to agree to reimburse their expenses incurred in the promotion and formation once the company has been incorporated.

A accountant or other **professional** who acts in their professional capacity in connection with the formation of a company is not a promoter on that basis. Whether someone is a promoter is a question of fact.

Duties

A promoter owes a **general duty of reasonable skill and care**. Where some or all of the shares are to be allotted to persons other than the promoter, they also owe the customary fiduciary duties of an **agent**. It follows that promoters must not put themselves in a position where their own **interests conflict** with those of the company and they **must account for any benefits** they receive through acting as promoter.

They must make a **full** and **proper disclosure** of any **personal advantage** to existing and prospective shareholders or to an independent board of directors. The promoter will be in **breach** of their fiduciary duty if they profit personally from a contract as promoter but not where they acquire property and then sell it to the promoted company at a **profit** (which they have disclosed).

In the event of a **breach of duty**, the company may **rescind** the contract and **recover its money**. If rescission is not possible, the promoter must account for their **wrongful profit** and may also be **sued for damages**. The general rule is that a promoter is **personally liable** on any completed pre-incorporation contract (see (b)) entered into with a third party.

(b) **Pre-incorporation contracts**

A **pre-incorporation contract** is a contract purported to be made by a company or its agent at a time before the company has received its certificate of incorporation. Since the company does not exist at the time the contract is made, it cannot be held liable in respect of its terms, nor can it ratify it. It may however enter into a new contract on identical terms after incorporation ('**novation**'). Mere recognition of the pre-incorporation contract by performing it or accepting benefits under it is not sufficient to constitute a new contract.

Promoter liability

Section 51 CA 2006 provides that **the person purporting to act for the company shall be personally liable on the contract subject to any agreement to the contrary**. Any agreement to the contrary must be an **express agreement** and cannot be implied. It is irrelevant whether the other party knew that the company did not exist or whether the contract is made in the company's name or in the agent's name.

The **promoter** might seek to **avoid liability** by **postponing completion** of the contract until after incorporation of the company or by providing that their liability shall cease as and when the newly incorporated company enters a new contract on identical terms.

Question 6

Text reference. Chapter 20.

Top tips. This is another two-part 'explain' question. Part (b) of this question is probably more tricky than part (a), particularly because it might be tempting to talk about resolutions rather than the mechanics of voting. Remember, no matter how learned you are on your chosen specialised subject, always, always, always answer the question set. Answers which sadly do not answer the question will win no marks at all.

Easy marks. Good marks can be gained for relatively simple and short explanations of polls and show of hands.

Marking scheme

			Marks
(a)	AGM called by directors	1	
	Timing requirements	1	
	General meetings (1 mark for each possibility)	4	
			6
(b)	Show of hands	1	
	One person one vote	1	
	Poll	1	
	Depends on shareholdings	1	
			4
			10

(a) **Meetings**

Annual general meeting

An annual general meeting ('AGM') must be called by the **directors** of **public companies once in each calendar year** (within **six months** of the company's **year end**). Private companies are not required by law to hold AGMs unless their constitution requires it.

General meetings at other times

A general meeting that is not an AGM may be called in any of the following ways:

- By the **directors** whenever they see fit. This power is usually conferred to them in the articles.
- Under s303 CA 2006 by the directors on the requisition of **members holding at least 10% of the paid up share capital carrying voting rights** or (if there is no share capital) 10% of the voting rights, in which case the meeting must be called within 28 days of the requisition being deposited. If the directors fail to call the meeting within 21 days of the members' requisition being issued, the members may themselves convene the meeting for a date within 3 months of the requisition. Where the company is **private** and no meeting has been held for **12 months** the requisite percentage is **5%**.
- By the **court**, on the application of a director or member (s306 CA). This is usually in the case of deadlock (for example where one member of two refuses to attend and so provide a quorum).
- By an **auditor** who gives a statement detailing the circumstances for their resignation or other loss of office and requires their explanation to be considered by the company (s518 CA).
- **Compulsorily**, by the directors of a public company where the **net assets fall to half or less of the amount of its called up share capital** (s656 CA).

(b) **Votes**

Unless a poll is demanded, a resolution is decided upon by a **show of hands**, where every **person** and **proxy** present has **one vote**. On a poll, each share normally carries one vote, so a member or their proxy may use as many votes as their shareholding grants them. It need not be held at the time, but can be postponed so that arrangements to hold it can be made. In either case, the number of votes cast determines the result and votes which are available but not used are disregarded.

A **poll** may be demanded by not less than **5 members** or members representing at least **10%** of the total **voting rights** or members holding shares which represent at least **10%** of the **paid up capital**. When a poll is held, any previous vote on a show of hands is disregarded and the votes cast are checked against the register of members.

Question 7

Text reference. Chapter 23.

Top tips. Don't duplicate your effort by going into detail in part (a) on the terms that are requested in part (b).

Easy marks. A solid general explanation of the offence in part (a) will earn you the bulk of the easy marks.

Examiner's comments. Although this topic has been examined on a number of occasions in the past, the structure of the presentation seemed to throw candidates...... Some candidates were confused about the very nature of insider dealing and thought that it was related to directors' conflict of interest.

Marking scheme

This question requiring a general explanation of the offence of Insider Dealing and in particular the terms used in regard to the offence, is divided into four parts. Marks will be allocated as indicated in the paper: four marks for part (a), and two marks for each element in part (b).

(a)	3-4 marks	Good general understanding of the area.
	1-2 marks	Some but limited knowledge.

(b) Marks will be awarded in line with thoroughness of explanation of each part.

(a) **Insider dealing**

Insider dealing is the name given to the offence where someone buys or sells securities as a result of having received **confidential information** which affects the value of those securities. Usually they are in possession of that confidential information because of some connection they have with the company, perhaps as an employee, director or professional adviser to the company.

Clearly with such **information**, someone can profit from buying shares at a time when they know of an anticipated increase in their **market value** and from selling shares when they have foreknowledge of a decrease in the shares' market value.

The **Criminal Justice Act 1993** makes it an offence:

- To **deal in securities** while in possession of inside information as an insider, the securities being price-affected by the information (s52);
- To **encourage another to deal** in them knowing, or having reasonable cause to believe, that dealing would take place. It is irrelevant whether the person encouraged realises that the securities are price-affected and whether any dealing actually takes place; and
- To **disclose the information** to another person other than in the proper performance of their employment, office or profession.

'Securities' include **shares** and **associated derivatives**, **debt securities** and **warranties** (s54).

Breach of the Act is a **criminal offence** but it will not in itself invalidate contracts which have been entered into in contravention of its provisions. On indictment, the offence carries an unlimited fine and/or imprisonment for up to seven years.

Defences

The Act lays down a number of **general** and **special defences**. It is a general defence if the offender can show that they **did not expect there to be a profit** or **avoidance of loss**, or that they had **reasonable grounds** to believe that the **information had been widely disclosed**, or that they **would have done what they did even if they had not had the information** (s53). In an offence of disclosing the information, it is a defence to show that the offender did not expect any person to deal or, if dealing was expected, that no profit or avoidance of loss was expected.

(b) (i) '**Dealing**' is defined (s55) as acquiring or disposing of or agreeing to acquire or dispose of relevant securities whether directly or through an agent or nominee or a person acting according to direction.

(ii) '**Inside information**' is defined (s56) as 'price-sensitive information' relating to a particular issuer of securities that are price-affected and not to securities generally. They are 'price-affected' if the information, being made public, would be likely to have a significant effect on price.

(iii) '**Insider**' **means** (s57) a person who has information which is (and they know it to be) inside information where they have that information, knowingly, from an inside source either (i) through being a director, employee , shareholder or issuer of securities or (ii) through access because of employment, office or profession or (iii) if the direct or indirect source falls within category (i) or (ii).

Question 8

Text reference. Chapter 5.

Top tips. In a complex scenario question like this one it is important that you follow our suggested procedure:

- **Identify** the issue
- **State** the law
- **Apply** the law
- **Conclude** on the given scenario

You can either do this separately for each part of the question, or you can do it in the way our answer does, by discussing all of the aspects of the law first and then applying it to the specific parts of the question.

Easy marks. Get the easy marks by making sure that you tackle each of the situations outlined in the question. Try to explain the legal principle and to quote at least one case in support of each.

Marking scheme

This question asks candidates to analyse the problem scenario in terms of the rules relating to the waiver of existing contractual rights generally and it also requires an explanation of the doctrine of promissory estoppel.

9-10 marks	A thorough to complete understanding of the legal issues in the question together with a clear analysis of the problem scenario and a correct application of the law to it.
7-8 marks	Good understanding of the law and supporting analysis and application.
5-6 marks	Some, if limited, knowledge of the law. Perhaps lacking in analysis and application.
0-4 marks	Little understanding of the legal issues arising from the question.

Issue

This question covers the **doctrine of consideration**, and specifically whether it is possible for consideration in a contract to be different from that originally agreed.

Consideration

One of the essential elements of a contract is **consideration** except where a contract is made by deed. One of the consequences of this principle is that, if an additional promise is made by one party to a contract, that additional promise must equally be supported by consideration. It does not matter whether this is a promise to do more than under the original contract or to do less, ie a waiver of some kind.

Forbearance

Two of the best-known definitions of consideration both include reference to the concept of **forbearance** and make it clear that the courts consider that **forbearance** (eg to pursue part of a debt) can amount to consideration. If a party to a contract agrees to waive their right to a part of a debt, it is clear under the general principles of contract law that this promise must itself be supported by consideration.

In *Foakes v Beer 1884*, the defendant had obtained judgement against the claimant for a debt. By written agreement, the defendant agreed to accept payment by instalments of the sum due, with no mention being made of interest which was also due. The claimant paid off this amount and the defendant then claimed the interest as well, arguing that their written agreement did not prevent them from claiming the interest as this promise was not supported by consideration. It was held that they were indeed entitled to the debt with interest, as the claimant had provided no consideration for any waiver of rights.

There are, however, exceptions to the rule that the debtor must give consideration if the waiver is to be binding that are relevant to Adam's situation.

For example:

- If the debtor offers and the creditor accepts **anything to which the creditor is not already entitled**, the extra thing will be sufficient consideration for the waiver. This may be for example, goods instead of cash (*Anon 1495*) or payment before the date payment is due (*Pinnel's case 1602*).
- The principle of **promissory estoppel** may prevent the creditor from retracting their promise with retrospective effect. This doctrine of equitable or promissory estoppel was developed in *Central London Property Trust v High Trees House 1947* to provide a more general safeguard to the promisee against the risk that the promisor may withdraw their waiver.

Promissory estoppel

The doctrine applies when a person **promises** (without consideration) **not to enforce** in full their existing rights and intending that the promisee shall act on the promise by altering their position in reliance on it. If the promisee does act on the promise the promisor is **estopped** from withdrawing the promise. In some circumstances however they may, on giving reasonable notice of their intention, restore the original position for the future. In other words the doctrine may operate to suspend rights which may be enforced once again if reasonable notice has been given.

The doctrine only applies to a **promise freely given** (*D and C Builders v Rees 1966*). In this case, claimants were forced to accept lower sums because of financial difficulties of which the creditor was aware. It also only applies to a promise to waive existing rights and it is a 'shield not a sword', which means that the doctrine does not create new causes of action where none existed before *(Combe v Combe 1951)*.

Applying these principles to the facts of the case involving Adam, the following conclusions are suggested:

Bob

In Bob's case, Adam agreed to accept servicing of his car as a payment in kind. He may not recover any further sum from Bob *(Anon 1495)*. Consideration need not be '**adequate**' at law but must be **sufficient** so the question of whether servicing of the car is valuable enough is not relevant.

Dawn

Prima facie, Adam's agreement to accept only half of the debt appears to be unsupported by consideration and therefore Adam may still claim the remaining amount. However, Dawn may claim he cannot do so because of the doctrine of **promissory estoppel**, since she acted on the strength of his waiver by spending the remaining debt money on her recording.

If Adam can show that he did not accept part payment voluntarily or that she took advantage of his financial difficulty, he may be entitled to recover following *D and C Builders v Rees 1966*. Alternatively, it may be argued that following the success of her recording, her reliance on the waiver was not to her detriment and it would be inequitable to allow her to avoid her obligations. The circumstances are such that it may be just to allow Adam to enforce his legal rights *(Combe v Combe 1951)*.

Question 9

Text reference. Chapters 15 and 17.

Top tips. Make sure that you notice the different mark allocations for each of the parts, and spend the appropriate time on each.

Easy marks. Make sure that you tackle all of the issues identified in the question, and cite at least one case in support of each.

Marking scheme

This question requires candidates to explain a number of company law areas. A company's constitutional documents, fixed charges and passing off.

		Marks
(a)	Four differences, 1 mark each	4
(b)	1 mark per valid point on fixed charges	3
(c)	1 mark per valid point on passing off or case	3
		10

(a) **Articles of association**

A company's **articles of association** deals mainly with matters affecting the **internal conduct** of the company's affairs including the issue and transfer of shares and class rights, dividends and alterations of capital structure, the convening and conduct of general meetings, the appointment, powers and proceedings of directors and company accounts.

A company may have its own full-length special articles or it may adopt **model articles under the** Companies Act. Model articles will be deemed to apply to the extent that the company does not submit its own articles in substitution.

A company's articles of association, along with any resolutions or agreements that it may make, **binds its members to the company**, **the company to its members** and **its members to each other** (s33 CA 2006).

Memorandum of association

The **memorandum** is a **document** which is signed and dated by the **subscribers** of the company. It states that the subscribers wish to **form a company** and that they undertake to **subscribe for at least one share**.

(b) **Fixed charges**

A **fixed or specific charge** attaches to the relevant asset as soon as the charge is created. For example a charge over named property given as security for a loan to the owner of the property. If the company needs to dispose of the charged asset, it will either repay the secured debt out of the sale proceeds so that the charge is discharged or dispose of the asset subject to the charge. A fixed charge may be over land or other company assets, from buildings and chattels to book debts. Where the assets charged are to be dealt with without reference to the chargee, usually on a regular basis (for example goods held in inventory), the appropriate form of charge is a floating charge. Holders of fixed charges, properly created and registered, rank in priority to subsequent claimants against the company's charged assets.

(c) **Passing off**

A company cannot be **registered** with a **name** which is the **same** as that of any **existing company** which appears in the statutory index at the Companies Registry. However, a company may carry on business under a name other than its registered name.

At common law, a company can be prevented from using a name if the use of that name causes the company's goods to be **confused** with those of another company.

The court may grant an injunction in a **passing off** action brought by that other company and may also force the defendant company to **change its name** (*see Ewing v Buttercup Margarine Co Ltd 1917* where a sole trader was prevented from using the business name 'The Buttercup Dairy Co' in the north of England because of confusion with the business in the London area of Buttercup Margarine Co Ltd).

Mat

Mat is likely to be **liable** for an action in passing off, particularly as he has declared that his aim is to benefit from the goodwill of an existing company. He is advised not to call his new company Netscope Ltd.

Question 10

Text reference. Chapter 15.

Top tips. You must be very well-prepared to be able to earn a good proportion of 10 marks on the *ultra vires* doctrine. Ensure you are familiar with the law in this area and plan your answer carefully.

Easy marks. Explain S39 CA 2006 in as much detail as you can.

Marking scheme

This question requires candidates to consider, explain and apply the *ultra vires* doctrine.

8-10 marks	Thorough to complete answers, showing a detailed understanding of the doctrine of *ultra vires* as it applies in the problem scenario.
5-7 marks	A clear understanding of the topic but perhaps lacking in detail or application.
2-4 marks	Some knowledge although perhaps not clearly expressed, or very limited in its application.
0-1 marks	Little or no knowledge of the topic.

Company capacity

The contractual capacity of a registered company is usually **unrestricted** and it may enter into any lawful contract. However the members may resolve to restrict the activities of the company (the objects), or the articles may have included restrictions at the time the company was registered.

Ultra vires

Any contract entered into which is affected by restrictions is in theory *ultra vires* (and void). However, given that the validity of a company's acts cannot be questioned on the grounds of it having lacked legal capacity (s39 CA 2006), the *ultra vires* rule is of very limited effect insofar as third parties are concerned.

Internally, the *ultra vires* rule is still relevant. Under s171 CA 2006 the directors owe a duty to exercise their powers and use the company's assets **in accordance with the company's purposes or objects**. A member can obtain an injunction to restrain the doing of an *ultra vires* act before it is done. However, in the event that the directors are in breach of this duty, the action can be ratified by **ordinary resolution** (and their liability relieved by a separate resolution).

Externally, s39 CA 2006 provides that 'the validity of an act done by a company shall not be called into question on the ground of lack of capacity by reason of anything in the company's constitution'. Neither the company nor the third party can plead *ultra vires* to escape their obligations and under s40 as long as the third part acts in good faith they can safely assume the directors have any power that they profess to have. Therefore, the *ultra vires* rule has effectively been abolished in relations to acts done between a company and a third party **unless the third party acts in bad faith and the directors exceed their authority**. Now almost all such acts will be capable of validation at the instance of either party.

Any *ultra vires* transaction between a **company** and a **director** will **be voidable** at the instance of the company **unless ratified** or third party rights intervene or where restitution can no longer be made (s.41).

Meg

Applying this to the scenario, it appears that the **intention** to market the new cleaner is *ultra vires.* Meg may therefore seek to restrain her colleagues from proceeding with this venture. However, under s39, any transaction with outsiders will be **binding** on the company. Internally, Meg's colleagues may well seek to unrestrict the company's objects by **special resolution** which, since they control 80% of the shares, would be successful.

ACCA Fundamentals Level
Paper F4
Corporate and Business Law
(Eng)

Mock Examination 2

Question Paper	
Time allowed	
Reading and Planning Writing	**15 minutes** **3 hours**
ALL TEN questions are compulsory and MUST be attempted	
During reading and planning time only the question paper may be annotated	

DO NOT OPEN THIS PAPER UNTIL YOU ARE READY TO START UNDER EXAMINATION CONDITIONS

All TEN questions are compulsory and MUST be attempted

Question 1

Assess the importance of delegated legislation as a source of contemporary law paying particular attention to the powers of the courts with respect to it. **(10 marks)**

Question 2

In relation to the law of contract:

(a) Distinguish between express and implied terms **(4 marks)**
(b) Explain the circumstances under which terms may be implied in contracts **(6 marks)**

(Total = 10 marks)

Question 3

Explain in relation to remedies for breach of contract:

(a) The difference between liquidated damages and penalty clauses **(5 marks)**
(b) The duty to mitigate losses **(5 marks)**

(Total = 10 marks)

Question 4

In relation to the dismissal of employees, explain:

(a) The grounds on which dismissal may be fair **(5 marks)**
(b) The grounds on which dismissal will be automatically unfair **(5 marks)**

(Total = 10 marks)

Question 5

Explain the meaning of the following terms when found at the end of the names of business organisations:

(a) & Co **(3 marks)**
(b) Ltd **(3 marks)**
(c) plc **(4 marks)**

(Total = 10 marks)

Question 6

In terms of the tort of negligence, briefly explain:

(a) Causality and the 'but for' test **(4 marks)**
(b) The circumstances that may break the chain of causality **(6 marks)**

(Total = 10 marks)

Question 7

In relation to company law explain:

(a) The meaning of winding up **(3 marks)**

(b) The procedures involved in

(i) a members' voluntary winding up **(3 marks)**

(ii) a creditors' voluntary winding up **(4 marks)**

(Total = 10 marks)

Question 8

Amy always took her car to be serviced at Brakes Ltd and did so again in January. On the three previous occasions, before handing her car over to the garage, Amy had always been required to sign a contractual document which contained the following statement.

'Brakes Ltd accepts no responsibility for any consequential loss or injury sustained as a result of any work carried out by the company, whether as a result of negligence or otherwise.'

On the most recent occasion, due to the fact that the garage was very busy when she arrived, Amy was not asked to sign the usual document. She was, however, given a receipt for the car, which she accepted without reading. On the back of the form was printed Brakes Ltd's usual business terms including the above statement.

After collecting the car after its service, Amy was driving home when she suddenly lost control of the car and crashed into a tree. As a consequence, Amy was severely injured and was unable to work for three months and the car was completely destroyed. It subsequently emerged that that the accident had been caused by a mechanic at Brakes Ltd who had failed to properly reconnect the car's steering mechanism. Brakes Ltd have accepted that their employee was negligent but deny any liability, relying on the exclusion clause.

Required

Advise Amy:

(a) Whether the exclusion clause was incorporated into her contract with Brakes Ltd **(8 marks)**

(b) Assuming it has been, whether it exempts Brakes Ltd for liability for all or any of the damage suffered as a result of the crash **(2 marks)**

(Total = 10 marks)

Question 9

Hilary is the managing director of Artworks Ltd, a company which distributes and sells the work of modern artists. Chris and Martin are the other directors. In her capacity as managing director of Artworks Ltd, Hilary ordered 10,000 paintings from Oilprojects Ltd. Oilprojects Ltd paid Hilary a personal commission for the order.

Required

Advise Chris and Martin as to whether Artworks Ltd has any claim against Hilary in relation to the commission paid by Oilprojects Ltd. **(10 marks)**

Question 10

Two years ago Fin inherited some money and decided to invest the money in company shares.

At that time he heard that Heave Ltd was badly in need of additional capital and that the directors had decided that the only way to raise the needed money was to offer fully paid up £1 shares to new members at a discount price of 50 pence per share. Fin thought the offer was too good to miss and he subscribed and paid for 20,000 new shares on this basis. However, Heave Ltd has since gone into insolvent liquidation, owing a considerable sum of money to its unsecured creditors.

With the remaining money of his investment Fin subscribed for 10,000 shares in Irk plc. Although they were nominally £1 shares, he was required to pay a premium of £1 for each share he subscribed for. The shares are currently trading at £2 per share.

Apart from the above shares, Fin has absolutely no other wealth.

Required

Advise Fin as to the following matters.

(a) His potential liability for the debts of Heave Ltd **(5 marks)**

(b) The prospect of his recovering his premium payment from Irk plc **(5 marks)**

(Total = 10 marks)

(Total = 100 marks)

Answers

DO NOT TURN THIS PAGE UNTIL YOU HAVE COMPLETED THE MOCK EXAM

A plan of attack

If this were the real Corporate and Business Law exam and you had been told to turn over and begin, what would be going through your mind?

Perhaps you're having a panic. Stop that now! What you should do is spend a good five minutes looking through the paper in detail, thinking about the topics and working out the order in which to attempt the questions. So turn back to the paper and let's sort out a plan of attack.

Looking through the paper

You have no choices in this paper and must attempt all questions. During reading and planning time you should decide the order that you will attempt them.

The questions in the Paper are as follows

- Question 1 is on delegated legislation.
- Question 2 asks for an explanation of the terms of a contract.
- Question 3 asks for an explanation of some terms relating to remedies for breach of contract.
- Question 4 is on fair and unfair dismissal.
- Question 5 asks for an explanation of terms that form parts of business names.
- Question 6 is a thorough examination of the concept of causality in the area of professional negligence.
- Question 7 asks about different types of winding-up of a company.
- Question 8 is a scenario-based question examining aspects of the law relating to exclusion clauses.
- Question 9 is a scenario-based question on directors' duties.
- Question 10 is a fairly complicated scenario-based question on share capital, the ability to recover it and the liability of shareholders for debts of a company.

Tackling the paper

You can answer the questions in any order, but we would advise you to **take the first seven questions first**. This is because the questions are more straightforward than the last three scenario questions and you can build up marks quickly, by ensuring that you get the simple marks in each of the questions you undertake. Also, if you do miscalculate your time apportionment and you have done the scenario questions first, you run the risk of missing a knowledge-based question out, and consequently losing the straightforward marks in that question, in favour of marks which are harder to get in other questions.

Here are some points to note:

- It is not wise to ignore a syllabus area when revising, as you reduce your potential score by 10% for each question you cannot answer in the exam.
- If you think that there are any questions that you cannot do, look through them all carefully. Do any of the questions have parts that you think you can attempt? At least attempt the parts you can answer.

The last three scenario questions are longer than the seven knowledge-based questions and usually require you to apply legal principles to situations. We suggest that you tackle them second when you have 'warmed up' by answering the knowledge-based questions.

A key skill is to be able to break down the larger questions into the components within them, to see where you will build up your marks.

Allocating your time

BPP's advice is always allocate your time according to the marks for the question in total and for the parts of the question. That means for paper F4 that you should spend 18 minutes on each question. However, use your common sense. If you are doing a question but know you can't answer part (c), allocate those minutes to another question, where you may be able to pick up more marks.

Forget about it!

And don't worry if you found the paper difficult. More than likely other candidates will too. If this were the real thing you would need to forget the exam the minute you left the exam hall and think about the next one. Or, if it is the last one, celebrate!

Question 1

Text reference. Chapter 2.

Top tips. It is important that you notice that the question effectively has two requirements running into each other: to consider the importance of delegated legislation and to consider how it is controlled. Don't make the mistake of simply writing all that you know about delegated legislation: try and tailor your answer to the requirements of the question. Why do the advantages of delegated legislation make it important?

Easy marks. In this 10 mark question you should be able to earn at least five marks by considering the advantages of delegated legislation and relating them to its importance. So, for example, it saves parliamentary time, so that parliamentary attention can be spent on other matters. Give some time to addressing the other aspect of the question, ie control. Even a brief attempt at discussing this should earn you a mark or two.

Examiner's comments. Most candidates were able to fulfil the first requirement, to assess the importance of delegated legislation, but many made little or no attempt to discuss the issue of control, or became irrelevant when doing so.

Marking scheme

This question asks candidates to explain both what delegated legislation is and its importance in the contemporary legal system. It specifically requires a consideration of the way in which the courts seek to control it, but mention should also be made of Parliamentary control.

6-10 marks	A thorough answer which explains the meaning of delegated legislation and how it is introduced. The perceived advantages and disadvantages should be considered and all aspects of control should be mentioned. For full marks reference should be made to the Human Rights Act 1998.
0-5 marks	A less complete answer, perhaps lacking in detail or unbalanced in that it does not deal with some aspects of the question.

Delegated legislation

The complexity of much modern legislation means that, in many instances, there is a great deal of **detail** which cannot conveniently be included in an Act of Parliament. The **time** available to Parliament is limited and the volume of legislation that is required to regulate a complex modern society is extremely high. Therefore, much modern legislation contains sections allowing for the full scope of legal rules to be completed by others, normally **ministers**, **government commissions** or **local authorities**.

The legislation is often **enabling** in nature, which means that it sets out the broad objectives and purpose of the Act, leaving the detail to be delegated to individuals or bodies outside Parliament. This is the means by which delegated legislation is made. There are various **forms** of **delegated legislation**.

Statutory instruments

Most often, delegated legislation takes the form of **statutory instruments**, with power having been delegated by Act of Parliament to a government minister. Different component parts of much legislation, such as employment legislation, are brought into effect by statutory instrument;

Bye-laws

Bye-laws are made by local authorities and apply within a specific locality.

Rules of court

Rules of Court may be made by the judiciary to **control court procedure**.

Professional regulations

Parliament also gives powers to various **professional bodies**, such as the Law Society, in connection with the regulation by the professional body of the conduct of its members.

Orders in council

Orders in Council contain rules which are laid down by the Privy Council, circumventing the need to go through the full Parliamentary process. However this may reduce the popularity of the government and is likely to be used only in instances of national emergency.

Delegated legislation is **important** for a number of reasons.

Volume of work

Without delegated legislation, Parliament would be **overwhelmed by the volume of work**. Delegated legislation enables Parliament to concentrate on the broader principles of the legislative framework, rather than getting bogged down in details.

Speed

The use of delegated legislation enables new laws to be passed much more **quickly**, which is especially advantageous in times of **emergency**.

Expertise

The subject of new legislation is often highly **detailed, technical and complex**. It makes sense, therefore, for the exact content and wording to be arrived at by consultation with professional, commercial or industrial groups outside parliament.

Tidier primary legislation

It also means that the **primary legislation is less voluminous** because the details are left to other delegated legislation documentation.

Flexibility

Delegation leads to greater **flexibility**, because regulations can be altered later without the need to revert to Parliament.

Disadvantages of delegated legislation

The volume of delegated legislation means that it can become difficult for Parliament to keep track of the effect of the legislation that it has enabled. Also, although Parliament is ultimately responsible for the legislation that is in force, it is likely that much of the detail has actually been drafted and finalised by individual ministers or by **civil servants**. Since civil servants are unelected, the degree to which lawmaking powers should be delegated to them is a matter for some debate.

Control over delegated legislation

It is therefore important that delegated legislation is **properly controlled** and that control is exercised by the courts and by Parliament.

Ultra vires

The **power** to make delegated legislation is conferred by the **enabling Act of Parliament** and this also defines the extent of that power. A statutory instrument may be challenged in the courts on the grounds that it is *ultra vires* – in other words that it exceeds the prescribed limits, or that it has been made without due compliance with the correct procedure. In this way, the courts exercise some degree of control or influence over it.

Human Rights Act 1998

The **Human Rights Act 1998** introduced an additional check on delegated legislation. In any proceedings in which a court determines whether a provision of delegated legislation is compatible with a right set out in the European Convention on Human Rights, it may declare the delegated legislation to be invalid and strike it out.

Parliament

Control over delegated legislation is also exercised by Parliament. This is achieved by means of providing for statutory instruments to be **laid before Parliament for 40 days** before they take effect and for members to propose a resolution of veto if there are objections. Alternatively, some regulations must be affirmatively approved by Parliament before they take effect. In addition, there are Scrutiny Committees whose duty it is to examine statutory instruments with a view to raising objections if necessary.

Question 2

Text reference. Chapter 6.

Top tips. The key to the difference between express and implied terms is the court's approach to them. Don't dwell too much on implied terms in part (a) as you can discuss them at length in part (b).

Easy marks. Try to quote as many cases as possible to maximise your marks, otherwise it is a rather narrow question, and quite difficult to find enough to say.

Examiner's comments. Not many candidates were able to explain the importance of the court's approach, and many just rephrased the question, adding little else. A significant minority confused representations and implied terms. Few candidates referred to case law or gave examples in part (b).

Marking scheme

			Marks
(a)	Terms can be settled by the court	1	
	Cases/examples	1	
	Express terms description	1	
	Implied terms description	1	
			4
(b)	Desire to maintain the contract	2	
	The Moorcock (or example)	1	
	'Bystander test' (or example)	1	
	Terms implied by SOGA 1979	1	
	Terms implied by custom	1	
			6
			10

(a) **Contractual terms**

As a general principle, the parties to a contract may include in their contract **whatever terms they choose**. The agreement reached on the terms must be **complete** in order to be legally binding and those terms must be sufficiently **clear and precise** (*Scammell v Ouston 1941*). However, it is always possible for the parties to leave an essential term to be settled by specified means outside the contract, for example by agreeing to sell at open market value on the day of delivery or to invite an arbitrator to determine a fair price (*Hillas & Co Ltd v Arcos Ltd 1932*). If, however, the parties defer an essential term for later negotiating (rather than specifying a means for its ascertainment), there is no binding agreement.

Express terms

An **express term** may be defined as any term which has been included by the parties. It may be written or oral and the court will ascertain as a question of fact whether any oral statement constitutes a term of the contract or simply a representation. However, if a contract exists and contains all necessary terms to make it an effective contract, generally speaking oral evidence will not be admitted in order to add to, vary or contradict any of the written terms.

Implied terms

An **implied term** is one which is deemed to form part of a contract even though not expressly stated by the parties, whether orally or in writing. Some terms are implied by the courts as necessary to give effect to the parties' presumed intentions or by statute or in accordance with relevant trade practices. Implied terms can normally be excluded or varied by the parties save where this is prevented by relevant statutory provisions.

(b) **Implying terms into contracts**

The usual reason for a court to imply a term in a contract is in order to give **business efficacy** to that contract. In such cases the term which is implied will be one which, it appears to the court, the parties inadvertently omitted or which is so obvious that it goes without saying and it can be assumed that the parties simply took it for granted that such a term would apply. The courts will be **keen to prevent the failure of an otherwise sound contract** and to implement the manifested intention of the parties (*The Moorcock 1889*).

Bystander test

This test was formulated in *Shirlaw v Southern Foundries 1940*. It allows terms to be implied into contracts which the parties did not express because they are so obvious that they go without saying. So if, while the parties were making their bargain, an officious bystander were to suggest some express provision for them in their agreement they would say 'why should we put that in, that's obvious'.

The court may imply terms which it considers to be required implicitly by the **nature of the contract** itself. In *Liverpool City Council v Irwin 1977*, the defendants were tenants of a maisonette in a tower block owned by the claimants with no formal tenancy agreement. The defendants withheld rent, alleging that the claimants had breached implied terms because the lifts did not work and the stairs were unlit. The court concluded that since tenants could only occupy the building with access to stairs and/or lifts, therefore terms needed to be implied on these matters, including an implied obligation on the landlord's part to keep these parts reasonably safe.

The courts have also established a number of **implied terms into employment contracts** concerning employers' and employees' duties.

Statute law

Terms will be implied by statute where that is the expressed intention of the legislation, for example under The Sale of Goods Act 1979, terms are implied as to the vendor's **title** and the **description** and **quality** of the goods in a contract for the sale of goods. In some cases, the statute provides that the implied terms cannot be overridden (there are several instances of this in SOGA 1979, but in others, express provisions to the contrary will prevail).

Custom and practice

The parties may be considered to have entered into a contract subject to a **custom or practice of their trade**. In *Hutton v Warren 1836*, the defendant landlord gave the claimant, a tenant farmer, notice to quit the farm. They insisted that the tenant should continue to farm the land during the period of notice. The tenant asked for 'a fair allowance' for seeds and labour from which they received no benefit (as they left before harvest time). It was held that by custom they were bound to farm the land until the end of the tenancy, but they were also entitled to a fair allowance for seeds and labour. However, any express term overrides a term which might be implied by custom (*Les Affreteurs v Walford 1919*).

Question 3

Text reference. Chapter 7.

Top tips. Make sure that you give the appropriate amount of time to the two halves of this question, that is nine minutes each. You cannot earn more than half marks on this question if you devote all your energies to part (a) and produce a wonderful answer but don't make a proper attempt at part (b). Try to focus on the precise requirements of the question: it is not about remedies for breach of contract generally but about specific aspects.

Easy marks. Explain what liquidated damages, penalty clauses and mitigation are, and try to quote a case as an illustration of each. By doing that you should earn more than half marks on the question.

Examiner's comments. In part (a) some candidates wrote a general essay on remedies for breach of contract rather than focusing on the precise requirements of the question. Part (b) was generally answered badly. Some candidates confused mitigation with the measurement of damages.

Marking scheme

This question requires an explanation of two aspects of the law relating to damages for breach of contract. It is split into two parts and the marks will be awarded equally.

(a)	3-5 marks	A good explanation of the difference between liquidated damages and penalty clauses with perhaps some examples or cases.
	0-2 marks	Some, if little, knowledge or both elements of the question or unbalanced in only dealing with one of the elements.
(b)	3-5 marks	A thorough explanation of the duty to mitigate losses with examples or cases.
	0-2 marks	Some, if little, knowledge of the duty but not clear or lacking in detail

(a) **Liquidated damages**

The parties to a contract may seek to avoid complicated calculations of loss and disputes as to damages by providing a **formula for the calculation** of such damages in the contract itself, for example a daily rate of payment in the event of late completion or late delivery of goods. A **liquidated damages clause** will be upheld by the court in the event of breach provided it is a genuine attempt to anticipate the appropriate level of damages *(Ford Motor Co (England) Ltd v Armstrong 1915)*.

Penalty clauses

Any term which amounts to a **penalty clause** will be **void**. In determining whether the clause in question is a penalty clause or a liquidated damages provision the courts will look to see if the clause represents a **genuine pre-estimate of loss** *(Dunlop Pneumatic Tyre Co Ltd v New Garage & Motor Co Ltd 1915)*. If so, the clause will be upheld, even if the actual loss is greater or smaller. In the Dunlop case, the garage sold tyres at below a minimum retail price, arguing that the £5 per tyre which the manufacturer was entitled to under the contract was in fact a penalty rather than a genuine pre-estimate of loss. Although the court stated that, generally, when a fixed amount is payable for breaches of different kinds, some more serious than others in their consequences, the clause would be void as a penalty clause, it held that here the formula was a genuine attempt to agree on liquidated damages.

In *Bridge v Campbell Discount Co 1962*, a clause in a hire purchase contract required the debtor to pay on termination both arrears of payments due before termination and an amount which, together with payments made and due, amounted to two-thirds of the total hire purchase price, and to return the goods. It was held that this was a penalty clause – and therefore void. In most circumstances, the creditor would receive on termination more than 100% of the value of the goods.

(b) **Mitigation**

In the event of a breach of contract, the injured party must take reasonable steps to **mitigate their loss** or they may not receive their full losses. This means that they must take reasonable steps to put themselves in **as good a position as if the contract had been performed**. For example, where goods are not delivered the buyer must take steps to buy the same goods from elsewhere as cheaply as possible. Equally, if the seller of goods does not receive payment, they are required to obtain as good a price as possible for them elsewhere.

In *Payzu Ltd v Saunders 1919*, the buyer in a contract for delivery of goods by instalments failed to pay for the first instalment within the agreed credit period. The seller refused to make any further deliveries unless the buyer paid cash in advance on the remaining instalments. The buyer refused to accept delivery on those terms, the price of the goods rose and the buyer sued for breach of contract. It was held, first, that the seller had no right to repudiate the original contract and, secondly, that the buyer should have mitigated its loss by accepting the seller's offer of delivery against cash payment. Damages were therefore limited to the amount that the buyer would have lost if they had paid in advance, which amounted to the interest that would have been foregone over the period of any pre-payment.

The **injured party** does not have to take discreditable or risky measures to mitigate their loss *(Pilkington v Wood 1953)*. In this case, which involved negligence by a solicitor in checking title of a property, the buyer of the property sued the solicitor, claiming the difference between the valuations with good and defective title respectively. The solicitor argued that the buyer should have mitigated their loss by claiming against the previous owner of the property, but it was held that the claimant was under no duty to embark upon complicated litigation which might well not have succeeded.

Question 4

Text reference. Chapter 11.

Top tips. Before you start to write take a minute to think through the grounds for both fair and unfair dismissal. Be as specific as you can in the examples that you give: vague references to bad behaviour are not sufficiently detailed.

Easy marks. In each of the two parts of the question try to think of five specific examples, and you should pick up a good proportion of the marks available.

Examiner's comments. In part (a) the weaker candidates tended to give rather vague examples of unsuitable behaviour without referring specifically to the Employment Rights Act. Candidates who could just list the statutory reasons scored full marks. In part (b) those candidates who had done well in part (a) tended to do so again, but most were not able to explain the topics in any detail.

Marking scheme

This question requires candidates to explain the provisions of the Employment Rights Act 1996 relating to the statutory grounds covering both fair and unfair dismissal. It is divided into two parts and the marks will be allocated equally.

(a)	3-5 marks	A good explanation of the grounds upon which dismissal may be fair.
	0-2 marks	Some awareness of the area but lacking in detailed knowledge.
(b)	3-5 marks	A thorough explanation of the grounds upon which dismissal will be automatically unfair.
	0-2 marks	Some awareness of the area but lacking detailed knowledge.

Unfair dismissal

The relevant legislation governing **unfair dismissal** is the **Employment Rights Act 1996**. Some grounds for dismissal are **potentially fair**, while others are **automatically unfair**. Even if a reason is potentially fair, the tribunal may find that the dismissal is unfair if the employer did not act in a **reasonable** manner.

(a) **Potentially fair grounds for dismissal**

To defeat a claim for unfair dismissal the employer must show that their main or sole reason for the dismissal was related to one of the following:

A lack of capability or qualifications

The employee lacks the necessary capacity or qualifications to perform the work of the kind which they are employed to do. The employee's competence will be judged with reference to the requirement of the contract, the work standards achieved by employees generally and by the standard achieved by the employee in question. The **Employment Rights Act 1996** states that 'capability is to be assessed by reference to skills, aptitude, health or any other physical or mental quality'. The level of incompetence must be sufficient to justify dismissal *(Lewis Shops Group Ltd v Wiggins 1973)*. Qualification means 'any academic, technical or professional qualifications relevant to the position that the employee holds'.

The **employer** must have **behaved reasonably**, for example by consulting with the employee, allowing time for improvement, providing training if necessary and considering alternatives to dismissal. If the employer relies on ill-health as the grounds for incapability, there must be proper medical evidence and they are entitled to consider their own business needs *(International Sports Ltd v Thomson 1980).*

Misconduct

A distinction is sometimes made between 'gross misconduct', which may justify dismissal on the first occasion (such as theft) and 'ordinary misconduct, which is usually not sufficient grounds unless it is persistent (such as rudeness to customers or persistent absence from work). Assault on a fellow employee, conduct endangering others, unpleasant behaviour towards customers and persistent absence from work have been regarded as sufficient misconduct to justify dismissal.

Redundancy

This is a fair reason for dismissal as long as the employer has implemented a **redundancy procedure** in accordance with good industrial relations practice. This requires consultation and objective criteria of selection. The criteria set out in *Williams v Compair Maxam Ltd 1982* are widely accepted as laying down the required standards of behaviour (including giving warnings, offering alternative employment and consulting with any trade union).

Illegality

Dismissal may be fair where **continued employment would be illegal** (for example if an in-house solicitor is barred by the Law Society or an employee who is employed as a driver is banned from driving).

Some other substantial reason

A reason other than these may suffice if is it substantial, for example refusal to accept changed working practices agreed by a majority of the workforce.

(b) **Automatically unfair reasons for dismissal**

Some grounds put forward for dismissal will be automatically unfair, as follows.

Pregnancy

Regardless of the length of service, a dismissal on grounds of **pregnancy** or a pregnancy-related illness, or any matter related to childbirth.

Trade Union activities

A dismissal on the grounds of an employee's actual or proposed membership of an independent **trade union**, their taking part at an appropriate time in the activities of such a trade union, or their refusal to be a member of a trade union.

Spent convictions

An employee dismissed on the basis of a conviction which is actually **spent** under the **Rehabilitation of Offenders Act 1974**.

Health and Safety

Where an employee takes steps to carry out **health and safety** related activities as requested by their employer or brings health and safety risks or dangers to the employer's attention or where they leave work reasonably believing themselves to be in danger.

Enforcing statutory rights

Where an employee takes action against an employer to enforce **statutory rights and duties** and the employer dismisses them as a result.

Whistleblowing

Where an employee is dismissed dismissal for **'whistleblowing'** – ie for making a protected disclosure in the public interest, according to the procedure laid down in the Public Interest Disclosure Act 1998.

Question 5

Text reference. Chapter 13.

Top tips. This is an extremely straightforward question. A well-prepared student should score extremely well on a question like this. However, as the examiner points out (below) there is also scope to make mistakes, for example, thinking plcs are all listed companies. Of course, this is not the case. You must ensure that you have a good understanding of the basics of these legal entities. Also note the comments made below about the style of answers.

Easy marks. Notice the mark allocation: if there are three marks for each of (a) and (b) make sure that you make three points. Likewise, make four points for part (c).

Examiner's comments. This was a very popular question, answered by the vast majority of candidates, and in general it was done competently with most candidates earning a clear pass mark. The main weakness was the failure of some candidates to cite case law and statute in support of their arguments. Candidates must try to quote the relevant legal authority to substantiate the points that they make. A discursive essay style is preferable to a list of bullet points, although appropriate credit was given for the latter.

One of the main errors was to state that a public company and a listed company are effectively the same thing. Candidates should expect this type of question to feature frequently in forthcoming exams, and they provide an excellent opportunity for earning high marks.

Marking scheme

			Marks
(a)	Identification of '& Co.'	1	
	Definition of a partnership	1	
	Limited liability partnerships	1	
			3
(b)	Identification of private limited company	1	
	Explanation of limited liability	2	
			3
(c)	Public limited company	1	
	Constitution must state a plc	1	
	Can offer shares to the public	1	
	Examples of more stringent regulations	1	
			4
			10

(a) **Partnership**

The words '& Co' show that the business organisation is a **partnership**. A partnership is the relation which subsists between persons carrying on a business in common with a view of profit (Partnership Act 1890 s 1).

A partnership is not a separate legal entity but merely the partners as a group working in a particular relationship with each other. In a partnership, **every partner is liable without limit for the debts of the partnership**. A partnership may exist without any written agreement – though it is normal practice to have a written agreement – in fact a partnership may even arise without the persons concerned intending it to do so.

The **Limited Liability Partnership Act 2000** provides for limited liability partnerships which are to have separate legal personality and therefore some of the attributes of registered companies.

(b) **Private company**

'Ltd' shows that the business organisation is a limited company, and, in particular, a **private limited company** as opposed to a public limited company. The essential characteristic of a company is the distinction between the corporation and its members (*Salomon v Salomon & Co Ltd 1897*) which means that its assets and liabilities are its own and a company can enter into and enforce contracts in its own right without members into the bargain. Following on, therefore, a company is liable for breach of contract and may have to pay damages or suffer some other remedy against it.

The significance of the word 'limited' is that the **liability of the company's members is limited to such amount as is unpaid on their shares**. Once shares are fully paid up, the owners of those shares have no further liability in respect of the debts of the company. A company will not cease to exist on a change in its membership.

(c) **Public company**

'Plc' denotes a **public limited company** which is also a separate legal entity distinct from its members, whose liability is limited to the amount outstanding on their shares. A public company must state in its constitution that it is a public company and its name must end with the words ' public limited company' or 'PLC' or 'plc' or its Welsh equivalent.

Unlike a private company, a public company can raise capital from the public. Many are listed on the Stock Exchange. Generally speaking, a public limited company is subject to more stringent accounting and other regulations than a private limited company.

Question 6

Text reference. Chapter 8.

Top tips. Keep to the subject matter of the question. Any answers that venture into remoteness of damage will not attract high marks.

Easy marks. Stating the circumstances that will break the chain of causality.

Marking scheme

			Marks
(a)	Explain the concept of causality	1	
	Explain the 'but for' test	2	
	Use of case to illustrate answer	1	
			4
(b)	One mark per circumstance explained up to a maximum of six marks		6
			10

(a) **Causality and the 'But for' test**

Liability for negligence will only be proved if the claimant can show that a **chain of events** occurred that began with the defendant's negligent action and that resulted directly with the damage caused to the claimant. This concept is know as **causality**.

To satisfy the requirement that harm must be caused by another's actions, the 'but for' test is applied. The claimant must prove that **'but for'** the other's actions they would not have suffered damage. Therefore claimants are unable to claim for any harm that would have happened to them anyway irrespective of the defendant's actions.

This concept is illustrated in the case of *Barnett v Chelsea and Kensington HMC 1969*. In this case a casualty doctor sent a patient home without treatment. The patient died of arsenic poisoning. The court held that the doctor was negligent, but the negligent action did not cause the death – the patient would have died anyway, therefore there is no chain of causality.

(b) **Circumstances that break the chain of causality**

Multiple causes

Where an injury has a **number of possible causes** including the negligent action, the chain of causality will be broken where the negligent act is not the most likely to have caused the injury. For example in *Wilsher v Essex AHA 1988*, a claimant could not prove that a doctor's negligence was the most likely out of six causes to have caused blindness in a baby.

Novus actus intervieniens

Courts will only impart liability where there is a chain of events that are a probable result of the defendant's actions. Defendants will not be liable for damage when the chain of events is broken. There are **three types** of intervening act that will break the chain of causation.

Act of the claimant

The actions of the claimant themselves may break the chain of causation. The rule is that where the act is **reasonable** and in the **ordinary course of things** an act by the claimant will not break the chain. In *McKew v Holland, Hannen and Cubbitts (Scotland) Ltd 1969*, a worker who was prone to falls could not claim for negligence as they did not seek assistance when negotiating a flight of stairs.

Act of a third party

Where a **third party intervenes** in the course of events the defendant will normally only be liable for damage until the intervention.

Natural events

Natural events that are **unforeseeable** will break the chain of causality. By their nature, they are unforeseeable circumstances that the defendant could not avoid. However, a foreseeable event will not break the chain.

Question 7

Text reference. Chapter 21.

Top tips. Make sure that you allocate your time appropriately to the parts of this question. You should not be spending much more than five minutes on a 3 mark section. Notice that part (b) is asking you about the distinction between members' and creditors' voluntary winding up, so you needn't go into too much detail about them in part (a).

Easy marks. Part (b) asks for the procedures involved in the two forms of winding up, so go into as much detail as you can, for example on resolutions and filing requirements. There will be marks available for all of these points.

Examiner's comments. Although some candidates did this question really quite well, others clearly had some knowledge of winding up but not enough to be able to talk in detail about the two types requested in the question. Part (a) tended therefore to be better done than part (b). Many candidates were obviously confused between creditors' and compulsory winding up.

Marking scheme

This question requires candidates to explain what is meant by winding up generally before going on to consider the two specific forms of winding up.

(a) 3 marks are available for explaining what is meant by winding up generally and will be awarded pro rata with regard to clarity of understanding.

(b)

5-7 marks	Clear explanation of both members' and creditors' voluntary liquidation. The two types must be mentioned to get all 7 marks.
2-4 marks	Lacking in knowledge or clarity or unbalanced.
0-1 marks	Little if any knowledge

(a) **Winding-up**

'**Winding-up**' refers to the process of **liquidation** of a company, leading to **dissolution**, where the life of a company is brought to an end, its debts are paid and any surplus assets distributed among its members and/or creditors. The rules governing a winding up are set out in the Insolvency Act 1986.

A company liquidation may be **compulsory** or **voluntary**, **solvent** or **insolvent** and will be governed by the relevant provisions of the Insolvency Act.

A **voluntary winding-up** is where the members in general meeting resolve to wind up the company. Whether it is a members' or creditors' voluntary winding-up will depend on whether the directors believe that the company will or will not be able to pay its debts in full. Only an ordinary resolution is required where the articles provide for liquidation on the expiry of a given period or the happening of a specified event, but more commonly a special resolution is required.

A **compulsory winding up**, by contrast, is made by the court in certain circumstances.

(b) (i) **Members' voluntary winding-up**

A **members' voluntary winding-up** occurs only where all the directors, or a majority of them, make and deliver to the Registrar a **declaration of solvency**, including a statement of the company's assets and liabilities. Such a declaration must state that, having made full enquiries into the company's affairs, they believe that it will be able to pay its debts together with interest, within a specified period (up to 12 months). It is a criminal offence punishable by fine or imprisonment, for a director to make a declaration of solvency without having reasonable grounds for it.

The **liquidator** is **appointed by the members** and their task is to wind up the company's affairs, realise the assets and distribute the proceeds. A voluntary liquidation is generally quicker, simpler and less expensive than a compulsory winding-up.

Once the liquidator has wound up the company affairs and performed their duties, they call a final meeting of members and deliver their final account, following which they send a copy of the accounts to the Registrar who **dissolves the company** 3 months later, by removing the company name from the Register.

(ii) **Creditors' voluntary winding-up**

Where no declaration of solvency is filed, the liquidation proceeds as a **creditors' voluntary winding up**. In this case, the directors convene a general meeting for the passing of a **special resolution** and also convene a meeting of the creditors, giving at least 7 days' notice. Although the members will appoint a liquidator at their meeting, the creditors (who normally meet 14 days later) have the final say in selecting and appointing a liquidator. They may also appoint a **liquidation committee** to work in conjunction with the liquidator.

Once the **liquidator** has **wound up the company affairs** and performed their duties, they call a final meeting of members (and creditors if appropriate) and deliver their final account, following which they send a copy of the accounts to the **Registrar** who dissolves the company 3 months later, by removing the company name from the Register.

Question 8

Text reference. Chapter 6.

Top tips. Read the question carefully at least twice. Highlight the question paper for key points or annotate the margin. Make sure that you identify the issues involved and are fully familiar with the scenario before you start your answer.

Easy marks. Try to have some breadth in your thought processes here. Most candidates will think quite easily of the common law rules regarding exclusion clauses, but don't forget the statutory rules as well. There are easy marks available for referring to the Unfair Contract Terms Act.

Marking scheme

This question requires candidates to decide whether or not an exclusion clause was incorporated into a contract and whether or not it is effective.

			Marks
(a)	2 marks for explaining exclusion clauses		
	Up to 2 marks for explaining the following (cases must be quoted to gain 2 marks)		
	Proper incorporation	2	
	Parties must both be aware	2	
	Nature of liability	2	
	Previous dealings	2	8
(b)	Clauses void	1	
	Clauses included if reasonable	1	2
			10

(a) **Exclusion clauses**

An **exclusion clause**, or **exemption clause**, can be defined as 'a clause in a contract which purports to exclude liability altogether or to restrict it by limiting damages or by imposing other onerous conditions.'

As a general principle of contract law, the **courts will not usually interfere** where two parties negotiate a contract from positions of **comparable bargaining strength**. However, the law will seek to protect a weaker party, for example in the case of **standard term contracts** put forward by the party in the stronger bargaining position. The validity of exclusion clauses is governed by the common law, the **Unfair Contract Terms Act 1977** and a number of other statutory regulations.

It is first necessary to determine whether the exclusion clause that Brakes Ltd is seeking to rely on has been **properly incorporated** into the contract with Amy.

Incorporating exclusion clauses

The common law provides that an exclusion clause must be **properly incorporated into a contract**, or in a document which is an integral part of the contract, before it can be effective *(Chapelton v Barry UDC 1940)*. Provided this is the case, a term cannot usually be disputed if the document has been signed, even if the signatory could not read the terms *(L'Estrange v Graucob 1934)*. This is unless the party putting forward the document gives a misleading explanation of the term's effects *(Curtis v Chemical Cleaning Co 1951)*.

Unsigned contracts

In the case of an **unsigned contract**, it must be shown either that the party affected actually **knew of the clause** or that the person seeking to rely on the exemption clause has taken reasonable steps to bring the existence of the clause to the attention of the other party at the time of or before the contract was made. Therefore a sign on a hotel room wall was not incorporated into the contract between hotel and client since it was not seen until after the contract was made *(Olley v Marlborough Court 1949)*.

Liability

The court will have regard to the **nature of the liability** which is being excluded when deciding whether a clause has been effectively incorporated. If the terms are particularly unusual or wide, a more prominent notice may be necessary *(Thornton v Shoe Lane Parking Ltd 1971)*.

Prior notice

Prior notice of the terms is not necessary, however where the parties have had **previous consistent dealings** and the documents used previously contained similar terms, they will be incorporated (even if the claimant has never read them *(J Spurling Ltd v Bradshaw 1956)*).

Where there have been **previous dealings**, but **not on a consistent basis**, then the party to be bound by the term must be sufficiently aware of it at the time of making the latest contract *(Hollier v Rambler Motors 1972)*. A particularly **unusual** or **onerous term** must be highlighted if it is to be incorporated into the contract *(Interfoto Picture Library Ltd v Stiletto Visual Programmes Ltd 1988)*.

Amy

In this case, it is apparent that Amy has **signed contractual documents** containing the relevant exemption clause on previous visits to Brakes Ltd. However, because she did not sign a contract on this visit, Brakes Ltd is unable to rely on *L'Estrange v Graucob*. The company will therefore seek to rely on the existence of a previous course of dealings (and *J Spurling v Bradshaw*), but will need to show that Amy was **actually aware** of the exclusion clause on this occasion.

(b) **Liability of Brakes Ltd**

Under the **Unfair Contract Terms Act 1977, liability for personal injury or death due to negligence may never be excluded**. Therefore **Brakes Ltd would not be able to rely on the exclusion clause** to avoid liability for the injuries to Amy which arose from its **negligence** due to the actions of the mechanic.

Exemption for **other types of loss** are valid only insofar as they are **reasonable** with regard to the parties' obligations of **skill and care**. The company would also be most unlikely to succeed in avoiding liability for damage to Amy's car since it is reasonable to expect the garage to exercise reasonable skill and care.

Question 9

Text reference. Chapter 19.

Top tips. In tackling a question like this:

- **Identify** the **issues** (directors' duties)
- **State** the law (what their duties are)
- **Apply** the law (to this situation)
- **Conclude** (advise the parties)

Easy marks. This is a straightforward question on directors' duties with many easy marks available for stating the law in this area.

Marking scheme

	Marks
Directors must avoid conflicts of interest	2
Directors must show undivided concern for the company's interests	2
Case or illustration	1
Directors cannot obtain personal advantage	2
Case or illustration	1
Directors cannot accept benefits from third parties	1
Hilary must account to company	1
	10

Directors' duties

Two of the main duties owed by a director to a company are to **avoid conflicts between company** and **personal interests,** and **not to accept benefits from third parties.**

Avoid conflicts of interest

Under s175 Companies Act 2006 a director has a **duty to avoid circumstances** where their **personal interests conflict**, or may possibly conflict, **with the company's interests**. Conflicts are inevitable where a director has an interest in a contract with their company, for example a contract between the company and one of its directors employing that director in the management of the business. A statutory framework exists enabling directors to be interested in contracts with the company but only subject to certain safeguards.

Directors' personal advantage

The principal common law condition is that a director **cannot obtain personal advantage** from their position as director unless permitted by the company. In *Regal (Hastings) Ltd v Gulliver 1942* the directors of one company, which owned one cinema, subscribed for shares in a new company which purchased two further cinemas since the first company had insufficient funds for the acquisition. The directors made substantial profits from the later sale of their shareholdings in the new company.

The then House of Lords held that the directors were accountable to the company for their profits since they had obtained it from an **opportunity** which **came** to them as directors. The fact that the company had lost nothing since it was unable to make the acquisition itself was irrelevant. Had the company agreed by resolution passed in general meeting, the directors could have retained their profits and, in the absence of fraud, their controlling shareholdings could have been used to pass such a resolution.

Not to accept benefits from third parties

Under s176 of the Companies Act 2006 a director must **not accept benefits** for doing or not doing something as a director. However, if they do so, the members have a right to authorise it.

Hilary's position

In the present case Hilary, as a director,received a commission from Oilprojects Ltd for placing an order with them. This sum, therefore, came to her as a result of her directorship and represents a **conflict of interest**. Consequently any profit can only be retained with the **consent** of the **company** in general meeting. She is also in breach of her duty not to accept benefits from third parties. As there is no suggestion that any such approving resolutions have been passed, Hilary will be required to account to the company for the commission.

Question 10

Text reference. Chapters 16 and 18.

Top tips. Read a question like this at least twice and make certain that you have fully absorbed all of the information in it before you put pen to paper.

Easy marks. Set out as clearly as possible the law relating to each part of the question, for example that shares cannot be issued at a discount on their nominal value.

Marking scheme

This question requires candidates to consider various issues relating to the issuing of shares by companies, the requirement for those shares to be paid for by shareholders and shareholders' potential liabilities for the debts of their companies. It is divided into two parts with each part being awarded 5 marks.

8-10 marks	Full and thorough treatment of both parts.
6-7 marks	Good treatment of both parts but perhaps lacking balance and knowledge.
4-5 marks	Lacking in detail in some or all parts.
0-3 marks	Little knowledge of either of the parts.

(a) **Shareholder liability**

It is possible for **part of the payment for shares to be deferred** to a future date – either fixed or on demand from the directors for example – or to be payable in instalments. In such cases the shares are referred to as **'partly paid'**. In the event of the shares being transferred, the unpaid capital passes with the shares as a debt payable by the holder at the time when payment becomes due.

The legal position is set out in the Companies Act 2006. If a company contracts to **issue shares** to an allottee at a **discount**, it is unable to enforce the contract against the proposed allottee. However if the allottee does enter into the contract, they are then bound to pay the full amount due. In respect of the shares issued at a discount, they are liable to pay the full nominal value together with interest at the appropriate rate. This **prevents** a company from issuing shares at a discount to the **disadvantage** of the **company's creditors**. It should be noted that the issue of shares at a price which is less than the **market value** (but equal to or more than the nominal value) of existing shares does not contravene the provision.

Fin

Applying this to the scenario, it is apparent that Fin is liable to Heave Ltd for the **unpaid element** of 50p per share. He will therefore have to pay up to a maximum of £10,000 to Heave Ltd, depending on the actual liabilities of the company.

(b) **Share premium**

A company may issue shares for a price in excess of the nominal value of those shares. The excess is called the **'share premium'** and must be credited to a share premium account. It is not necessary for the articles of association to include a power to issue shares at a premium since it is implied. The general rule is that reduction of the **share premium account** is subject to the same restrictions as reduction of share capital. No part of the account can be distributed as dividend. The account can be used to pay up fully paid shares under a **bonus issue** since this operation simply converts one form of fixed capital into another. It can also be used to **pay issue expenses** and **commissions** in respect of a **new share issue**.

Fin

Applying the above to the present scenario, it is apparent that Irk plc **cannot** repay in cash any amount of the share premium account to Fin or any other shareholders.

ACCA Fundamentals Level

Paper F4

Corporate and Business Law

(ENG)

Mock Examination 3

Question Paper	
Time allowed	
Reading and Planning Writing	**15 minutes** **3 hours**
ALL TEN questions are compulsory and MUST be attempted	
During reading and planning time only the question paper may be annotated	

DO NOT OPEN THIS PAPER UNTIL YOU ARE READY TO START UNDER EXAMINATION CONDITIONS

ALL TEN questions are compulsory and MUST be attempted

Question 1

In relation to the English legal system:

(a) Explain and distinguish between:
  (i) Primary legislation; and
  (ii) Secondary/delegated legislation. **(6 marks)**

(b) Explain the powers of the courts in relation to challenging the validity of primary and secondary/delegated legislation. **(4 marks)**

(Total = 10 marks)

Question 2

State and explain the remedies available for breach of contract. **(10 marks)**

Question 3

In relation to the law of tort explain:

(a) The neighbour principle **(4 marks)**
(b) Remoteness of damage **(4 marks)**
(c) Liability for economic/financial loss. **(2 marks)**

(Total = 10 marks)

Question 4

In relation to the issuing of company shares explain:

(a) Pre-emption rights **(3 marks)**
(b) Rights issues **(3 marks)**
(c) Bonus issues. **(4 marks)**

(Total = 10 marks)

Question 5

In relation to the Companies Act 2006:

(a) State, and explain the purpose of, the various registers that have to be kept by a company. **(4 marks)**
(b) Describe what accounting records will have to be produced and maintained by a company. **(6 marks)**

(Total = 10 marks)

Question 6

In relation to company law, explain the duties owed by directors to their companies. **(10 marks)**

Question 7

In relation to employment law explain:

(a) The meaning of unfair dismissal; and **(6 marks)**
(b) The remedies available for unfair dismissal. **(4 marks)**

(Total = 10 marks)

Question 8

In January 20X9, Amy started a business as an independent website designer.

To give her a start in her career her brother Ben, who ran a retail business, said he would give her £1,000 if she updated his business website. At the same time, her friend Che asked her to do work for his business, also for a set fee of £1,000.

However, by the time Amy had completed the two projects her design business had become a huge success and she had lots of other clients. When Ben and Che discovered how successful Amy's business had become they both felt that they should not be asked to pay for the work they had commissioned.

Ben said he would not pay anything as he had only offered the work to help his sister out. Che said he would not pay anything either, on the basis that he had only given her work to do on the basis of their friendship.

Required

Advise Amy as to whether she can insist on Ben and Che paying the full amounts of their initial promises.

(10 marks)

Question 9

Dee and Eff are major shareholders in, and the directors of, the public company Fan plc. For the year ended 30 April 20X8 Fan plc's financial statements showed a loss of £2,000 for the year.

For the year ended 30 April 20X9 Fan plc made a profit of £3,000 and, due to a revaluation, the value of its land and buildings increased by £5,000.

As a consequence, Dee and Eff recommended, and the shareholders approved, the payment of £4,000 in dividends.

Required

Advise Dee and Eff as to:

(a) The legality of the dividend payment; and **(6 marks)**

(b) Any potential legal liability in regard to the dividend payment. **(4 marks)**

(Total = 10 marks)

Question 10

Geo, Ho and Io formed a partnership three years ago to run a hairdressing business. They each provided capital to establish the business as follows:

Geo £20,000;

Ho £12,000; and

Io £8,000.

The partnership agreement stated that all profits and losses were to be divided in proportion to the capital contribution.

After 18 months Geo provided the partnership with a loan of £3,000 in order to finance the purchase of more stock. The loan was to be paid back from the profits of the business.

Unfortunately the business was not successful and the partners decided to dissolve the partnership rather than risk running up any more losses. At the time of dissolution of the partnership its assets were worth £20,000. Its external debts were £7,000 and none of the debt to Geo has ever been paid.

Required

Advise the partners as to how the financial aspects of the dissolution will be conducted and how the assets will be distributed.

(10 marks)

(Total = 100 marks)

Answers

DO NOT TURN THIS PAGE UNTIL YOU HAVE COMPLETED THE MOCK EXAM

A plan of attack

If this were the real Corporate and Business Law exam and you had been told to turn over and begin, what would be going through your mind?

Perhaps you're having a panic. Stop that now! What you should do is spend a good five minutes looking through the paper in detail, working out the order in which you are going to attempt the questions. So turn back to the paper and let's sort out a plan of attack.

Looking through the paper

You have no choice in the paper, so in your 15 minutes reading time, read all the questions carefully to decide what order you are going to do them in. The questions in this paper are as follows:

- Question 1 asks you to explain primary and secondary legislation and how the courts have an element of control over them by challenging their validity.
- Question 2 is a simple question that requires you to explain the remedies for breach of contract.
- Question 3 tests your knowledge of three aspects of the tort of negligence.
- Question 4 is a straightforward question testing your recall of three issues relating to share capital.
- Question 5 comprehensively tests the main aspects relating to company registers and accounting records.
- Question 6 is looking for you to explain the duties of directors under company law.
- Question 7 is concerned with unfair dismissal: its meaning and the remedies a person subject to such a dismissal is entitled to.
- Question 8 is a contract law scenario question testing intention to enter into legal relations.
- Question 9 is a scenario question which tests your knowledge of the rules relating to the payment of dividends.
- Question 10 is a scenario question which is concerned with the dissolution of a partnership and how capital is distributed.

The questions

You can answer the questions in any order, but we would advise you to **undertake the first seven, non-scenario questions first**. This is because the questions are more straightforward and you can build up marks quickly, by ensuring that you get the simple marks in each of the question you undertake in this section. Also, if you do miscalculate your time apportionment and you have done the scenarios first, you run the risk of missing a complete knowledge question out, and consequently losing the straightforward marks in that question.

Additionally you can sometimes find that the fact that you will consider seven areas of law will act as a trigger to **enable you to recall relevant areas of the law** when you move on to the scenarios.

Here are some points to note:

- You cannot ignore a syllabus area when revising because you have no choice of questions.
- If you think that there are some questions that you cannot do, look through them all carefully. Do any of the questions have parts that you think you can attempt?

If you have revised the syllabus fully, we would advise that you do questions 2, 3, 4, 6 and 7 in that order, as these are the most straightforward. Question 5 is potentially tricky as it is on two small areas of the syllabus which you may not have revised in enough detail. You may wish to leave question 1 until later in the exam when you have 'warmed up' on the other questions, as students often struggle with questions on the English legal system.

The scenario questions usually require you to apply legal principles to situations. We suggest that you tackle them once you have answered the more straightforward questions.

A key skill in scenarios is to be able to break down the questions into the components within them, to see where you will build up your marks.

Question 8 is a question on **intention to create legal relations.** If you have revised contract law well then the solution is probably obvious to you. However, remember that you won't get many marks for just stating the outcome – you must go through the process of identifying the issue, stating the law and applying the law as well.

Question 9 is quite a short scenario but the issue is the rather narrow area of **dividend law**. Unless you revised this part of the syllabus thoroughly then you are likely to struggle with it. However, if you just remembered that plcs cannot distribute unrealised profits as dividends then you would be well on your way to earning some good marks.

Question 10 looks, on first glance, like a standard **partnership law** question – and it is. The twist this time is that it's not just about partnership debts or partners' liability. The main issue is the dissolution of the partnership and distribution of its assets to creditors and owners.

Allocating your time

BPP's advice is always allocate your time according to the marks for the question in total and for the parts of the question. That means for paper F4 you should spend just over 2 hours on the knowledge style questions and an hour on the scenarios. However, use your common sense. If you are doing a question but know you can't answer, say part (c), allocate those minutes to another question, where you may be able to pick up more marks.

Forget about it!

And don't worry if you found the paper difficult. More than likely other candidates will too. If this were the real thing you would need to forget the exam the minute you left the exam hall and think about the next one. Or, if it is the last one, celebrate!

Question 1

Text reference. Chapter 2.

Top tips. You must read the question carefully. Notice in part (a) that you are required to distinguish as well as explain the two types of legislation. If you fail to do so then you will be missing out on a number of important marks.

In part (a) you would also earn marks if you mentioned the structure of the Houses of Parliament and/or the role of the Monarch in the creation of legislation. You could have mentioned the doctrine of parliamentary sovereignty in part (b).

Easy marks. Stating that under the HRA 1998 the courts can strike out delegated legislation but can only declare primary legislation incompatible.

ACCA examiner's answers. The ACCA examiner's answer to this question can be found at the back of this kit.

Marking scheme

This question asks candidates to explain both what delegated legislation is and its importance in the contemporary legal system. It specifically requires a consideration of the way in which the courts seek to control it. The question is divided into two parts but may be answered globally.

(a)	5–6 marks	A thorough answer, which explains the meaning of primary and secondary/delegated legislation. The perceived advantages and disadvantages may be considered but are not necessary for full marks to be awarded.
	2–4 marks	A less complete answer, perhaps lacking in detail or unbalanced in that it does not deal with some aspects of the question.
	0–1 mark	Little if any awareness of the topic.
(b)	3–4 marks	A thorough answer dealing with the powers of the courts in relation to legislation. For full marks reference should be made to the Human Rights Act 1998 and judicial review.
	1–2 marks	Some, but limited knowledge.
	0 marks	No knowledge whatsoever.

(a) (i) **Primary legislation**

Whilst the judiciary is responsible for the creation of case law, **Parliament** creates **statute law** by following a process of developing and refining proposed legislation.

A proposal for legislation can be brought by the Government, a backbench MP, or a peer. A Government Bill may be aired in public in a **Government Green** or **White Paper** and may be introduced into either the House of Commons or the House of Lords. When it has passed through various stages in one House it must then go through the same stages in the other House.

Statute law is usually made in areas so **complicated** or **unique** that suitable common law alternatives are unlikely, or would take an unacceptable length of time to develop. Company law is one example of an area of law created by statute.

In addition to making new law, Parliament may make the law clearer by passing **codifying** statutes. These put case law on a statutory basis (such as the Sale of Goods Act 1979). It may also pass **consolidating** statutes that incorporate an original statute and its successive amendments into a single piece of legislation (such as the Employment Rights Act 1996 or the Companies Act 2006).

(ii) **Secondary/delegated legislation**

Where Parliament gives powers to a minister, or public body such as a local authority, to make law, the resulting law is known as **secondary** or **delegated legislation**. This is because Parliament has delegated the creation of that law to them and this is the main difference between primary and delegated legislation. The delegation is usually conferred within a particular 'enabling' statute that Parliament has created.

The other difference is found in the **types of law created**. Unlike a new statute, codified statute or consolidated statute which Parliament creates, examples of delegated legislation include statutory instruments, bye-laws, rules of court, orders in council and professional regulations.

Delegated legislation has the **same force of law** as statute but it is often used where the law is highly technical (requiring expert input) or where it is too time-consuming for Parliament to go into enough detail.

As delegated legislation is often created by unelected individuals or bodies there are controls over it. It may have to be approved by an **affirmative resolution** of Parliament or be **laid** before Parliament for 40 days before it takes effect.

(b) **Powers of the courts**

The power of the courts in relation to **challenging the validity of legislation** depends on the type of legislation in question.

Delegated legislation may be **challenged** by judicial review in the courts, firstly on the grounds that Parliament exceeded its authority to delegate and acted *ultra vires*, and secondly on the grounds that the legislation has been made without **due compliance** with the correct procedure.

As Parliament (the supreme law maker in the UK) creates **primary legislation** the courts have less power to challenge it. However, under the **Human Rights Act 1998**, Parliament may not enact laws that are incompatible with it. In addition, when a court interprets an existing statute it must do so in a way which is compatible with rights under the European Convention on Human Rights. If a court finds that it cannot interpret a statute in such a way then it may **declare the statute incompatible with the Convention right**. This does not mean the law is invalid but it brings the lack of compatibility to the attention of Parliament which may amend it.

This is in contrast to the courts' role in relation to **delegated legislation**. Under the Human Rights Act, courts have the power to **strike out** any delegated legislation that is incompatible with it.

Question 2

Text reference. Chapter 7.

Top tips. Before you start to write, take a minute or two to run through the different remedies for breach of contract in your head. Do not restrict yourself purely to damages or you will miss out on the majority of the marks available.

Easy marks. For each remedy that you discuss, make sure that you cite a case or an illustration in support.

ACCA examiner's answers. The ACCA examiner's answer to this question can be found at the back of this kit.

Marking scheme

This question requires candidates to consider the various remedies for breach of contract.

8–10 marks	A very good answer revealing a thorough to complete understanding of all of the remedies available for breach of contract, although a concentration on damages is to be expected.
5–7 marks	A good answer but perhaps unfocused or lacking in detail as to the specific nature of the remedies. Perhaps simply a list of remedies with no consideration might warrant the lowest mark in this category.
2–4 marks	Weak answer, unfocused or lacking in knowledge or detail.
0–1 mark	Very little, if any, knowledge of the topic.

Breach of contract

A party is said to be in **breach of contract** where they **fail to perform their contractual obligations fully and precisely** without lawful excuse. Breach of contract always gives rise to an obligation to **compensate** the other party for losses sustained. In certain cases, the breach may also entitle the innocent party to treat the contract as discharged.

The **remedies** available are as follows.

Damages

Damages are a **common law remedy** primarily intended to restore the person who has suffered loss to the same position they would have been in had the contract been performed. Where there is no contractual provision for liquidated damages (a genuine pre-estimate of losses arising from breach of contract agreed at the time of contract formation), the courts will determine the damages payable with reference to the following factors:

- The remoteness of damage
- The measure of damages

Remoteness of damages

With regard to **remoteness**, the courts consider how far down the chain of cause and effect the consequences of breach should be traced before they become so remote that no compensation should be awarded in respect of them.

Under the rule in *Hadley v Baxendale 1854*, damages may be awarded in respect of losses which **arise naturally**, according to the **usual course** of things, or which arise in a manner which the parties may **reasonably be deemed to have contemplated** as the probable result of breach of contract.

If the resulting loss is of an **unusual type**, that is, outside the natural course of events, it may be claimed only if the defendant was aware of the unusual circumstances which might give rise to that abnormal loss *(Victoria Laundry (Windsor) v Newman Industries 1949)*.

Measure of damage

In assessing the **measure of damages**, it should be noted that damages are intended to **restore** the wronged party to the position they would have been in if the contract had been performed, but not to put them in a better or more profitable position nor to be punitive. Measurement of financial loss is usually made with reference to the 'available market' rule.

Action for the price

If the breach of contract is one party's **failure to pay the contractually agreed sum**, the other party should bring a personal action for the price against the party in breach. This is subject to the proviso that the property in the goods has passed to them unless the price has been agreed to be paid on a specific date.

Quantum meruit

A 'quantum meruit' award may be sought as an **alternative to damages** where, for example, one party has already performed part of their obligations and the other party then repudiates the contract. Provided the injured party elects to treat the contract as terminated, they may claim a reasonable sum in respect of the work done *(De Bernardy v Harding 1853)*. A quantum meruit award, unlike damages which is a compensatory award, is a restitutory award and aims to restore the claimant to the position they would have been in if the contract had never been made.

Specific performance

An order of specific performance is an **equitable remedy** and is an order to the party in breach to **perform their part of the contract**. It is at the discretion of the court and will only be awarded where damages would not be an adequate remedy. It will not be awarded where performance would be required over a period of time and the court could not properly supervise the performance, for example in a contract for employment or personal services, or building contracts.

Injunction

An injunction, like specific performance, is an **equitable remedy** at the discretion of the court. The court can require the defendant to **observe terms** in the contract which are in substance negative restraints. The court may award an injunction in cases where specific performance would be refused, for example in a contract of personal service *(Warner Bros Pictures Inc v Nelson 1937* and *Metropolitan Electricity Supply Co v Ginder 1901)*. An injunction will not be granted merely to restrain the defendant from acts inconsistent with their positive obligations *(Whitwood Chemical Co v Hardman 1891)*.

Rescission

Rescission entails **setting the contract aside** as if it had never been made. Rescission is an **equitable remedy** which seeks to ensure that the parties are restored to their position before the contract was made. The right to rescind is lost where:

- A misled person affirms the contract after discovering the true facts
- The parties can no longer be restored to their original positions
- The rights of third parties would be prejudiced by rescission
- So much time has elapsed that allowing rescission would be inequitable.

Question 3

Text reference. Chapters 8 and 9.

Top tips. Avoid the temptation to write everything you know about negligence. The question is quite specific and addresses three narrow areas. Answers which drift off target will not earn any marks.

Easy marks. Briefly explaining the neighbour principle, remoteness of damage and financial loss.

ACCA examiner's answers. The ACCA examiner's answer to this question can be found at the back of this kit.

Marking scheme

This question requires candidates to explain three distinct but related aspects of the law of tort.

(a) This part of the question refers to the neighbour principle in the determination of a duty of care in the law of negligence.

3–4 marks A thorough understanding of the issues involved. It is likely that the best answers will focus on the cases, although examples might be used.

1–2 marks Some, but limited, understanding of the issue, perhaps not referring to any cases to support the explanation.

0 marks No knowledge of the topic.

(b) This part of the question refers to the issue of remoteness of damage in the law of negligence.

3–4 marks A thorough understanding of the issues involved. It is likely that the best answers will focus on the cases, although examples might be used.

1–2 marks Some, but limited, understanding of the issue, perhaps not referring to any cases to support the explanation.

0 marks No knowledge of the topic.

(c) This part of the question focuses specifically on the issue of liability for purely economic or financial loss as a result of a tortious action.

1–2 marks A good understanding of the issues involved. It is likely that the best answers will focus on the cases, although examples might be used.

0 marks No knowledge of the topic.

(a) **Duty of care and the neighbour principle**

In the tort of negligence an individual is not liable for every action they take, only to those to whom they owe a duty of care. Whether or not a duty of care exists in any situation is generally decided by the courts on a **case by case basis**, with each new case setting a precedent based on its own particular facts.

In the landmark case of *Donoghue v Stevenson 1932,* the House of Lords ruled that a person might owe a duty of care to another even though there is **no** contractual relationship between them.

In this case, the claimant purchased a bottle of **ginger beer** for consumption by another person. This other person drank part of the contents, which contained the remains of a decomposed snail, and became ill. The manufacturers argued that as there was no contract between themselves and the person who drank the ginger beer, they owed them no duty of care and so were not liable.

The House of Lords refuted this and laid down the general principle that **every person** owes a duty of care to his '**neighbour**', to 'persons so closely and directly affected by my act that I ought reasonably to have them in contemplation as being so affected'.

(b) **Remoteness of damage**

Even where it is proved that a **defendant's negligence** caused damage to a claimant, a **negligence claim** can still **fail** if the actual damage caused is **'too remote'**. This rule, which is comparable to remoteness of damage in contract cases, is important as it **restricts a defendant's liability** for damage to those losses which they should **reasonably have foreseen**. It would be unfair for a party to be held liable for **damage** which, although they may have caused it, was unforeseeable and therefore in theory impossible to prevent.

The **test** of **reasonable foresight** developed out of *The Wagon Mound 1961.* Liability is limited to **damage** that a **reasonable man could have foreseen**. This does not mean the exact event must be foreseeable in detail, just that the eventual outcome is foreseeable.

In the case of *The Wagon Mound 1961* a ship was taking on oil in Sydney harbour. Oil was spilled onto the water and it drifted to a wharf 200 yards away where welding equipment was in use. The owner of the wharf carried on working because they were advised that the sparks were unlikely to set fire to furnace oil. Safety precautions were taken. A spark fell onto a piece of cotton waste floating in the oil, thereby starting a fire which damaged the wharf. The owners of the wharf sued the charterers of the Wagon Mound. The court decided that the claim must fail. Pollution was the foreseeable risk: fire was not.

The test has since developed further. In *Jolley v London Borough of Sutton 2000* it was held that the remoteness test can be passed if some **harm is foreseeable,** even if the exact nature of the injuries could not be. In this case the defendants should have removed a boat which had been dumped two years previously. A teenage boy was injured while attempting to repair it. The court decided that even though the precise incident was not foreseeable, the authority should have foreseen that some harm could be caused since they knew children regularly played on the abandoned boat.

Invariably it **is up to the court** concerned to decide what damage is foreseeable given all the **circumstances** and **facts** available.

(c) **Liability for economic/financial loss**

Claimants are able to claim for **financial loss** providing it is a consequence of physical injury or damage to property. Pure financial loss is rarely recoverable. However, in *Hedley Byrne & Co Ltd v Heller and Partners Ltd 1963* liability for financial loss was **extended** to situations unconnected with physical damage or injury where a duty is owed in respect of **negligent misstatement** made by a party to another with whom they have a **special relationship**.

Question 4

Text reference. Chapters 16 and 18.

Top tips. If you can expand on the basic definitions in each part, by linking them to the rules on capital maintenance, then you will be well on your way to a high mark. There is a certain amount of overlap between parts (a) and (b) so be careful not to duplicate your answer.

Easy marks. Defining pre-emption rights, rights issues and bonus issues.

ACCA examiner's answers. The ACCA examiner's answer to this question can be found at the back of this kit.

Marking scheme

This question requires candidates to consider the various procedures relating to the issuing of shares to existing members. It is in three parts, although it is likely to be answered globally. Credit will be given for worked accountancy examples.

8–10 marks	A very good answer revealing a thorough to complete understanding of all three elements of the question.
5–7 marks	A good answer but perhaps unbalanced or lacking in detail.
2–4 marks	Weak answer, unfocused or lacking in knowledge or detail.
0–1 mark	Very little, if any knowledge of the topic.

(a) **Pre-emption rights**

Pre-emption rights are the rights of existing ordinary shareholders to be offered new shares issued by the company *pro rata* to their existing holding of that class of share. This right is created where a company proposes to allot ordinary shares wholly for cash and the offer must be on the same or more favourable terms as the main allotment.

A **private** company may by its articles permanently exclude these rules so that there is no statutory right of first refusal (s 567) and **any company** may, by special resolution, resolve that the statutory right of first refusal shall not apply to a particular issue: s 570.

(b) **Rights issue**

A **rights issue** is a right given to a shareholder to subscribe in cash for further shares in the company, usually *pro rata* to their existing holding in the company's shares.

The offer of shares must be made **in writing** by the company and specify a period of **not less than 21 days** during which it may be accepted but may not be withdrawn. If not accepted or renounced in favour of another person within that period the offer is deemed to be declined. Equity securities which have been offered to members in this way but are **not accepted** may then be allotted to non-members. Shares issued under a rights issue are subject to the **normal rules** of allotting shares – they may be issued at a discount to their market value but not to their nominal value.

(c) **Bonus issue**

Bonus issues (also known as '**capitalisation issues**' or **'scrip issues'**) are the **capitalisation of the reserves** of a company by the issue of additional shares to existing shareholders, in proportion to their holdings. Such shares are normally fully paid-up with no cash called for from the shareholders.

Bonus issues are subject to the normal rules of **issuing shares** and must be paid for, if not by the members, then out of **distributable profits**.

The **share premium account** may be used to fund a bonus issue. This is one of its few permitted uses due to the rules on **capital maintenance**. The reason it is permitted lies in the fact that the process merely involves a transfer from one undistributable reserve (share premium) to another (share capital).

Question 5

Text reference. Chapter 14.

Top tips. In part (a) you do not have to list every register – just enough to earn the four marks on offer. Note that keeping a register of debentureholders is not a legal requirement, although there are statutory provisions covering it if a company wishes to do so.

Easy marks. Listing the various company registers in part (a).

ACCA examiner's answers. The ACCA examiner's answer to this question can be found at the back of this kit.

Marking scheme

This question requires candidates to explain the various registers and accounts that companies are required to maintain.

(a) This part of the question relates to registers.

4 marks	A very good answer, not only detailing the main registers, but explaining their purpose.
2–3 marks	A fair to good answer but perhaps unbalanced or lacking in detail.
0–1 mark	Very little, if any, knowledge of the topic.

(b) This part of the question relates to accounting records.

4–6 marks	A very good answer, explaining in some detail the various accounts required to be maintained by companies.
2– 3 marks	A fair to good answer but perhaps unbalanced or lacking in detail.
0–1 mark	Very little, if any, knowledge of the topic.

Credit will be given for accountancy records not strictly required by the legislation.

(a) **Company registers**

Under the Companies Act, companies are bound to keep a number of **statutory registers** available for public inspection and normally held at the company's registered office (although companies can nominate a single alternative inspection location or SAIL).

The **register of members** contains the name and address of each member and the class to which they belong, the number of shares held by them and the date on which they became and (when appropriate) ceased to be a member.

The **register of charges** contains details of all fixed and floating charges affecting the company's property or undertaking, setting out brief descriptions of property charged, the amount secured and the name of the chargee.

The **register of directors** contains details of each individual's name and address (usually a service address), nationality, business occupation, and date of birth.

Records of service contracts are copies or written memoranda of all service contracts for directors, including contracts for services other than in the capacity of director.

Additional information

You may also have mentioned the following registers:

Register of secretaries

Register of directors' indemnities

Records of resolutions and meetings

Register of disclosed interests in shares (plcs only)

(b) **Accounting records**

A company is required to keep **accounting records** sufficient to **show and explain** the company's transactions. At any time, it should be possible:

- To **ascertain** with reasonable accuracy the **company's financial position** at intervals of not more than six months
- For the directors to ensure that any accounts required to be prepared **comply** with the **Act** and **International Accounting Standards**

Certain **specific records** are required by the Act.

- Daily entries of **sums paid** and **received**, with details of the source and nature of the transactions.
- A **record** of **assets** and **liabilities.**
- **Statements of stock** held by the company at the end of each financial year.
- **Statements of stocktaking** to back up the records above.
- **Statements of goods bought and sold** (except retail sales), together with details of buyers and sellers sufficient to identify them

Accounting records must be kept for **three** years (in the case of a **private** company), and **six** years in that of a **public** one.

Question 6

Text reference. Chapter 19.

Top tips. From the mark scheme it is clear that you need to have explained all or most of the duties to earn the highest marks. Do not go into too much detail on each otherwise you risk running out of time so keep your explanations short.

Easy marks. Stating each of the duties – making them into a header with a short explanation below will make them easily visible to the marker.

ACCA examiner's answers. The ACCA examiner's answer to this question can be found at the back of this kit.

Marking scheme

This question requires candidates to consider the duties owed by directors to their companies and requires some explanation of the duties rather than just listing them.

8–10 marks	Clear explanation of all or at least most of the duties.
5–7 marks	Fair knowledge of the duties, but perhaps lacking in detailed explanation.
2–4 marks	Some knowledge of the duties, perhaps merely dealing with one or two elements of the answer.
0–1 mark	Very little, if any knowledge of the topic.

The Companies Act 2006 introduced **seven statutory duties** that directors must meet.

Duty to act within powers (s 171)

This duty requires directors not to exceed the powers given to them by the company in its constitution. In particular they must only exercise powers for the purpose for which they were conferred.

Duty to promote the success of the company (s 172)

The principle of 'enlightened shareholder value' requires directors to act in a way which is most likely to promote the success of the company for the benefit of the members as a whole, but they must show consideration for other stakeholders (such as employees, suppliers and customers) as well.

Duty to exercise independent judgement (s 173)

Directors must exercise independent judgement. They must not delegate their powers or be swayed by the influence of others.

Duty to exercise reasonable skill, care and diligence (s 174)

Directors have a duty to exercise the same standard of care, skill and diligence that would reasonably be expected of a reasonably diligent person with:

- The knowledge, skill and experience which may be reasonably expected of a person in their position and
- The knowledge, skill and experience they actually have.

Duty to avoid conflicts of interest (s 175)

The Act suggests a number of circumstances where a director's personal interests may conflict with the company's interests. Directors have a duty to avoid such circumstances.

Duty not to accept benefits from third parties (s 176)

This duty prevents directors from accepting benefits from parties outside the company (usually bribes). It supports the duty under s 175 by preventing a potential conflict of interest.

Duty to declare an interest in proposed transactions or arrangements (s 177)

Directors must declare the nature and extent of any proposed arrangement or transaction they may be involved in with the company either personally or through a third party. Disclosure may be given by written or general notice or at a board meeting, but must be made to the directors, as disclosure to the members is not sufficient to discharge the duty.

Question 7

Text reference. Chapter 11.

Top tips. The answer below covers just about everything that you could have mentioned on unfair dismissal and therefore is more detailed than what you would be expected to write as an exam answer. When judging how many marks to award yourself you should apply the mark scheme below.

If you got stuck in deciding what would/wouldn't count as unfair dismissal then you could resort to your common sense. For example it should be reasonably obvious that dismissing someone for being pregnant is going to be an example of unfair dismissal.

You would also earn marks if you mentioned the possibility of constructive dismissal giving rise to a claim of unfair dismissal.

Easy marks. Defining unfair dismissal and the three remedies.

ACCA examiner's answers. The ACCA examiner's answer to this question can be found at the back of this kit.

Marking scheme

This question relating to issues in employment law is divided into two parts.

(a) This part of the question requires candidates to explain what is meant by unfair dismissal.

4–6 marks	A clear, concise explanation perhaps citing cases or examples.
2–3 marks	A clear understanding, but perhaps lacking authority or examples.
0–1 marks	Unbalanced, or may not deal with all of the required aspects of the topic. Alternatively the answer will demonstrate very little understanding of what is actually meant by unfair dismissal.

(b) This part of the question requires candidates to explain the remedies available for unfair dismissal.

3–4 marks	Thorough to complete answers, showing a detailed understanding of all or certainly most of the remedies available.
1–2 marks	A clear understanding of the remedies, but perhaps lacking in detail.
0 marks	No knowledge of the topic whatsoever.

(a) **Unfair dismissal**

The relevant legislation governing **unfair dismissal** is the **Employment Rights Act 1996**. Some grounds for dismissal are **potentially fair**, while others are **automatically unfair**. Even if a reason is potentially fair, the tribunal may find that the dismissal is unfair if the employer did not act in a **reasonable** manner.

Potentially fair grounds for dismissal

To defeat a claim for unfair dismissal the employer must show that their main or sole reason for the dismissal was related to one of the following:

A lack of capability or qualifications

The employee lacks the necessary capacity or qualifications to perform the work of the kind which they are employed to do.

Misconduct

This is behaviour by the employee which warrants disciplinary action. However, a distinction must be made between 'gross misconduct', which may justify dismissal on the first occasion (such as theft), and 'ordinary misconduct, which is usually not sufficient grounds unless it is persistent (such as rudeness to customers or persistent absence from work).

Redundancy

This is a fair reason for dismissal as long as the employer has implemented a redundancy procedure in accordance with good industrial relations practice.

Illegality

Dismissal may be fair where continued employment would be illegal (for example if an in-house solicitor is barred by the Law Society or an employee who is employed as a driver is banned from driving).

Some other substantial reason

A reason other than the above may suffice if is it substantial, for example refusal to accept changed working practices agreed by a majority of the workforce.

Automatically unfair reasons for dismissal

The following grounds for dismissal are classified as automatically unfair:

Pregnancy

Regardless of the length of service, a dismissal on grounds of pregnancy or a pregnancy-related illness, or any matter related to childbirth.

Trade Union activities

A dismissal on the grounds of an employee's actual or proposed membership of an independent trade union, their taking part at an appropriate time in the activities of such a trade union, or their refusal to be a member of a trade union.

Spent convictions

An employee dismissed on the basis of a conviction which is actually spent under the Rehabilitation of Offenders Act 1974.

Health and Safety

This includes dismissals related to an employee carrying out health and safety related activities or bringing health and safety risks or dangers to the employer's attention. It also applies where an employee leaves work reasonably believing themselves to be in danger.

Enforcing statutory rights

Where an employee takes action against an employer to enforce statutory rights and duties and the employer dismisses them as a result.

Whistleblowing

Where an employee is dismissed for 'whistleblowing' – ie for making a protected disclosure in the public interest, according to the procedure laid down in the Public Interest Disclosure Act 1998.

(b) **Remedies for unfair dismissal**

Remedies for a successful claim for unfair dismissal include **reinstatement**, **re-engagement** and **compensation**.

Reinstatement

Reinstatement is return to the same job without any break of continuity by order of the employment tribunal.

Re-engagement

Re-engagement occurs when the employment tribunal orders that the employee is given new employment with the employer on terms specified in the order.

When deciding whether to exercise powers of **reinstatement** and **re-engagement**, the tribunal must take into account whether the complainant wishes to return to work for their employer and whether it is practicable and just for the employer to comply. **Such orders are in fact very infrequent**.

Compensation

If the tribunal does not order reinstatement or re-engagement the tribunal may award **compensation**, which may be made in three stages.

- **Basic award**

  A **basic award** calculated as follows. Those aged 41 and over receive one and a half weeks' pay (up to a maximum of £380 gross per week) for each year of service up to a maximum of 20 years. In other age groups the same provisions apply, except that the 22-40 age group receives one week's pay per year and the under 22 age group receives half a week's pay.

- **Compensatory award**

  A **compensatory award** for any additional loss of earnings, expenses and benefits on common law principles of damages for breach of contract. This is limited to £66,200 by the Employment Rights Act 1996.

- **Punitive award**

  If the employer does not comply with an order for reinstatement or re-engagement and does not show that it was impracticable to do so a **punitive additional award** is made of between 26 and 52 weeks' pay (again subject to the £380 per week maximum).

- **Reduced award**

  The employment tribunal may reduce the amount of the award if the employee **contributed** in some way to their own dismissal, if they **unreasonably refused** an offer of reinstatement, or if it is **just and equitable** to reduce the basic award by reason of some matter which occurred before dismissal.

Question 8

Text reference. Chapter 5.

Top tips. As with all scenario questions – avoid jumping straight to the conclusion even if it is obvious to you from the start. Work through the issues following the ISAC approach to maximise your marks.

Easy marks. Stating the two presumptions on intention.

ACCA examiner's answers. The ACCA examiner's answer to this question can be found at the back of this kit.

Marking scheme

This question requires candidates to explain and apply the rules relating to intention to create legal relations.

8–10 marks	A very good answer revealing a thorough to complete understanding of the rules relating to intention to create legal relations, together with the ability to apply them accurately. It is very likely that cases will be referred to, although appropriate examples will be recognised.
5–7 marks	A good answer but perhaps unfocused or lacking in detail as to the specifics of the appropriate law.
2–4 marks	Weak answer, unfocused or lacking in knowledge or detail.
0–1 mark	Very little, if any knowledge of the topic.

Issue

As part of her business, Amy has undertaken some work for her brother and a friend. Both are now refusing to pay for the work done stating that they only offered her the work due to their relationships as brother and friend. Amy needs to know whether or not the agreements she made are enforceable contracts.

Intention

A **contract** is a **legally binding agreement** resulting from the **valid acceptance** of a **valid offer** supported by **consideration**. In addition, no agreement can constitute a contract unless there is evidence, express or implied, of the **intention** of the parties that their agreement should give rise to legally binding obligations.

The parties may make an **express statement** in making an agreement, that it is or it is not intended to create legal relations. In one leading case, a written agreement stated that the agreement itself was 'not subject to legal jurisdiction' *(Rose & Frank v Crompton 1923)* and that statement was legally effective.

However, in many cases the parties do not express any intention and in those circumstances the **courts** must **interpret the agreement** which the parties have made by objective criteria and legally rebuttable presumptions, depending on the relationship of the parties.

There are **two basic presumptions**, the first relating to **family** and **social arrangements** and the second relating to **commercial agreements**. Both presumptions may be rebutted by evidence to the contrary.

Domestic and social agreements

Domestic agreements are generally regarded as **informal** rather than contractual, unless the facts indicate otherwise. Therefore an agreement by a husband to pay an allowance to his wife during his absence abroad was not legally binding *(Balfour v Balfour 1919).*

The **presumption** is, however, **rebuttable** and the courts may decide that there is an intention to create legal relations in an agreement between husband and wife, especially if they are no longer living together and/or if there is other evidence that legal relations were intended, for example, where the agreement is formally drawn up and signed *(Merritt v Merritt 1970).* Also, where the agreement relates to property matters, it is perhaps more likely that the courts will infer an intention to create legal relations.

Business agreements

In **commercial agreements**, the **courts** will normally infer that there **is an intention to create legal relations** unless there is evidence to the contrary. In *Edwards v Skyways 1964* an agreement entered into to make an 'ex-gratia' payment as part of a larger negotiation was held to be legally binding. In *Carlill v Carbolic Smoke Ball Co 1893* the manufacturer argued, unsuccessfully, that their offer to pay a sum of money to any user of their medicine (who was not protected by it) was a mere 'puff' not intended to create a legally binding agreement. The court held that their assurance that they had deposited money in a bank account to meet claims was evidence of an intention to create legal relations.

Some commercial agreements may be described by the parties as '**binding in honour only**'. This amounts to an express denial of intention to create legal relations and is effective to rebut the presumption *(Jones v Vernon Pools 1938).* As mentioned above, in *Rose and Frank v Crompton 1923*, a statement that the arrangement was not subject to legal jurisdiction was held to be effective.

Application of law

Applying the above **principles** to the facts of the scenario, the following may be observed.

(a) **Amy and Ben**

Amy and Ben are sister and brother and so it may be thought that the presumption that this is a '**domestic and social' arrangement**, involving family relations, should apply. However, it is clear from the facts of the case that there is an intention to enter into a business relationship as Ben's business provided Amy's business with work for a fee of £1,000.

(b) **Amy and Che**

The same principles which apply to Ben also apply to Che and perhaps Amy has an even stronger case as there is no family connection with her.

Conclusion

Amy can insist that both Ben and Che pay her the full amounts that they promised.

Question 9

Text reference. Chapter 18.

Top tips. Never forget that where assets are revalued, any excess is transferred to a revaluation reserve which is not a distributable reserve for dividends.

Easy marks. Stating what counts as distributable profist for a plc and the liability for directors and shareholders who declare or receive unlawful dividends.

ACCA examiner's answers. The ACCA examiner's answer to this question can be found at the back of this kit.

Marking scheme

This question requires candidates to explain the rules relating to the lawful distribution of company dividends. The question is divided into two parts, but is likely to be answered globally.

8–10 marks	A thorough understanding of law relating to dividends as it applies specifically to public companies. Cases may well be cited and will be credited.
5–7 marks	A clear understanding of the general law but perhaps lacking in detail or application.
2–4 marks	Some, but limited, understanding of the law and poor application.
0–1 mark	Little or no knowledge of the topic.

Issue

Dee and Eff are directors and shareholders of Fan plc. In the current financial year the company distributed **dividends** of £4,000 when it had made £3,000 profit and revalued its assets up by £5,000. The issue is whether or not the dividend payment is legal and if not who is liable.

Dividend law: declaring dividends

All companies have the power to **declare dividends**. This is the return given to members for their investment in the company. The directors may authorise the payment of **interim dividends** during the financial year but the **final dividend** must be **approved by the members**, usually by **ordinary resolution** with a simple majority at a public company's AGM or by **written resolution** of private companies.

Dividends are **usually declared payable** on the **paid up amount of share capital** and are usually paid in **cash**. They may however be paid wholly or partly by the distribution of non-cash assets.

Dividend law: funding

The **general rule** applicable to all companies is that **dividends may not be paid out of capital**. The Companies Act 2006 sets out specific rules that must be followed which essentially mean that dividends must be paid out of profits that they have available for that purpose, in other words **distributable profit.**

'Distributable profit' is defined in the Companies Act as 'accumulated realised profits, so far as not previously utilised by distribution or capitalisation, less accumulated realised losses, so far as not previously written off in a reduction or reorganisation of capital duly made'. Only profits realised at the balance sheet date shall be included in the calculation.

'Accumulated' means that any losses of previous years must be included in reckoning the current distributable surplus. In order to be treated as 'realised', a profit or loss must be deemed to be realised in accordance with generally accepted accounting principles prevailing when the accounts are prepared.

In addition to the rules stated above, a **public company** can only make a distribution if its **net assets**, at the time are **equal** to or **greater** than the **aggregate of its called up share capital and undistributable reserves**. The amount of any dividend cannot exceed such amount as would leave its net assets at not less than that aggregate amount.

Undistributable reserves comprise the **share premium account**, the **capital redemption reserve**, the **revaluation reserve** and any reserve which the company is prohibited from distributing by statute or its own constitution.

Dividend law: breach of dividend rules

If a dividend is paid otherwise than out of distributable profits the **company**, the **directors and** the **shareholders** may be involved in making good the unlawful distribution.

The directors are held **responsible** since either they recommended to members in general meeting that a dividend should be declared or they declared interim dividends.

The directors may however **honestly** rely on proper accounts which disclose an apparent distributable profit out of which the dividend can properly be paid. They are not liable if it later appears that the assumptions or estimates used in preparing the accounts, although reasonable at the time, were in fact unsound.

The company can **recover from members** an **unlawful dividend** if the **members knew** or had **reasonable grounds** to believe that it was unlawful: s847. If the directors have to make good to the company an unlawful dividend they may claim **indemnity from members** who at the time of receipt knew of the irregularity.

Application of law and conclusion

(a) **Legality of the dividend payment**

Accumulated profit is a **distributable reserve**. In Fan plc's case the total is £3,000 for the year less any brought forward losses or plus any brought forward profits. We are not told the accumulated amount brought forward - just that a loss was made in the previous year. If the company had accumulated profits of over £2,000 before the previous year then it could distribute the full profit for the year of £3,000 plus any surplus profits brought forward. If the £2,000 from the previous year created or added to a loss brought forward then this would be deducted from the £3,000 profit when calculating the amount of profit available for distribution.

The **profit on revaluation** of land and buildings is credited to the revaluation reserve, not to the profit and loss reserve and is not distributable.

For the year in question, £4,000 was paid as a dividend but, as we said earlier, we do not know what the accumulated profit or loss brought forward is. The payment would only be legal if the company had **accumulated realised profits** equal to or greater than £4,000 brought forward.

Additionally, as a plc, the company can only make the distribution if its **net assets**, at the time, are **equal** to or **greater** than the **aggregate of its called up share capital and undistributable reserves**. It is not evident from the scenario whether this is or is not the case.

(b) **Potential liability**

Dee and Eff will be liable as **directors** (for declaring unlawful dividends) and as **shareholders** (who knew or had reasonable grounds to believe the dividend was unlawful) if the dividend paid was in excess of the company's distributable profit. However, as stated above, it is not clear from the scenario whether or not this is the case.

Question 10

Text reference. Chapter 13.

Top tips. As a general rule the law seeks to protect creditors and it would be a reasonable guess (if you did not know the rules) that the external debts would be paid off first. Whether or not you knew that partners' loans would be paid off next, you should have realised that any balance would be distributed to the partners in accordance with their capital contributions – otherwise the information would not have been included in the question! So you can see with a little common sense you can often pick up marks where on first glance you think that you do not know the answer.

You would also have earned some marks for referring to the provisions of the Partnership Act, partnership agreements and the nature of partnerships generally.

Easy marks. Stating the order that partnership assets are distributed on termination.

ACCA examiner's answers. The ACCA examiner's answer to this question can be found at the back of this kit.

Marking scheme

This question requires candidates to explain and apply the rules governing liability for debts on the dissolution of a partnership.

8–10 marks	This should provide a clear understanding of the legal rules and apply them accurately to the facts of the situation.
5–7 marks	This may show some detailed knowledge of the legislation but unable to apply it accurately.
2–4 marks	Some, but limited, understanding of the law and poor application.
0–1 mark	The poorest candidates will provide nothing but the briefest reference to the legislation and fail to apply it to the problem scenario.

Issue

Geo, Ho and Lo have set up in partnership together. They have a partnership agreement and debts in the name of the partnership and wish to dissolve the business. The partnership does not have enough assets to repay all its partners' capital in addition to its external debts. Therefore the issue is how to **apportion out what assets** it does have.

The law

In the event of the **termination** of a partnership, a partnership's **assets are realised** and the proceeds applied in this order.

- Paying off **external debts**
- Repaying to the **partners** any **loans** or **advances**
- Repaying the partners' **capital contribution**
- Anything left over is then **repaid** to the **partners** in the **profit sharing ratio**.

Application of the law

The **partnership's total assets** are **£20,000**. The first item to be repaid is the **£7,000 external debts** which leaves a balance of £13,000. Next on the list is the **£3,000 loan advance** provided by Geo. As there are sufficient funds to repay it in full, Geo will receive a full repayment of the loan, leaving a **£10,000 balance** to be distributed among the partners in accordance with their capital contribution.

The **partners' capital contributions** in percentage terms are:

Geo 50% (£20,000 out of £40,000 initial capital)

Ho 30% (£12,000 out of £40,000 initial capital)

Lo 20% (£8,000 out of £40,000 initial capital)

Conclusion

Each of the partners shall receive the following amounts:

Geo

£8,000 (50% of the remaining assets plus £3,000 loan repayment).

Ho

£3,000 (30% of remaining assets).

Lo

£2,000 (20% of remaining assets).

ACCA examiner's answers:
June 2010 paper
December 2010 paper

Note. The ACCA examiner's answers are correct at the time of going to press but may be subject to some amendments before the final versions are published.

1 The civil court structure in ascending order of authority is as follows:

Magistrates' courts

Magistrates' courts have a significant, if limited, civil jurisdiction. They hear family proceedings and in such cases the court is referred to as a 'family proceedings court'. More generally, magistrates' courts have powers of recovery in relation to the council tax arrears and charges for water, gas and electricity. They also hear appeals against refusal by local authorities to grant licences for selling liquor in their area. Importantly the magistrates' courts have no jurisdiction over claims in contract or tort.

County courts

The network of county courts was introduced in 1846 to provide for local adjudication of relatively small-scale litigation. There are currently 243 county courts. The county court jurisdiction extends to probate, property cases, tort, contract, bankruptcy, and insolvency.

Of particular importance with regard to the county court is the provision of a small claims procedure operated under its auspices. This procedure essentially allows for an arbitration hearing to be conducted by a district judge in most cases involving claims of no more than £5,000. This small claims procedure is designed to be quicker, less formal and less expensive than a county court hearing.

The High Court of Justice

The High Court has three administrative divisions: the Court of Chancery, the Queen's Bench Division and the Family Division.

The Queen's Bench Division

This is the main common law court and is the division with the largest workload. It has some criminal jurisdiction and appellate jurisdiction, but its main jurisdiction is civil concerning contract and tort cases.

The Queen's Bench Divisional Court

This court, as distinct from the Queen's Bench Division, exercises appellate jurisdiction on a point of law by way of case stated from magistrates' courts, tribunals and the Crown Court. It also exercises the power of judicial review of the decisions made by governmental and public authorities, inferior courts and tribunals.

The Chancery Division

The jurisdiction of the Chancery Division includes matters relating to: the sale or partition of land and the raising of charges on land; mortgages; trusts; the administration of the estates of the dead; contentious probate business, such as the validity and interpretation of wills; copyright, company law, partnership and revenue law; and insolvency.

Chancery Divisional Court

Comprising one or two Chancery judges, this appellate court hears appeals from the Commissioners of Inland Revenue on income tax cases, and from county courts on certain matters like bankruptcy.

The Family Division

The Family Division of the High Court deals with all matrimonial matters both first instance and on appeal. Amongst other matters, it deals with issues relating to minors, legitimacy, adoption, and proceedings involving domestic violence.

The Family Divisional Court

The Family Divisional Court, consisting of two High Court judges, hears appeals from decisions of magistrates' courts and county courts in family matters.

The Court of Appeal (Civil Division)

The Court of Appeal was established by the Judicature Act 1873. The court hears appeals from the three divisions of the High Court; the divisional courts; the county courts; the Employment Appeal Tribunal; the Lands Tribunal and the Transport Tribunal. The most senior judge is the Master of the Rolls. Usually, three judges will sit to hear an appeal although for very important cases five may sit.

The Supreme Court

The Supreme Court, which came into operation in the autumn of 2009, is the highest court within the English civil system. It replaces the House of Lords as the highest judicial forum and exercises all of that court's functions. It was felt that the previous location of the highest court in the land in the legislature was contrary to the separation of powers and consequently the members of the Supreme Court no longer sit in the House of Lords. It consists of 12 justices and hears appeals on the most important legal issues.

2 (a) *Offer*

An offer sets out the terms upon which an individual is willing to enter into a binding contractual relationship with another person. It is a promise to be bound on particular terms, which is capable of acceptance. The essential factor to emphasise about an offer is that it may, through acceptance by the offeree, result in a legally enforceable contract. The person who makes the offer is the offeror; the person who receives the offer is the offeree.

Offers, once accepted, may be legally enforced but not all statements will amount to an offer. It is important, therefore, to be able to distinguish what the law will treat as an offer from other statements, which will not form the basis of an enforceable contract. An offer must be capable of acceptance. It must therefore not be too vague (*Scammel* v *Ouston* (1941)). In *Carlill* v *Carbolic Smoke Ball Co* (1893) it was held that an offer could be made to the whole world and could be accepted and made binding through the conduct of the offeree.

In addition an offer should be distinguished, from the following:

(i) a mere statement of intention, which cannot form the basis of a contract even although the party to whom it was made acts on it (Re *Fickus* (1900)).

(ii) a mere supply of information, as in *Harvey* v *Facey* (1893) where it was held that the defendant's telegram, in which he stated a minimum price he would accept for property, was simply a statement of information, and was not an offer capable of being accepted by the claimant.

(b) (i) *Counter-offer*

A counter-offer arises where the offeree tries to change the terms of the original offer that has been made rather than directly accepting it. The consequence of making a counter-offer is to bring the original offer to an end so it is no longer possible for that original offer to be accepted at a later time. For example, in *Hyde* v *Wrench* (1840), Wrench offered to sell his farm for £1,000. Hyde offered £950, which Wrench rejected. Hyde then informed Wrench that he accepted the original offer. It was held that there was no contract. Hyde's counter-offer had effectively ended the original offer and it was no longer open to him to accept it.

A counter-offer must not be confused with a request for information. Such a request does not end the offer, which can still be accepted after the new information has been elicited. See *Stevenson* v *McLean* (1880), where it was held that a request by the offeree as to the length of time the offeror would give for payment did not terminate the original offer, which he was entitled to accept prior to revocation.

(ii) *Unilateral offer*

A unilateral offer is one where one party promises something in return for some action on the part of another party. In relation to unilateral offers, revocation is not permissible once the offeree has started performing the task requested. Reward cases are examples of such unilateral promises. There is no compulsion placed on the party undertaking the action but it would seem to be unfair if the promisor were entitled to revoke their offer just before the offeree was about to complete their part of the contract. An example of unilateral contracts may be seen in *Carlill* v *Carbolic Smoke Ball Co* (1993), where the company promised to pay £100 to anyone who caught influenza after using their product. No one was forced to buy the product but once they did and started using it, the company was bound by its promise. In *Errington* v *Errington* (1952), a father promised his son and daughter-in-law that he would convey a house to them when they had paid off the outstanding mortgage. After the father's death, his widow sought to revoke the promise. It was held that the promise could not be withdrawn as long as the mortgage payments continued to be met.

3 An individual is not automatically liable for every negligent act that he or she commits and in order to sustain an action in negligence it must be shown that the party at fault owed a duty of care to the person injured as a result of their actions.

Consequently, the onus is on the claimant to establish that the respondent owed them a duty of care.

The test for establishing whether a duty of care exists was initially set out in *Donoghue* v *Stevenson* (1932), the snail in the ginger beer bottle case. In putting forward the test to establish a duty of care Lord Atkin stated that:

'You must take reasonable care to avoid acts and omissions which you could reasonably foresee would be likely to injure your neighbour. Who, then, in law is my neighbour? ... any person so closely and directly affected by my act that I ought reasonably to have them in contemplation as being so affected when I am directing my mind to the acts and omissions which are called in question.'

It can be seen that this neighbour test for deciding the existence of a duty of care is an objective, rather than a subjective one. It is not a matter of what the respondent actually considered, but what they ought to have considered. Nor does the test require the contemplation of the resultant effect on the specific individual injured, but merely requires that identity of a class of individuals who might be injured as a consequence of the respondent's lack of care.

The idea of the neighbour, or proximity, test was extended in *Hedley Byrne* v *Heller* (1964), which established the possibility of liability for negligent misrepresentation causing economic loss, where a party gave inaccurate advice or information to another party, within a special relationship, and that party subsequently and reasonably relied on it.

The test in *Donoghue* v *Stevenson* was extended further in *Anns* v *Merton LBC* (1978), Lord Wilberforce introducing a two stage test for establishing the existence of a duty, as follows:

- Is there a sufficient relationship of proximity or neighbourhood between the alleged wrongdoer and the person who has suffered damage such that, in the reasonable contemplation of the former, carelessness on his part may be likely to cause damage to the latter?
- If the first question is answered in the affirmative, are there then any considerations which ought to negate, reduce or limit the scope of the duty or the class of persons to whom it is owed or the damages to which a breach of duty may give rise?

The impact of *Anns* led to the expansion of negligence, as the policy reasons acted only to limit liability once a duty had been found to exist, as opposed to limiting the existence of the duty itself. However, there was gradual criticism of, and retreat from the approach taken by Lord Wilberforce. Thus in *Peabody Donation Fund* v *Sir Lindsay Parkinson & Co Ltd* (1984), it was stressed that the proximity test had to be satisfied before a duty of care could be found to exist.

The decision in *Anns* was eventually overruled by *Murphy* v *Brentwood DC* (1990).

In *Caparo Industries plc* v *Dickman* (1990), a three stage test for establishing a duty of care was recommended. This requires consideration of the following questions:

- Was the harm caused reasonably foreseeable?
- Was there a relationship of proximity between the defendant and the claimant?
- In all the circumstances, is it just, fair and reasonable to impose a duty of care?

As regards the final element above see *Marc Rich & Co* v *Bishop Rock Marine Co Ltd (The Nicholas H)* (1996), for a subsequent application of the *Caparo* approach. In that case the House of Lords relied on policy reasons for not imposing a duty of care.

The present position appears to be that in establishing the existence of a duty of care in negligence, an incremental approach must be taken. The claimant must show that the defendant foresaw that damage would occur to the claimant, that is, that there was sufficient proximity in time, space and relationship between the claimant and the defendant. In practical terms, foreseeability of damage will determine proximity in the majority of personal injury cases. The courts will then, where appropriate, consider whether it is just and reasonable to impose a duty and whether there are any policy reasons for denying or limiting the existence of a duty, for example, under the floodgates argument.

4 Section 7 Companies Act 2006 (CA) sets out the method for forming a company, which is that one or more persons must subscribe their name to a *memorandum of association* and comply with the requirements of the provisions of the Act as to registration. Under s.9, the *memorandum of association* must be submitted to the companies' registrar together with an *application for registration*, which in turn lists other documents that must be submitted. As a result the following documents are required to be submitted.

(a) *The memorandum of association*

Although the 2006 Act retains the previous requirement for individuals wishing to form a company to subscribe their names to a memorandum of association it nonetheless significantly reduces the importance of the memorandum and as a consequence it is no longer possible to amend or update the memorandum of a company formed under the 2006 Act. Nonetheless the memorandum of association, which must be in the prescribed form, remains an important, document to the extent that, as required by s.8, it evidences the intention of the subscribers to the memorandum to form a company and become members of that company on formation. Also in relation to a company limited by shares, the memorandum also provides evidence of the members' agreement to take at least one share each in the company.

(b) *Application for registration*

Although the 2006 Act only requires the memorandum and application for registration to be submitted, s.9 sets out other documents as well as the specific information that must be delivered to the registrar when an application for registration is made.

Section 9 provides that in *all* cases the application for registration must state:

- the company's proposed name;
- whether the company's registered office is to be situated in England and Wales (or Wales), in Scotland or in Northern Ireland;
- a statement of the intended address of the company's registered office (that is, its postal address as opposed to the preceding statement confirming the jurisdiction in which the company's registered office is to be situated);
- whether the liability of the company's members is to be limited and if so whether it is to be limited by shares or by guarantee;
- whether the company is to be a private or a public company.

(c) *Statement of capital and initial shareholdings*

This document is required where the company is to have a share capital. Alternatively a statement of guarantee is required where that is not the case (CA 2006 ss.10 & 11 set out the detailed provisions in these regards).

(d) *A statement of the company's proposed officers*

Section 12 explains that this requirement relates to:

- any person/persons who are to be the first director or directors of the company
- the person/s who is/are to be the first secretary.

9

(e) *A copy of any proposed articles*

As the model articles apply by default this requirement operates to the extent that the company does not intend to use the model articles.

(f) *A statement of compliance*

This requirement to the effect that the rules relating to registration have been followed is as set out in s.13. Such a statement does not need to be witnessed and may be made in either paper or electronic form. Under s.1068, the registrar is authorised to specify the rules relating to, and who may make, such a statement. Section 1112 makes it a criminal offence to make a false statement of compliance, as is the case in relation to all documents delivered to, or statements made to, the registrar.

The appropriate fee must accompany the foregoing documents and once the registrar is satisfied that the requirements of the Act have been met, he shall issue a certificate that the company is duly incorporated. As previously, once issued the certificate is conclusive evidence that the requirements of this Act as to registration have been complied with and that the company is duly registered under the Act.

5 Companies ordinarily raise the money they need to finance their operations through the issue of share capital, but it is equally common for companies to raise additional capital through borrowing.

(a) Debentures

A debenture is a document, which acknowledges the fact that a company has borrowed money. The use of the term debenture, however, has been extended to cover the loan itself. A debenture may be issued to a single creditor or to a large number of people, in which case each of the creditors has a proportionate claim against the total 'debenture stock'.

As creditors of the company, debenture holders receive interest on their loans and are entitled to receive payment whether the company is profitable or not. As regards repayment, debts rank in order of creation, so earlier debentures have to be paid before those created later. Where debentures are issued as part of a series, it is usual for a *pari passu* clause to be included in the document creating the debt, with the effect that all of the loans made within the series rank equally with regard to repayment.

Debentures which have no security are referred to as 'unsecured loan stock'. It is usual, however, for debentures to provide security for the amount loaned. Security means that if the company is wound up, the secured creditor will have priority in terms of repayment over any unsecured creditor. There are two types of security for company loans: fixed charges and floating charges.

(b) Fixed charge

In this situation a specific asset of the company is made subject to a charge in order to secure a debt. Once the asset is subject to the fixed charge the company cannot dispose of it without the consent of the debenture holders. The asset most commonly subject to fixed charges is land, although any other long-term capital asset may also be charged. It would not be appropriate, however, to give a fixed charge against stock-in-trade, as the company would be prevented from freely dealing with it without the prior approval of the debenture holders. Such a situation would obviously prevent the company from carrying on its day-to-day business. If the company fails to honour the commitments set out in the document creating the debenture, such as meeting its interest payments, the debenture holders can appoint a receiver who will if necessary sell the asset charged to recover the money owed. If the value of the asset that is subject to the charge is greater than the debt against which it is charged then the excess goes to pay off the rest of the company's debts. If it is less than the value of the debt secured then the debenture holders will become unsecured creditors for the amount remaining outstanding.

(c) Floating charge

This category of charge is peculiar to companies and represents one of the advantages of the company over other business forms. The floating charge is most commonly made in relation to the 'undertaking and assets' of a company and does not attach to any specific property whilst the company is meeting its requirements as stated in the debenture document. The security is provided by all the property owned by the company, some of which may be continuously changing, such as stock-in-trade. Thus, in contrast to the fixed charge, the use of the floating charge permits the company to deal with its property without the need to seek the approval of the debenture holders. However, if the company commits some act of default, such as not meeting its interest payments, or going into liquidation, the floating charge is said to crystallise. The value of the assets subject to the charge may be realised in order to pay the debt owed to the floating charge holder, although the Enterprise Act 2002 introduced a new procedure to limit the powers of floating charge holders to appoint administrative receivers and requires them to make use of the general administration procedure.

All charges, including both fixed and floating, have to be registered with the Companies Registry within 21 days of their creation. Failure to register the charge as required has the effect of making the charge void, i.e. ineffective, against any other creditor, or the liquidator of the company. The charge, however, remains valid against the company, which means in effect that the holder of the charge loses their priority as against other company creditors. In addition to registration at the Companies Registry, companies are required to maintain a register of all charges on their property. Although a failure to comply with this requirement constitutes an offence, it does not invalidate the charge.

In relation to properly registered charges of the same type, they take priority according to their date of creation. However, as regards charges of different types, a fixed charge takes priority over a floating charge even though it was created after it.

6 This question requires candidates to consider the important role of the company secretary in relation to the operation of companies. The corporate governance structure specifies the distribution of rights and responsibilities among different participants in the corporation, such as, the board, managers, shareholders and other stakeholders, and spells out the rules and procedures for making decisions on corporate affairs. The essence of corporate governance is to ensure that companies are properly run and that its officers are accountable and subject to control. Whilst it is usual to focus on directors when considering the idea of corporate governance, it should be remembered that company secretaries also have an important function to perform in relation to the proper conduct of company affairs.

Every public company is required to have a secretary, who is one of the company's officers for the purposes of the Companies Act 2006 and who, in addition, may, or may not, be a director of the company. Private companies are no longer required to appoint company secretaries, although they still can do so if they wish.

Appointment

Section 1173 Companies Act (CA) 2006 includes the company secretary amongst the officers of a company. Every public company must have a company secretary and s.273 of the CA requires that the directors of a public company must ensure that the company secretary has the requisite knowledge and experience to discharge their functions. Section 273(2) & (3) sets out the following list of alternative specific minimum qualifications, which a secretary to a public limited company must have:

- they must have held office as a company secretary in a public company for three of the five years preceding their appointment to their new position;
- they must be a member of one of a list of recognised professional accountancy bodies, including ACCA;
- they must be a solicitor or barrister or advocate within the UK;
- they must have held some other position, or be a member of such other body, as appears to the directors of the company to make them capable of acting as company secretary.

Duties

The duties of company secretaries are set by the board of directors and therefore vary from company to company, but as an officer of the company, they will be responsible for ensuring that the company complies with its statutory obligations. The following are some of the most important duties undertaken by company secretaries:

- to ensure that the necessary registers required to be kept by the Companies Acts are established and properly maintained;
- to ensure that all returns required to be lodged with the Companies Registry are prepared and filed within the appropriate time limits;
- to organise and attend meetings of the shareholders and directors;
- to ensure that the company's books of accounts are kept in accordance with the Companies Acts and that the annual accounts and reports are prepared in the form and at the time required by the Acts;
- to be aware of all the statutory requirements placed on the company's activities and to ensure that the company complies with them;
- to sign such documents as require their signature under the Companies Acts.

With specific regard to the Combined Code on Corporate Governance company secretaries are required:

- to ensure the flow of necessary information within the board of directors and its committees;
- to ensure that new board members are properly inducted into their positions;
- to ensure the professional development of company directors;
- to provide advice and guidance to the board and its chair on all matters relating to corporate governance.

Powers

Although old authorities, such as *Houghton & Co* v *Northard Lowe & Wills* (1928) suggest that company secretaries have extremely limited authority to bind their company, later cases have recognised the reality of the contemporary situation and have extended to company secretaries potentially extensive powers to bind their companies. As an example consider *Panorama Developments Ltd* v *Fidelis Furnishing Fabrics Ltd* (1971). In this case the Court of Appeal held that a company secretary was entitled 'to sign contracts connected with the administrative side of a company's affairs, such as employing staff and ordering cars and so forth. All such matters now come within the ostensible authority of a company's secretary.'

7 Employees are people working under a contract of service. Those who work under a contract for services are independent contractors. They are not employees, but are self-employed. It is essential to distinguish the two categories clearly, because important legal consequences follow from the placing of a person in one or other of the categories. For example, although employees are protected by various common law and statutory rights in relation to their employment, no such wide-scale protection is offered to the self-employed.

Given the importance of the distinction the courts have developed a variety of test for distinguishing the employee from the self-employed.

(i) *The control test*

The first test to be applied by the courts was known as the control test and depended upon the degree to which the person who is using the other's services actually controls; not only what they do, but how they do it (in *Walker* v *Crystal Palace Football Club* (1910) a professional football player was held to be an employee of his club). The main shortcoming in the control test was its lack of subtlety. Highly skilled professionals, such as surgeons, by necessity have a high level of control over how they perform their day-to-day work, which meant that, under the control test, they were deemed to be self-employed rather than employees. Consequently, they were personally liable for any negligence in their performance, rather than the Health Authority, which used their services.

(ii) *The integration test*

The integration test shifted the emphasis from the degree of control exercised of an individual to the extent to which the individual was integrated into the business of their employer (in *Whittaker* v *Minister of Pensions & National Insurance* (1967) a circus trapeze artist who was required to do other general tasks in relation to the operation of the circus was held to be an employee). However, even the integration test was not without problems, with some employers attempting to give the impression of using a self-employed work-force whilst effectively still controlling what that work-force did.

(iii) *The multiple, or economic reality test*

The economic reality test was first established in *Ready Mixed Concrete (South East) Ltd* v *Minister of Pensions and National Insurance* (1968). In that case, rather than relying on one single factor the court held that there were three conditions supporting the existence of a contract of employment:

- the employee agrees to provide his own work and skill in return for a wage,
- the employees agrees, either expressly or impliedly, that they will be subject to a degree of control, exercisable by the employer,
- the other provisions of the contract are consistent with its being a contract of employment.

In deciding whether or not there is contract of employment the courts tend to focus on such issues as whether wages are paid regularly or by way of a single lump sum; whether the person receives holiday pay; and on who pays the due national insurance and income tax. However, there can be no definitive list of tests as the whole point of the multiple test is that it examines all aspects of the situation in order to reach a determination. For example in *Nethermore (ST Neots)* v *Gardiner & Taverna* (1984), a group of home workers, i.e. people who carried out paid work in their own homes, were held to be employees on the grounds that they were subject to an irreducible minimum obligation to work for their employer.

8 The provision of some form of consideration is an essential requirement in the establishment of contractual relationships. This question requires candidates to examine the operation of the rules relating to whether or not the performance of existing contractual duties can provide consideration for some new promise.

Bry and Cis entered into a contract with Ami to carry out the work for an agreed price. However, before the completion of the contracts Ami promised each of them a further payment, although she is now refusing to pay more than the original agreed sum of £5,000. The question is whether Bry and Cis can enforce Ami's promise to pay them the additional sums.

In order to require Ami to make payment at the new level, those claiming it must show that they provided legally 'sufficient' consideration for her promise. The question, therefore, is whether the performance of existing contractual duties can ever provide consideration for a new promise. The long-established rule of contract was that the mere performance of a contractual duty already owed to the promisor could not be consideration for a new promise. Thus in *Stilk* v *Myrick* (1809) when members of a ship's crew deserted, the captain promised the remaining members of the crew that they would share the deserter's wages if they completed the voyage. Subsequently, however, when the owners refused to make the promised payment it was held that the captain's promise could not be legally enforced as the sailors had only done what they were already obliged to do by their contracts of employment. Where, however, the promisee did more than they were already contractually bound to do then the performance of the additional task does constitute valid consideration for a new promise (*Hartley* v *Ponsonby* (1857)).

The more contemporary case of *Williams* v *Roffey Bros* (1991) expanded the category of consideration. In that case the Court of Appeal held that Roffey Bros had enjoyed practical benefits as a result of their promise to increase Williams' previously agreed payment for work under an existing contract, although Williams did no more than they were contractually bound to do. The benefits enjoyed were that the work would be completed on time, they would not have to pay any penalty; and they would not suffer the bother and expense of getting someone else to complete the work.

As a result it would now seem that the performance of an existing contractual duty can amount to consideration for a new promise in circumstances where there is no question of fraud or duress, and where practical benefits accrue to the promisor.

It remains to apply the preceding legal principles to the case in point. First of all as regards Bry, he had a contract with Ami to do the plastering, but insisted that Ami increase his money before he would complete the work. Bry might try to argue that his situation falls within the ambit of *Williams* v *Roffey Bros*, and that therefore he can enforce the promise. He would point out that Ami did enjoy practical benefits in that the gallery was finished on time thus allowing her to open her exhibition. It is clear, however, that this situation is significantly different in that whereas in *Williams* v *Roffey Bros* the plaintiff did not exert any undue pressure on the defendants to induce them to make their promise of additional money, in this situation Bry has clearly exerted a form of economic duress on Ami to force her to increase the contract price: Ami was left with no real choice but to agree to Bry's terms or else she would have suffered a potentially substantial loss. Such unfair pressure would take the case outside of *Williams* v *Roffey Bros*, and the old rule as stated in *Stilk* v *Myrick* would apply, and Bry would be unable to enforce the promise for the additional £1,000.

As regards Cis, it would appear that he did no more than he was required to do under his contract with Ami. Consequently he would be subject to the operation of *Stilk* v *Myrick* and could not enforce the promise for the additional £1,000.

12

9 This question can be divided into three distinct sections.

The first element of this question requires a consideration of Fi's situation with respect to her potential liability. Partnerships do not normally provide their members with limited liability, unless the partnership has been registered as a limited partnership under the Limited Partnerships Act 1907 or registered as a limited liability partnership under the Limited Liability Partnerships Act 2000.

The situation in the problem scenario indicates that the partners have not gone through the appropriate procedure for the establishment of a limited partnership or a limited liability partnership. As a result, as far as outsiders are concerned, Fi is fully liable for any debts of the partnership and could be required to pay more than her agreed maximum payment of £100,000. Fi would, however, be entitled to rely on the internal partnership agreement to limit her liability within the partnership. This would mean that although she could be liable to outsiders beyond the £100,000, she would be able to claim reimbursement of any payments made above that limit from the other two partners, always assuming that they were in a position to make such a payment.

Chi has clearly used her powers for an unauthorised purpose. Unfortunately for the other partners, they cannot repudiate her transaction with the bank, even although it was outside her actual authority. The reason being, that it is within his implied authority as a partner to enter into such a transaction. As a trading partnership, all the members have the implied authority to borrow money on the credit of the firm and the bank would be under no duty to investigate the purpose to which the loan was to be put. As a result the partnership cannot repudiate the debt to the bank and each of the partners will be liable for its payment. It has to be stated, however, that Chi will be personally liable to the other partners for the £10,000 and as a further consequence of her breach of his duty not to act in any way prejudicial to the partnership business, the partnership could be wound up.

Di's purchase of the books was also clearly outside of the express provision of the partnership agreement. However, nonetheless the partnership would be liable as the transaction would be likely to be held to be within the implied authority of a partner in a gallery business (*Mercantile Credit* v *Garrod* (1962)). Once again, Di, the partner in default of the agreement, would be liable to the other members for any loss sustained in the transaction.

As regards any partnership debt owing, that is clearly within the ambit of the partnership and the members are all liable for non-payment.

If the partnership cannot pay the outstanding debts then the individual partners will become personally liable for any outstanding debt. Although under s.9 of the Partnership Act 1890 partnership debts are said to be joint, the Civil Liability Act 1978 provides that a judgement against one partner does not bar a subsequent action against the other partners. Once the debts owed to outsiders have been dealt with, only then the internal financial relationships of the partners amongst themselves will be dealt with according to the partnership agreement.

10 This question raises issues relating to the duties owed by company directors to their companies and the consequences of any breach of such duties. Before the Companies Act 2006 directors' duties were considered as an aspect of the fiduciary relationship that existed between those directors and their companies. Certain duties follow from a person being fixed as a fiduciary, and these fiduciary duties are analogous to the duties owed by a trustee to a beneficiary under a trust.

Under the previous regulation, directors were required to act honestly and with good faith for the benefit of the company in discharging their duties. This general duty to the company was sub-divided into the three further heads: the duty to act *bona fide* in the best interests of the company, the duty to exercise their powers for a proper purpose, and the duty not to allow his personal interests to conflict with his duties to the company.

Those common law rules/equitable principles have now been given statutory effect under the provisions of chapter 2 of the Companies Act 2006. Somewhat paradoxically, although subsection 171(3) of that Act clearly states that the statutory rules replace the previous rules, nonetheless subsection 171(4) provides that the statutory rules have to be interpreted and applied in the same way as the previous common law and equitable rules/principles from which they were derived, and thus retains those previous rules and principles.

There are two particular issues that emerge from the problem scenario. The first relates to the fact that Harry has taken a facility fee from Itt plc and the second relates to the fact that the board of directors has used its general power to allot shares to pursue the particular end of assuring the successful takeover of their company.

These issues will be considered in turn below.

(i) *Harry's facility fee*

The rule that directors should not allow a conflict of interest to arise was strictly enforced by the courts in the United Kingdom and it can be clearly stated that directors were forbidden from entering into any arrangement which would involve, even the possibility of, a conflict between their personal interests and the interests of their company. The simplest statement of the rule is that directors were not permitted to profit personally from their position without full disclosure and the prior approval of the company (*Regal (Hastings)* v *Gulliver* (1942) and *Boardman* v *Phipps* (1967)).

There can be no clearer instance of a conflict of interest than the situation of a director taking a bribe. This general prohibition has been given specific statutory form in s.176 of the Companies Act 2006, which sets out the categorical duty of directors not to accept benefits from third parties (s.176 CA 2006).

Under s.176, a director must not accept a benefit from a third party, which is conferred by reason of his being a director or his doing, or not doing anything as director. For the purposes of s.176 CA 2006 a third party is any person other than the company, an associated company or a person acting on behalf of the company or the associated company.

13

By virtue of s.176(4), however, there is no breach of duty if the acceptance of the benefit by the director cannot reasonably be regarded as likely to give rise to a conflict of interest. As a result, immaterial benefits and those which are entirely unrelated to the affairs of the company will not be covered by s.176. The statute retains the previous civil law remedies available under the common law or equity, as specifically stated in s.178 so directors in breach of the provision will be held liable to account to the company for any benefit received.

Applying the foregoing to Harry, it is unarguable that s.176 applies to his situation, as, no matter how the payment is referred to, it is nonetheless a benefit from a third party, Itt plc, to induce Harry to use his influence as a director to further the merger. As a result he has breached his duty to Gilt Ltd and not only will he be liable to be dismissed from the board by a simple majority vote (CA 2006 s.168), but he may also be required to pay any money received to Gilt Ltd.

(ii) *The allotment of shares to Itt plc*

Once again the Companies Act 2006 restates a previous fiduciary duty in statutory form, with s.171(b) setting out the long-standing common law rule that directors' powers should be used only for the purposes for which they were conferred. This rule is known as the 'proper purposes doctrine' and was developed by the courts in order to ensure that directors use their powers for the purpose for which those powers were given to them and not for any ulterior or improper purpose. Most of the cases on this point have related to the exercise by directors of their power to issue new shares in an attempt to assist or, alternatively to prevent, potential takeover bids for their companies. Thus in *Howard Smith* v *Ampol Petroleum* (1974) directors preferred one takeover bid as opposed to another, which was supported by the majority shareholding. In order to defeat the bid they disliked, the directors issued new shares, effectively reducing the existing majority to a minority holding in the company, incapable of blocking their preferred takeover bid. This was clearly an abuse of the directors' powers and a breach of their duty to act *bona fide* in the interests of the company (See also *Hogg* v *Cramphorn* (1966) and *Bamford* v *Bamford* (1969)).

Another aspect of this general fiduciary duty is that directors must not act in such a way as will fetter the exercise of their discretion in relation to decisions that affect the operation of the company. For example, directors might enter into a contractual agreement with some outsider to use their vote in a particular way at board meetings. Once again, such an agreement is a clear breach of their fiduciary duty, although it must be recognised that if directors enter into contract on behalf of the company, which they genuinely consider to be in the company's best interests, then they may bind themselves to vote in favour of any subsequent resolutions necessary to achieve the successful completion of the contract.

Applying the above to the facts of the problem, it is apparent that the board of directors have contravened the provision of s.171 of the Companies Act 2006 in that they have used their power to allot shares, not for the primary purpose of raising capital for their company, but for the ulterior purpose of facilitating the take-over. As a result, although their exceeding their powers could be ratified by a vote at a subsequent general meeting, nonetheless without that ratification, May could apply to the court to have the share allocation declared invalid and Itt plc's use of those shares to vote in favour of the takeover bid would also be invalidated. In any subsequent vote to ratify the improper use of the directors' powers, Itt plc would not be permitted to vote.

14

1 (a) (i) **Primary legislation**

Legislation refers to law that has been created by the legislative body within a constitution. In the United Kingdom that body is Parliament, constituted by both the House of Commons and the House of Lords and Bills have to be considered in, and approved by, both houses before they become law, subsequent to the formality of its receiving royal approval. Under UK constitutional law, it is recognised that Parliament has the power to enact, revoke or alter such, and any, law as it sees fit. Even the Human Rights Act (HRA) 1998 reaffirms this fact in its recognition of the power of Parliament to make primary legislation that is incompatible with the rights provided under the European Convention on Human Rights (ECHR). Such primary legislation takes the form of Acts of Parliament; however, the role of delegated or secondary legislation, as a source of law, should not be underestimated.

Contemporary practice has seen the reduction of general and definitive Acts of Parliament that attempt to lay down detailed provisions covering every perceived possibility. Instead, the modern form of legislation tends to be of the enabling type, which simply states the general purpose and aims of the Act. Such Acts merely lay down a broad framework, whilst delegating to ministers of state the power to produce detailed provisions designed to achieve those general aims through secondary, delegated legislation.

(ii) **Delegated (secondary) legislation**

Generally speaking, delegated legislation is law made by some person or body to whom Parliament has delegated its general law-making power. A validly enacted piece of delegated legislation has the same legal force and effect as the Act of Parliament under which it is enacted.

Thus delegated legislation is law made by some person, or body, to whom Parliament has delegated its general law-making power. The output of delegated legislation in any year greatly exceeds the output of Acts of Parliament and, therefore, at least statistically it could be argued that delegated legislation is actually more significant than primary Acts of Parliament.

There are various types of delegated legislation including:

(i) *Orders in Council* permit the government, through the Privy Council to make law without the need to go through the full parliamentary process.

(ii) *Statutory Instruments* are the means through which government ministers introduce particular regulations under powers delegated to them by parliament in enabling legislation.

(iii) *Bye-laws* are the means through which local authorities and other public bodies can make legally binding rules and may be made under such enabling legislation as the Local Government Act (1972).

The use of delegated legislation has advantages over primary legislation:

(i) *Time-saving.* Delegated legislation can be introduced quickly where necessary in particular cases and permits rules to be changed in response to emergencies or unforeseen problems.

(ii) *Flexibility.* The use of delegated legislation permits ministers to respond on an *ad hoc* basis to particular problems as and when they arise.

(iii) *Access to particular expertise.* Given the highly specialised and extremely technical nature of many of the regulations that are introduced through delegated legislation it is necessary, therefore, that those authorised to introduce delegated legislation should have access to the external expertise required to make appropriate regulations. In regard to bye-laws, local knowledge should give rise to more appropriate rules than general Acts of Parliament.

There are, however, some disadvantages in the prevalence of delegated legislation:

(i) *Accountability.* Parliament is presumed to be the source of statute law, but with respect to delegated legislation government ministers, and the civil servants, who work under them to produce the detailed provisions, are the real source of the legislation. As a consequence, it is sometimes suggested that the delegated legislation procedure gives more power than might be thought appropriate to such unelected individuals.

(ii) *Bulk.* Given the sheer mass of such legislation, both Members of Parliament, and the general public, face difficulty in keeping abreast of delegated legislation.

(b) **Judicial control of legislation**

Section 4 HRA 1998 expressly retains the principle of parliamentary sovereignty in stating that the courts cannot declare primary legislation invalid as being contrary to the rights protected by the Act. The only way the courts can challenge such legislation is by issuing a declaration of incompatibility in such circumstances (*Bellinger* v *Bellinger* (2003)). It is then for Parliament to act on such a declaration to remedy any shortcoming in the law if it so wishes (the *Bellinger* case led to the enactment of the Gender Recognition Act 2004). However, such limitation does not apply to secondary legislation, which the courts can now declare invalid on the grounds of not being compatible with the HRA.

Furthermore, a validly enacted piece of delegated legislation has the same legal force and effect as the Act of Parliament under which it is enacted; but equally it only has effect to the extent that its enabling Act authorises it. Consequently, it is possible for delegated legislation to be challenged, through the procedure of judicial review, on the basis that the person or body to whom Parliament has delegated its authority has acted in a way that exceeds the limited powers delegated to them or has failed to follow the appropriate procedure set down in the enabling legislation. Any provision in this way is said to be *ultra vires* and is void.

It should also be recalled that the primacy of European Union law over domestic law, means that any domestic law made in contravention of European Union law is subject to challenge and overturning in the courts.

2 This question invites candidates to examine the various remedies that may be available to innocent parties when they suffer as a consequence of a breach of contract.

Breach of a contract occurs where one of the parties to the agreement fails to comply, either completely or satisfactorily, with their obligations under it. A breach of contract may occur in three ways:

(i) where a party, prior to the time of performance, states that they will not fulfil their contractual obligation;
(ii) where a party fails to perform their contractual obligation;
(iii) where a party performs their obligation in a defective manner.

Any breach will result in the innocent party being able to sue for an appropriate remedy. In addition, however, some breaches will permit the innocent party to treat the contract as discharged. In this situation they can refuse either to perform their part of the contract, or to accept further performance from the party in breach.

The principal remedies for breach of contract are:

– damages;
– *quantum meruit*;
– specific performance;
– injunction.

Damages

Every failure to perform a primary obligation is a breach of contract. The secondary obligation on the part of the contract-breaker, by implication of the common law, is to pay monetary compensation to the other party for the loss sustained by him in consequence of the breach (*Photo Productions Ltd* v *Securicor Transport Ltd* (1980)).

Such monetary compensation for breach of contract is damages. There are two issues to consider: remoteness and measure.

(i) Remoteness of damage

This involves deciding how far down a chain of events a defendant is liable. The rule in *Hadley* v *Baxendale* (1854) states that damages will only be awarded in respect of losses which arise naturally, i.e. in the natural course of things; or which both parties may reasonably be supposed to have contemplated, when the contract was made, as a probable result of its breach.

The effect of the first part of the rule in *Hadley* v *Baxendale* is that the party in breach is deemed to expect the normal consequences of the breach, whether they actually expected them or not.

Under the second part of the rule, however, the party in breach can only be held liable for abnormal consequences where they have actual knowledge that the abnormal consequences might follow. Thus in *Victoria Laundry Ltd* v *Newham Industries Ltd* (1949) the plaintiff was able to claim for damages with respect to the normal profits, but could not claim abnormal profits which would have resulted from an especially lucrative contract, which the defendant knew nothing about.

(ii) Measure of damages

Damages in contract are intended to compensate an injured party for any financial loss sustained as a consequence of another party's breach. The object is not to punish the party in breach, so the amount of damages awarded can never be greater than the actual loss suffered. The aim is to put the injured party in the same position they would have been in had the contract been properly performed.

Even damages of a non-financial nature can be recovered (*Jarvis* v *Swan Tours Ltd* (1973)).

It is possible, and common in business contracts, for the parties to an agreement to make provisions for possible breach by stating in advance the amount of damages that will have to be paid in the event of any breach occurring. Damages under such a provision are known as liquidated damages. They will only be recognised by the court if they represent a genuine pre-estimate of loss, and are not intended to operate as a penalty against the party in breach (*Dunlop* v *New Garage & Motor Co* (1915)).

Quantum meruit

Quantum meruit means that a party should be awarded 'as much as he had earned', and such an award can be either contractual or quasi-contractual in nature. If the parties enter into a contractual agreement without determining the reward that is to be provided for performance, then in the event of any dispute, the court will award a reasonable sum.

Payment may also be claimed on the basis of *quantum meruit*, where a party has carried out work in respect of a void contract (*Craven-Ellis* v *Canons Ltd* (1936)).

Specific performance

An order for specific performance requires the party in breach to complete their part of the contract. The following rules govern the award of such a remedy.

8

(i) specific performance will only be granted in cases where the common law remedy of damages is inadequate. It is most commonly granted in cases involving the sale of land, where the subject matter of the contract is unique.
(ii) specific performance will not be granted where the court cannot supervise its enforcement. For this reason it will not be available in respect of contracts of employment or personal service (*Ryan* v *Mutual Tontine Westminster Chambers Association* (1893)).
(iii) specific performance, as an equitable remedy, will not be granted where the plaintiffs themselves have not acted properly.

Injunction
This is also an equitable order of the court, which directs a person not to break their contract. An injunction will only be granted to enforce negative covenants within the agreement, and cannot be used to enforce positive obligations (*Whitwood Chemical Co* v *Hardman* (1891)). However, it can have the effect of indirectly enforcing contracts for personal service (*Warner Bros* v *Nelson* (1937)).

Quasi-contractual remedies are based on the assumption that a person should not receive any undue advantage from the fact that there is no contractual remedy to force them to account. An important quasi-contractual remedy is an action for money paid and received. If no contract comes into existence for reason of a total failure of consideration, then under this action, any goods or money received will have to be returned to the party who supplied them.

3 **(a)** The neighbour principle is the test for establishing whether a duty of care exists in relation to the tort of negligence. It was initially set out in *Donoghue* v *Stevenson* (1932), the snail in the beer bottle case. In putting forward the test to establish a duty of care Lord Atkin stated that:

'You must take reasonable care to avoid acts and omissions which you could reasonably foresee would be likely to injure your neighbour. Who, then, in law is my neighbour? ... any person so closely and directly affected by my act that I ought reasonably to have them in contemplation as being so affected when I am directing my mind to the acts and omissions which are called in question.'

It can be seen that this neighbour test for deciding the existence of a duty of care is an objective, rather than a subjective one. It is not a matter of what the respondent actually considered, but what they ought to have considered. Nor does the test require the contemplation of the resultant effect on the specific individual injured, but merely requires that identity of a class of individuals who might be injured as a consequence of the respondent's lack of care.

(b) Just as in contract law, the position in negligence is that the person ultimately liable in damages is only responsible to the extent that the loss sustained was considered not to be too remote.

The test for remoteness was established in *The Wagon Mound (No 1)* (1961). The defendants negligently allowed furnace oil to spill from a ship into Sydney harbour, which subsequently caused a fire, which spread to, and damaged, the plaintiff's wharf. Although the defendants were held to be in breach of their duty of care, they were only liable for the damage caused to the wharf and slipway through the fouling of the oil. They were not liable for the damage caused by fire because damage by fire was at that time unforeseeable (the oil had a high ignition point and it could not be foreseen that it would ignite on water).

The test of reasonable foresight arising out of *The Wagon Mound* clearly takes into account such things as scientific knowledge at the time of the negligent act. The question to be asked in determining the extent of liability is, 'is the damage of such a kind as the reasonable [person] should have foreseen?' This does not mean that the defendant should have foreseen precisely the sequence or nature of the events.

This is illustrated in the case of *Hughes* v *Lord Advocate* (1963), where employees of the Post Office, who were working down a manhole, left it without a cover but with a tent over it and lamps around it. A child picked up a lamp and went into the tent. He tripped over the lamp, knocking it into the hole. An explosion occurred and the child was burned. The risk of the child being burned by the lamp was foreseeable. However, the vaporisation of the paraffin in the lamp and its ignition were not foreseeable. It was held that the defendants were liable for the injury to the plaintiff. It was foreseeable that the child might be burned and it was immaterial that neither the extent of his injury nor the precise chain of events leading to it was foreseeable.

(c) There are two categories of economic/financial loss, which may form the basis of a claim in negligence. First, there is economic loss arising out of physical injury or damage to property; and, secondly, there is what is known as 'pure' economic loss, which is the sole loss sustained, unconnected with physical damage (*Spartan Steel and Alloys Ltd* v *Martin and Co* (1973)). Only the former is now recoverable, unless the claimant can show that there was a 'special relationship' between them and the defendant, in which the defendant assumed responsibility for the claimant's economic welfare (*Hedley Byrne & Co* v *Heller and Partners* (1964) & *Williams* v *Natural Life Health Foods Ltd* (1998)).

4 **(a)** Pre-emption rights refer to the rights of existing shareholders to be offered any new issue of shares before those shares can be offered to non-shareholders.

The purpose of pre-emption rights is to ensure that existing shareholders have an opportunity to maintain their interest in their company by preventing their percentage holding being watered down by the issue of shares to new members. There is, of course, no compulsion on the part of the shareholder to take the shares if they do not wish to.

In the UK there was no statutory requirement as to pre-emption rights before the European Community second company law directive (77/91) made it necessary for the law of the UK to be changed to introduce such rights.

Currently, by virtue of s.561 Companies Act (CA) 2006, a company cannot offer new shares for cash unless the existing shareholders have been offered the chance to buy the shares in proportion to their existing holding. Section 565 specifically exempts pre-emption rights where non-cash consideration is involved.

As it is not always cost effective to offer new shares to all existing members, pre-emption rights can be waived by provision in the articles of association or by a special resolution of shareholders.

Pre-emption rights may also be included in a company's articles of association and it is not unusual in the case of private companies to offer a form of pre-emption right to existing members when others wish to sell their shares.

(b) A rights issue is the procedure through which a company raises new capital by offering new shares to its existing members. As the shares are offered to the existing shareholders in proportion to their existing holding, it can be seen as respecting and giving effect to the shareholders' pre-emption rights, even in situations where those rights have been suspended, as indicated previously. As the purpose is to raise new capital for the company, either because it is in difficulty, or needs the additional capital to expand its business, the shareholders who are offered the new shares are required to pay for them. However, as an inducement to engage in the deal, it is usual for the new shares to be offered at a discount to the current *market* value of the existing shares. It is essential to note that the discount is not on the *nominal* value of the shares, which is required by the rules of company law to be fully-paid as companies cannot issue shares at a discount.

Once again there is no compulsion to participate in the rights issue and often the rights to participate in the allotment of new shares are usually tradeable securities in themselves. Consequently shareholders who do not want to buy the new shares themselves may sell the rights to a third party.

(c) A bonus issue of shares, sometimes referred to as a scrip issue or more accurately a capitalisation issue is similar to a rights issue in that existing members receive new shares in proportion to their existing holdings, but it differs in one essential point: the individuals who receive the new shares usually do not have to pay anything for them; they are received free. However, as already pointed out in (b) above, it is a strict rule of company law that shares must be paid for and cannot be issued at a discount. This apparent anomaly is explained by the fact that the shares are paid for, but they are paid for by the company itself, rather than the members. It is perfectly possible for the company to issue partly paid-up bonus shares, in which case the recipients may have to make some contribution in the future.

In effect what the issue of bonus shares amounts to is a capitalisation of the company's reserves, some of which could have been distributed to the members in some other way such as dividends. This is not the case with all reserves as some non-distributable ones, such as the share premium account and the capital redemption reserve may be used to fund the bonus issue. Bonus issues must never be funded from a company's ordinary capital.

5 This question requires candidates to set out and explain the various registers and accounting records that companies are required to maintain.

(a) *Statutory Registers*

Companies are required to maintain a number of important registers, which are usually kept at the registered office and are open to public inspection. The registers are as follows:

Register of members. Under s.113 Companies Act (CA) 2006 every company is under the obligation to keep a register of its members and to include the following information in that register: the names and addresses of the members, the date on which each person was registered as a member and the date at which any person ceased to be a member. It must also indicate the number and class of shares held and the amount paid on those shares.

Registers of directors and secretaries. This requirement is set out in the CA 2006, ss.162–165 for directors and ss.275–278 for company secretaries. Section 163 sets out the details that have to be included in relation to directors and includes their present and former names, date of birth, nationality, a service address which need not be the home address of the director, and occupation. Under s.165 the company must keep a separate register of directors' residential addresses, but this is not open to either ordinary members of the company or members of the public.

Register of charges. Section 876 CA 2006 requires all limited companies to keep a register of all fixed charges affecting the property of the company and all floating charges on the undertaking or property of the company. Such registers must contain a short description of the property, which has been charged, the amount of the charge and the names of the persons who hold it. Companies are not required to maintain a separate register of debenture holders but where they do maintain such a register it shall be open to inspection (CA s.743).

Register of interests in shares. This register is required under s.808 and relates to interests of a substantial nature in the voting shares of public limited companies. The level is currently set at 3%.

In addition to the registers, companies also keep records of directors' service contracts and indemnities, and records of resolutions and meetings of the company.

10

(b) *Accounting records*
Section 386 CA 2006 requires every company to keep accounting records and sets out what those records should be designed to achieve. They must be sufficient to

- show and explain the company's transactions, disclosing with reasonable accuracy, at any time, the financial position of the company at intervals of not more than six months;
- enable the directors to ensure that any accounts required to be prepared comply with the CA and International Accounting standards.

In particular the accounting records must contain:

- entries from day-to-day of all sums of money received and expended by the company and the matters in respect of which the receipt and expenditure takes place;
- a record of the assets and liabilities of the company; and where the company deals in goods;
- statements of stock held by the company and the end of each financial year of the company;
- all statements of stocktaking from which any statement as is mentioned above has been prepared; and
- except in the case of goods sold by way of ordinary retail trade, statements of all goods sold and purchased showing the goods and the buyers and sellers in sufficient detail to enable them to be identified.

Under CA s.394 a company's directors must prepare accounts for each accounting reference period, usually 12 months. These accounts must include a balance sheet and a profit and loss account (s.396) and must show a true and fair view of the company's state of affairs.

Accounting records must be kept for a period of three years for private companies and six years for public companies.

6 The Companies Act (CA) 2006 sets out a new statutory statement of seven general duties owed by directors to their companies as follows:

- *Duty to act within their powers*
  Section 171 CA replaces existing similar common law duties and requires directors to act in accordance with the company's constitution. Section 17 of the Act provides that a company's constitution includes not only the company's articles of association but the resolutions and agreements specified in s.29, which includes special resolutions passed by the company and any resolutions or agreements that have been agreed to, or which otherwise bind classes of shareholders.

  Directors are also required to use powers only for the purposes for which they were conferred. This is a restatement of the long-standing 'proper purposes doctrine'.
- *Duty to promote the success of the company for the benefit of members as a whole*
  Section 172 CA 2006 replaces the previous common law duty on directors to act in good faith in the best interests of the company. In the course of making their decisions under Part 1 of the section, then, directors are now required to have regard to each of the following list of matters:
  - the likely consequences of any decision in the long term,
  - the interests of the company's employees,
  - the need to foster the company's business relationships with suppliers, customers and others,
  - the impact of the company's operations on the community and the environment,
  - the desirability of the company maintaining a reputation for high standards of business conduct, and
  - the need to act fairly as between members of the company.

  The above list is non-exhaustive and directors must also have regard to other non-specific matters.
- *Duty to exercise independent judgement*
  This duty, stated in s.173 CA 2006, reflects the previous rule prohibiting directors from fettering their discretion unless acting in accordance with an agreement duly approved by the company.
- *Duty to exercise reasonable skill, care and diligence*
  Section 174 CA 2006 codifies and replaces the previous common law duty but in a way that reflects the recent tightening of control over directors in line with the standard set out in relation to wrongful trading in the Insolvency Act 1986, s.214.
- *Duty to avoid conflicts of interest*
  Section 175 CA 2006 reflects the long-standing common law rule that directors, as fiduciaries, must respect the trust and confidence placed in them and should do nothing to undermine or abuse their position as fiduciaries. The practical effect of the rule is that any conflict of interest must be authorised by the members of the company, unless some alternative procedure is properly provided. In the case of a private company, a conflict can be authorised by the other directors of the board unless the company's constitution provides to the contrary. The position is the same for public companies, except that the constitution must expressly permit authorisation by the board.
- *Duty not to accept benefits from third parties*
  Under s.176, a director must not accept a benefit from a third party, which is conferred by reason of (a) his being a director or (b) his doing (or not doing) anything as director. This duty is an aspect of the previous general duty to avoid conflicts of interest, but it has been stated separately in order to ensure that the obtaining of a benefit from a third party by a director can only be authorised by members of the company rather than by the board.

– *Duty to declare to the company's other directors any interest a director has in a proposed transaction or arrangement with the company*
Under s.177 CA 2006 a director must declare to the other directors any situation in which they are in any way, directly or indirectly, interested in a proposed transaction or arrangement with the company. Again this further emphasises the duty to avoid a conflict of interests by ensuring that directors are transparent about personal interests, which could, even remotely, be seen as affecting their judgement.

7 **(a)** Under the Employment Rights Act (ERA) 1996 employees have a right not to be unfairly dismissed. A number of situations are considered automatically to be unfair, however, once the employee has to show that they have been dismissed the onus is placed on the employer to show that they acted reasonably in dismissing them for a potentially fair reason within s.98 ERA.

The following are situations where dismissal is automatically unfair:

(i) Dismissal for trade union reasons. This applies where an employee has been dismissed for actual, or proposed, membership of a trade union, or is dismissed for taking part in trade union activities. It also applies where an individual has refused to join a trade union.
(ii) Dismissal on grounds of pregnancy or childbirth or other reason connected to her pregnancy or following her maternity leave period.
(iii) Dismissal in relation to health and safety issues, such as bringing to the employer's attention any reasonable concern related to health and safety matters or leaving their place of work in the face of a reasonably held belief that they faced serious danger.
(iv) Dismissal for making a protected disclosure to the appropriate authorities. This action, otherwise known as 'whistle blowing', covers criminal activity, breach of legal obligations, breach of health and safety provisions, and activity damaging to the environment on the part of the employer.
(v) Dismissal for asserting a statutory right governing such aspects of employment as the length of working time or minimum wage payment.

On the other hand, the following five categories may be counted as fair:

(i) Lack of capability or qualifications. However, even in this situation, the employer must show that not only was the employee incompetent but that it was reasonable to dismiss them.
(ii) Misconduct. Any such behaviour must be sufficient seriousness to merit the description 'gross misconduct'. Examples of such conduct might involve assault, drunkenness, dishonesty or a failure to follow instructions, or safety procedures, or persistent lateness.
(iii) Redundancy is a *prima facie*, a fair reason for dismissal as long as the employer has acted reasonably in introducing the redundancy programme.
(iv) In situations where continued employment would constitute a breach of a statutory provision, for example, if a driver is banned from driving then they may be fairly dismissed.
(v) Some other substantial reason such as a clash of personalities. This final general provision means that it is not possible to provide an exhaustive list of all grounds for 'fair dismissal'. However, none of the above reasons are sufficient in themselves to justify dismissal and under all instances the employer must act as would be expected of a 'reasonable employer'.

(b) In relation to a successful claim for unfair dismissal, an Employment Tribunal may award any one of the following remedies:

(i) reinstatement,
(ii) re-engagement or
(iii) compensation.

Reinstatement is where the dismissed employee is treated as not having been dismissed in the first place.

Re-engagement means that the dismissed employee is re-employed under a new contract of employment.

The calculation of a *basic* award of compensation is calculated in the same way as for redundancy payments and is subject to the same maximum level of payment. The actual figures are calculated on the basis of the person's age, length of continuous service and weekly rate of pay subject to statutory maxima. Thus employees between the ages of 18 and 21 are entitled to ½ week's pay for each year of service, those between 22 and 40 are entitled to 1 week's pay for every year of service, and those between 41 and 65 are entitled to 1½ weeks' pay for every year of service. The maximum number of years service that can be claimed is 20 and as the maximum level of pay that can be claimed is £350, the maximum total that can be claimed is £10,500, (i.e. 1·5 x 20 x 350).

In addition, however, a *compensatory* award of up to £66,200 may be made at the discretion of the tribunal and an *additional* award of up to £18,200 may be made where the employer ignores an order for re-employment or re-engagement, or the reason for dismissal was unlawful discrimination.

12

8 This question relates to the issue of whether the parties to an agreement can enforce its terms through court action. By definition, a contract is a binding agreement, but the important thing for this question is that not all agreements are contracts. In order to limit the number of cases that might otherwise be brought, the courts will only enforce those agreements, which the parties intended to have legal effect. Although expressed in terms of the parties' intentions, the test for the presence of such intention is an objective, rather than a subjective, one. For the purposes of this question in regard to intention to create legal relations, agreements can be divided into two categories, in which different presumptions apply.

Domestic and social agreements
In domestic and social agreements, there is a presumption that the parties do not intend to create legal relations.

In *Balfour* v *Balfour* (1919), a husband returned to Ceylon to take up his employment and he promised his wife, who could not return with him due to health problems, that he would pay her £30 per month as maintenance. When the marriage later ended in divorce, the wife sued for the promised maintenance. It was held that the parties had not intended the original promise to be binding and therefore it was not legally enforceable.

Another situation where it held that there was no intention to create legal relations can be seen in *Jones* v *Pandavatton* (1969), in which a mother was not held liable to maintain an agreement to pay her daughter a promised allowance.

It should be emphasised, however, that the presumption against the intention to create legal relations in such relationships is only that, a presumption and that, as with all presumptions, it may be rebutted by the actual facts and circumstances of a particular case as may be seen in *Merritt* v *Merritt* (1970). After a husband had left the matrimonial home, he met his wife and promised to pay her £40 per month, from which she undertook to pay the outstanding mortgage on their house. The husband, at the wife's insistence, signed a note agreeing to transfer the house into the wife's sole name when the mortgage was paid off. The wife paid off the mortgage but the husband refused to transfer the house. It was held that the agreement was enforceable as in the circumstances the parties had clearly intended to enter into a legally enforceable agreement.

Commercial agreements
In commercial situations, the strong presumption is that the parties intend to enter into a legally binding relationship in consequence of their dealings.

In *Edwards* v *Skyways* (1964), employers undertook to make an *ex gratia* payment to an employee whom they had made redundant. It was held that in such a situation the use of the term *ex gratia* was not sufficient to rebut the presumption that the establishment of legal relations had been intended. The former employee, therefore, was entitled to the payment promised.

As with other presumptions, this one is open to rebuttal. In commercial situations, however, the presumption is so strong that it will usually take express wording to the contrary to avoid its operation. An example can be found in *Rose and Frank Co* v *Crompton Bros* (1925) in which it was held that an express clause stating that no legal relations were to be created by a business transaction was effective.

Applying the above law to the facts in the problem scenario provides the following conclusions:

Amy and Ben
Although they are brother and sister it is clear from the facts of the situation that they entered into a business relationship with regard to the provision of the updating of the web site. Amy was to do the work for Ben's business and Ben was expected to, and indeed agreed to pay £1,000. In such circumstances there was a clear intention to create legal relations and Ben cannot avoid his liability to pay Amy on the basis of their familial relationship. He may have wanted to help his sister, but he did so by entering into a business contract with her; one which she can enforce against him.

Che
The position in this instance is even stronger in Amy's favour. Even if he did have the motive to benefit Amy as his friend, Che can hardly claim that his agreement with her was a purely social one. It was clearly a business transaction and as such he is bound to comply with the original terms of the contract and pay the full contractual price of £1,000.

9 **(a)** Dividends are the return received by shareholders in respect of their investment in a company. Subject to any restriction in the articles of association, every company has the implied power to apply its profits in the distribution of dividend payments to its shareholders. The long-standing common law rule is that dividends must not be paid out of capital (*Flitcroft's case* 1882). The current rules relating to the payment of dividends are to be found in part 23 Companies Act (CA) 2006. The Act governs, and imposes restrictions on distributions made by all companies, both public and private. Section 829 defines distribution as **any** payment, cash or otherwise, of a company's assets to its members, except for the categories stated in the section, which include the issue of bonus shares, the redemption of shares, authorised reductions of share capital, and the distribution of assets on winding up.

Section 830 goes on to provide the basic condition for distribution, applying to **all** companies, which, in essence, is that they must have 'profits available for that purpose'. This term is defined in the section as accumulated realised profits less accumulated realised losses, with profit or loss being either revenue or capital in origin.

It is important to note that the use of the term accumulated means that any previous years' losses must be included in determining the distributable surplus, and that the requirement that profits be realised prevents payment from purely paper profit resulting from the mere revaluation of assets. Section 841 provides that all losses are to be treated as realised except where a general revaluation of all fixed assets has taken place.

The foregoing realised profits test applies to both private and public companies, but public companies face an additional test in relation to distributions, in that s.831 requires that any distribution must not reduce the value of the company's net assets below the aggregate of its total called up share capital plus any undistributable reserves. The effect of this rule is that public companies have to account for changes in the value of their fixed assets, and are required to apply an essentially balance-sheet approach to the determination of profits.

(b) Under the rule in *Flitcroft's case* any directors of a company who breached the distribution rules, and knowingly paid dividends out of capital, were held jointly and severally liable to the company to replace any such payments made. The fact that the shareholders might have approved the distribution did not validate the illegal payment (*Aveling Barford Ltd* v *Perion Ltd* (1989)). Also at common law shareholders who knowingly received, or ought to have known that they had received an unlawful dividend payment were required to repay the money received, or to indemnify the directors for payments they might have already been required to have made (*Moxham* v *Grant* (1900)). Section 847 Companies Act 2006 restates the common law rule, providing that shareholders, who either know or have reasonable grounds for knowing that any dividend was paid from capital, shall be liable to repay any such money received to the company.

Applying the foregoing to the problem at hand it is apparent that the loss from 2008–2009 cannot be ignored, as the company is required to take accumulated losses into account. Nor can the paper profit of £5,000 generated by the asset revaluation be taken into account as it is unrealised. As a result the realised trading profit of £3,000 for the year 2009–10 has to be set against the loss of £2,000 from the previous year, which means that Fan plc only had £1,000 available for distribution to its members by way of dividend.

As dividends amounting to a total of £4,000 was paid, it is apparent that £3,000 too much was paid in dividends.

As a result any shareholder who either knew or had reasonable grounds for knowing that the dividends were improperly paid will have to recompense the company to the extent that their dividends were overpaid. In the final analysis Dee and Eff will be personally liable to make good the difference to the company for any payments made to shareholders who do not fit into that category.

10 As with companies business assets must be used to pay the debts of a partnership. However, unlike most companies, members of partnerships do not benefit from the advantage of limited liability and consequently their personal wealth may be called upon to pay off business debts. Upon dissolution, the value of the partnership property is realised and the proceeds are applied in the following order:

(i) in paying debts to outsiders;
(ii) in paying to the partners any advance made to the firm beyond their capital contribution;
(iii) in paying the capital contribution of the individual partners.

Any residue is divided between the partners in the same proportion as they shared in profits (s.44 of the Partnership Act (PA) 1890).

If the assets are insufficient to meet debts, partners' advances and capital repayments, then the deficiency has to be made good out of any profits held back from previous years, or out of partners' capital, or by the partners individually in the proportion to which they were entitled to share in profits.

Applying these rules to the partnership in question, the first step is for the value of the partnership assets to be realised in order to pay off the debts owed to the various outside creditors. As stated, the partnership assets are worth £20,000 and it has debts to outside creditors of £7,000. As the value of the assets is sufficient to cover all of these debts, the creditors will be paid their debts in full before any allocation between the partners.

The next stage in the problem is to consider Geo's advance of £3,000 to the partnership and as stated above he is entitled to receive repayment of that sum before any further distribution to the partners.

The effect of these payments is that amount left for distribution between the partners is only £10,000 (£20,000 less £7,000 to the outside creditors, less the £3,000 advance owed to Geo). This means that the partnership has actually suffered a loss of £30,000 on the original capital contributed by the members. That total loss will be allocated, according to the partnership agreement, in proportion to the capital contribution. As the total capital contribution was £40,000, Geo who provided £20,000 must suffer half of the loss (i.e. 20/40ths), Ho, who provided £12,000 must suffer 3/10ths of the loss (i.e. 12/40ths) and Io, who provided £8,000, will suffer 1/5th of the loss (i.e. 8/40ths). In terms of money, the losses will be: £15,000 for Geo, £9,000 for Ho and £6,000 for Io.

In practice these losses will merely reduce the amount of capital returned to the partners. Thus Geo will receive £5,000, Ho will receive £3,000 and Io will receive £2,000.

14

Notes

Notes

Review Form – Paper F4 Corporate and Business Law (UK) (01/11)

Name: ______________________ **Address:** ______________________

____

____

How have you used this Kit?
(Tick one box only)

☐ Home study (book only)
☐ On a course: college ______________________
☐ With 'correspondence' package
☐ Other ______________________

Why did you decide to purchase this Kit?
(Tick one box only)

☐ Have used the complementary Study text
☐ Have used other BPP products in the past
☐ Recommendation by friend/colleague
☐ Recommendation by a lecturer at college
☐ Saw advertising
☐ Other ______________________

During the past six months do you recall seeing/receiving any of the following?
(Tick as many boxes as are relevant)

☐ Our advertisement in *Student Accountant*
☐ Our advertisement in *Pass*
☐ Our advertisement in *PQ*
☐ Our brochure with a letter through the post
☐ Our website www.bpp.com

Which (if any) aspects of our advertising do you find useful?
(Tick as many boxes as are relevant)

☐ Prices and publication dates of new editions
☐ Information on product content
☐ Facility to order books off-the-page
☐ None of the above

Which BPP products have you used?

Text	☐	*Success CD*	☐	*Learn Online*	☐
Kit	☑	*i-Learn*	☐	*Home Study Package*	☐
Passcard	☐	*i-Pass*	☐	*Home Study PLUS*	☐

Your ratings, comments and suggestions would be appreciated on the following areas.

	Very useful	*Useful*	*Not useful*
Passing F4			
Planning your question practice			
Questions			
Top Tips etc in answers			
Content and structure of answers			
'Plan of attack' in mock exams			
Mock exam answers			

Overall opinion of this Kit *Excellent* ☐ *Good* ☐ *Adequate* ☐ *Poor* ☐

Do you intend to continue using BPP products? *Yes* ☐ *No* ☐

The BPP author of this edition can be e-mailed at: stephenosborne@bpp.com

Please return this form to: Lesley Buick, ACCA Publishing Manager, BPP Learning Media Ltd, FREEPOST, London, W12 8BR

Review Form (continued)

TELL US WHAT YOU THINK

Please note any further comments and suggestions/errors below.